A Very Courageous Decision

A Very Courageous Decision

THE INSIDE STORY OF

YES MINISTER

Graham McCann

Aurum
Press

First published in Great Britain
2014 by Aurum Press Ltd
74–77 White Lion Street
Islington
London N1 9PF
www.aurumpress.co.uk

A catalogue record for this book is
available from the British Library.

ISBN 978 1 78131 189 9

1 3 5 7 9 10 8 6 4 2
2014 2016 2018 2017 2015

Typeset in Adobe Garamond by SX Composing DTP Ltd
Printed by CPI Group (UK) Ltd, Croydon, CR0 4YY

For Silvana

CONTENTS

Prologue

*Mystery is the antagonist of truth. It is a fog of human invention,
that obscures truth, and represents it in distortion. Truth never
envelops itself in mystery, and the mystery in which it is at any time
enveloped is the work of its antagonist, and never of itself.*
Thomas Paine

*As yet the few rule by their hold, not over the reason of the multitude,
but over their imaginations, and their habits; over their fancies as to
distant things they do not know at all, over their customs as to near
things which they know very well.*
Walter Bagehot

*It is a good thing to be laughed at.
It is better than to be ignored.*
Harold Macmillan

Prologue

The day – Monday, 25 February 1980 – unfolded, in the context of British politics, much like any other day. Government, in those days, happened rather like a tree falling in a forest when there was no one there to witness it. For those among the Great British Public who wanted to believe that something was happening, the assumption was that something was indeed most probably happening, while for those who still needed to see it, or hear it, to believe it, there remained a high degree of doubt that anything was happening at all.

The scepticism was far more understandable than the faith, because there was, in those days, no live coverage of formal political proceedings on television. There were no rolling news channels, no Internet, no online feeds, no text messages, blogs or tweets, and, apart from half an hour of 'highlights' tucked away late at night on BBC Radio 4's *Today in Parliament* programme, not even very much on the wireless.[1] What went on in Westminster and Whitehall that day in 1980, therefore, would remain, as far as the vast majority of the British public was concerned, as formidably obscure and bemusingly inscrutable as the rest of Britain's political system.

The House of Commons met, as usual, at 2.30 p.m., when prayers were said, and then various Ministers stood up and gave run-of-the-mill answers to run-of-the-mill questions, ranging from the general pace of industrial progress ('Whilst the Government have made a good start on getting the right climate for economic growth, it will take time for their policies to be fully implemented and to take effect'[2]) to the specific prospects for British Steel ('Whatever the British Steel Corporation's record in forecasting it cannot conceivably be as bad as the forecasts of successive Governments who over-expanded the industry'[3]), with a tantalisingly brief aside on the topic of telephone tapping ('I have at present nothing to add'[4]).

The House of Lords, meanwhile, was at its ermine-swathed, arcane best, pondering at great length the most prudent possible response to a year-old 'consultative document' ('My Lords, the time for consultation on the Consultative Document was to end originally in January 1979 and that was later deferred. Do the Government intend to continue consultation in view of the change of Government in the meantime?'[5]), and exploring the minutiae of the new Education Bill ('Doubtless the liability of individual governors in respect of claims could be covered by some form of insurance, but it seems an unfortunate second best when the opportunity to make the governing body a body corporate was there'[6]), while also finding time to acknowledge receipt of a report regarding some proposed legislation concerning the promotion of better health within Britain's population of bees.

Deeper still into the darkest shadows cast by the political Establishment, the denizens of dusky committee rooms in Whitehall were keeping themselves similarly busy by even more byzantine means, with various officials poring over recent speeches by leading political figures on the future of the EEC budget, while another clique was assessing plans for a national shelter policy designed to help the country cope with a potential nuclear attack. Elsewhere in the same set of buildings, a coterie of kingmakers was mulling over the respective merits of several candidates for the soon-to-be-vacant position of Head of the Diplomatic Service. Whatever the specific details aired in these many meetings of mandarins, it was safely assumed that not so much as a scintilla of information would reach the ears or eyes of any humble outsider until any disclosure was deemed to be wise and worthwhile.

None of this was at all out of the ordinary. None of this was in danger of intruding too noticeably onto the day's main news agenda.

This day, in short, was how such days were done. The sheer opacity of the political system, and the barely audible hum of its hidden machinery, was still treated by the vast majority of the population as part and parcel of how the country was run.

True, there were brief annual spasms of distant visibility, when the three main parties set up stalls at the seaside for their respective conferences, and longer periods of staged accountability mixed with sundry redundant intimacies that happened every few years during the run-up to each General Election, but neither of these events afforded the public a genuinely rich and vivid opportunity to analyse the actions of their elected representatives, let alone lend them any insight into the ancillary activities of their unelected civil servants. The best (or worst) any typical day in British politics could expect to elicit, in terms of exposure, was the tiny amount of trickle-down enlightenment tucked away in the 'serious' pages of the following morning's papers.

While some contemporary critics complained that such a tradition of secrecy, muddled with mystery, represented a deep-rooted 'English disease' and 'the chronic ailment of the British Government',[7] others – noting the peculiarly, and potentially unnervingly, ambiguous nature of an 'organic' constitution partly unwritten and entirely uncodified – continued to echo the more cautious Victorian view that a certain degree of impenetrability was actually quite beneficial, acting as a discreet but invaluable counterweight to the average citizen's propensity for 'irritable activity',[8] thus maintaining the 'great union of spur and bridle, of energy and moderation'[9] that inspired the best kind of British character.

This particular day, however, would end up making all of the days to come seem a little different to all of those that had gone before, because, right in the middle of the mainstream television that was being broadcast that evening, a new situation comedy was screened that, as if out of nowhere, appeared to lay bare the real workings of British government. Even though it was presented as a 'mere' comedy rather than something 'worthy' from the realms of drama or current affairs, and even though it was placed there primarily to provoke some laughs rather than spark serious debate, once it had arrived, the show, called *Yes Minister*, would provide the British public with arguably *the* quintessential piece of public service broadcasting on the subject of practical politics: something that informed, educated *and* entertained people about the prosaic processes of power.

It would have made a mark on TV even if it had been just one more British sitcom, because the British sitcom, back in those days, was in something of a rut, having recently seen the great wave of 1970s series slowly recede (*Dad's Army* and *Porridge*, for example, had both ended in 1977, with *The Good Life* and *Rising Damp* bowing out in 1978 and *Fawlty Towers* following suit in 1979), leaving, at the start of the new decade, a distinctly barren-looking beach littered with such evanescent seaside-postcard fare as *Hi-de-Hi!*, *Terry and June*, *Only When I Laugh* and the long-running but visibly flagging duo of *It Ain't Half Hot Mum* and *Are You Being Served?*. In such a context, therefore, any new sitcom that boasted better-quality scripts, more elegant comic acting and a greater degree of intelligence would have been more than welcome, but *Yes Minister* brought all of that and more. What made it still more notable and admirable was the combination of the seriousness of its subtext and the lightness of its touch.

This, after all, was still an era in which the mainstream TV sitcom was supposed to know its place. After a brief period of bold and confident creativity in the mid-1960s, when Galton and Simpson blended raw emotion with playful humour in *Steptoe and Son* and Johnny Speight brutally satirised bigotry in *Till Death Us Do Part*, the genre had appeared to lose its nerve. Perhaps this was partly due to the messy failure of lesser efforts: Speight's own spectacularly clumsy *Curry and Chips* in 1969, for example, and Vince Powell and Harry Driver's depressingly lazy *Love Thy Neighbour* from 1972 to 1976, both of them bungling the opportunity to mock rather than mirror the racial prejudices of their time. There may also, though, have been a disinclination among TV executives to continue dealing with the controversies that such shows had provoked. There rarely seemed to be a day during the second half of the 1960s, for example, when the BBC's Director-General, Hugh Carleton Greene, escaped public censure from British broadcasting's self-appointed moral arbiter, ombudswoman and would-be Platonic guardian Mary Whitehouse, along with her clique of easily piqued 'Clean Up TV' acolytes, for supposedly condoning programmes that undermined 'the moral, mental and physical health of the country'.[10]

The consequence was that, while the 1970s was in many ways a continuation of a golden age for British sitcoms (with new heights being reached in terms of both the standard of the ensemble acting and the consistently high quality of the humour), the genre as a whole preferred to err on the side of caution when it came to choosing its subject matter, with imitation mattering more than ideas as sitcoms aimed to encourage social identification far more assiduously than they did intellectual engagement. The arrival of *Yes Minister* early in 1980 thus represented, in this sense, a welcome return to the ambitious populism of the 1960s, eschewing zany escapism or cosy suburban domesticity and choosing instead to engage directly with arguably the most complicated, contentious, divisive and – as far as many members of the public were concerned – driest topics imaginable, and make it not only comprehensible and colourful but also consistently funny.

Suddenly, the kind of subject matter that television usually treated as something self-consciously sober and serious, communicated via the stiff-necked, straight-faced style it had always associated with the industrious domain of 'hard' news rather than the playful preserve of 'light' entertainment, was now being made accessible to everyone, regardless of background or bias. Now everybody was being invited to explore, understand and evaluate a process that had previously seemed aloof, obscure and obfuscatory.

Minute by minute, as that first engrossingly amusing episode of *Yes Minister* unfolded, the nobility of its comic novelty grew more evident and admirable. It respected the intelligence of its audience, it shared with them its secrets and it conspired with them to create a new and populist critique. What it showed them – all of them – was a part of their lives that should have been monitored constantly, but, until now, had been left shrouded in myth and mystique.

Here was a Minister: the restless, rash Jim Hacker. Here was a Civil Servant: the calm, cautious Sir Humphrey Appleby. Here, inside the generic government department, was the context within which they came into contact with each other. Here, in essence, was British politics and administration, in tandem, in action. Yes, it was exaggerated and embellished in places for comic effect, and yes, it was nipped and tucked in terms of detail, but, more importantly, it was still the moment when, in a popular cultural sense, the curtains were first parted to reveal the routine interaction between Westminster and Whitehall.

It would be misleading, however, to suggest that *Yes Minister* emerged, fully formed, from nowhere. Although its particular approach and focus was strikingly and invaluably novel, as a comic commentary on certain aspects of the Establishment it was actually founded on two largely distinct but very significant satirical traditions: one that targeted our elected representatives, and the other their unelected associates.

The failings of Britain's politicians, in particular, had been the subject of accessible satire since at least the eighteenth century, when William Hogarth and James Gillray captured all of the corruption in caricatures that even the illiterate lower classes could comprehend. The trend continued, albeit in a more decorous and discreet style, throughout the Victorian era, when such notable works of fiction as Anthony Trollope's series of *Palliser* novels personalised the political machinations of their age, poking fun, as they did so, at the institutionalised indolence of Parliament ('[Palliser] had spoken for two hours together, and all the House had treated his speech with respect – had declared that it was useful, solid, conscientious, and what not; but more than half the House had been asleep more than half the time that he was on his legs'[11]), the aimlessness of most administrations ('I never knew a government yet that wanted to do anything'[12]), the shameless self-absorption of the ambitious politician ('The rising in life of our familiar friends is, perhaps, the bitterest morsel of the bitter bread which we are called upon to eat'[13]) and the degree of cynicism demanded of those who desire to rise all the way to the top ('When a man wants to be Prime Minister he has to submit to vulgarity, and must give up his ambition if the task be too disagreeable to him'[14]).

By the early twentieth century, with pictures now proving to be at least as powerful as prose, political cartoonists such as David Low ensured that no popular newspaper would fail to inject at least a degree of irreverence into its coverage of the existing crop of MPs. Portraying politicians as, among other things, flea-ridden dogs, spitting cats, creeping insects, bawling babies, interchangeable fashion mannequins and a wide array of human grotesques, these daily cartoons gleefully deconstructed every new attempt at striking a proud and ingratiating pose. Winston Churchill, one of Low's favourite (and, to his great credit, most respectful) targets, reacted stoically to the rise of such visual critiques by describing Low in 1931 as a 'truly Laboucherian jester' (the allusion is to the waggish Liberal politician and critic Henry Labouchère) and his style of cartoon as 'the regular food on which the grown-up children of today are fed and nourished', adding for the benefit of the more mature among his Parliamentary peers: 'Just as eels are supposed to get used to skinning, so politicians get used to being caricatured'.[15]

A similarly dissident comic spirit was evident, here and there, in the theatre and cinema of that time, communicating a common message that echoed Thomas Carlyle's bitterly dismissive view of Parliament as 'a poor self-cancelling "National Palaver"'.[16] Such plays as the Unity Theatre's subversive take on the pantomime *Babes in the Wood* (a 1938 attack on Chamberlain's policy of appeasement) and William Douglas-Home's class-conscious confection *The Chiltern Hundreds* (a 1947 burlesque of recent election campaigns), and films ranging from the knockabout farce of *Old Mother Riley, MP* (a 1939 mockery of corrupt politicians) to Frank Launder and Sidney Gilliat's far more sophisticated mixture of romance and satire *Left Right and Centre* (a 1959 take on by-election opportunism), all contributed to such a consensus, and, in doing so, sported a succession of nods and winks to the gradual decline of the country's deferential political culture. Even radio, hindered though it was during the early post-war years by the notorious list of so-called 'taboos' collected in the BBC's policy guide, known informally as the 'Green Book', was prepared to insist on the right of its comic contributors to 'take a crack at the Government of the day and the Opposition so long as they do so sensibly, without undue acidity, and above all funnily'.[17]

By the start of the 1960s, a more confrontational spirit was abroad in the land and enjoying subversive success on the stage in the form of the intelligently irreverent revue *Beyond the Fringe*. Here, Peter Cook not only impersonated the then Prime Minister, Harold Macmillan, but also, on one memorable occasion, did so in his presence, staring out straight at him while saying: 'There's nothing I like better than to wander over to a theatre and sit there listening to a group of sappy, urgent, vibrant young satirists with a stupid great grin spread all over my silly face'.[18] Finally ready to air its own style of biting critique, television followed suit and launched the topical *That Was The Week That Was* in 1962 to inspire a new age of small-screen political satire. While leaving the real, intricate workings of Westminster largely an unexamined mystery, this and other shows' countless biting jibes about individual MPs certainly helped to popularise, if not quite democratise, the assessment of particular political performances.

Whitehall, meanwhile, was by no means exempt from the evolution of such irreverence (one thinks, for example, of the nepotistic, nit-picking Barnacle family, plodding around in circles within the Circumlocution Office in Charles Dickens' *Little Dorrit*,[19] and the Pharisaical Sir Gregory Hardlines, straining for ways to achieve greater respectability inside the Department of Weights and Measures in Trollope's *The Three Clerks*[20]), but, for a surprisingly long time, its officials seemed to be subjected to far less cultural abuse than did their Westminster counterparts. What made this satirical sluggishness so surprising was the fact that, in more formal critical circles, the creeping increase in the power and influence of the Civil Service had long been a topic of urgent and anxious discussion, with Max Weber – a German social theorist whose practical career unusually saw him straddle the bureaucratic and political divide – warning darkly as far back as the start of the twentieth century of the 'inescapable' and 'progressive' rise of a specially trained, unelected and therefore unaccountable administrative class, whose growing de facto dominance within the system came mainly from the fact that they were the 'permanent residents of the house of power', while any particular set of politicians were merely transient and amateurish players dependent on the vicissitudes of occasional reshuffles and regular elections.[21]

Because of their invisibility, however, there was perhaps something inevitable about popular culture's struggle to depict these figures as anything more vivid and vulnerable than either a sparely sketched troupe of interchangeable turnspits or a charcoal-smudged vignette of brollied, bowler-hatted and pinstriped éminences grises. While the caricaturists were busy individuating the most prominent members of the political class, their focus on the Civil Service tended to fix on the form instead of the content, mocking the institution rather than any of its members.

Often reduced to little more than a comical synecdoche, be it a sober suit, a lofty sneer perched on top of a starched wing collar or a solitary rubber stamp, the individual civil servant's identity, and accountability, thus remained protected for some time by the shield of his cultural and social obscurity. The *Daily Mirror's* William Haselden, for example, produced a series of cartoons early on in the twentieth century, entitled 'The Public Money and the Public Man', which treated Britain's mandarins as human beings who had been worn down into anodyne anonymity by their meek submission to rigid routine (with one sequence charting the process whereby the newly enlisted bureaucrat was gradually mummified by red tape[22]), leaving little else to ridicule except for the supposed point-lessness of the profession as a whole ('One of Mr Bureaucrat's first acts is to engage a huge staff,' another caption declared, 'then to provide them with a suitable number of forms to send out to the public'[23]).

Arguably something of a breakthrough occurred shortly before the start of the Second World War, with the arrival on Britain's airwaves of the radio comedy show *It's That Man Again* (usually abbreviated as *ITMA*[24]), where, for a while, much of the action took place in a shambolic war-time bureaucracy called 'The Office of Twerps' (which was situated next door to the real-life Office of Works).[25] Soon hugely popular with mil-lions of listeners, this fast-paced, pun-addicted, catchphrase-crazy show starred Tommy Handley as the 'Minister of Aggravation and Mysteries' ('We've been very busy in the Office of Twerps – making out official forms and scribbling all over them, issuing orders one day and cancelling them the next!'), who presided over such eccentric and overzealous officials as a strait-laced Permanent Secretary named Fusspot (whose standard response to any request was the startled exclamation: 'Most irregular!'). The absence of vision obliged both the writers and performers to transcend the old cartoonists' Whitehall stereotype and make an effort instead to craft a set of distinctive comic characters. It was still a blatantly broad-brush style of satire, but at least Britain's bureaucrats were now beginning to be treated as potentially intriguing personalities rather than completely flat and unin-teresting cardboard clichés.

This mildly progressive trend continued after the war, when many recently demobbed young performers showed a keen appetite for treating authority figures as potential targets for satire. A whole generation of clever character actors, such as John Le Mesurier, had encountered at first hand all kinds of meddling mandarins during their years of military service, and returned to stage and studio much more able to personalise their portrayal of any Civil Service type – ranging from the most risibly incompetent to the most chillingly efficient – who happened to pop up in a script. There was even a minor movie, the comedy *Dear Mr Prohack* (1949), that had Cecil Parker playing a senior Treasury official as a man who was hopelessly ill equipped to cope with the world outside of the Whitehall womb.

Meanwhile, in the variety halls and on the wireless, countless stand-up and sketch comedians, surveying a social scene in which all of the newly nationalised industries seemed in danger of being smothered by the remorseless, rapid spread of red tape, now rushed to include Britain's bureaucrats among the regular objects of their most biting jokes and routines. Indeed, by 1950, the then Head of the Civil Service, Sir Edward Bridges, noting the recent proliferation of gags and parodies ('I take this to be part of the Englishman's reaction against authority'), felt moved to make the sad prediction that he and his colleagues 'shall continue to be grouped with mothers-in-law and Wigan Pier as one of the recognised objects of ridicule'.[26]

Film-makers certainly wasted little time in trying to fulfil Sir Edward's prophecy on the cinema screen. The 1949 sardonic political fable *Passport to Pimlico* had already reunited Basil Radford and Naunton Wayne (familiar to audiences as the cricket-obsessed pair of old coves Charters and Caldicott in Alfred Hitchcock's 1938 comedy thriller *The Lady Vanishes*) playing a couple of clueless, chronically buck-passing civil servants ('A rather abstruse constitutional issue has now arisen,' declares one of them desperately, 'and I'm afraid we shall have to pass it on to the Law Offices Department . . .'), and now the artfully owlish Richard Wattis added further failings as an irascibly fatalistic Ministry of Education official called Manton Bassett in a series of popular comedies, beginning with *The Belles of St Trinians* (1954) and *Blue Murder at St Trinians* (1957).

The Boulting brothers, those masters of post-war film comedy, did much the same, deploying a mini-repertory company of crafty character actors to breathe life into the many bureaucrats who bungled about in the background of their socially acerbic movies, before placing the profession centre stage and casting Terry-Thomas as a hopelessly inept, nepotism-tainted, aimless Foreign Office diplomat in their 1959 satire *Carlton-Browne of the F.O.* ('It'll mean that I shall miss Ascot!' he gasps, on learning that he is being sent out on an important mission abroad right in the middle of the flat season). *Carlton-Browne* was arguably the most notable cinematic take on the Civil Service thus far, simply because, although it featured far more comedy than realism, it did at least purport to depict a whole network of officials, rather than just an individual apparatchik, at work within the walls of Whitehall, and thus projected to the public an artist's impression of the wheels and pulleys that worked the previously unseen machine.

Mainstream radio responded soon after with the BBC's *The Men from the Ministry* – a sitcom, written primarily by Edward Taylor, featuring Wilfrid Hyde-White (later replaced by Deryck Guyler) and Richard Murdoch as 'Number One' and 'Number Two', a pair of bumbling bureaucrats in the fictional 'General Assistance Department' of an unnamed Ministry. Running for fourteen series from 1962 to 1977,[27] the show proved very popular both at home and abroad without ever really threatening to say anything sharply incisive about the institution it was supposed to be mocking.

NUMBER ONE: Have you seen that memo from the Ministry of Regional Development?

NUMBER TWO: The one about that campaign against pollution?

NUMBER ONE: Yes, that's it. Did you take the appropriate action?

NUMBER TWO: Yes, I folded it up very small and put it under the leg of my desk to stop it rocking about.[28]

Formulaic and increasingly repetitive, too many of the episodes relied on the plot conceit of crossed wires within Whitehall (such as an order for '5,000 rubber boats' for an army exercise being misread as '5,000 rubber boots',[29] or a scribbled note about a dilatory secretary being 'due for a rocket' being mistaken as an official bulletin about the space programme[30]), but, every now and again, the odd barbed remark would slip in (such as the comment that a missile had been nicknamed 'The Civil Servant' – because 'it wouldn't work, they couldn't fire it and it cost the taxpayer a fortune').

There was even a similarly themed but short-lived ITV television sitcom *If It Moves, File It*, written by Troy Kennedy Martin, broadcast in 1970.[31] Starring John Bird and Dudley Foster as a pair of obsessively secretive but indolent British bureaucrats, it was as insular as its radio predecessor, making the same sort of mildly irreverent jokes without any real sense of point or purpose.

By 1980, therefore, there was nothing new or revolutionary per se about satirising either Britain's politicians or its bureaucrats. Both of these traditions were firmly established in the country's popular consciousness. What *was* new and, indeed, revolutionary about *Yes Minister* was the fact that it brought these two particular comic traditions together, synthesised them and then, in a very important sense, transcended them to create something much richer, more ambitious and much more insightful.

Yes Minister did not just go beyond what had passed for political satire in the past by featuring both politicians and civil servants. Crucially, it also went beyond the mere coexistence of these two types of public official, consigning to entertainment history the notion of them taking turns to pop in and out of the picture like the husband and wife inside a weather clock, and focused instead on the relationship *between* them. Here on show, for the first time in popular culture, was the clandestine connection, the hidden hyphen, at the heart of the British system of government – the living, meaningful, dynamic relationship between politician and bureaucrat.

The effect was akin to finding chess pieces that moved of their own volition. Suddenly, all of the old familiar snapshots that stood in for real political insight – all those multiple but interchangeable images of sober-looking suits slipping in and out of the big black shiny door of Number Ten, or gesticulating self-consciously from behind the conference podium, or posing awkwardly with random members of the public while out and about on the hustings – looked as flat and fake and shamelessly meretricious as they had, really, always been, and in their place now came a coherent and compelling vision of how the business of British government was actually done. The conversation was at last being covered.

Here, on the screen, were the scenes behind the scenes. Here was the real battle for power, the struggle for supremacy. Finally exposed were all the cogs and springs of the political clock, the proper nature of the tick and the tock.

Viewers saw the threat to progress and innovation posed by the likes of Sir Humphrey and his bureaucratic battalion of specialists without spirit, doing their best to bring about Max Weber's notorious vision of an 'iron cage' of cool and clinical efficiency that locked in more and more individuals while leaving all matters of political will and principle locked outside to perish in the 'polar night of icy darkness'.[32] Viewers also saw the contiguous threat to continuity and stability posed by the likes of Hacker and his horde of party political activists, who, as the ever-prescient nineteenth-century critic Walter Bagehot had once warned that they would, now seemed to oscillate wildly and bewilderingly between the arrogant desire that 'an eager, absolute man might do exactly what other eager men wished, and do it immediately',[33] and the cowardly inclination to allow any dubious version of 'vox populi', even when distorted into 'vox diaboli', to dictate the answers to the weightiest and most urgent of their decisions.[34]

Not since the stand-up comic Frankie Howerd, back in the early 1960s, contrived to reduce the analysis of high-level British politics to something that could be gossiped about over the garden wall ('Everyone blames Harold Macmillan for sacking half the Government last year,' he tittle-tattled. '*I* don't. No. I'm sorry, I don't blame *him*. I blame *her*. No, I do. It's Dot. Yes, *Dot*. Dotty Macmillan!'[35]), had the core of the country's institutional conflict seemed so engagingly comprehensible and comically credible. The major difference now was that the insight provided by *Yes Minister* was founded firmly on truth rather than just playful speculation, and what was being laughed at today could be taken away and reflected upon far more seriously tomorrow.

This, however, was only the first of several layers that contributed to the show's great and enduring appeal. Lurking beneath the pertinent but ultimately parochial comic casing were other, universal and timeless, themes that had more to do with political theory than political science. A wide range of topics, relating to truth, honour, prudence, accountability, personal integrity and the pursuit and preservation of power, were persistently picked at and probed under the surface as the show continued to progress.

There was, for example, the nagging matter of how political actors competed, through their mastery of the art of rhetoric, to present the public with a very partial version of what was supposed to pass for the truth. Such an issue had been a constant source of contention ever since ancient times in Athens, when the conservative Thucydides, on being asked whether he or the democrat Pericles was the more formidable political fighter, conceded glumly but promptly that Pericles was by far the better, because, even when he knew that he had been defeated, he still managed to convince the audience that he was in fact the victor.[36]

In the British context, the same theme had been evident since at least the middle of the seventeenth century, when Thomas Hobbes, alarmed as he watched the country collapse into civil war, warned about the combined dangers of dogmatism, unwarranted credulity and the cynical misuses of eloquence. 'For words,' he remarked darkly, 'are wise men's counters, they do but reckon by them; but they are the money of fools'.[37] Surveying the various factions that were fighting to win the bitter ideological battles of the time, he feared that the 'powerful Eloquence' of those in authority, which enabled them to 'procure[th] attention and Consent', was ever more likely to seduce most people's rational faculties into mistaking mere opinions and passions for the 'principles of Truth'.[38]

The point was echoed soon after by Hobbes' equally eminent theoretical contemporary, John Locke, when he complained that the art of rhetoric is 'nothing else but to insinuate wrong Ideas, move the Passions, and thereby mislead the Judgement', thus making such skills amount to the 'perfect cheat'. The conclusion, once again, was to demand that this deviousness be avoided 'in all Discourses that pretend to inform or instruct'.[39]

Three centuries on, and much the same kind of critique was being amplified by George Orwell shortly after the end of the Second World War, when he raged against the institutionalised insincerity that clanked and clunked as the machinery of each party's political claptrap continued to click and whir. 'When there is a gap between one's real and one's declared aims,' he warned, 'one turns as it were instinctively to long words and exhausted idioms, like a cuttlefish spurting out ink'. Surveying the weaselly rhetoric of his own age, he lamented that much of mainstream political discourse had been reduced to 'a mass of lies, evasions, folly, hatred, and schizophrenia', adding that when 'the general atmosphere is bad, language must suffer'.[40]

By the late twentieth century, in an age of all-encompassing mass media, this anxiety was more intense than ever, with orators now being supplemented by public relations-savvy 'post-orators', or, as they were soon to be called, 'spin doctors', giving another twist to what had already been twisted and thus making the means of communication seem more intricate, slippery and bewildering than ever before. In this sense, the ability of Yes Minister to feature regular scenes in which policies were packaged, messages massaged and errors explained away could not have been more welcome or apposite, mirroring so precisely as it did the growing prominence of advertising and PR as part and parcel of modern politics.

Here, the significance of the satire within *Yes Minister* stretched out far beyond the British Isles and spoke to audiences, and governments, all over the world. As Saatchi & Saatchi set about rebranding Margaret 'Milk Snatcher' Thatcher as 'The Iron Lady' in the UK, and similarly assiduous image makers in America started work on elevating Ronald Reagan to a level of stardom in Washington that he had never managed to achieve in Hollywood, and a whole new breed of fiercely ambitious communications officers began to buzz about trying to 'clarify' what had been 'misspoken' by their political bosses, *Yes Minister* highlighted the whole message-manipulation phenomenon, and in so doing underlined the irony of a process that appeared to treat honesty as the only intolerable policy in politics.

The sitcom's deepest and most weighty subtext of all, however, explored an issue that had preoccupied theorists and activists alike since classical times: namely, the problem of 'dirty hands'.[41] The deceptively simple-sounding question posed in Jean-Paul Sartre's 1948 play, *Les Mains Sales* – 'Do you think you can govern innocently?'[42] – has niggled away at any and every political figure when faced with the prospect of exercising what Trollope termed 'beneficent audacity'[43] and doing what feels like the 'wrong' thing in order to achieve what feels like the 'right' thing for the community as a whole.

At least three conflicting ethical answers have been articulated over the centuries. There is the deontological (whereby the likes of Immanuel Kant argued that, as no crisis ought to compel us to respond in a way that contravenes the dictates of our absolute moral principles, we should solve the problem of dirty hands simply by never getting our hands dirty[44]); the utilitarian (whereby the likes of John Stuart Mill contended that, as no particular moral code can be considered incontrovertible in absolute terms, we should go ahead and get our hands dirty to ensure we achieve the greatest good for the greatest number[45]); and the value plural-ist (whereby the likes of Isaiah Berlin claimed that, as there are different spheres of value between which crucial and potentially incommensurable conflicts are possible, we should only get our hands dirty if and when we are convinced that enough members of the community, here and now, expect us to do so[46]).

There is also a fourth, amoral, answer, championed most notoriously by Machiavelli, which insists that, as we cannot even be sure that there are enough people around who believe in a moral code, let alone enough people who will adhere to it consistently, we have no choice but to get our hands dirty if we want to acquire and hold onto political power. The crucial thing to do, in this sense, is not to do bad things badly, but rather to do bad things well: '[H]ow men live is so different from how they should live,' wrote Machiavelli, 'that a ruler who does not do what is generally done, but persists in doing what ought to be done, will undermine his power rather than maintain it. If a ruler who wants always to act honourably is surrounded by many unscrupulous men his downfall is inevitable. Therefore, a ruler who wishes to maintain his power must be prepared to act immorally when this becomes necessary'.[47]

Part of the brilliance of *Yes Minister* as a political satire was the way that it managed to weave this grandest of themes deep into the texture of its own episodic comedy, and use the regular tussles between a Minister and his Permanent Secretary as a delightfully subtle Socratic dialogue about the extent to which, if at all, our governors – and administrators – should dirty their own hands. Without the kind of strain or stress that one would find in an academic textbook or abstruse philosophical monograph, the show choreographed Hacker and Sir Humphrey through one ethical conundrum after another, as the hidden complexities of each idea were revealed and the obstacles in the way of its execution addressed.

It was this, and all the rest, that impressed itself upon the consciousness of the viewer on that dark and chilly evening back in February 1980. Its effect, as a consequence, was revelatory.

Suddenly, the ailing British sitcom seemed rejuvenated. Suddenly, Britain's shrouded political system seemed unveiled. Now Britain's television audience had a new show that not only entertained, informed and educated them, but also, in so doing, treated them with rare respect.

This book will tell the story of how this happened, how it developed and how it helped to change the way that popular culture engaged with contemporary politics. It is the story of a very courageous decision that for once, quite spectacularly, paid off.

PART ONE

*Laws, like sausages, cease to inspire respect in proportion
as we know how they are made.*
John Godfrey Saxe

1

The Writers

Humour is not a mood but a way of looking at the world.

It all started back in 1962. Two men, one a thirty-two-year-old BBC current affairs editor named Antony Jay and the other a nineteen-year-old Cambridge law undergraduate called Jonathan Lynn, were both drawn, quite independently of each other, to the widespread media coverage of a political saga that, as it developed, seemed to epitomise the strange effect that the political system could have on a supposedly ordinary individual.

The story concerned the Labour MP Sir Frank Soskice, a sober-minded and well-regarded barrister turned politician (praised by the press for 'his disdain for intrigue and his indifference to flattery'[1]) who was at that time the Shadow Cabinet's spokesman for Home Affairs and a well-known campaigner against capital punishment. Sir Frank had just helped start a petition to secure a posthumous pardon for Timothy Evans, a semi-literate van driver with an estimated mental age of ten and a half, who had been executed back in March 1950 for the murder of his daughter inside the family's top-floor flat at 10 Rillington Place in Notting Hill Gate, west London.

During his trial, Evans had accused one of the chief witnesses against him, his downstairs neighbour, John Christie, of being the real killer of his wife as well as his daughter, but his claims had been dismissed. Three years after Evans' execution, however, Christie was finally exposed as a serial killer who had murdered at least eight women in the same house, secreting some of their bodies in various parts of the building. Shortly before his own execution in July 1953, Christie confessed to murdering Evans' wife, and, although he continued to deny it, was strongly suspected also of strangling the daughter.

As public unrest over the soundness of the original ruling mounted, a private inquiry, led by John Scott Henderson QC, was promptly set up to examine the possible miscarriage of justice in Evans' hanging. The result of the almost risibly perfunctory week-long investigation, however, was deemed such a whitewash in favour of the police that, far from defusing the situation, it only served to make it seem even more incendiary than before.

Questions continued to be raised in Parliament over the handling of the matter and, in 1955, the editors of the *Observer*, the *Spectator*, the *National and English Review* and the *Yorkshire Post* formed a delegation to petition the Home Secretary to grant a new inquiry. In the same year, a book about the case, *The Man on Your Conscience* by the solicitor Michael Eddowes, provided a compelling argument suggesting that Evans had actually been innocent, thus further stimulating widespread debate. Although the demand for a new inquiry was denied,[2] the campaign for justice continued into the next decade, when another book on the subject, the television journalist Ludovic Kennedy's *10 Rillington Place* (1961), dramatically revived public interest in the case.

A large number of politicians, citing the evidence that had been set out so clearly and powerfully in Kennedy's recent book, urged the then Home Secretary, R.A. Butler, to order a second inquiry, but Butler stood firm and refused. Claiming that 'witnesses' recollection of the events of 1949 must inevitably have been dimmed by the [passage] of time', and deeming Kennedy's book to be of interest only 'in its presentation of the case for believing Evans to have been innocent rather than in its addition to the information already available', he concluded that 'a further inquiry could not bring any new information to light'.[3] This only exacerbated the anger among many Opposition MPs, and one of them, Patrick Gordon Walker, initiated a new House of Commons debate on the subject in June 1961.

Sir Frank Soskice, predictably, was one of the first MPs to rise and contribute to the proceedings. 'I desire to make a most earnest appeal to the Home Secretary,' he said, 'to accept the suggestion that there should be a further investigation into the circumstances of this case. [. . .] If ever there was a debt due to justice, and to the reputation both of our own judicial system and to the public conscience of many millions of people in this country, that debt is one that the Home Secretary should now pay'.[4]

Once again, the Opposition was defeated and the controversy dragged on, with Sir Frank and others pledging their support the following year for the petition demanding that Evans be granted a posthumous pardon. It was at this point, as the various media summaries of the saga so far started to circulate, that Antony Jay and Jonathan Lynn, along with many other people, refreshed their memories of the case and looked forward with interest to how it might finally be resolved.

It did not seem as though they would have long to wait. When the Labour Leader Hugh Gaitskell died at the beginning of 1963, he was replaced by the more incisive Harold Wilson, who, among other things, was an outspoken opponent of capital punishment and a strong critic of how the Evans case had been handled. One of the first promises he made, as the new Leader of the Opposition, was a vow to do whatever he could to push through a bill that abolished the death penalty.[5] It seemed only a matter of time, therefore, once Labour won the October 1964 General Election, that Sir Frank Soskice and his fellow campaigners would finally see Evans declared innocent.

The next time the issue was raised in Parliament, however, in February 1965, the new Home Secretary summarily declined the request, explaining without any sound or sign of regret that too many years had passed 'to elicit the truth about this tragic case', claiming that he himself was ambivalent about the matter ('I certainly think it would be kinder not to express views one way or the other'), and then adding: 'Even if the innocence of Evans were established, I have no power to make an official declaration of it'.[6] In spite of a succession of loud and passionate pleas to think again, he flatly refused to relent, insisting: 'I think it is much better that the matter should be left as it is'.[7] Many people both inside and outside of Parliament would have been surprised at the Home Secretary's ruling, no matter who he happened to be. In this particular instance, however, they were especially shocked, because this new Home Secretary happened to be none other than Sir Frank Soskice.

The sheer irony of the situation was astounding. Here was a Home Secretary effectively snubbing himself, or at least his slightly younger self, after years of campaigning, now that he finally had the power to do what he had always demanded.

The most cynical of insiders put this seemingly bizarre volte-face down simply to the exigencies of ambition: 'Such are the unfortunate effects of office in general,' observed the Conservative MP Norman St John-Stevas, while betraying more than a trace of a smirk, 'and the Home Office in particular'[8]. More idealistic voices raged at what they regarded as Sir Frank's brazen hypocrisy (a visibly furious Ian Gilmour, a Conservative MP who had formerly campaigned alongside Sir Frank for justice on this very matter, asked him to explain to the House 'why it would be kinder to the relatives of Timothy Evans not to say that he was innocent if he was, in fact, innocent'[9]). While Roy Jenkins, the man who would soon replace him as Home Secretary, was content to explain it away as the consequence of personal incompetence (claiming that Sir Frank had 'practically no political sense and an obsessive respect for legal precedent'[10]).

The most common explanation, among the broader public, was simply that here was yet another politician whose principles had proven to be far more pliable than his passion for self-preservation. Following on from such recent political embarrassments as Tam Galbraith's entanglement in a sex and espionage scandal;[11] Harold Macmillan's self-serving purge of one-third of his own Cabinet;[12] John Profumo's Parliamentary perjury when challenged about his alleged affair with the mistress of a Soviet spy;[13] and the 14th Earl of Home's eager use of the new Peerage Act – which he had formerly seemed so disinclined to support during its passage through the Lords – in order to disclaim his title and return to the House of Commons as Prime Minister;[14] Sir Frank's perverse case of self-betrayal struck many disenchanted onlookers as more or less par for the course in British politics.

A thoughtful few, however, were left pondering what could possibly go on within the country's dimly lit and labyrinthine political system to convince such characters that there was any real logic to their illogicality. Antony Jay and Jonathan Lynn were certainly among those whose imaginations were captured by this question.

It made them think more rigorously about politics. It also made them think more carefully about comedy. This was, after all, a sequence of events that, while very serious, also seemed, in a sense, far more strangely, sardonically amusing than anything most playwrights might have plotted. Truth, it appeared, really could be much funnier than fiction.

What both of these men shared, at this stage, was a perspective on such things that owed much to the modus operandi cultivated at their shared alma mater. Marked by a stringency less urbane and more restlessly reductive than the equivalent intellectual culture evident at Oxford at the same time, the dominant disposition in Cambridge, during that post-war age, was, as far as the humanities were concerned, the kind of dogged and disciplined disputatiousness epitomised by the followers of F.R. Leavis and the disciples of Ludwig Wittgenstein. Every discussion, at every level, seemed to rock to the same relentless rhythm of the classic Cantabrigian conjunction: 'But what do you mean by . . . But could it . . . But should it . . . But what if . . . ?'

Antony Jay had gone to Cambridge in 1949 to study Classics and Comparative Philology at Magdalene College. Jonathan Lynn had arrived in 1961 to read Law at Pembroke College.

Both of them witnessed at close hand the kind of characters who were already intent on becoming part of Britain's political Establishment, rushing to sign up to the student version of their favoured political party and wasting no time before making their voice heard in the main debates. Jay was a contemporary of future Conservative Party Cabinet Ministers Douglas Hurd, John Biffen, Norman St John-Stevas and Cecil Parkinson, as well as the Labour MP Greville Janner. Lynn found himself stuck in the middle of a veritable glut of future Thatcherites that included Norman Lamont, Michael Howard, John Selwyn Gummer, Peter Bottomley and Peter Lilley, as well as a Liberal-leaning economist called Vince Cable.

Although both Jay and Lynn were, if anything, just as preoccupied by political ideas, neither was impressed by the naked ambition and tunnel vision these contemporaries all displayed. Lynn, in particular, found the vast majority of them 'smug young men' who oozed the kind of confidence that suggested they saw themselves as predestined for prominence in Parliament.

Their natural habitat was the unnatural habitat of the Union Society's debating chamber, situated behind the Round Church in Bridge Street. A wooden-floored, leather-seated, stuffy Victorian construction modelled loosely on the House of Commons, it was the place where these young men, looking prematurely middle-aged with their flat, brilliantined hair, bow ties and dinner jackets, spouted their 'pimply puerility' on a regular basis. 'Their unwarranted confidence in their own abilities,' Lynn would later recall, 'was a sight to behold'.[15]

It was, in its own quaint way, a kind of theatre, but this was a theatre devoid of all deliberate irony. The only appeal it held for Jay and Lynn was of a limited anthropological nature, suited to a short period of study before being consigned to the mind as a memory. The only effect that it had on either of them was to push them away from conventional political participation and towards critical commentary: 'It became clear to me,' Lynn would recall, 'that my only role in politics could be to ridicule the system'.[16]

Jay, outside of his formal studies, preferred to seek out the kind of pastimes that would relax and refresh him, rather than frittering away his free hours squabbling with the student politicians. His extra-curricular interests included 'cricket, hockey, bridge, squash and editing the college magazine. I did think about joining the Footlights – my parents were both on the stage – but it would have meant abandoning my hopes of a decent degree, which considering I had a major classical scholarship seemed a pity. After all, I could act later, but I couldn't get a degree later'.[17]

He also began to feed what would be a lifelong fascination with the politics of organisations, quickly understanding, in his own environment, how the image of Cambridge as one big university ruling over a collection of little colleges obscured a reality that was its opposite, with the colleges (which he likened to 'feudal baronies'[18]) combining to keep the university impotent and thus ensure that any proposed reforms (unless the biggest and wealthiest colleges really wanted them) would be thwarted.

Jonathan Lynn, once alienated from the Union debates (the fact that his parents had paid for him to be a life member, in the hope that he might end up as its president, obliged him to linger a little longer than he would otherwise have liked), was soon drawn to the more conventional and inclusive form of theatre provided by the University's Footlights Society. He continued to find elements of interest in his studies (and was particularly impressed by the teachings of Brian King, an unusually progressive Lecturer in Jurisprudence, who brought a more worldly, sociological and psychological perspective to how laws actually work in practical reality[19]), but, increasingly, it would be the Footlights that consumed most of his time. It was here, along with such talented contemporaries as future

Pythons John Cleese, Graham Chapman and Eric Idle, and Goodies Graeme Garden, Tim Brooke-Taylor and Bill Oddie, as well as future director Richard Eyre, writer/actor Tony Hendra and producers David Hatch and Humphrey Barclay, that Lynn first explored his potential both as a writer and performer.

It was certainly propitious that he was based at Pembroke, because, in those days, the place had acquired the informal name of 'the comedy college'. The huge influence of its most precociously talented alumnus Peter Cook, who had graduated in 1960 and immediately gone on to find national fame as part of the *Beyond the Fringe* quartet, remained rich and widespread in Cambridge when Lynn, along with his friend Eric Idle, performed a sketch together at a Pembroke 'smoker' (an annual revue that served as a showcase for new talent), which led in turn to a reprise at a Footlights smoker and earned them entry into the University's broadest-based comedy troupe.

There was no instant impact: at the end of Lynn's second year as a student, his first contribution to a Footlights revue (*A Clump of Plinths*), saw him limited to playing the drums (he was a keen jazz drummer) down in the orchestra pit. He did much better at the end of his third and final year, however, appearing onstage as a bona fide member of the cast in a revue entitled *Stuff What Dreams Are Made Of*, which also featured Graeme Garden, Eric Idle, John Cameron (later known for his work on TV and in movies as a composer and arranger), David Gooderson (an actor and director who would end up being best known for playing 'Davros' in *Dr Who*), Sue Heber-Percy, Flick Hough, Mark Lushington (who went on to serve as a union leader for the NUT in Hackney) and Guy Slater (another member who would forge a career as an actor, writer and director).

As with so many students whose attention was distracted from their formal studies by the glare and glamour of the Footlights, Lynn ended up in the summer of 1964 underperforming academically with a disappointing Lower Second degree, and consequently abandoned the idea of a life in Law in favour of pursuing his interest in writing and performing. Jay, on the other hand, had graduated in 1952 with a flawless First and, after a couple of years of compulsory National Service in the Royal Signals (where he rose to the rank of 2nd Lieutenant), had embarked on a broadcasting career at the BBC.

Jay would later describe his outlook during the nine years that he spent working in talks and current affairs at the Corporation as that of 'a card-carrying media liberal',[20] and, according to his own recollections, such an outlook was fast becoming the norm in Britain's metropolitan culture. He was part of a new generation of young writers, editors, producers and reporters who, having grown up during an era defined by a world war, in a country ruled by censorship, identity cards, rationing and relentless regimentation, were now, as adults, eager for greater freedom and deeply suspicious of those who seemed content with the status quo.

Jay's first major job was to help bring to the screen a new kind of current affairs programme that reflected the change in the national mood away from deference and paternalism towards a more informal, critical and questioning attitude. Championed by two of the BBC's most innovative and iconoclastic young programme-makers, Donald Baverstock (a future Controller of BBC1) and Alasdair Milne (a future Director-General), this new programme, which was to be called *Tonight* and would be broadcast live five nights a week, was designed to sweep away British television's traditional approach to covering the news and current affairs – an approach which relied on a starchy, stiff-lipped style that Baverstock and Milne found far too dull, submissive and condescending – and replace it with something that was lively, varied, relaxed, seriously journalistic, occasionally very playful but also essentially moral.[21] The idea, as one of their bosses Grace Wyndham Goldie would later put it, was to create a programme that was firmly and clearly on the side of the viewer rather than the rulers, and would speak up for them rather than down to them. 'Power,' she wrote, 'even the power endorsed by election in a democratic society, did not confer wisdom, and those who wielded it could be questioned'.[22]

Jay could not have been more suited to supporting such a venture, and, initially as film director, later as editor, he would help make the programme one of the great success stories of British television's post-war era, launching the careers of a tidal wave of memorably distinctive reporters (including Cliff Michelmore, Alan Whicker, Fyfe Robertson, Magnus Magnusson, Julian Pettifer, Michael Cockerell, Cynthia Judah, Macdonald Hastings, Brian Redhead and Kenneth Allsop). First broadcast on 18 February 1957, the *Tonight* programme grew rapidly in popularity – to the point where it attracted a nightly audience of around seven million viewers – and won unprecedented critical prestige. Perhaps inevitably, given that it began just over a year after Harold Macmillan arrived at Number Ten and ended in 1965 about twenty months after he departed, the new Prime Minister became one of the most enduring targets of its opprobrium – but he was far from being alone.

'[We] were not just anti-Macmillan,' Jay would recall, 'we were anti-industry, anti-capitalism, anti-advertising, anti-selling, anti-profit, anti-patriotism, anti-monarchy, anti-Empire, anti-police, anti-armed forces, anti-bomb, anti-authority'.[23] This was a somewhat misleading exaggeration – the programme sought to apportion praise as well as blame, and could be constructive as well as destructive – but it certainly did refuse to accept, prima facie, any explanation by the Establishment designed to justify its actions. What it showed politicians, in particular, was that, from this point on, television existed to make them accountable rather than merely visible, and, as a consequence, the programme set a new and higher standard for the way current affairs was covered.

While Antony Jay was making his name as an editor and producer, Jonathan Lynn was beginning to establish himself on the stage and screen as an entertainer. Shortly after graduation, he had been recruited by his old Footlights colleagues John Cleese, Graham Chapman, Tim Brooke-Taylor and Bill Oddie, who had renamed their old *Clump of Plinths* revue *Cambridge Circus* and restaged it in London's West End. One of their fellow cast members, Chris Stuart-Clark, had since dropped out to pursue other interests, and so, in May 1964, Lynn was enlisted just in time to join them on a short tour of New Zealand before transferring in September to New York; first for a short run at the Plymouth Theater on Broadway, and then, for the remainder of the year, at a cosier café theatre in Greenwich Village.

Encouraged by the experience, which had not only exposed him to large theatre audiences but also given him his television debut on the hugely popular *Ed Sullivan Show*, Lynn returned to Britain and began working steadily over the next few years as an actor in repertory, spending time in companies based in Leicester, Edinburgh and at the Bristol Old Vic, as well as the odd production in London, appearing in everything from *The Taming of the Shrew* to *Fiddler on the Roof* and receiving a nomination for a *Plays and Players* award as 'Most Promising New Actor' for his performance in Paul Ableman's 1965 two-act comedy *Green Julia*.

He also joined his old Cambridge contemporaries Bill Oddie, Graeme Garden and Tony Buffery, along with Oxford graduates Terry Jones and Michael Palin, to make a short-lived but memorable sketch show called *Twice a Fortnight*. Produced and directed by Tony Palmer ('in front of a tanked-up audience'[24]), it was screened on BBC1 during 1967, ran for ten editions and featured not only the kind of fresh, irreverent and unconventional humour that would help create the culture in which the likes of *Monty Python's Flying Circus* would soon thrive, but also, with its regular musical guests (which included Cream, The Who and The Small Faces), paved the way for a new style of youth-oriented variety show that mixed comedy with popular music.

By the end of the decade, however, Lynn was looking to develop a second, complementary career as a writer, and he got his chance after joining the cast of a new ITV sitcom (adapted by, among others, Lynn's fellow Footlights alumni John Cleese, Graham Chapman, Bill Oddie and Graeme Garden from the bestselling stories by Richard Gordon, and produced by another old college friend Humphrey Barclay), called *Doctor in the House* (1969). Although he was dropped as an actor when the show returned for a second series, entitled *Doctor at Large* (1971), the friendship that he had formed with one of the show's main stars, George Layton, led to them collaborating (with Layton using his occasional pseudonym of 'Oliver Fry') on a script for one of the episodes.[25]

It helped that Lynn came from a family of doctors, so he could draw on a fund of real-life medical stories, but there was also a freshness and paciness about the comedy that he crafted with Layton. The episode slipped slyly from a mundane-sounding first act about nurses 'with big bazookas' into a surprising second act that mocked male hypocrisy and consequently stood out. Barclay, indeed, was so impressed with their writing that he went on to use them regularly in future series, including *Doctor in Charge* (1972–3), *Doctor at Sea* (1974) and *Doctor on the Go* (1975), and they also started supplying scripts for a number of other sitcoms, including several episodes in 1972 of ITV's creakily coarse but consistently popular *On the Buses*.

Even though he was confined by the context of such formulaic fare, Lynn still showed an intriguing ability to slip in some detail, exchange or sequence that gave an otherwise anodyne scenario a little more character and clout. In a predictably farcical episode of *Doctor in Charge* entitled

'Which Doctor', for example, viewers were treated to a brief but unusu-ally sardonic glimpse (for ITV at least) of the old boys' network, as one insufferably smug senior Harley Street surgeon, after cheerfully bidding farewell to a now useless dying patient ('I'll miss his money'), brags to his NHS equivalent about his busy practice ('business is booming') and recent knighthood, and hints that a lesser gong might be obtainable via one of his glamorous cocktail parties ('We'll get an OBE for you yet, Geoffrey!'). It was this good sense of when and how to give such conventional shows a bit of bite that made producers increasingly appreciative of Lynn's ability to shape a script.[26]

It did not take too long, however, for him to feel as though, in spite of such signature touches, he was fast becoming the servant of the sitcom 'sausage machine',[27] stuffing in a tiny bit of meat with plenty of filler and artificial flavourings, to keep each familiar format going. He wanted to try to write episodes that were more 'grown up', featuring less conventional and more satirical themes and situations, but, time and again, the produc-ers of existing sitcoms kept passing on such proposals. Eventually, for want of another option, he and Layton decided to create a show of their own.

Entitled *My Brother's Keeper*, it was envisaged by Lynn as a fairly daring affair that explored the idea, which he had been pondering ever since his undergraduate days, that there was a surprisingly slender psychological line separating law enforcers from law breakers (a criminology study of identical twins separated at birth had found that, of thirteen persistent offenders, nine of their long-lost brothers had also grown up to be persis-tent offenders, while the other four had become policemen[28]). He planned to play a petty criminal, called Pete Booth, whose twin brother Brian, played by Layton, was a dutiful policeman. Slowly but surely, however, the premise was prodded and poked by ITV producers until it was deemed safer and more suitable for one of its prime-time comedy slots, with the criminal being replaced by a comically militant student.

Reaching the screen in 1975, it ran for two series and performed well in the ratings, but, given the knowledge of what it might have been, it proved a profoundly frustrating experience for Lynn, who felt that a career was being crushed. Looking back to trace the trajectory of his writing partnership with Layton, he would later describe it as evolving up to this point in the following manner: 'Initially, enthusiasm. Later, gloom. Not about him, though. My own depression'.[29] His mood was made worse as he surveyed so many of his old Footlights friends doing work that, in his eyes, seemed much more distinctive and rewarding, such as John Cleese's achievements on TV, first with *Monty Python* and now *Fawlty Towers*, and Richard Eyre's efforts in the theatre, where, in his capacity as artistic director of the Nottingham Playhouse, he was commissioning and directing a succession of interesting new plays, including Trevor Griffiths' critically lauded *Comedians*.

Ready for a change but unsure of what to do, on 29 April 1976 Lynn glanced, quite by chance, at an advertisement in the latest edition of the weekly industry publication *The Stage*. It was for someone to fill the vacant position of artistic director of the Cambridge Theatre Company. Tired of being a 'joke machine', and impatient to stretch himself, Lynn decided the time was right for him to apply.[30]

The career of Antony Jay, meanwhile, was developing in a different direction. He left the BBC (where he had risen to the lofty position of Head of Television Talk Features) in 1964, although he remained so highly thought of at the Corporation that he was given a succession of long-term contracts that retained his services as a consultant. Working for a number of companies as a freelance writer, adviser and producer, he helped develop several arts programmes, contributed satirical material for *The Frost Report* (BBC1, 1966–7), wrote the commentary for the dramatic 'let in daylight upon magic' documentary *Royal Family* (BBC1, 1969), and assisted in a wide variety of other projects. He also popularised his views on politics, bureaucracy and individual liberty via a number of best-selling books, which included the elegantly analytical *Management and Machiavelli* (1967), the quasi-anthropological *Corporation Man* (1972) and a drily amusing self-help pamphlet entitled *The Householder's Guide to Community Defence against Bureaucratic Aggression* (also 1972).

His great gift, as it emerged from all of these diverse enterprises, was to be able to deconstruct complex institutions and processes as if they were tangible mechanisms, grasping the intricacies of their internal structure and then not only explaining, simply and clearly, how they functioned, but also suggesting how, if at all, they might be made more effective. On his own classically educated terms, he was more of a hedgehog than a fox, more of a man who knew one big thing rather than one who knew many

little things; in the sense that wherever he looked, be it business or government or any other organised form of activity, he felt that it could be
reduced to the way that the formal rules of engagement were interpreted
and enacted.

Rather like Walter Bagehot had done before him, Jay had a rare flair
for connecting the paper description to the living reality. It was this gift
for animated enlightenment that provided the pattern that united all of
his projects.

He found yet another venture through which he could channel his
ideas and expertise when, in 1972, he teamed up with John Cleese and
two old BBC colleagues, Peter Robinson and Michael Peacock, to form
Video Arts, a production company designed to make concise but exceptionally engaging training films for a wide range of business organisations.
Dealing with everything from committee meetings to consumer complaints, the films would use humour to demonstrate how the dynamics
of any typical situation could best be managed to everyone's advantage.
Using an impressive unofficial repertory group of well-known performers,
including Terence Alexander, Tim Brooke-Taylor, Connie Booth, Nigel
Hawthorne, Prunella Scales, Andrew Sachs and John Cleese himself, the
company soon established itself as the leader in its field, garnering numerous awards, plenty of critical plaudits and countless contented customers.[31]

There was still a restless curiosity about Antony Jay, and it was therefore no surprise when, in 1974, he accepted an offer to become a member
of Lord Annan's Committee on the Future of Broadcasting. Launched by
the Labour Government's Roy Jenkins, it was charged with the challenging task of assessing the extent to which Britain's broadcasting industry,
organisationally, technologically and financially, could and should be
modernised and democratised. The process, which lasted for three years,
turned Jay temporarily from outsider to insider, and afforded him the
priceless opportunity to gorge himself on privileged gossip and insights,
and to assess at close quarters the routine connections between Whitehall
and Westminster.

It was during this period that the paths of Antony Jay and Jonathan
Lynn finally came to cross. When Video Arts started making its first few
training films, Lynn was one of the people John Cleese persuaded to get
involved (for an initial sum of 'thirty quid plus a deferred fee'[32]) both

as a writer and performer. This work, which included such titles as the award-winning *Who Sold You This, Then?* (1972),[33] *It's All Right, It's Only a Customer* (1973) and *Selling on the Telephone* (1975), also brought him into contact with Cleese's fellow director, Antony Jay.

Lynn's first impression of Jay, looking at him through the eyes of someone well used to casting characters, was that of 'a typical BBC producer or an Oxbridge don': 'He was tall with thinning, wispy, long greying hair, a tweed sports jacket, worn-down suede shoes and a characteristic, slightly knock-kneed stance. He talked very fast in a voice that became slightly squeaky when enthusiastic'.[34] Jay, in turn, already recognised Lynn from his television and stage performances, and, face to face, warmed to his quick wit and unforced expertise. 'I was rather impressed,' he later remarked, 'by his professional knowledge of actors and audiences'.[35] In some ways, they made an unconventional pair. Although they shared a common cultural background of public school (Jay at St Paul's in London and Lynn at Kingswood in Bath) and Cambridge, they were, in many respects, very different.

There was, for example, a thirteen-year age gap between them (Jay was born in London in 1930, and Lynn in Bath in 1943), and while Jay had experienced growing up in an era that had witnessed Britain going to war, Lynn had grown up in a period that had seen the country struggle to cope with the austerities of peace. Jay had been through the enforced regimentation of post-war National Service, while Lynn reached the same age just after the compulsory call-up had been cancelled. The effect, arguably, was to give Jay's youthful liberalism something of a nostalgic character, yearning for a 'glorious revolution' that would restore the freedom of the pre-war years, while lending Lynn's early rebelliousness more of an inchoate, anticipatory feel.

They also projected, unaffectedly, quite distinct kinds of social personae: Jay was actually an unusually complex soul who was the product of a lineage that was part quintessentially English (on his mother Catherine's side) and part Jewish immigrant (on his actor father Ernest's side[36]), but, superficially, he exuded the kind of effortless assuredness that epitomised a creature of the Establishment. Conversely, Lynn, whose awkward teenage years had been marked by him being the only Jewish boy at a Methodist school ('If you want to create an outsider,' he would later observe, 'that's a good way to go about it'[37]), had settled into the image of an obvious and somewhat prickly anti-Establishment figure.

The snapshot impression was thus of contrasts: tall and short, reserved and outspoken, conservative and radical, insider and outsider. Jay, on top of all of this, was primarily an analyst and an observer, a man who had made his mark behind the scenes, while Lynn was an actor and an artist, best known for what he had contributed out on the stage and in front of the cameras.

Once the two men had spent some time in each other's company, however, they found that they complemented each other surprisingly well. Each had acquired a degree of specialist expertise and a range of experiences that impressed and interested the other. Each had the kind of character that had a pleasingly moderating effect on the other. Even their respective political outlooks, which, with Jay's located recognisably to the right of centre and Lynn's some way to the left, appeared at first sight to suggest a possible conflict, were in fact far closer than they looked, as Jay's sceptical and strongly libertarian brand of conservatism had more in common with Whig traditions than Tory ones, while Lynn's radical instincts were far more redolent of Paine than Tawney or Marx.

They were thus, beneath the superficial contrasts, kindred spirits. Both of them were deeply suspicious of privilege and power. Both were passionately egalitarian and meritocratic. Both had an instinctive sympathy for the individual, the eccentric and the outsider against any form of oppressive hegemony. Both hated hypocrisy and humbug. They could tell, as they talked, that they were on the same side.

The two of them got to know and like each other even better once John Cleese became distracted by his work on *Fawlty Towers* and, in his absence, Jay started collaborating with Lynn. By the time that Lynn had taken on the role of artistic director at the Cambridge Theatre Company, Video Arts was doing so well that it was looking to increase its annual output significantly, so when Jay invited him to contribute on a more regular basis, Lynn, whose theatre position was aesthetically rewarding but poorly paid, saw it as 'an insurance policy'.[38] 'It was,' Jay would say, 'a very happy and successful partnership.'[39]

It was at this time, during a break from writing, that Jay began to reminisce with Lynn about one of the strongest and sharpest political memories they shared: that extraordinary moment, about a decade before, when Sir Frank Soskice stood up in the House of Commons and dismissed the demands of Sir Frank Soskice. They laughed again about the absurdity of the saga, and were further amused when they reflected on the fact that, soon after, Sir Frank was rewarded for his troubles by being elevated to the House of Lords as Baron Stow Hill of Newport.

Warming to the subject, Jay then proceeded to tell Lynn other stories he had heard about the various ways that politicians, once they became drawn deep into Whitehall's maw, had their plans rethought or thwarted. He talked, for example, about a memorably candid lecture that the redoubtable Labour MP Barbara Castle had given at the Civil Service College at Sunningdale in 1972, bemoaning all of the problems that she had encountered, when Secretary of State for Transport, with her Department's Permanent Secretary, and warning that the Civil Service ('the best spying organisation I have ever known') had now become 'a state within a state'.[40] He also recounted the various recent broadsides that Castle's colleague, Tony Benn, had fired at Britain's unelected bureaucracy for having the effrontery to undermine the plans of its elected representatives.[41] It was through thinking about such things, Jay said, that he had come to the realisation that 'there was something called "Ministry policy" which was not the Minister's policy',[42] and that, as a consequence, he now saw 'the conflict between the politicians in government and the civil servants as being far more interesting and far less understood in Britain than the conflict between Government and the Opposition'.[43]

Jay then went further, and told Lynn that he found this dynamic so intriguing, so revealing and so rich in satirical potential, that it had given him an idea. It had given him an idea for a sitcom.

2

The Situation

For fifty years he listened at the door.
He heard some secrets and invented more.
These he wrote down, and women, statesmen, kings,
Became degraded into common things.

Antony Jay's idea for a sitcom concerned 'the corridors of power'.[1] It would be set in Whitehall, in a typical Ministerial Department, and would feature the chronic tug of war between a leading politician and a senior civil servant. Illuminating what had hitherto been secreted deep in the system's Stygian gloom, this sitcom would be different, revealing, controversial and, potentially, very, very funny.

There was only one problem. Jonathan Lynn did not want to do it: 'I thought that was really the most boring suggestion that had come my way for a long time,' he later explained.[2] 'Furthermore, I had just renounced sitcom writing. I told him I wasn't interested'.[3] That, it appeared, was that. Jay, for all his polymathic capacities, had no experience of writing a situation comedy, nor, on his own, did he feel confident about attempting to create one, and so, reluctantly, he shelved the idea and got on with his other projects, while, quite amicably, Lynn went off to concentrate on his new role at the Cambridge Theatre Company.

The idea, however, did not fade away. As various new political stories came and went, Jay could not stop wondering how they might have been covered in his sitcom. Lynn, meanwhile, recharged his batteries through his stage work, and, slowly but surely, started having second thoughts.

The two men got back in touch with each other early in 1977. Both of them agreed that, on reflection, this was indeed an idea that merited further consideration.

Why did Lynn now want to pursue it? The answer, he had realised, in a cool hour, was that he had unfinished business as a writer of sitcoms. Once he had stopped obsessing over what had gone wrong with his previous efforts, and once (after overseeing other writers' work in the theatre) he had regained some of the old hunger to write something himself, he realised that Jay's idea might be worth reappraising.

This time, the conversation was positive. They reacquainted each other with the basic premise, played around with possible options and reflected on real-life inspirations. The case of Sir Frank Soskice came up again, inevitably, as did a few more recent examples of politicians being caught with their hands looking distinctly dirty. Jay also related some of his memories of working with political guests during his early days at the BBC in Current Affairs ('I realised how much difference there was between the way politicians spoke on air – as if they were responsible for everything – and the fact that behind the scenes they were constantly turning to their Private Secretary and asking, "What's the answer to this?"[4]) as well as the moans and groans about the struggles between political and bureaucratic officials that he was hearing while working with the recently retired Harold Wilson on his forthcoming television series, *A Prime Minister on Prime Ministers*.[5] Reflecting on the obvious comic potential that lurked in such anecdotes, the pair of them laughed at the enduring truth of Will Rogers' old saying: 'There's no trick to being a humorist when you have the whole government working for you'.[6]

Eagerly expanding on his theme, Jay talked more about the work that now went on in Whitehall instead of Westminster, and how the real discussions, debates and decisions were made there, behind closed doors, rather than out in the playhouse of Parliament as such. The power of the sitcom, therefore, would come from the fact that it would, in effect, be taking the audience behind the curtain, backstage, to show them what goes on in rehearsal before each polished political performance is put on.

It would not only peel off all the masks and show politicians in a different, and far more realistic, light. It would also, Jay insisted, finally show civil servants as they really were, as individuals, as a community, in situ, behind the familiar but hopelessly old-fashioned caricature.

This was something that seemed particularly pertinent, as far as the novelty of the proposed sitcom was concerned. Up to this point, as Lynn would acknowledge, 'All comedy shows that featured civil servants portrayed them as boring people who wore bowler hats and drank a lot of tea'.[7] Jay, though, was determined to change that perception once and for all. Having served on a government committee (and seen, next to one of his own suggestions, the word 'RESIST' underlined twice in sober mandarin handwriting[8]), he had first-hand knowledge of who these people were, how they acted and interacted, not only with each other but also with politicians. 'He had drafted part of the Annan Report,' Lynn noted, 'and after working with some senior civil servants he knew that the popular image of them was false.'[9]

It was this drive for accuracy as well as comedy, this conviction that the humour would be rooted in the truth, that most excited the two writers. This was going to be a sitcom very different from the normal formulaic fare. It was going to be about insight instead of escapism; a fiction founded on fact.

As a consequence, the first step would be to do some serious research to get the details right. Jay knew some tantalising bits and pieces, but to write a proper sitcom, to structure a series of episodes, they would have to dig deeper, court some insiders and piece together the bigger picture.

In this sense, it was their good fortune that an exceptionally rich, vivid and informative source had recently emerged in the public domain. Richard Crossman, a Labour Party politician and former Minister (who first served in the Cabinet at the same time as Sir Frank Soskice), had been a lifelong opponent of his country's culture of secrecy, and of the multiple means whereby information was withheld from the masses in order to keep the demon of democracy safely at bay. In a principled act of rebellion, therefore, he had broken the Cabinet code of omertà and bequeathed to the nation an insider's account of the workings of British politics.

Since 1951, as a backbench MP and then as a Cabinet Minister during the second half of the 1960s, he had religiously recorded his experiences in a series of diaries. A disciple of Walter Bagehot (whom he hailed as 'the only Englishman who saw right through our politics without losing faith in freedom'[10]), his original intention had been to use the material selectively and reasonably discreetly as a source not only for his memoirs but also as the basis of a twentieth-century version of Bagehot's 1867 classic, *The English Constitution*. By the early 1970s, however, when his health was failing rapidly and he realised that such projects were now beyond him, he changed his mind and resolved instead to publish the diaries as they were, in order to provide the public with 'a daily picture of how a Minister of the Wilson Government spent his time, exactly what he did in his Department, in Cabinet Committee and in Cabinet itself, and . . . outside his office'. It would, he vowed, be 'a true record of how one Minister thought and felt' and would thus be of 'quite special historical value'.[11]

Crossman died in April 1974 at the age of sixty-six, but plans for the publication went ahead – much to the horror of the British political Establishment, which proceeded to do all it could to stifle the spilling of its secrets. Advance excerpts, scheduled to appear in *The Sunday Times* during the autumn of 1974, were delayed repeatedly by the Cabinet Office (which had insisted on assessing the proofs, extremely slowly, for possible breaches of confidentiality), and the publication date for the first of three intended volumes was also pushed back indefinitely due to various legal objections and veiled threats. Eventually, on 1 October 1975, after endless debates in Parliament and the press, the Lord Chief Justice brought the high-profile saga to an end when he refused to grant the Attorney General an injunction to prevent publication, ruling that an outright ban would not be in the public interest, and, at long last, the books began to appear.[12]

The Diaries of a Cabinet Minister (1975, 1976 and 1977) had very much the great impact that Crossman had expected and many of his former colleagues had feared, demystifying Cabinet government to an unprecedented extent and inviting the public not only to reflect on all the stories of unseemly political infighting but also, and more importantly, to consider the hitherto largely hidden influence of the Civil Service. The reviewers duly hailed the diaries as 'a plain man's guide to the political jungle',[13] bringing out the difference 'between the way we are governed and the way our governors wish us to suppose that we are governed',[14] and the 688-page first volume sold more than twenty-five thousand copies within weeks of its publication.[15]

What immediately engaged the reader was Crossman's vivid depiction of himself as a newly appointed Cabinet Minister in October 1964:

tumbling down the Whitehall rabbit hole and finding himself dazed and confused inside an unfamiliar office that seemed 'like a padded cell', feeling as though he had been 'suddenly certified a lunatic' who was 'cut off from real life and surrounded by male and female trained nurses and attendants'.[16] It was in these first few diary entries that he shared with his readers the growing realisation about 'the tremendous effort it requires not to be taken over by the Civil Service'.[17]

Uprooted and disoriented, he reflected with a mixture of awe and alarm how the venerable machinery of each Whitehall department was more than capable of rumbling on, regardless of who the latest arrival was from Westminster. The new Minister might be male or female, young or old, left wing, right wing or centrist, but the undeniable fact was that they were a transient part of a permanent process, and 'one has only to do absolutely nothing whatsoever in order to be floated forward on the stream'.[18] This view was soon reinforced by the obliging Private Secretary who assured Crossman that, in every instance, his civil servants would draft every option for his consideration and, if ever he preferred not to make a choice, all he needed to do was move everything from his in tray to his out tray 'and if you put it in without a mark on it then we will deal with it and you need never see it again'.[19]

What further focused the attention as the entries continued was the growing significance of the relationship between the Minister and his Permanent Secretary. Crossman's first Permanent Secretary was a strikingly redoubtable woman named Dame Evelyn Sharp, who had been in the Civil Service since 1926 and, in 1955, was the first woman to have reached the highest executive position within a Ministry. Having already served and seen off four Ministers, and achieved a level of expertise in her Department's field of responsibility (Housing and Local Government) that by this stage in her long career was probably second to none, she looked upon her latest Minister, who (fresh from a stint in Opposition as Education spokesman) had neither the experience nor the expertise to stamp his signature on his new subject, with ill-disguised disdain.

Crossman's initial opinion of her, in turn, was similarly negative. He described her as a 'tremendous patrician' who was 'utterly contemptuous and arrogant', treating local authorities as 'children which she has to examine and rebuke for their failures', most external experts as 'utterly worthless', the general public as 'incapable of making a sensible decision' and her own Minister as a lowly creature of 'stupidity and ignorance' who represented a threat to the efficiency of a Department that she treated like her own 'personal domain'.[20]

As a consequence, the earliest stage of Crossman's time as Minister was marked by his chronicling the constant tension and struggles between his Permanent Secretary and himself, with his retiring at the end of each day, bloodied and bruised, to record the many times when she had failed to consult him, or furnish him with information, or blocked his access to outside advisors and alternative ideas and generally contrived, albeit very discreetly, to frustrate all of his personal schemes. Complaining bitterly of how her loyalty was obviously exclusively to the Civil Service rather than even partially to him, he ended up, after no more than a month, exclaiming to his Prime Minister: 'I have had enough of the Dame'.[21]

In time, the dynamic, and mood, began to change. She warmed, subtly, to his indefatigable commitment to certain policies, and he (after realising that she had been fighting hard to prevent their Department from being broken up and abolished) came to admire, just as subtly, her desire to do what she believed was the right thing.

He actually started to feel a strange kind of affinity with her, acknowledging that, although both of them had started off wanting to see the back of each other, they had come, in time, to see each other as something more like kindred spirits. '[We] really do quite like each other,' he wrote in his diary, 'and regard each other as exceptions to a dreary rule,' adding that 'we are two people who know their own value and know the other's value'.[22]

There was also a more pragmatic reason for the change of heart. Dame Evelyn, who was edging ever closer to retirement, knew that it was not in her interests to antagonise her latest Minister too acutely when her beloved Department badly needed stability. Crossman, meanwhile, realised that any sign from him to suggest that he was planning to push her out would mean that 'the whole of Whitehall hierarchy would be against me', as well as 'questions in Parliament' and 'a hell of a row'. Moreover, he was reminded, privately but somewhat brusquely by the Head of the Civil Service, that a new Permanent Secretary would last much, much, longer than a new Minister ever would (the average was several years compared to several months[23]), and that it was therefore deemed far more important that any replacement should suit the Department over whoever happened to be its current Minister.[24]

The result was that, until Dame Evelyn finally moved on, the two of them continued working together, while working apart, to ensure that their Department remained intact. She guided him, and sometimes manipulated him, as well as she could, while he drew on her expertise, and sometimes defeated her preconceived designs, as well as he could.

During this uneasy truce, Crossman reflected on the routine processes that linked Whitehall with Westminster, and realised, as a consequence, how quietly effective the Civil Service was at influencing government policy. It achieved it, he believed, mainly through two basic means: first as the 'keeper of the muniments', and second via the imposition of a single 'official' view on all of the Ministers.[25]

The Civil Service was keeper of the muniments in the sense that, through the Cabinet Secretariat, it not only recorded but also minuted Cabinet discussions. This duty, quite unintentionally, bestowed on permanent officials, in Crossman's view, an extraordinary power of discretionary prerogative. As only what was recorded ranked officially as precedent, it followed that precedent had become whatever the Civil Service chose to recognise as such.

It also imposed its own 'official' view on politicians, in two intimately linked ways. First, each Permanent Secretary could work to convince his or her own Minister of a certain opinion about a policy, and then, if anything remained disputed, some discreet coordination could ensure that a 'cohesive interdepartmental view' would be echoed by most if not all of the other Ministers once they assembled together in Cabinet.

First-hand experience of this deft, devious and discreet manner of manipulating the decision-making process more or less convinced Crossman, within six months or so of arriving in Whitehall, that unless an individual Minister had the full backing of the Prime Minister, or at least one of his most eminent lieutenants, 'the chance of prevailing against the official view is absolutely nil'.[26] Here, he concluded, 'is the way in which Whitehall ensures that the Cabinet system is relatively harmless.'[27]

This insight was more than enough to guide Jay and Lynn a fair distance in the right direction. It gave them an invaluably authentic model for the basic situation, dynamics and key relationship of the sitcom that they wanted to craft, and would remain an essential source of authoritative information ('We referred continuously to it,' Jay would confirm[28]).

Crossman's diaries also provided them with a title. On the very first page of the first volume he had talked about the deceptive obsequiousness of the civil servants who greeted him in his Department, all of them saying, 'Yes, Minister! No, Minister! If you wish it, Minister!' while clearly thinking the opposite.[29] 'Tony suggested that *Yes Minister* would be a good, ironic title for our show,' Lynn later recalled, and he agreed. *Yes Minister* would indeed be the name of their sitcom.[30]

Greatly encouraged by the insights they were gleaning from the Crossman diaries, the two writers started looking further afield for similarly enlightening sources. They wanted, ideally, more recent anecdotes and opinions from contemporary politicians, as well as perspectives from the other side of the institutional divide from well-established civil servants.

Their first significant living source was Marcia Falkender, the long-serving Political Secretary to Harold Wilson, whom Jay had got to know while working on the *A Prime Minister on Prime Ministers* series. An ever-present figure at Wilson's side since 1956, Falkender had been on the inside at Number Ten during two spells in government, as well as on the outside during Wilson's periods in Opposition, and had been privy to all of the major discussions, crises and strategies that had shaped the past thirty years of Labour's political history. Elevated to the House of Lords as a Baroness in 1974, a couple of years prior to Wilson's retirement, she was still active in public life and politics when Jay called on her for advice.

Lynn, meanwhile, found another promising contact in the form of an academic: Nelson Polsby, Professor of Political Science (and later Head of the Institute of Governmental Affairs) at Stanford University in California. Although he was an American who specialised in the study of the US Presidency and Congress, Polsby was currently based in England as a Visiting Professor at the London School of Economics, and, as a worldly, witty and well-informed outsider, he offered a refreshingly non-partisan, less parochial perspective on Britain's contemporary political system. Never distracted from patterns and processes by the dazzle of particular personalities, Polsby described his analytical, almost anthropological, approach as 'a job of fundamental importance, because facts rarely speak for themselves. There are usually too many facts and not infrequently too many different versions of the facts. Rather than speaking for themselves, various facts have what we have come to refer to as spokespersons'.[31] He was, as a consequence, well suited to engaging with what was fast becoming an age of spin.

It was actually through Polsby that Lynn was introduced to another invaluable adviser, Bernard Donoughue. A former LSE academic who in 1974 had moved into politics as founder and first Head of the Number Ten Policy Unit, where he worked as Senior Policy Adviser to Harold Wilson and his successor James Callaghan, Donoughue was not just eminently well placed to provide Lynn and Jay, very discreetly, with an up-to-the-minute account of the country's governing class, but was also blessed with a subtly mischievous spirit that made him unexpectedly well attuned to the sensibilities, and most urgent needs, of these two sitcom writers.

'It was all very hush-hush,' he would say of his role. 'I was very nervous initially, because I didn't want to appear publicly as an inside source, especially if something was going to be critical of the Civil Service, and so forth. But it was to be done on the grounds of anonymity, so that reassured me and, from that point on, I felt able to relax and talk fairly freely'.[32]

These three figures – Falkender, Donoughue and, to a much lesser extent, Polsby ('I did meet Nelson,' Antony Jay would say, 'but he didn't have any particular influence on me'[33]) – would form the unofficial think-tank on which Jay and Lynn would rely for their most reliable off-the-record insights and advice. Each had something different to offer, each had a wealth of experience and admirable expertise and each trusted the writers to use, rather than abuse, whatever they cared to share.

The writers were careful to ensure that no source would be distracted by anxieties about what the others might be saying. Polsby, as an individual academic transplanted from his natural habitat, never presented a problem (and only really spoke at any length with Lynn), but the other two, as creatures of the same intensely competitive political culture, were always kept strictly apart and, to some extent, in the dark. 'We never mentioned to either of them that we were also regularly talking to the other,' Jonathan Lynn would later reveal. 'This was not difficult. We kept all our sources completely confidential, and still do. The only people who are known to be our sources are those who have publicly identified themselves. Also, although we had a slight sense that [Falkender and

Donoughue] didn't get along with each other, we had no idea how acri-
monious their relationship really was.'[34]

The strategy worked. Each of the sources proved to be an invaluable
guide.

Lady Falkender, for example, not only furnished them with numerous
tales of what used to go on inside Number Ten, the hotels at party conferences and the ministerial cars, but she also 'decoded' current events,
explaining what was really happening and how and why it was being mis-
represented for public consumption. Donoughue, similarly, not only fed
them snippets of information (such as the story about how, on his first
day inside Number Ten following the General Election of February 1974,
a civil servant had proposed a Prime Ministerial visit to China because, as
one world-weary colleague put it, 'civil servants are only interested in trips
abroad'[35]), but also, extremely discreetly, opened doors for them within
Westminster, introducing them to an increasingly wide range of gossipy
grandees.

Jay and Lynn would meet these figures at a good central London restaurant for a long and well-lubricated lunch ('with some fine wine, they'll
tell you plenty'[36]). The tactic generally proved to be hugely effective. 'We
discovered they would tell us practically anything we wanted to know,'
Lynn would recall, 'firstly, because they knew that they were not going to
be quoted; secondly, people had a political axe to grind and wanted a particular view aired; and, thirdly, we discovered the higher up people were,
the closer they were to real power, the more indiscreet they would be.'[37]

Nelson Polsby, meanwhile, was always available as a sounding board if
ever there was a need to find universal themes in specific occurrences. 'He
was full of insight,' said Lynn.[38]

Having secured these three invaluable political contacts, Jay and Lynn
still needed to find sources for the bureaucratic side of their research,
but, predictably, Whitehall proved far less receptive than Westminster to
requests for regular advice. They were thus left with no choice but to flit
from one figure to another, battling wits as they tried to prise stories from
out of the notoriously tight-lipped members of the Civil Service.

Realising that most civil servants would only volunteer information
that they assumed Jay and Lynn already knew, the pair resorted to various
kinds of subterfuge to trick their quarry into admissions. For example, Jay

had a strong suspicion that there was a rivalry, to the point of antipathy, between the Home Civil Service and the Foreign Civil Service, so, rather than ask an insider to confirm it, he asked them to explain it: 'I said, "Why do the Home Civil Service dislike the Foreign Civil Service so much?" And he said: "Well, I think it's partly because . . ." and admitted it by default.'[39]

The nearest the writers came to finding the Civil Service equivalent of a Crossman was by reading Leslie Chapman. Like Crossman, Chapman was a well-placed whistle-blower whose revelations about the institution to which he once belonged caused widespread controversy and debate.

Until recently, he had been a regional director of what in those days was the Ministry of Public Buildings and Works, where, from 1967 to 1974, he had made it his business to identify and suggest ways to eliminate instances of inefficiency and waste, saving in the process some £3.5 million out of an annual budget of £10 million in his own area of authority. His repeated attempts to get his methods adopted nationally, however, had always been thwarted by his superiors. Even when he persuaded Ministers (Labour and Conservative alike) of the potential scope for cutting waste nationally, instructions from them were either blocked high up in Whitehall or heavily watered down. Chapman, growing frustrated by such stubborn resistance, decided eventually that it was no longer worth fighting for his cause on the inside, and resolved instead to retire and continue the fight on the outside.

Writing became his weapon, and, early in 1978, his first book, *Your Disobedient Servant: The Continuing Story of Whitehall's Overspending*, was published. A bestseller for which he declined to take payment, it was an excoriating critique of how the Civil Service was run, supplying the reader with an extraordinary collection of shaming cases of incompetence and irrationality. Among his many eye-catching examples were the twelve dockets that had to pass through eighty-two bureaucratic processes before a tap could be mended; the use of ministerial cars by junior staff when taxis would have been cheaper; the continued use of a depot railway system when public roads would have served just as well for a fraction of the cost; the pointless insistence on heating stores that were the size of aircraft hangars to normal office temperatures; an army depot that stored enough mule shoes to fight another Crimean War; and welfare officers travelling up to two hundred miles a day to see staff who had no desire to be visited.

The conclusion was that the institution was guilty not only of a lack of care but also a lack of contrition. 'The trouble is,' he complained bitterly, 'the Civil Service in this country hates to admit that it is wrong and will do almost anything rather than admit that it has erred.'[40]

Just like the Crossman diaries had done to Parliament, Chapman's book – which was backed up by two hard-hitting television documentaries (in the form of special editions of BBC2's *Man Alive* and ITV's *World in Action*[41]) and then followed by an equally caustic sequel, *Waste Away*, in 1981 – put the Civil Service under the harsh media spotlight, alarming many people (the new Conservative leader Margaret Thatcher, most notably, among them) – with its depiction of a Whitehall that was complacent, profligate, overmanned and overindulged. At a stroke it pushed the subject of bureaucratic waste (and secrecy) high up on the political agenda, where it would stay throughout the next decade.

Jay and Lynn could not believe their luck: here, landing in their laps, was a treasure trove of raw material that was ripe for comedic dramatisation. Although Chapman himself had been adamant that nothing in his account should be regarded as a laughing matter – 'To make jokes of such examples,' he warned, 'obscures the seriousness of the waste involved'[42] – to the two writers the satirical value of his revelations was plainly apparent. 'We absolutely devoured them,' Antony Jay later said of the two books, 'and in fact we got ideas for plots which we altered to fit our needs.'[43]

Having amassed such a wealth of material on both sides of the Westminster–Whitehall divide, the writers could now start to collate it and shape it into the basis of a believable fictional world. They were ready to begin crafting their sitcom.

Antony Jay already knew how they should proceed, because, in a sense, they had done it before. The template, he reasoned, was the kind of training film that he and Lynn had made for Video Arts:

> It is not an accident that Jonathan and I had worked on the
> Video Arts training programmes because we had to do a lot
> of research [for them], the object of which was to find out
> what, for example, were the correct ways of running a meeting,

conducting an interview or a negotiation, or dealing with an angry customer. The bulk of research for these training films involved finding credible instances of situations being handled wrongly which were entertaining while at the same time were painfully recognisable, and then we would show salespeople what should have been done: that they should not stress the features rather than the benefits of something they were trying to sell; that they should not reel off a long list of a machine's revolutions per minute and oil consumption to an old lady who just wants to buy a hoover or lawnmower. [. . .] In a way in *Yes Minister* we just carried on doing what we had been doing except we did not show what the correct lessons were.[44]

It was in this spirit that the two writers set about creating their biggest and most important training film so far. The lesson on this occasion was: how not to govern a representative democracy.

Their first step was to fashion a context in which the action would happen. To succeed, this context needed to be two things: small enough to keep a sharp focus without losing the dramatic truth (anything that even tried to resemble a fully staffed government department, on screen, would have over-complicated the action as well as drained the budget), and pliable enough to justify it covering practically any and every area of domestic policy (a specific department would have restricted all the storylines to a specific subject).

Jay and Lynn met both of these requirements by inventing an 'umbrella' department of their own: the Department of Administrative Affairs. Simplified by keeping most of the staff off camera, and purified by eschewing any possible associations with actual and particular areas of specialisation, this fictional department was to symbolise 'the ultimate bureaucracy: that wing of the Civil Service that was only concerned with running the Civil Service; the administration that administered administrators'.[45]

The next thing they needed was to populate this context with a core group of characters, and, as far as this part of the process was concerned, the writers did at least have some precedents to consider from the sit-com tradition. Most of the classics of the genre, on British television, had, up to this point, been either 'buddy' comedies or 'family' comedies, thus relying on no more than four key characters: *Hancock's Half*

Hour, *Steptoe and Son*, *The Likely Lads* and *Sykes* made do with two; *Whatever Happened to the Likely Lads?* used three; and *Till Death Us Do Part*, *Porridge*, *Rising Damp*, *The Good Life* and *Fawlty Towers* had focused on four. The only really notable exceptions to this rule were the more American-style, 'gang show' sitcoms that David Croft made with Jimmy Perry and Jeremy Lloyd, such as *Dad's Army* and *Are You Being Served?*, which required an immense amount of planning (and plenty of diplomacy and tact) to ensure that all members of each troupe received their fair share of lines and screen time.

For *Yes Minister*, it was decided that a comic triangle of characters would be the most coherent and practicable option. Pitting one typical politician against one typical civil servant, the show was going to be, essentially, an 'anti-buddy' sitcom, so a third, intermediary, figure, whose loyalties and sympathies would flit back and forth from one to the other, was added to moderate the conflict and ensure that the centre would hold.

This template had the appeal of working on several levels: double act and stooge; only child and warring parents; solitary agnostic versus a duo of dogmatists; and an audience representative interacting with the main comedy couple. Most importantly, it allowed Jay and Lynn to turn a long shot into a close-up and still capture the truth of the dynamics that epitomised the workings of Whitehall.

The inspiration for the main two-man relationship within the triangle came from a number of sources. There was, obviously, the real-life partnership between Minister and Permanent Secretary that had been captured with such clarity by the likes of Richard Crossman, but there was also a rich heritage of comic combinations that influenced how the writers depicted the central union of their sitcom. There was, for example, the tussle between master and servant in Beaumarchais' *La folle journée, ou le Mariage de Figaro* (1784) and Mozart's *Le Nozze Di Figaro* (1786); between peer and butler in J.M. Barrie's *The Admirable Crichton* (1902) and between young gentleman and valet in P.G. Wodehouse's *Jeeves* stories (1915–74) – all of them sharing the comic conceit of the subordinate who outwits his superior.

This notion suited perfectly Jay and Lynn's own vision of a relationship defined by the contrast between its appearance and its reality, with a supposedly all-powerful Minister who is frequently tricked and trumped by his ostensibly meek and obedient Permanent Secretary. The world of Wodehouse, especially, did not seem too far away from the world of Whitehall, and it was fairly easy to imagine Bertie Wooster and Jeeves transplanted, *mutatis mutandis*, from the drawing room of a country house to the office of a government department, with Bertie, slumped behind the ministerial desk, bristling at the memory of the latest subtle show of impertinence by his deceptively humble assistant ('I don't want to seem always to be criticising your methods of voice production, Jeeves,' I said, 'but I must inform you that that "Well, sir" of yours is in many respects fully as unpleasant as your "Indeed, sir"'[46]) while realising how much he needed this unflappable mastermind to guide him away from trouble: 'It was one of those cases where you approve the broad, general principle of an idea but can't help being in a bit of a twitter at the prospect of putting it into practical effect. I explained this to Jeeves, and he said much the same thing had bothered Hamlet'.[47]

The language of Wodehouse, and in particular the contrast in styles of phrasing and cadence between his two main characters, was another obvious influence. Listening to Jeeves' elaborate, ornate and orotund orations, and Bertie's short, scatty and staccato responses, it was easy to imagine how the sound of such dialogues would suit the exchanges between a polished and poised civil servant and an impatient but poorly briefed politician:

JEEVES: The stars, sir.

BERTIE: Stars?

JEEVES: Yes, sir.

BERTIE: What about them?

JEEVES: I was merely directing your attention to them, sir. Look how the floor of heaven is thick inlaid with patines of bright gold.

BERTIE: Jeeves—

JEEVES: There's not the smallest orb which thou beholdest, sir, but in his motion like an angel sings, still quiring to the young-eyed cherubins.

BERTIE: Jeeves—

JEEVES: Such harmony is in immortal souls. But whilst this muddy vesture of decay doth grossly close it in, we cannot hear it.

BERTIE:	Jeeves—
JEEVES:	Sir?
BERTIE:	You couldn't possibly switch it off, could you?
JEEVES:	Certainly, sir, if you wish it.
BERTIE:	I'm not in the mood.
JEEVES:	Very good, sir.[48]

There was yet one more influence that helped crystallise the new relationship. Antony Jay, like Jonathan Lynn, had always been a great admirer of Ray Galton and Alan Simpson's sitcom *Steptoe and Son* – one of the truly great, groundbreaking contributions to the genre, in terms of both using character actors instead of comic personalities, and of blending drama with laughter – and, the more that they thought about their own show, the more the cruel but comical inextricability of the Steptoe scenario seemed to resonate with their own idea of what should root *Yes Minister* to the spot.

Steptoe and Son was all about the ties that bound two people together. It was about a father and son, both too poor to go it alone, and both (deep down) too attached to the other to part company, even though the relationship was polarised on a day-to-day basis by their respective personalities and ambitions. Theirs were the ties that trapped. Harold, the son, was always dreaming of soaring off to the stars, while his father, Albert, constantly reminded him that he had grown up in the gutter, and it was always painfully clear that neither was going to go anywhere other than back out onto the streets to collect junk.

The dynamic was quintessentially British: idealism undermined by realism, optimism by pessimism, pretentiousness by irreverence. When Harold tries to intimidate with forced verbosity – 'You frustrate me in everything I try to do. You are a dyed-in-the-wool, fascist, reactionary, squalid, little know-your-place, don't-rise-above-yourself, don't-get-out-of-your-hole, complacent little turd!' – Albert smacks him down with casual brevity: 'What d'yer want for yer tea?' Similarly, when Harold attempts to impress with his ethereal ambitions, such as when he talks of transforming his shared junkyard hovel into a fashionable salon, a 'powerhouse of intellectual thought' so full of 'choice wines, superb food and elegant conversation' that the likes of 'C.P. Snow and Bertrand Russell will be busting a gut to get in', Albert punctures the inflated pose with his earthbound actualities: 'Oh *yeah*! There'll be *plenty* for them to do *here*: table tennis, rat hunting . . . I can see you all now, going for long tramps across the yard deep in intellectual conversation and horse manure!'[49]

The contrasts struck a chord for the writers of *Yes Minister*. 'If you think about it,' Jay would say, 'young Steptoe was the minister, having lots of bright ideas which wouldn't work, and old Steptoe was a kind of secretary just deflating everything, going, "Nah, that won't work!" He was the Sir Humphrey. It was the conflict between the two of them that seemed to me could be just as well translated into Whitehall.'[50]

Just like in *Steptoe*, they reasoned, the explicit division was counterbalanced by an implicit interdependence. As Jay put it:

> Comedy, like drama, comes from the tension between characters in conflict of intention. Therefore it seemed to me that the two characters, the Minister and the Permanent Secretary, symbolised the two halves of the conflict perfectly and what made the comedy, and indeed the drama, work was that although the two had quite different and often opposing ambitions, nevertheless, each needed the other. The Minister needed the Permanent Secretary for support, to get the facts right, for briefings, for the provision of the necessary administrative back-up and for advice. The Permanent Secretary needed the Minister to publicise the things the Department had done well – and thus to get kudos for himself. He also needed the Minister to fight the Department's corner in Cabinet and to fight for its share of the budget at the public expenditure round. They could not just walk out on each other. Their relationship was like a marriage and they both had a great deal invested in it. Therefore, if the story line could put strong pressures to force them to the point of separation, the drama and the comedy would be created.[51]

There was, however, a third person in this marriage: the Principal Private Secretary. Another ingredient inspired primarily by the contents of the Crossman diaries, which had described this figure as the key link between the Minister and his Permanent Secretary, he was the obvious

choice to serve as their comic foil. According to Crossman, the Principal
Private Secretary's job was 'to make sure that when the Minister comes to
Whitehall he doesn't let the side down or himself down and behaves in
accordance with the requirements of the institution'.[52]

Crossman's own Principal Private Secretary was a young, tall, owlish-
looking man named John Delafons, whom he depicted as a kind of amiable
double agent. Positioned in the office outside that of the Minister, like the
host of 'a grand vizier's waiting room', he liaised between his political and
bureaucratic bosses, advising both on how best to deal with the other.
Delafons, wrote Crossman, was thus able to appear simultaneously as one
of 'us' and one of 'them', part friend and part foe. It was a role whose
essential ambiguity clearly fascinated, and more than a little unnerved,
the Minister, who valued the way that Delafons 'really does try to get my
ideas across to the Department', but also feared that 'his main job is to get
across to me what the Department wants'.[53]

It was for this reason, rich in comic potential, that Jay and Lynn saw
the Principal Private Secretary as the obvious third point of the triangle.
Never entirely under the control of either one of his two superiors, he
would, as a consequence, undermine the authority and composure of both
of them simply by standing between them instead of behind them.

He would also serve as a natural means to elicit exposition. Whereas
the line of least resistance with the Minister would result in his hiding
behind the jargon of policy, and with the Permanent Secretary would
result in him playing with the parlance of procedure, the Principal Private
Secretary could be relied on to step in and ask each of them to explain
himself plainly and simply, and thus provide the audience with whatever
background information they might require.

Another invaluable aspect of his role involved him serving as confidant
to each of his two bosses. 'You had to have scenes of them apart,' Antony
Jay would say of Sir Humphrey and Hacker, 'because you had to tell the
audience what Jim was planning that he didn't want Humphrey to know,
or Humphrey was planning that he didn't want Jim to know, so that was
where Bernard came in. He was piggy in the middle. He was confided in
by both of them, trying to be loyal to both of them, and it made his part
a very funny one'.[54]

When it came to shaping these three characters, the writers remained,

for a while, relatively cautious. Lynn, in particular, as the sitcom veteran of
the duo, knew how each part only really started to grow and evolve once
an actor had been assigned to play it, and so, at this early planning stage,
the focus remained on building up the bare bones rather than adding too
much of the fleshy substance.

They decided to call the Minister 'Gerry Hacker',[55] because, as Lynn
would later explain, the name Hacker (in that pre-Internet era) 'evoked
an image of a lost and desperate politician, blindly and hopelessly hacking
his way through the undergrowth of the Whitehall jungle'.[56] There was
no particular reason why he was dubbed 'Gerry' other than the fact that it
sounded socially non-specific.

Some would speculate, once the show was up and running, that Hacker's
character was modelled on one particular politician or combination of politicians, and it became something of a game in the bars and tea rooms of the
House of Commons to guess who the most likely 'Hacker' might be. The
writers, however, always remained adamant that their minister was never
modelled on anyone in particular. Hacker, Jonathan Lynn would stress, 'is
completely fictional. But we did want him to be a centrist politician who
could have belonged to either party, like Jim Prior or Roy Jenkins. He's not
as intelligent as either of them, though, and rather more venal.'[57]

The Permanent Secretary, meanwhile, was christened 'Humphrey',
because, when Lynn tried to think of someone suitably upper class, urbane
and incisive, his old Cambridge and broadcasting colleague, Humphrey
Barclay, came to mind. The surname of 'Appleby' was chosen because 'it
seemed suitably English and bucolic', and the knighthood – as usually happened in real life – came with the job.[58] Once again, as Antony Jay would
make clear, the character of Sir Humphrey, just like that of Hacker, was
dreamed up from what struck him and Lynn as most typical of each tribe:
'They were [both] drawn from imagination, and from the logic of the job that
they were in and the constraints and opportunities that those jobs created.'[59]

As for the Principal Private Secretary, Lynn resorted to a spot of nominative determinism, calling him 'Woolley' to signal his vague nature. His
first name, 'Bernard', had no conscious inspiration, but it did benefit from
its connotations of hard-working and helpful St Bernard dogs.

The only real decision the writers made, at this early stage, as to their
characters' respective backgrounds, concerned their academic training and

the impact it had had on their personalities. They saw Sir Humphrey as a classicist and Hacker as an economist because, as Lynn would put it, 'A classicist lives within certain established principles and attitudes. An economist exists on quicksand.'[60]

Sir Humphrey would have been educated at Balliol College, Oxford, it was decided, because 'Oxbridge represented privilege' and so many senior civil servants were Oxonians or Cantabrigians in real life (the estimated figure at the time was 75 per cent[61]). His Classics training would have furnished him not only with a deep appreciation of history, tradition, continuity and change, but also a mastery of the mechanics of language and culture, enabling him to remain calm in the face of any local crisis while deciphering, or dissembling, his way to an acceptable solution.

Gerry Hacker, on the other hand, was deemed to have been educated at the London School of Economics, where he would have learned, both as a student and as a fledgling lecturer, how to claim, and sometimes feign, authority in a subject that, notoriously, can never quite forgive practical human reality for not being as predictable as mathematics. As Lynn explained:

> There was a famous joke about a successful economist who went
> back to see his old professor at Cambridge. He saw his professor
> marking exam papers and commented that the questions were
> the same ones set for his own finals 30 years before. The old
> economist said, 'I set the same questions every year. The students
> know that the questions are the same.' 'Then why don't they
> all get 100 per cent?,' asked his former student. 'Because,' the
> professor replied, 'each year the answers are different.'
>
> Therefore, it seemed very suitable that Hacker should be an
> economics lecturer at the LSE. We also wanted him to be more
> typical of most members of the House. A great many of them are
> teachers, university lecturers and journalists. We did not want
> him to have the same mental framework as Sir Humphrey. We
> wanted him to approach questions from a different perspective.[62]

Woolley, meanwhile, was handed the Civil Service's standard Oxbridge background, but, as befitted his name and nature, little else was considered relevant about him at this stage in the process. Such sparseness of biographical detail did indeed suit a figure whose role would rarely warrant the need to volunteer much, if any, personal information. Richard Crossman, when writing after about a year of daily interaction with his own Principal Private Secretary, had reflected on the fact that 'we don't know each other much better [now] than we did on the first day',[63] so it made perfect sense to allow for an air of mystery to surround young Bernard. The only notable distinguishing characteristic that the writers did decide to give him was an obsession – 'to a fault'[64] – with language, causing him to play with it via 'comically irritating' puns or pedantically pause it in order to parse it. This would be the main means whereby his puppy-like gaucheness would be revealed, contrasting quite endearingly with the enculturated self-awareness of his two superiors.

With Woolley now formed as an outline alongside Hacker and Sir Humphrey, the writers were finally in a position to start working on their first script. It was at this moment, though, that a degree of doubt started to creep in.

They knew that they would soon have to pitch the idea to a broadcaster, but, in an age when there were only three television channels – BBC1, BBC2 and ITV – the competition for commissions was intense. The more they reflected on their own proposed programme and compared it to the range of recently launched sitcoms that were currently succeeding on the screen (such as the cartoon-like *Citizen Smith*, the creakily crude *George and Mildred* and the sugary *Robin's Nest*), the more they feared that *Yes Minister* 'had none of the ingredients for a popular television show'.[65]

'There was no target audience,' Lynn would recall, shaking his head at the seeming naivety, or bravery, of it all. 'Antony and I had an idea for a comedy show, but we did not think anyone would be much interested. It was about three middle-aged men sitting around and talking about the government of Britain. It had no sex, no violence, no action.'[66]

It still made sense, however, to Jay and Lynn. They still believed that it could work. They were determined to make it work.

They were ready to sell it. They just had to hope that someone, somewhere, would be willing to buy into their vision.

3

The Pitch

Where there is error, may we bring truth. Where there is doubt,
may we bring faith. And where there is despair, may we bring hope.

The idea was pitched during the summer of 1977. Jay and Lynn typed up
a brief outline of what *Yes Minister* was going to be about and sent it off
to the BBC's Head of Comedy, James Gilbert. He opened it, read it and,
contrary to their fears, he liked it. He wanted to sign this sitcom up.

What followed would come to seem like a deliciously ironic echo of the
Sir Frank Soskice saga. Gilbert, in order to get the green light for the project,
needed to have his decision ratified by his immediate superior, the BBC's
Head of Light Entertainment. By the time it was submitted to him, however,
the BBC's Head of Light Entertainment was none other than James Gilbert.

The proposal had arrived only a few days before the BBC was due to
make one of its periodic executive reshuffles, with the then Head of Light
Entertainment, Bill Cotton, being promoted to Controller of BBC1,
Gilbert succeeding him as Head of Light Entertainment and a young producer, John Howard Davies, succeeding him as Head of Comedy. Gilbert,
therefore, was able simply to take the proposal with him from one office
to the other, sit down behind his new desk, reach into his in tray and
then, in stark contrast to Sir Frank Soskice, show perfect consistency by
rubber-stamping his own request.

It was happening. The proposal had been accepted and, on 13 October,
a pilot would be formally commissioned with a view to making a series for
screening on BBC2.[1]

'We were very pleasantly surprised that BBC 2 wanted it,' Lynn would
say. 'I was very surprised that anybody wanted it.'[2]

The next step, now that a pilot script had been requested, was to settle down and actually write it, so Jay and Lynn started to plan their first
story. 'Hypocrisy was the name of the game,' Lynn later remarked on their
starting point for this, and every subsequent, story-making session. '[We
would focus on] the contrast between the public face and the private face;
the difference between what was being fed to the public and the reality.'
The next stage, Jay would say, would be to tighten the focus further by
looking for the most pertinent context: 'The guiding factor always was to
explore themes that would produce conflict between the political side and
the administrative side of government.'[3]

The two writers would then search through these scenarios for the
ones that offered a 'hideous dilemma' that would generate the right degree
of dramatic tension: 'There had to be a truly appalling situation for Jim
Hacker or Sir Humphrey, or preferably both of them,' Lynn would recall,
'there had to be a sword of Damocles hanging over their heads. Without a
hideous dilemma you do not have an uproarious comedy, and if we could
not find the dilemma we would put the subject aside, because we did not
want to write a preachy programme.'[4] The final stage, Lynn added, was to
narrow down the remaining options 'to particular themes that amused or
annoyed us, after which we would go out and find sources.'[5]

For their first script, they decided, the topic would be what seemed like
the most fundamental issue of all: open government. A newly elected government would come to power in part due to its promise to replace secrecy
with transparency. Gerry Hacker, once given ministerial responsibility for
Administrative Affairs, would be the politician whose task it would be to
turn this promise into a reality, while Sir Humphrey, as the Permanent
Secretary attached to Hacker's Department, would be the bureaucrat
whose task it was to ensure that the promise went unfulfilled.

It seemed the ideal set-up. The main political theme would be introduced
explicitly and immediately, and the basic dynamic of the Westminster versus
Whitehall, Hacker versus Sir Humphrey, relationship would be animated
right from the start. It was a plot that both writers were happy to tackle.

What still had to be decided, however, was how they would write it
together. There were no rules about how any pair of writers should collaborate on a sitcom. It depended on their respective personalities, typing
skills and creative habits.

Some liked to do it standing up and others liked to do it sitting down. Some preferred to type and then read out loud, others to improvise and then transcribe. Some wrote separately and then met up to synthesise the sections; others worked face to face and bounced ideas off each other until every line had been agreed.

Ray Galton and Alan Simpson created both *Hancock's Half Hour* and *Steptoe and Son* inside a large and airy office in London, with Simpson seated behind a desk with a typewriter and Galton usually stretched out on the floor, staring up at the ceiling.[6] David Croft and Jimmy Perry gradually changed how they collaborated on *Dad's Army*, starting out by meeting up to agree on a series of plots and then going their separate ways to write several whole episodes each, and then, in later years, teaming up at Croft's country home in Suffolk to work on each story together.[7] Dick Clement and Ian La Frenais cobbled together many of their scripts for *The Likely Lads* in the former's house in Kentish Town, with Clement writing in longhand at the kitchen table while La Frenais walked back and forth over the lino.[8] John Cleese and Connie Booth wrote most of *Fawlty Towers* while sitting side by side at a large desk in an upstairs room at their home in Kensington, with Booth scribbling on a notepad and Cleese poised over a typewriter.[9]

The crucial difference for Jay and Lynn, however, was the fact that, unlike these illustrious predecessors, creating a sitcom was not their primary concern. They would have to write it, so to speak, 'on the side'.

Their own particular modus operandi as a writing team was thus largely determined by the demands that their respective solo careers placed on their time together. Jay continued to be Chairman of and chief writer for Video Arts, while Lynn was still Artistic Director at the Cambridge Theatre Company, so neither had much room left for a new project, and what little they did have was further constrained by the fact that Jay had a strict policy of reserving evenings and weekends solely for rest and relaxation ('Life has most people by the throat,' John Cleese often said of his friend. 'Tony has life by the throat'.)[10] Matters were further complicated by geography: Jay, at the time, lived in Ealing, while Lynn was based about ten miles away in Hampstead Garden Suburb, and, thanks to the fact that they were connected by a North Circular Road that seemed to be in a permanent state of reconstruction, the drive to one or the other's home would often take up to an hour each way.

There was no choice but to eschew all creative self-indulgence and approach writing *Yes Minister* in the most disciplined and businesslike manner they could devise. A strict schedule was agreed: no more than two weeks to construct a story, and no more than five mornings to write a script. Alternating between one home and the other, they would start work between 8.30 a.m. and 9 a.m.; if Jay had an appointment at Video Arts, they would finish at noon; if Lynn was rehearsing a play they would stop at 11.15 a.m. On those very rare occasions when both men had a relatively clear day in the diary, they would work on together until 12.30 p.m. or 1 p.m., but, even then, never any later. 'For Tony,' Lynn would recall, 'afternoons were *Yes Minister*-free zones. They were for Video Arts, sitting in his garden or napping.'[11]

Physically, both of them favoured the desk-bound writing tradition, sitting opposite each other across a table and verbally exchanging ideas. After working hard to refine that morning's material, whichever one of them felt the more energetic would pick up a pen and start writing out what they had talked through so far. Then the pad would be passed over to the other, who would study it, cross out the odd word, revise a sentence here and there and sometimes add a small detail, comic line or telling phrase. Occasionally one of them would stare at the page for a while and then decide, on reflection, that they had drifted off in the wrong direction, at which point they would scribble over the whole section and start all over again.

The relationship was kept scrupulously equal – each had the right to veto the other's ideas – and admirably equable. 'There were no rules,' Lynn would say, 'and no hurt feelings. Mostly, by the time the script was completed, we genuinely didn't know who had written what, and we didn't care.'[12] They never rowed, always encouraged and supported each other's efforts and certainly regarded their collaboration as mutually beneficial. 'Tony often says that he learned how to write comedy from me,' Lynn would recall, 'but I don't think that could be true, for he is a very funny man and a very experienced writer. I do know that I learned from him how the world works. I learned a little detachment, too, though that's never been my strong suit and still isn't.'[13]

If there was any unofficial division of labour between them, it concerned the management of the two main characters. Jay would come to describe himself, somewhat tongue in cheek, as 'the guardian of Sir Humphrey's soul', while Lynn, he said, was the guardian of Hacker's. Although they always wrote both characters – and everything else – together, Lynn would agree that the distinction did indeed make some sense. 'Tony,' he observed, 'like Sir Humphrey, has a First in Classics, is fluent in Latin and Greek and has an academic, analytical mind. He would probably have become a Permanent Secretary, had he joined the Civil Service instead of the BBC.'[14] Lynn also accepted that, at least at first glance, he was not unlike Hacker: 'a frustrated and disappointed idealist who regularly fails to practise what he preaches.'[15]

As they wrote together, therefore, Jay would sometimes be the one to suggest how Sir Humphrey might act, or what he might say, and Lynn would then seize on that to develop some comic dialogue between him and Hacker. The best ideas for Bernard Woolley's donnish interjections, however, would come about far more naturally and accidentally over the course of a writing session.

One example of this, which arose during work on a later episode,[16] concerned an exchange between Sir Humphrey and Hacker about a policy that might prove to be a vote winner. Hacker declared that, if that was indeed the case, he would not want to look a gift horse in the mouth. This prompted Jay to give Sir Humphrey the line, 'I put it to you, Minister, that you are looking a *Trojan* horse in the mouth', which in turn caused Lynn to have Hacker say, 'You mean, if we look closely at this gift horse we'll find it's full of Trojans?'

When Lynn then slid the writing pad back over to Jay, his partner frowned at the latest line and then said, 'Well, no. If one had looked the Trojan horse in the mouth one would have found Greeks inside, because the Greeks gave the horse to the Trojans. So technically it wasn't a Trojan horse at all, it was a Greek horse. Hence the tag *Timeo Danaos et dona ferentes*, which is usually and somewhat inaccurately translated as "Beware of Greeks bearing gifts".'

Lynn could not resist asking his partner what a better translation of the Greek tag might be. 'No,' Jay replied, warming to his theme, 'it's a Latin tag. It's obvious, really, the Greeks would hardly have advised other people to beware of Greeks. But there's another way you can tell: the tag is clearly Latin rather than Greek, not because *timeo* ends in "o", because the Greek first person also ends in "o" – actually, there is a Greek word *timao* meaning "I honour" – but because the "os" ending is a nominative singular termination of the second declension in Greek and an accusative plural in Latin. Incidentally, *Danaos* is not only the Greek for Greek but the Latin for Greek, too.'

Lynn, listening to this, realised that it was perfect for one of Bernard Woolley's jaw-droppingly irrelevant yet well-meaning contributions to a conversation, so, as Jay went on, he quickly scribbled it all down and slipped it into the latest script.[17] It would end up getting some of the loudest laughs of the episode. 'Tony,' Lynn later recalled, 'was benignly pleased that his arcane academic knowledge struck other people as amusing.'[18]

The bulk of their work on the pilot script, though, involved making the situation, as well as the characters, seem as believable as possible, so they had to think carefully not only about what was going to happen but also who, on screen, would be involved. Neither Sir Humphrey nor Woolley, it was felt, would require any real glimpse into their lives beyond Whitehall, as having civil servants seem permanently in situ was part of the point, but it was felt that Hacker, as a public figure, would need to be shown to have some kind of life, and a separate set of relationships, outside of his department.

He was therefore given a wife (and later on a daughter) because the pilot needed to see him at home waiting to know his fate as far as the new Cabinet was concerned, and also because the tensions between a Minister's real family and the surrogate one inside his department promised plenty of future comic opportunities. He was also given a political ally, his special adviser Frank Weisel (pronounced 'Wy-sel'), partly because Ministers did indeed like to make use of such outside figures, and partly because Permanent Secretaries tended to hate them.

Some of the biggest, and most common, clashes between the Minister and his Permanent Secretary that were recounted in Richard Crossman's diaries concerned his attempts, as a painfully isolated social democratic politician surrounded by conservative-minded bureaucrats, to seek out advice from beyond the walls of Whitehall, and Dame Evelyn's strenuous attempts to stop him from doing so. It was a relatively new phenomenon at the time, and something that struck many senior civil servants – bristling at the prospect of more and more outsiders undermining and second-guessing them from a constitutionally questionable position – as the cue for chaos unless they could snuff the fashion out as swiftly as possible.

One of Crossman's early favourites was Arnold Goodman, a left-leaning lawyer who later became Lord Goodman and one of the country's most influential political grandees. When Dame Evelyn first heard that her Minister had been acting on Goodman's unofficial advice, after he intervened in a bill that their Department was in an advanced stage of drafting, she burst into his office incandescent with rage, telling him that she had never been so insulted in her life, and had almost resigned in protest.[19] Although shaken by the severity of her reaction, Crossman continued to crave ways to challenge the Civil Service's monopoly on guidance and advice, and Dame Evelyn continued to devise more and more devious ways to defeat him.

By the mid-1970s, however, the fashion for special advisers (who were now starting to be nicknamed 'spads') had grown far more widespread, with no fewer than thirty-eight being appointed by the Labour Government following its 1974 election victory. Not everyone on the political side liked them – James Callaghan, for example, viewed them with intense suspicion and blamed them for government leaks – and not (quite) everyone on the bureaucratic side disliked them – sometimes the value of their specialist knowledge and insight was simply impossible to deny – but, at the time when *Yes Minister* was brought to life, they were indubitably newsworthy and controversial.

Jay and Lynn (who, of course, had the benefit of two of the most eminent exemplars of the breed – Marcia Falkender and Bernard Donoughue – as their guides) believed that Hacker's special adviser would have a similarly unsettling effect on Sir Humphrey to that which the likes of Goodman had had on Dame Evelyn, so they wove the figure of Frank Weisel into the picture. A passionate, persistent, pushy little party dogmatist, Weisel could be relied on to bully Hacker into taking on the bureaucrats, and to berate him whenever he seemed in danger of settling for pragmatism before pure principle. Sir Humphrey would not even bother to hide his contempt for such an interloper, deliberately mispronouncing his name as 'Weasel' and suggesting that he base himself a safe way away in darkest Walthamstow, while Weisel would be open in his eagerness to see 'Sir Humphrey Bloody

Appleby and Mr Toffee-Nosed Private Secretary Snooty Woolley' taken tightly 'by the short and curlies'.

One thing that neither Jay nor Lynn wanted to add to the sitcom was the identity of Hacker's own political party. They would scrupulously avoid any mention of its name, called its headquarters 'Central House' – an amalgam of the Conservative's Central Office and Labour's Transport House – had Hacker wear a white rosette when attending his election count, and (since Margaret Thatcher's rise to the top of the Tory Party had finally made gender a feature of the political firmament) only referred to his leader as 'the Prime Minister'.

This apparent coyness was mainly to satisfy the BBC policy to strive for political impartiality, even in a sitcom, but, as Jay later explained, it also helped to keep the focus on the fundamentals of the fiction:

> The party in power was bound to be either Conservative or
> Labour – there was no other option at the time of devising it.
> Or there were the Liberals, if you count them as an option, but
> no one would have done. If we had identified the party then it
> could have been construed as a consistent and unremitting attack
> on one or other political party; obviously we did not want to do
> that. However, we also did not want to identify the party because
> we did not see the series as being about how the Labour Party or
> the Conservative Party when in government interacted with the
> Civil Service. Moreover, between some opposition politicians
> and government ministers there was often only a tiny gap in
> terms of their political beliefs and practice: as, say, between the
> Conservative William Whitelaw and Labour's Merlyn Rees as
> Home Secretary. Therefore, following BBC policy was useful for
> our purposes.[20]

Once the pilot script was completed it was sent, at the end of 1977, on to the BBC's new Head of Comedy, John Howard Davies, to review. Davies was a sharp-witted, imaginative and very experienced programme-maker who had produced and/or directed such hugely successful comedy shows as *Monty Python's Flying Circus*, *The Goodies*, *Steptoe and Son*, *The Good Life* and, most notably, *Fawlty Towers* before rising up the ranks as an executive. He was, as a consequence, supremely confident in his own ability to judge the potential of any new sitcom, and, when he read the pilot script of *Yes Minister*, he felt sure that it had the 'legs' to be a success.

Not only did Davies like the idea of the show, but he also already had some fairly clear ideas concerning which actors to cast as the two leads – and his views on such a subject tended to be treated as authoritative. The son of the scriptwriter Jack Davies and a former child actor himself (making his debut in 1948 as the eponymous young hero of David Lean's adaptation of *Oliver Twist*), and described by John Cleese as 'a very, very good judge of comedy',[21] he had an impressive track record for picking the right performers for the right roles. While planning *Fawlty Towers*, for example, he had taken primary responsibility for choosing most of the members of the cast (selecting, among others, Prunella Scales as Sybil Fawlty, Andrew Sachs as Manuel and Ballard Berkeley as Major Gowen), and had also brought together the talents that worked so well as a team in *The Good Life*.

When, in January 1978,[22] he first met up with Jay and Lynn in his office at Television Centre, he was keen to get straight down to business. He wanted to discuss the casting.

Jay and Lynn had some ideas of their own about the cast. 'The person I originally had in mind for Sir Humphrey,' Jay later revealed somewhat whimsically, 'was an actor called Cecil Parker. He was not available for two reasons: one was that he was too expensive, and the other was that he was dead [he died in 1971]. He was marvellous at playing anguished butlers who were superior to their employers but had to cloak it in deference. His style was very funny as it thinly concealed the fury and contempt that were hiding, stifled, beneath.'[23]

Given the absence of Parker, Jay agreed with Lynn that the actor now most suited to playing Sir Humphrey was Nigel Hawthorne ('We each think we suggested him first'[24]), and the one best equipped to capture Hacker was Paul Eddington. They would therefore be very relieved to discover that John Howard Davies, completely independently, had come to exactly the same conclusion.

Jay and Lynn had seen Hawthorne onstage playing a frustrated schoolmaster in Simon Gray's *Otherwise Engaged* (1975) and a Blimpish major in Peter Nichols' *Privates on Parade* (1977), as well as on television in numerous productions, and they had already worked with him briefly in a Video Arts film called *Decisions, Decisions* ('He'd been terribly good,' Jay would say[25]). His ability to play calm, cool-headed, superior types, who were nonetheless prone to the odd apoplectic explosion, convinced them that he would be perfect for the part of their Permanent Secretary.

Lynn, meanwhile, had been an admirer of the artful and amiable Paul Eddington ever since, as a teenager, he had seen him at the Bristol Old Vic in the 1961 production of George Bernard Shaw's *The Apple Cart*, and had got to know him a little when, in 1975, he joined him in one episode of *The Good Life*.[26] Jay had also seen and admired Eddington over the years in countless plays and programmes, and, like Lynn, was very keen to have him as Hacker.

Davies knew both actors well, and, indeed, had been the one who had chosen Eddington for *The Good Life* (and had promised to find him another vehicle for his talents[27]). So when Jay and Lynn began the meeting by proposing Paul Eddington for Hacker, Davies agreed immediately. In turn, when Davies suggested Nigel Hawthorne for Sir Humphrey, Jay and Lynn were similarly quick to accede. At which point both parties agreed that that was that, and the meeting was deemed to be over. 'It was the easiest casting session in my career,' Lynn later said.[28]

What would prove to be far from easy, however, was convincing the actors. Neither, it would soon seem, was particularly keen to commit himself to the project.

Jay and Lynn had no real reason to anticipate such reluctance, so they pressed ahead with their plans. After making one small revision to the pilot script – on John Howard Davies' advice, Hacker's first name was changed from 'Gerry' to 'Jim', in order to avoid associations with Eddington's previous sitcom incarnation, Jerry Ledbetter – they sent off a copy to each of their two targets.

According to Nigel Hawthorne's later recollection of his first sight of the initial script ('It was like being handed a pot of gold'[29]), he was immediately impressed by the 'brilliance of the dialogue' and was fascinated by the 'central, complex relationship' between the politician and the civil servant: 'I recognised the potential in Sir Humphrey the moment I'd reached the end of the first page and, long before finishing the last, had decided to do the job.'[30] Paul Eddington would end up saying much the same thing: he loved the script and was drawn just as quickly to the project, even though he 'thought the appeal would be very small'.[31] It seems, though, that neither actor's memory was entirely reliable on this point.

Their actual reaction at the time, according to John Howard Davies, was positive, but curbed by a certain degree of caution. 'They wanted to see more scripts,' Davies would later reveal. 'Both of them really liked the first one – Nigel, especially, was pretty dazzled by it, in fact – but I think because of that, they wanted to be reassured that it wasn't a one-off, a flash in the pan. They wanted to see if that quality could really be sustained.'[32] Eddington in particular was, it seems, very wary about getting carried away by the accomplishments of a first script. He was painfully aware of other actors who had signed up for a series on the basis of a solitary sample script – unaware that it had actually taken several months to shape, hone and polish – only to discover, soon after the contract had been signed, that the writing on subsequent episodes fell far below the standard of the original.

Eddington also let it be known that, on the evidence of this first script, he would much rather play Sir Humphrey than Hacker, because he had noticed that Sir Humphrey always had the last line. Davies assured him, however, that the writers had always envisaged him as the actor who could best make Hacker seem real, and pointed out that, while Sir Humphrey would always be more or less the same, Hacker offered much more chance for character development. This seemed to satisfy him, but, like Hawthorne, he continued to harbour doubts about agreeing to do a series.

The result was that, on 7 February 1978, Davies commissioned a second script from Jay and Lynn (for a joint fee of £1,350[33]), which they duly wrote and submitted by the agreed deadline of 13 March, and which he then sent on to the actors. Eddington and Hawthorne responded in much the same manner as before, praising what they had read but asking for more. Thus began a cycle.

On 13 April a third script was commissioned. This time Jay and Lynn were paid an increased joint fee of £1,450 (with an additional £50 being sent to an unnamed 'third party' for assisting the writers with their research). The deadline was 5 June.[34]

A fourth script was then ordered on 26 May. Jay and Lynn were again paid £1,450 between them. The deadline on this occasion was 18 August.[35]

Eventually, after submitting their fourth meticulously researched and stylishly written episode, an exasperated Jay and Lynn decided to draw the line. 'No,' Lynn would recall the two of them saying to John Howard Davies as he began, somewhat sheepishly, to suggest yet another submission, 'four scripts are enough, they must make up their minds, yes or no.'[36] Davies put the question to the two actors at the end of August, and both of them finally came up with an answer: 'Yes'.

The sense of relief on all sides was palpable. Neither Eddington nor Hawthorne, in spite of their anxieties, had really wanted to pass on such an enticing part, and neither Jay nor Lynn (nor Davies) had wanted to lose them. The prevarication had been agonising to endure, but, now that the decision was made, the worries disappeared and the confidence came through. The two main characters had been cast.

Davies then commissioned two more scripts from Jay and Lynn, bringing the total to what he thought, at that stage, would be a series of six episodes.[37] He could now concentrate on moving ahead with the rest of the production.

Most pressingly, the actor to play Bernard Woolley still had to be chosen, and, in stark contrast to the two leads, there was no immediate consensus as to who should be at the top of the list. John Howard Davies had a famously bulging book of TV and theatrical contacts, and, in such situations, could always be relied on to draw up an impressive collection of candidates (he had, for example, considered a list of fifteen possibilities to play Sybil in *Fawlty Towers* before settling on Prunella Scales[38]), but, given that the role was at this stage deliberately underwritten, the sheer range of options was almost overwhelming.

Initially Jonathan Lynn had considered putting himself forward for the part. There was, after all, a precedent for such a move, as his friend John Cleese had written Basil Fawlty for himself with great success. There was also, on the other hand, a precedent for resisting such a temptation: Jimmy Perry had been blocked from playing the role of Private Walker in *Dad's Army* (even though he had conceived it expressly for himself) because, it was decided, having a writer among the cast might have caused resentment over the distribution of lines.[39] In the case of *Yes Minister*, however, the issue was soon rendered redundant because, after some reflection, Lynn decided to put his Cambridge Theatre Company commitments first and withdrew from consideration.

John Howard Davies then sounded out several candidates for the role, but all of them declined because, as they saw it, on paper the part seemed far too insubstantial. Undaunted, Davies persisted, trying a number of other actors, but he kept getting the same negative response: the character said little, did little and thus held little appeal.

It took a chance encounter to solve the problem. There is, however, a difference of opinion between the two main protagonists as to when and where that chance encounter took place.

According to Jonathan Lynn's recollection, the setting was Holloway Prison, where he was one of the guests at a dinner party hosted by the Governor and his wife. Seated next to him was the actor Derek Fowlds, who had worked in theatre and television on a wide range of productions over the course of about eighteen years, but who, at that stage, was best known to the general public for being the much-loved human sidekick to a hand puppet in the very popular children's series *The Basil Brush Show*, from 1969 to 1973. Lynn liked him personally, and knew that his open, understated and amiable manner made viewers warm to him rapidly. He decided then and there that Fowlds would be just right for this new role.

According to Derek Fowlds himself, however ('I *have* been to Holloway Prison – the Governor and his wife, Tony and Patricia Heald, were friends of mine – and I *did* meet Jonathan there for a dinner, but that *wasn't* when he mentioned anything to me about playing Bernard. He might have been *thinking* about me for the role, but that wasn't when he first *mentioned* it'[40]), the encounter took place a little later in the considerably more conventional and respectable environment of the West End of London in the foyer of a theatrical agency:

> Johnny [Lynn] and I had the same agent. And I was there at the office, sitting waiting to go in and see our agent, when I saw Johnny come out. I knew him then as an actor. So I said, 'Hello, Johnny, how are you?' You know, the usual. And then he left and I went in and said to my agent, 'What's *he* doing here?' And my agent said, 'Oh, he's so pleased, because they're doing a new series, he's co-writing it, and he's thrilled because they've just cast Nigel Hawthorne.' So I said, 'Well, what *is*

it? Is there something in it for *me*?' And he said, 'No, I don't think so.' So we chatted about other things, and then I went home.[41]

Wherever the chance encounter really happened, what is clear is that the next morning Lynn talked to Antony Jay and then called John Howard Davies to suggest Fowlds for Bernard Woolley. Davies agreed, and sent him a script.

Fowlds, unlike all of the previous candidates, would immediately see the part's potential, realise how he could help develop it, and would not hesitate before calling to accept:

> My agent had phoned me and said, 'Well, we have a script, because I asked Johnny Lynn and he said, "There *is* a part, and let Derek have a look at it".' So I said, 'What *is* it? What's it called?' He said, 'It's called *Yes Minister*.' So I said, 'Oh, is it about *vicars*?' I thought it must be some Derek Nimmo-style, *All Gas and Gaiters* sort of thing! He said, 'No, no, it's *political*, it's very new, very different. Read the script – the part is Bernard.'
>
> So he sent me the script, and I read it, and I just wet my breeches, really. I thought, 'This is so *exciting*!' And I knew Paul and Nigel – I'd worked with Paul and I knew Nigel as a friend – and I really couldn't wait to team up with them to do it.[42]

The comic triangle had its trio of players. Now the rest of the casting could be concluded.

Diana Hoddinott was hired (for a fee of £165 per show[43]) to be Hacker's wife, Annie. She had been working fairly steadily in television since the early 1960s, mainly in dramas rather than comedies, popping up in one-off episodes of such popular shows as *Suspense*, *Maigret* and *Dixon of Dock Green*. John Howard Davies chose her mainly because, with her ability to blend a cool demeanour with subtle wit, she could portray a typical modern politician's wife: a liberated woman forced to hide behind a submissive-looking image, realistic enough to know that she was obliged to seem pleasantly anodyne when thrust into the public spotlight, one step behind him physically while one step ahead of him mentally. [44]

Davies also decided to cast Neil Fitzwiliam as Frank Weisel. This was, he would admit,[45] something of a gamble, as the actor had been more noticeable over the past decade or so as a dancer than as a thespian (his credits included spots on *The Eartha Kitt Show*, *Half a Sixpence* and *The Slipper and the Rose*), but Davies had also seen him in a few dramatic roles and had liked his portrayals of edgy, snappy types. He had wanted someone who could make Weisel seem as physically, verbally and irritatingly weaselly as possible, and Fitzwiliam seemed capable of fitting the bill.

Finally, Davies needed to find someone suited to playing the Civil Service's *capo di tutti capi*, the Cabinet Secretary Sir Arnold Robinson, a crusty, testy, imposing figure who needed to seem sufficiently threatening as to make even Sir Humphrey appear a little insecure. A number of actors were considered for this small but memorable part, but, eventually, Davies settled on selecting John Nettleton, a sober-looking man with a voice that sounded as though it had been marinated in Earl Grey tea and who, over the past couple of decades, had huffed, puffed and harrumphed his way through a wide variety of world-weary majors, colonels, admirals, barristers, spies and detective superintendents (as well as, in the sitcom *If It Moves, File It*, a senior civil servant). Davies felt Nettleton would bring just the right air of understated but menacing authority to such a formidable éminence grise.

Once Nettleton accepted the offer of the role – which he did quickly and eagerly – the casting, for this initial stage, was complete. Davies, reflecting on all of his choices, was satisfied with the company that he had assembled. They would make *Yes Minister* work.

Now everyone was keen to press on with the production process. They had the scripts and the stars and the supporting players. All of the key ingredients were, at last, in place. It was time for the pilot to be made.

4

The Preparation

Ever failed. No matter. Try again. Fail again. Fail better.

Filming started for the pilot episode on Sunday, 21 January 1979. The brief external scenes were being recorded well ahead of the rest, so the actors were out and about in Downing Street and Whitehall, walking up and down, looking suitably businesslike.[1]

The mood at the start of such a production is always a mixture of hope and apprehension. Anything can happen – good or bad.

It is the possibility of bad things happening that, inevitably, causes all of those involved to approach the early tasks with a high degree of anxiety. 'A pilot is *always* done under conditions of extreme nervous tension,' John Howard Davies would confirm. 'It doesn't matter how brilliant you think the script is, or how wonderful the actors are. Experience teaches you that anything could go wrong, or it might all go right and still, for some inexplicable reason, fall flat when it's finished and an audience finally sees it. Honestly, I can assure you, you're *always* frightened to death.'[2]

Actors can struggle to make their roles work, writers can have second thoughts about certain scenes, directors can change their minds about how to shoot particular sequences, permissions to film in specific locations can suddenly be withdrawn, topical events can intervene to change the situation: all kinds of unexpected hazards can be encountered. One can never quite know, from day to day, what fresh hell is set to be unveiled.

In the case of making *Yes Minister*, the first problem concerned the weather. All that the production team wanted to do was to cover, quickly and easily, the fleeting outside shots of Hacker hearing his election result and then heading off to his new Department. Everything else would be recorded on set, inside the studio. In January, the weather was predictably poor (with Londoners bracing themselves for the imminent arrival of the blizzards that were sweeping down the country from the north), and, while the various caravans and the make-up bus were stiflingly hot inside, the actors were left standing for hours outside in the bitterly cold wind and rain, trying hard not to look as if the weather was particularly seasonable at all.

The next day of filming was even worse, because Paul Eddington, along with his screen wife Diana Hoddinott and special adviser Neil Fitzwiliam, were obliged to stand in front of a crowd of extras on the balcony of Chiswick Town Hall, supposedly celebrating at Hacker's election count, while pretending that snow was not flying into their faces. There was no filming at all on the Tuesday, thanks to even heavier downfalls of snow and the traffic chaos caused by a rail strike, but they resumed on Wednesday at Euston Station, with Eddington joined by Neil Fitzwiliam to show Hacker and Weisel on their way to Whitehall. Eddington, already drained from having to appear on the West End stage eight times a week in the Alan Ayckbourn play *Ten Times Table*, had a previously arranged television commercial to record on the Thursday, and by Friday, thanks to the earlier exposure to the elements, he was forced to retire to bed with a bad bout of bronchitis.

After recuperating over the weekend, Eddington joined up with the rest of the team on Monday, when they reassembled in a large and echoey room (Room 161, to be precise) in the BBC's multistorey rehearsal block in Victoria Road, North Acton (known affectionately by those who used it as the 'Acton Hilton'), to begin work on the studio scenes. Facing the usual tight schedule for pilot productions, they set about their task with plenty of energy and discipline, rehearsing all week (mornings only on those days when Eddington had a matinee to perform in at the theatre) and then reconvened in a studio at Television Centre on the Sunday (4 February) for a final run-through before recording the pilot in the evening.

The session seemed to go reasonably well – the audience, composed mainly of Londoners curious to see a new sitcom being made for free, had been reassuringly positive in their reaction – but the performers were left somewhat flat and dissatisfied by the experience. It was not the script that had bothered them – far from it – but rather the direction.

It had not felt right. It had not felt right from the very first day of rehearsals.

The man responsible was Stuart Allen. An experienced producer/director, he had overseen plenty of sitcoms in the past, but none of them had been notable for their subtlety or scope. Specialising in ITV's distinctive brand of undemanding comedy – the kind that signalled each gag with all the mouthy, shouty, face-slapping, 'wakey, wakey' intrusiveness of a red-top tabloid front-page headline – Allen's creative nadir had been *Yus, My Dear* (an execrable 1976 sitcom, set in and around a council flat, that starred Arthur Mullard as a cockney bricklayer), but he was associated most strongly with *On the Buses*.

A weekly cacophony of leery laughs, mock moans and the inevitable 'I 'ate you, Butler!', the show (which co-starred the small and stocky Reg Varney and the tall and cadaverous Bob Grant as a pathetic pair of would-be Lotharios) had been one long wolf whistle to sexist, seaside humour, impressive only for the shameless way that it kept underestimating the intelligence of the audience it targeted. It had also, however, been remarkably popular, running for seven series comprising seventy-four episodes, between 1969 and 1973, and had spawned no fewer than three spin-off movies.

As soon as Jonathan Lynn heard that the normally judicious John Howard Davies had chosen Allen, of all people, to make the pilot of *Yes Minister*, his mind flashed back to the unhappy time that he and George Layton had spent writing a handful of scripts for *On the Buses* a few years earlier ('George did more than me,' Lynn later explained, admitting that it had been a sitcom which he 'found very hard to write'[3]). Relations between Lynn and the show's director had actually been good ('I had no problem with Stuart Allen. I liked him'[4]), but it had not been a happy working experience.

Lynn had been startled by how formulaic it all was – the strict rule was that no episode must contain more than one hundred and forty speeches, because, he was told, 'that's the speed the actors go at'[5] – and how low it had set its standards (on one occasion, for example, when he proposed a plot revolving around the show's resident female grotesque, Olive, flirting with the women's lib movement, it was explained to him that feminism was 'a middle-class fad', and that this was 'a workin' class show' that required 'jokes about the price of fish'[6]). It had been this kind of demoralising sitcom experience that had driven Lynn away from television to the theatre, and, as appreciative as he now was of the BBC's willingness to invest some of its time and money in filming the first *Yes Minister* script, it was hard for him not to feel anxious about having Allen (as amiable and well regarded though he was within the industry) at the helm.

Antony Jay, while not plagued by such painful personal memories, was also far from enthusiastic about the choice of director. 'I was not particularly impressed by him,' he later recalled, 'but I felt he would do. I didn't know his previous work.'[7]

It was not just the writers who were concerned. Neither Paul Eddington nor Nigel Hawthorne was happy about the selection, suspecting, as Eddington would later put it, that the 'sophistication of our show' would hold little appeal to a director more used to sitcoms about boobs, bums and buses.[8] Derek Fowlds agreed: 'There was nothing personal about it, but, knowing that the script called for something that would seem more factoid than fiction, we all thought that Stuart seemed a strange choice'.[9]

Their worst fears were confirmed during rehearsals, when Allen made it clear that he felt the show needed a few 'improvements'. His first idea, much to all the actors' horror, involved getting Diana Hoddinott, who as Annie Hacker was on her hands and knees searching for something or other under a coffee table, to waggle her bottom in the air as she did so. 'It's all dialogue,' Allen explained impatiently, 'we've got to get in some *visuals*.' Hawthorne sidled over to Eddington at the side of the rehearsal room and whispered, 'Surely the script's funny enough in itself, we don't have to try to *make* it funny?'[10] Eddington, rolling his eyes, nodded grimly in agreement. This was not how they wanted things to develop.

Allen pushed on regardless, seemingly intent on turning *Yes Minister* into *Yus Minister*. Listening to Sir Humphrey's elaborate monologues, he sighed, frowned and fidgeted, and then suggested things for the other actors to do to leaven the wordiness with a little action. Watching Hacker sit motionless at his desk, he suggested bits of physical business that might get one or two more laughs. He even started (without even thinking of consulting the writers first) dreaming up new lines, exchanges and scenes, claiming that it was all in the show's best interests.

It came as a profoundly unwelcome shock, therefore, when Jonathan Lynn arrived on the third day of rehearsals (Antony Jay was otherwise engaged on Video Arts business) and discovered what the director was actually doing. Upon entering the room and sitting quietly on a seat at the side, he watched as, to his horror, the actors worked on a scene that neither he nor Jay had written.

It featured Hacker, as the newly elected Minister, excitedly studying swatches of fabric as he prepared to choose a new sofa for his office. Once the scene was over, Lynn, trying hard to stifle the desire to scream and shout, walked over to Allen and asked what exactly he thought he was doing adding things to the script. 'But this new stuff is *funny*,' the director exclaimed with a smile. Lynn, still straining to be polite, questioned that assertion, pointing out that this was a sitcom that was supposed to seem realistic, and having Hacker fuss over sofas, on his first day as a Minister, simply made no sense.

He asked Allen to revert to the original script, exactly as it had been written, and stick to it, but the director was clearly disinclined to agree. 'It's *clever*,' he said of Jay and Lynn's script, with an expression on his face that suggested he was dealing with a sitcom neophyte. 'It's very *clever*. But we have an audience coming in on Sunday. We need to get some laughs.'[11]

Lynn, now positively bubbling with hot bursts of volcanic fury, assured him that the script, as written, would indeed get laughs. Allen looked at him pityingly and replied: 'Not very many.'[12]

By this stage, the rest of the team had drifted over and, hovering nearby, were listening in on the tense conversation. 'Look,' Lynn said, barely able to contain himself any longer, 'this is the script that the BBC bought, that Paul and Nigel signed on for, and that you agreed to direct.' He wondered to himself if he could speak on his absent writing partner's behalf, decided that he could and went on: 'We don't agree to your changing it. If you do, the show won't happen on Sunday night. Tony and I will see that it's stopped. We'll call our agents today. There will be no show.'[13]

Lynn, with his heart pounding, realised that he had possibly over-stepped the mark. He had no idea, off the top of his head, if he and Jay actually had the power, contractually, to carry out such threats, but he was far too angry to back down.

An awkward silence descended on the room as Lynn stared at Allen and Allen stared back at Lynn. It was only a few seconds, but it felt more like minutes, until Paul Eddington stepped forward and, bearing a slight diplomatic smile, said to Allen: 'I think, you know, if Jonathan feels that strongly, we should try it his way.'[14] Then Nigel Hawthorne and Derek Fowlds joined in and agreed. 'We all felt that it was wrong,' Fowlds would recall, 'because I think Stuart was directing it as the kind of sitcom that people would have been expecting – very light and slightly farcical. Whereas the beauty of Jonathan and Tony's script was that it was so brilliant that we really had to play it totally for the truth.'[15]

With great reluctance, the director reverted to the original script and resumed the rehearsal. Lynn watched for a while longer, making sure that all was well, and then left to call Antony Jay and explain what had happened. Jay, on hearing Lynn's account, congratulated him on his response and reassured him that he had done the right thing. It was their script, they agreed, and it would be their script that would end up being acted out on the screen.

Work continued through to the end of the week, with a fair amount of tension in the air. The actors did not trust the director, and the director did not trust the script. It was an uncomfortable situation in which no one seemed happy.

The mood barely improved on the Sunday, when the team met in the studio to prepare for the recording. As was the norm in those days at Television Centre, members of the audience were obliged to form a queue, on the ground floor, directly outside the dressing room windows. As Eddington, Hawthorne, Fowlds and the rest of the cast were getting themselves ready to perform, their concentration kept being interrupted by the snatches of conversation that were drifting up from the crowd outside. Hawthorne, especially, was rattled to hear some of them express regret that they had failed to get free tickets for a show they already knew, and the nervous actor suspected that 'many of them would have preferred to be coming to *George and Mildred*'.[16]

Hawthorne and Eddington were further irritated once the audience had been admitted to the studio and were being entertained by the warm-up man. Trusted by countless BBC producers over the years not only to get the audience ready to laugh as soon as the red light came on at the start of a recording, but also to return whenever there was a scene change or a technical hitch to maintain the positive mood, Felix Bowness (who would soon find a certain amount of fame himself by appearing in front of the cameras as the lugubrious ex-jockey Fred Quilly in the sitcom *Hi-de-Hi!*) had worked behind the scenes on some of the biggest light entertainment shows of the past decade. He was, as a consequence, the obvious choice to warm up any sitcom audience.

On this occasion, however, there was a problem. Both Eddington and Hawthorne hated the way he was doing it.

Hawthorne, for example, emerged from the make-up room to hear 'gales of laughter rocking the studio'. That would normally have delighted any sitcom actor, but in this case, as he hovered in the wings to listen to some of the material, it began to worry him. 'I realised a lot of the jokes were decidedly blue,' he later explained, 'and that Felix was gearing up the audience to expect a very different show from the one which we were to present.'[17]

Eddington, if anything, reacted even more negatively – mainly due to the fact that he had already had more than his fill of warm-up men during the years that he spent on the set of *The Good Life*. Raging at the typical practitioner's 'racist and honeymoon jokes and his invitations to the audience to shake hands with each other and shout out where they came from', he immediately resented Bowness' presence, scowling at the bawdy-sounding laughter and vowing that this would be the last time he would tolerate such a pre-show performance.[18]

'I liked old Felix,' Derek Fowlds would recall. 'He was funny, but on that particular night I must say he *was* being a bit blue, and I could see it was really rattling Paul and Nigel. They were pacing around backstage, listening to all of this, going: "What on *earth* is going *on* out there?"'[19]

Both men, however, were far too professional to dwell on such issues so close to a performance, and quickly returned their focus to the script. When everything was ready, they stepped onto the set in Studio 1, straight into character, and the recording duly began.

There were no significant mistakes. Each scene flew by according to plan and, as Lynn had promised, the original script elicited plenty of laughs. By the end, as all of the actors returned to take a bow before the loudly applauding audience, John Howard Davies had already decided to commission two more scripts and thus guarantee *Yes Minister* its first six-episode series.

Relieved and exhilarated ('A huge cloud of worry just blew away,' Antony Jay would say[20]), the writers and their stars went off to reflect on what had happened and plan for what was to come. Both parties had opinions that they wanted to air.

The stars, for example, were keen to compare notes with the writers as to how they might grow into their respective roles. After having to rush through the all-too-brief rehearsal period to get the pilot completed, there seemed to be a need, before the production process resumed, to use whatever breathing space was available to think more deeply about who each character was supposed to be.

It was probably inevitable that Paul Eddington would have strong ideas about his part because he himself was quite a political animal. Raised as a Quaker who believed passionately in George Fox's tenet that 'There is a God in every man',[21] he was a staunch pacifist who had been a conscientious objector during the Second World War and a keen supporter of the Labour Party until, under Clement Attlee's leadership, they decided to continue with conscription into peacetime: 'I ceremoniously burned my [membership] card and dropped it out the window'.[22] Now defiantly non-aligned in terms of parties, he remained firmly left of centre (quite Crossman-like, in fact) and followed the political coverage, both at home and abroad, with a keen interest.

Eddington said that he saw Jim Hacker as 'a sort of Candide – an innocent beset by these piratical civil servants', who was bound, in time, to be corrupted, to some extent, by the culture of the governing class.[23] This was surely in itself a little naive, as 'a sort of Candide' would struggle even to get selected as a prospective MP in the cut-throat, cynical world of modern British politics, let alone go on to get elected and then clamber over enough of his or her contemporaries to be made a Minister. Jonathan Lynn, however, while sympathising with the actor's perspective, endeavoured to deepen the depiction.

Lynn said that he thought of Hacker as a figure reminiscent of the 'whisky priest' portrayed in Graham Greene's novel *The Power and the Glory* – a disappointing man who neither desired to dirty his hands nor was strong enough to resist doing so, a character who, as Greene had put it, just 'gets caught up'.[24] Lynn explained: 'I think Hacker was very much a moralist, but I would say that he totally failed to live up to his morality.

I would argue that he was a sort of unfrocked priest. His problem was that he would always compromise – when the opinion polls told him he had to, or when Sir Humphrey warned him that he was being "courageous". As you know, to be controversial may lose votes, but being courageous could lose the next election.'[25]

There would be strong rumours at the time that Eddington, unbeknown to the writers, drew further inspiration for his portrayal of Hacker by studying the Conservative MP James Prior.[26] A Heathite member of the Thatcherite Shadow Cabinet, Prior – a stocky little figure with a round, red-cheeked face that suggested he had either just peered inside a piping-hot Aga or been scolded by his headmistress – bore a passing resemblance to the actor Ned Beatty, who was famous for playing the unfortunate fellow in *Deliverance* who was forced to 'squeal like a pig' (which was somewhat ironic, seeing as Prior was a farmer who had started out running a pig club during the war[27]). More of a Pooter than a Candide, he was, nonetheless, particularly fascinating, it seems, to Eddington for what in the shifting political climate of the time was coming to seem like an oxymoronic personality – a committed pragmatist, a defiant moderate, whose old-fashioned 'softly, softly' approach inside a Shadow Cabinet that now favoured a 'shrilly, shrilly' approach, made him seem as if on a collision course with his uncompromising leader, who had already branded him (off the record) as one of the 'wettest' of her current lieutenants.

Eddington always refused either to confirm or deny the link. There was certainly, however, a family resemblance between Hacker and Prior that would sometimes catch the eye as the fictional minister fretted over his latest political puzzle.

Nigel Hawthorne, meanwhile, was volunteering his own views on Sir Humphrey. Unlike Eddington, he claimed to have no interest at all in politics; although English-born, he had grown up in South Africa and only returned as a refugee from the apartheid regime, and, while he was an instinctive liberal, he would always feel something of an outsider when it came to domestic current affairs.[28] He was also not inclined to analyse his character as an individual. He preferred to think of him simply as an archetype, a kind of bureaucratic Everyman. Antony Jay, he was pleased to find, thought much the same, explaining that he and Lynn had performed a kind of 'principlectomy' operation on the figure, removing all of his moral principles and personal ethics, leaving him to 'operate entirely by what it took to succeed in the job'.[29]

When it came to the question of Sir Humphrey's motivation, Jay said that, as with politicians, there were two answers – the publicly acceptable one and the real one. 'The civil servant's declared motivation,' he said, 'is to carry out the wishes of the government efficiently, economically and impartially, working conscientiously and tirelessly to turn ministers' policies into just, beneficial and workable laws. Their real motivation is to raise their personal status, to enhance the importance of their department, to avoid blame, to gain credit, to minimise work, to resist change, and to retire with an index-linked pension, a knighthood and the chairmanship of a couple of quangos and a seat on the board of a blue-chip company.'[30] Hawthorne nodded in recognition; this was precisely how he had come to think of Sir Humphrey.

The differences in outlook between Eddington and Hawthorne would lead to Jay and Lynn employing different tactics to talk each one of them through the rest of their scripts. Eddington, always arriving for rehearsals with a well-thumbed copy of the *Guardian* folded tightly under his arm, could see the big picture as far as the show's satire was concerned, and so whenever he asked what the significance of any of the more arcane details might be, the writers were quick to place it in the broader political context. Hawthorne, on the other hand, would tend to look blank and bored in the face of such a strategy, and so Antony Jay hit upon an alternative method of exposition. If ever Hawthorne looked at an episode and said that he was puzzled by how Sir Humphrey was behaving, Jay would take him to one side and explain: 'Well, he's like Malvolio this week', or 'This week it's Iago'.[31] At this kind of insight, Hawthorne's eyes would light up, he would gasp a triumphant 'Aha!' and would be off and running.

The easy-going Derek Fowlds, on the other hand, was quite content to keep playing Bernard Woolley exactly as the pilot script had suggested, providing the link between the two main protagonists. Woolley, he agreed with the writers, was 'both sides of centre, with slight leanings to the right and left',[32] and he was there not just to act but also (and perhaps even more importantly) to listen and react. There was no need to build up much of a backstory for Bernard. 'You begin with the script, you end with the script,' Fowlds would say, 'and if you're a good actor you can just stand there and say the lines.'[33]

He had also, by this time, been admonished by Paul Eddington for attempting to act too much while they were filming the external scenes for the pilot. 'I don't know why, but I'd got these little glasses,' Fowlds would recall, 'and I put them on and I started to talk *a bit like thet*. And Paul and I were in the taxi, rehearsing, and he said, "Derek, why are you talking *funny?*" So I said, "Well, you know, Bernard's a PPS, so, er, I thought I'd do something *rather like thet.*" So he said, "*Why?*" And then he said, "And what have you got those *glasses* on for?" I said, "Well, it's all character stuff." So he said, "Derek, take the glasses off. Just be *you!*"'[34]

Apart from the characterisations, one other thing that everyone wanted to discuss were the caricatures that had formed part of the opening credits sequence. No one liked them. The actors, in particular, hated them.

Drawn – in something of a hurry – by a hastily hired hand,[35] the clumsiness of the execution had rather alarmed the performers.[36] It was not hard to see why: Hacker looked like a bloated Regency roué, Sir Humphrey resembled the bastard child of Sid James and Tony Hancock, and Woolley appeared to be a badly drawn Beatle.

A round-table discussion was duly held to determine what should be done to remedy the situation before the rest of the series was filmed. Hawthorne insisted that they hire another artist and, when asked who this should be, replied: 'There is only one, and that's Gerald Scarfe.'[37] The suggestion – of a man whose work was driven with the precision of a Gillray-like satirical eye – met with unanimous approval (although Jonathan Lynn had initially been considering contacting Ralph Steadman), and it was agreed that John Howard Davies would commission a new set of caricatures from the artist.

Another complaint concerned the theme tune. Written by Max Harris (an experienced composer who had written the music for Anthony Newley's experimental 1960 comedy series *The Strange World of Gurney Slade* as well as, more recently, *Porridge*, *Open All Hours* and the *On the Buses* movie), there had always been something half-hearted about the composition. Given little time to experiment, and little knowledge of the kind of show *Yes Minister* was likely to become, Harris had rushed to produce something – anything – that sounded right enough for the pilot edition. His piece had done the job without also doing what the best of such tunes did, namely capturing the real character of the sitcom. A jaunty yet aimless piece of music, dominated by trumpets and trombones, it had sounded rather like a marching band that had ended up in a cul-de-sac.

The consensus, once again, was that it needed to be replaced, and so John Howard Davies decided to commission (for the modest sum of £157.50[38]) a new theme tune from the doyen of sitcom composers, Ronnie Hazlehurst. The new piece that he eventually came up with – a far more polished and stately affair complete with Big Ben chimes, spoiled only by the kind of rickety guitar sounds that were practically de rigueur in 1970s television music – would, though arguably not quite matching Hazlehurst's very best work, certainly be deemed an improvement on its predecessor and was accepted as the new theme for the series.

Capitalising on this climate of constructive criticism and piecemeal change, Paul Eddington could not resist also requesting that they do away with the traditional warm-up man. *Yes Minister*, he insisted, was not the sort of show that needed its audience to be given a sugar rush of forced hilarity prior to every recording. It would do well enough by trusting the script and respecting the viewers' intelligence. Not everyone else felt as strongly about this as he did, and John Howard Davies certainly still believed that there had to be someone around to keep people alert and cheerful during the various lulls in action, but, after giving the matter some thought, he agreed to a compromise: they would use a warm-up man, but, rather than rely on a run-of-the-mill comedian (who would also have demanded a fee) they would instead settle for the more informal PR skills of the floor manager, Brian Jones (who would do it for nothing).

In addition to these internal notes and queries, there was also a polite intervention from a few BBC executives who, having heard rumours that this new show would be unusual in its use of British politics as the basis for a sitcom, started expressing their concerns about possible objections from Whitehall and Westminster on the grounds of some kind of alleged ideological bias. This was one anxiety that was assuaged not by John Howard Davies but rather by Antony Jay.

As a former editor of the *Tonight* programme, as well as the head of a current affairs documentary department, Jay – uniquely for a writer of a situation comedy – knew and understood the BBC's political policy a great deal better than anyone in its Light Entertainment department, 'who practically never came across it and who were terrified of it'. The result was that he could reassure the more nervous of Davies' colleagues that there would always be a safe pair of hands dealing with anything potentially controversial in the show's content. 'I took charge of that side of the script-writing,' Jay later confirmed, 'and so there was never a problem with BBC policy. It was rather like being a libel lawyer: a really valuable one can tell you what you can do and say. It was the same with BBC policy: the more familiar you were with it, the more things you knew were perfectly accept-able; so it enabled us to be less timid about what we said about politics and the political system.'[39]

The one other issue that, at this stage, needed to be addressed was the thorniest one of all: the director.

There was still deep dissatisfaction with the whole approach of Stuart Allen, which for some bordered on outright hostility. Even though the writers and actors had combined to force him to adhere to the words as written, he had still managed to make certain moments in the pilot seem just a little broader than had been intended – the bottom wiggling, though greatly subdued, was still glimpsed – and the overall impression had been of a director going through the motions.

It was clear, in fact, that the ill feeling was mutual. At that point Allen himself was well aware that he was not suited to this kind of material, or rather that this kind of material was not suited to him, and it therefore came as no surprise when he jumped at the chance to oversee another new ITV sitcom, *Mind Your Language*, which mainly revolved around immi-grants who spoke in 'funny' accents. The job of producer/director of *Yes Minister* was now vacant.

John Howard Davies, appreciating that his last choice had been a rare aberration on his part (although the main reason for it had been that none of the BBC's in-house producer/directors had been available[40]), took more time on this occasion to find a director who fitted, and, after consulting Jay and Lynn and the actors, and sounding out a number of experienced figures, he eventually came down in favour of Sydney Lotterby. A BAFTA-winning veteran of BBC sitcoms, Lotterby (who had joined the Light Entertainment department back in 1958) had worked on such successes as *Sykes and A . . .*, *Up Pompeii!*, *The Liver Birds*, *Some Mothers Do 'Ave 'Em*, *Last of the Summer Wine*, *Porridge*, *Going Straight* and *Open All Hours*, and his calm, good-natured professionalism (along with his dry wit) had won him the trust and affection of many writers and performers (including Marty Feldman,[41] who teased him in no fewer than three sketches for the *At Last the 1948 Show* – 'The Four Sydney Lotterbys', 'The Return of the Four Sydney Lotterbys' and 'Sydney Lotterby Wants To Know The Test Score' (all 1967)[42] – and John Cleese, who would go on to name one of the characters in his 1997 movie *Fierce Creatures* after him, as well as Ronnie Barker, who treated him as a mentor).

Davies knew that, first of all, Lotterby could be relied on to improve morale substantially. As Geoffrey Palmer (one actor who worked with him on numerous other projects) testified, he was 'immensely painstaking and just creates the most lovely working atmosphere'.[43] Davies also knew that, in the longer term, he would work hard to ensure that there was a smooth transition from script to screen.

A Lotterby sitcom could be trusted to avoid lurching towards one or other of the genre's two extremes: on the one hand, slapstick, overacting, and the mechanical repetition of set-up and punchline, and on the other, self-regarding artiness, aimless inaction and listless chatter. This is not, however, to suggest that there was anything meekly middle-of-the-road or cravenly mediocre about his programme-making approach. What he always aimed for was a well-written, well-paced, well-acted show that, as the BBC's traditional light entertainment dictum put it, gave 'viewers what they wanted – but better than they expected it'.[44] A man who had the utmost respect for those who contributed the words and the performances, Lotterby (like such similarly talented colleagues as Duncan Wood, John Ammonds and Dennis Main Wilson) regarded his role as being one that cultivated rather than commodified what the creative talents did. As a consequence, his appointment was warmly welcomed by all those involved.

With this and all of the other changes in place, the team could look forward at last to making the series. It was still going to be quite a logistical challenge, as neither of the writers (who were set to be paid a fee of £1,200 per script, minus agents' commission, between the two of them[45]) could afford to give up their day jobs, and all of the actors had various theatre commitments inked into their diaries, but everyone involved was now determined to bring this sitcom to the screen.

It was at that very moment of optimism that something strange happened. All of a sudden, the production was put on hold.

The Labour Government was beginning to crumble, the widespread industrial unrest (exacerbated by a failed attempt to maintain pay restraint for another year) was worsening by the week and there were increasingly urgent calls for a General Election. The BBC, panicking about the need to be seen to avoid political controversy during the run-up to voting, feared that *Yes Minister*, among its other overtly 'political' programmes, might well end up reaching the screen right in the middle of what was promising to be an exceptionally fierce and fractious campaign . . . so it pulled the plug.

This had been a sad tradition at the Corporation since the early 1960s, when *That Was The Week That Was* was abruptly cancelled when unofficial but nonetheless very intense pressure was brought to bear on the BBC to stop broadcasting satire in the months leading up to the 1964 General Election.[46] Ever since then, certain tabloid (and a couple of broadsheet) newspapers, notorious for their progressively bitter anti-BBC agenda, had seized on anything screened that might have been thought to cause political divisions during such periods, and all of the main political parties themselves, in a similar spirit of cynical opportunism, followed suit, protesting long and loud at the supposed BBC bias against them in anything from conventional current affairs programmes to playful sketch shows and sitcoms. The consequence was that, by the late 1970s, few people at the Corporation seemed to have the stomach for fighting such high-profile complaints, and the tendency was to err well on the side of caution. *Yes Minister*, alas, was one of those productions that ended up as collateral damage.

To be fair to those who reacted so rashly, the political portents did indeed seem exceptionally ominous at the start of 1979, just when the remaining episodes of *Yes Minister* were meant to go into production. The ailing Labour Government, which had been left with no overall majority following a by-election defeat in March of 1977, had only survived in subsequent months due to a fragile pact with the Liberal Party,[47] and that agreement finally snapped apart in September 1978. As a result, the Prime Minister, James Callaghan, was widely expected to call a snap General Election, but he decided instead to gamble and go on as the leader of a minority Government in the hope that circumstances would improve before he was forced to go to the polls.

The gamble, however, was destined to fail, and instead of the Prime

Minister the media had dubbed 'Sunny Jim' emerging revitalised into a much warmer and more benign political climate, he would instead be plunged into a so-called 'Winter of Discontent', when the country was plagued by industrial action, economic disarray and administrative incompetence. From the last few months of 1978 through to the beginning of 1979, Britain would effectively be strikebound, with public servants staging mass walkouts, leaving food and fuel supplies undelivered, rubbish uncollected and, most notoriously, bodies unburied.

While the BBC's decision to slip *Yes Minister* onto the shelf was hugely disappointing, it was hardly inexplicable. As the first sitcom to deal so openly, honestly and accurately with Britain's political system, it found itself the victim of its own novelty. It should have been allowed to go on, impartially satirising the system rather than mocking any of its constituent parts, but the backbone in broadcasting was no longer there.

Everyone involved with the show was left feeling angry, frustrated and depressed. Stranded at the start of 1979, with the Government dragging itself doggedly on, there was not even a light at the end of the tunnel. They would just have to wait for however long it took until, ludicrously, it was deemed safe again for the BBC to screen whatever it wished.

Reluctantly, the two writers went off to busy themselves with their other, solo concerns, and the actors, always anxious about 'resting', immersed themselves with diverse theatrical ventures. Nigel Hawthorne signed up to appear in a new production of *Uncle Vanya* (which was due to open in November at the Hampstead Theatre), while the similarly restless Paul Eddington was about to commit to co-starring with his old *Good Life* friend Richard Briers in the new Roger Hall comedy *Middle Age Spread* (which was set to start in the same month at the Lyric). Derek Fowlds, meanwhile, took on a number of one-off roles in various television dramas.

Everyone waited. Although the Government might have given up at any moment, time seemed to pass more slowly with each uneventful day. Calendars were studied; clocks were watched. All that anyone could do was keep reading the newspapers and hope for news of an election.

The papers, however, only added to the agony with their seemingly endless swathes of speculation. On 7 February, for example, it was widely reported that Labour Party whips, in response to the depressing-looking polls, were urging Callaghan to delay polling day until, at the very least, the autumn.[48] On 15 February, a vague-sounding 'concordat' (dismissed by the Opposition as a 'fig leaf') was announced that suggested the TUC was prepared to prop up the Government for the foreseeable future in return for certain sympathetic deals with the unions.[49] On 26 February, Callaghan took to the television, in a hastily arranged interview with BBC1's *Panorama* programme, to make a desperate attempt at countering the calamitous-sounding opinion polls that were still rushing in. Then, on 4 March, there were more reports that, in defiance of the mounting pressures to resign, he was planning to 'cling on until the autumn'.[50] The scattered *Yes Minister* team now knew that there might be months more to wait until they could all reunite and resume their project.

There were no doubts, Jonathan Lynn would say, that it would, eventually, be resumed, because the pilot had been so well received within the BBC. 'But I had doubts,' he later admitted, 'about whether the series would interest enough people. I predicted a total of six episodes on BBC2, and would have been quite happy with that.'[51]

The waiting game did not, as it happened, go on as long as was feared. It lasted until late on the night of 28 March, when the Government lost a motion of no confidence by a single vote.[52] A General Election was finally called for 3 May, and the campaign duly began.

The Conservatives won it, and a triumphant Margaret Thatcher stood on the steps of Number Ten and expressed the improbable wish that her Government would replace discord with harmony. She then stepped inside, the big black door shut behind her and life, officially, went back to normal.

Whatever else the *Yes Minister* team might have thought about the result – and, as the vast majority of them (with the notable exception of Antony Jay) were either Labour or Liberal supporters, it seems unlikely that the reaction was positive – they could at least look forward, after months of miserable inactivity, to getting back to work. This time the sitcom really was going to happen.

John Howard Davies signalled his intent by commissioning a seventh and final script for the series on the day after the election. Paying them a fee of £725 each, he set the writers a deadline of 30 September 1979.[53]

There was still a delay, however, as each member of the team needed to deal with their various other commitments and find space in their

respective diaries, and Davies himself still needed to negotiate an appropriate schedule for the production, but, after a few more months, everything,
and everyone, was back in place and the process was ready to be restarted.
There was little to be done to the scripts, because, although all but one of
them had been written during what was now an outdated period in politics, Jay and Lynn had always eschewed overt topicality, and so the themes
remained just as relevant as they had been the year before. The same was
true of the characters, who were never meant to be suggestive of any particular party or person, and so required no rethinking.

Once the whole team could reconvene, therefore, the hard work could
begin, and – after the longest tea break in sitcom history – production
started again towards the end of the year. Brian Wenham, the Controller
of BBC2, had made plans to start broadcasting the series in late February
1980, so there was no time to be lost.

First, the series fees had to be agreed. The actors were remunerated
mainly in terms of their perceived status within the show, so Eddington,
as its ostensible star, would receive £750 per episode (a modest figure compared to, say, the £1,500 that David Jason would soon be receiving for
Only Fools and Horses[54]), followed by Hawthorne on £550 and Fowlds on
£275, with the supporting cast receiving sums averaging around £165 per
programme. Jay and Lynn, meanwhile, received a modest increase for the
filming of their scripts, rising from the £600 each of them earned for the
pilot to £750 apiece for the subsequent episodes.[55]

The next priority was to record the external scenes and shots ahead of
the studio sessions, so all of them were filmed in one busy week from 9 to
16 December 1979. The Welsh Office in Whitehall was chosen to pass
for the outside of the Department of Administrative Affairs (a practice
that would continue for subsequent series), and other locations included
RAF Northolt in Ruislip, a street of shops in Kingston upon Thames, The
Metals Society in London's Carlton House Terrace and the north end of
Platform 1 at King's Cross Station.[56]

The new signature tune came next. Ronnie Hazlehurst recorded it in
one session at Lime Grove Studios on 18 December.[57]

Meanwhile, the set designers were taking great care to ensure that all of
the interiors within Whitehall would be as detailed and believable as possible. An indication of this can be found in the prop requests from this time.

For Hacker's office, for example, the items acquired included: one oval conference table; six upright chairs; two armchairs (one brown velvet and the other upright leather); twelve copies of Hansard; two Ministerial red boxes; two telephones; a selection of government stationery; a pair of large in and out trays; a desk writing set; a noticeboard; two zip-up document cases; a dictating machine; a copy of all the daily newspapers; a drinks cabinet; one bottle of Bell's whisky; one bottle of Queen Anne whisky; one bottle of Booth's gin; two bottles of Tio Pepe sherry; three small bottles of bitter lemon; three small bottles of dry ginger ale; two bottles of Malvern water; two bottles of ginger cordial; one bottle of blackcurrant cordial; six plain whisky tumblers; six gin glasses; six sherry schooners and a metal ice bucket with tongs. It was to be an office that did not seem to belong to any particular Minister, an office that was more suited to anxiously entertaining a wide range of visitors rather than satisfying its actual incumbent.[58]

Sir Humphrey's office was decorated with similar thoughtfulness. There were more books (usually leather-bound and mainly about the law), more tasteful paintings, more ashtrays and more expensive and elegant creature comforts. It was a lair, a den, a place for intrigue, introspection and, eventually, gloating. Even the contents of his own drinks cabinet were made to look distinct from Hacker's in order to complement his character: all of the glasses were mock crystal, with a choice of small and large ones for his better brands of sherry, and he was also given an expensive-looking soda syphon.

Rehearsals began back inside Room 601 at the 'Acton Hilton' on New Year's Day. Paul Eddington, by this time, was back on the West End stage as the star of *Middle Age Spread*, and so, as with preparations for the pilot episode, the schedule had to be nipped and tucked to cope with his occasional absences.

The actors would join Sydney Lotterby on a Tuesday for a read-through of the latest episode, followed by a first basic rehearsal; they met again on Wednesday morning for a few more hours' work before Eddington had to set off for a matinee; Thursday was the first full day for everyone to start really mastering their performances, and Friday would be another full day of rehearsal. Saturday would see them perform a technical run-through and another complete performance, and then they would reconvene on Sunday at 10 a.m. for a long sequence of technical and dress rehearsals. Then, at 8 p.m. (either in Studio 4 or 8) the recording would commence.

There would be a quick drink at 10 p.m. after the show, and everyone would drift off into the night.

This was the strict, rigorous, intense timetable, repeated week after week throughout January and most of February, which would enable *Yes Minister* to be ready and recorded in time to reach the screen. No one complained about the rush; after waiting for so long, there was, if anything, an impatience to get everything done.

A year of waiting had passed, but, at long last, all of the hard work was finally nearing completion. Nothing, after this, would ever be the same again.

PART TWO

Rational calculation . . . reduces every worker to a cog in this bureaucratic machine and, seeing himself in this light, he will merely ask how to transform himself into a somewhat bigger cog.
Max Weber

There is an enormous difference between an armed and an unarmed man; and it cannot be expected that a man who is armed will obey willingly a man who is unarmed, or that an unarmed man will be safe among armed servants. Since the latter will be contemptuous and the former suspicious and afraid, they will not be able to work well together.
Niccolò Machiavelli

5

Series One

*[A]n observer who looks at the living reality will wonder at the contrast to the
paper description. He will see in the life much which is not in the books;
and he will not find in the rough practice many refinements of the literary theory.*

It was better late than never. In fact, it was actually better late than on
time.

The first series of *Yes Minister* finally reached the screen on 25 February
1980 – one year later than planned. Instead of emerging, as intended,
into the Britain presided over by James Callaghan's floundering Labour
Government, it arrived in the Britain run by Margaret Thatcher's fledgling
Conservative Government. The delay, however, did nothing to diminish
the noteworthiness of its appearance: what it had to say about the system
as a whole remained just as relevant regardless of whether the current party
in power was red or blue, or left or right.

The issues on the domestic political agenda were much the same now
as they had been the year before: unemployment, inflation and industrial
unrest were still lodged firmly at the top of the list. Both Labour and the
Conservatives, in the run-up to the election, had pledged to cut all three,
but, as Labour remained distracted internally by a spate of ever more fierce
and bitter ideological schisms, it had been the Conservatives who had
fought the far cannier campaign, embellishing their nosegay of core commitments with such eye-catching and class-coordinated floral additions
as the promotion of a 'property-owning democracy' (by allowing council
house tenants to buy their own homes at a discount) and the provision of
incentives designed to reward those most eager to enrich themselves and
climb the social ladder. The result was a 5.2 per cent swing to the Tories,

ensuring that Margaret Thatcher and her colleagues came to power with an overall majority of forty-three seats.

If anything, this change in government actually made the conditions more propitious for a show like *Yes Minister* to strike a chord with the country. Back in the dark days of 1979's Winter of Discontent, it seems highly unlikely that the British public would have been in a mood remotely conducive to welcoming a new sitcom that required them, among other things, to care about, and to some extent sympathise with, the respective ambitions of a politician and a civil servant. Nothing coming out of Westminster or Whitehall in those days was considered to be a laughing matter.

With the stench of failure masked only partially by the cologne of contrition, the stock of the country's political Establishment had rarely sunk so low. Among the routine stories of price hikes and job losses, all through the winter there seemed to have been an unremitting blizzard of bitterly negative reports about the weakness of political leadership, the strength of union leadership, the lack of cohesion within the Cabinet and the opportunism of the Opposition. Matters worsened with James Callaghan's spectacular 'Crisis, What Crisis?' PR implosion in January 1979 when, in the middle of a lorry drivers' strike (and at the very moment when *Yes Minister* had originally been due to air), he arrived back in Britain from an economic summit in sunny Guadeloupe only to respond to the usual barrage of pointed press questions about various domestic crises first by babbling away cheerfully about his refreshing swims in the warm Caribbean waters, and then issuing a haughty warning to his inquisitors about not being so parochial in their perspective. As angry opinion pieces proliferated in the papers, and the strikes, squabbles and progressively ominous economic prognoses continued to dominate the daily news, the climate seemed more suited to agitprop drama than elegant comedy.

A year on, however, and some of the wounds were beginning to heal. While much of the pain and anger still remained, there was at least the recognition that the most culpable political protagonists had either been dumped, demoted or reshuffled, and there was now a readiness – perhaps even a desperation – to look forward rather than back.

The usual sense of freshness that informs the first few months of a reconstituted House of Commons, rendered even sharper on this occasion by the novel presence of Britain's first female Prime Minister at the Government Despatch Box, further encouraged the cultivation of a somewhat more benign and open-minded mood around the country. The material signs, in a sober sense, might have seemed, if anything, even bleaker for the country than before, but, after the cathartic experience of completing the electoral cycle, a spirit of stoicism had returned, albeit briefly, to the national mood.

In addition to all of this, the belated *Yes Minister* was also gifted a new Government in Westminster that appeared intent on waging a war on Whitehall, pledging to oversee the 'reduction of waste, bureaucracy and over-government' and to reassert 'the supremacy of Parliament' over the Civil Service.[1] The relationship between the two bodies, which had hitherto been kept so discreet, was now being discussed and debated openly, just as a new comedy show was about to unveil its dynamics for the scrutiny of a broader public. It was in this sense that *Yes Minister*, with its special subject matter, style and scope, could count itself fortunate to have had its debut delayed. Cometh the real-life power struggle, cometh the realistic and pertinent sitcom.

One thing that had not changed, though, was television's traditional reluctance to overburden new programmes with too much advance publicity – with the result that most of them slipped onto the screen like something of a secret. As with the vast majority of the great sitcoms that had preceded it, *Yes Minister* was left to find and develop a following largely via a combination of luck and word of mouth.

Back in that more basic broadcasting world of just three television channels, there were no preview screenings for the critics, nor any promotional campaigns for the public, such as have since come to be a normal part of the build-up to a brand new series. As the weeks and days were counted down before the show's arrival, the most helpful hype it received was a short article, focusing far more on the actors than on the themes, tucked away in the middle of the *Radio Times* – and even that modest piece of puffery managed to obscure what was most distinctive about the project by adopting a banner – 'The Men from the Ministry' – that would have prompted memories of the old radio series that centred exclusively on the Civil Service.[2]

When the time finally came, on Monday 25 February, for the show to make its debut, it was given a place in the schedules at 9 p.m. on BBC2.[3] This was by no means the most appealing of slots to occupy, as tradition showed that comedy programmes in general, and sitcoms in particular, tended to perform better in the second half of the working week (when the weekend loomed and moods improved), and attracted a much larger share of the audience (as well as, admittedly, a much larger share of the pressure to succeed) on BBC1 rather than BBC2. Monday on BBC2 was thus not the natural time for anything that promised to be, or even become, 'event TV'. This was the place for slow-burning dramas or sober-sounding documentaries. The message that the scheduling seemed to send out, to those who noticed such things, was that this show, with its unusual mix of high and low cultural associations, was set to be something of an experiment, to be highlighted gradually, or quietly dropped, depending on how the first few episodes fared.

The competition on that particular night, such as it was, had all the hallmarks of that gloomily fatalistic phase of the weekly schedules. BBC1 was offering an edition of the current affairs programme *Panorama* at 8.10 p.m. (revolving around a tentative examination of the new Government's industrial and economic policies), followed by the *Nine O'Clock News* and then an uninviting old movie (the critically panned 1975 remake of the classic 1946 thriller *The Spiral Staircase*). ITV seemed only slightly less resigned to the prospect of a grim-faced nation having an early night by serving up an edition of its own current affairs programme *World in Action* at 8.30 p.m. (about certain aspects of the aftermath of the Vietnam War), followed by an episode of its spy series, *The Sandbaggers*, that was more praised than watched. Over on BBC2, meanwhile, the opening instalment of *Yes Minister* itself was handed the challengingly ambiguous brief of holding onto an audience that, beforehand, had sat through the nostalgic light entertainment schmaltz of the hour-long *An Evening with Anthony Newley*, and was set to follow it with an edition of the science series *Horizon* that featured a report on the treatment of terminal diseases.

It was far from ideal, but at least the long wait was finally over. *Yes Minister* was about to be seen.

The series began with the original pilot episode, entitled 'Open Government', which sought to introduce all of the key characters and most of the key themes while engaging the interest of the mainstream audience. Although filmed back in January 1979, it reached the screen looking tailor-made for the here and now.

Instead of beginning in the conventional manner by going straight to the title sequence, the show started with a news-style 'outside broadcast' from a typical election night scene, with all the candidates and their respective partners standing out on a town hall balcony, huddling nervously around the returning officer as he announces the result: 'James George Hacker: 21,793'. As cheers are heard from the voters below, the unseen reporter remarks: 'So Jim Hacker is back with an increased majority, and, after many years as a shadow minister, seems almost certain to get a post in the new Government!'

After the title sequence, the episode moved fast to reassure an audience that was used to watching suburban-based family sitcoms by starting with a scene of instantly familiar domesticity, with Hacker, dressed casually in cardigan and slacks, sitting by the telephone in the living room while his similarly attired wife, Annie, walks in with a tray of teacups. Even though the actual reason why Hacker is hovering over the phone so anxiously is because he is hoping for the call from Number Ten that will confirm his place in the new Cabinet, it could just as easily have been *The Good Life*'s Jerry Leadbetter waiting for some beneficial news from his business, or *Hi-de-Hi!*'s Jeffrey Fairbrother twitching in anticipation of a report about disco night at his holiday camp. The message the scene sent out was that this sitcom was still going to be a sitcom about believable, recognisable people, even though they were mainly going to be shown trying to cope within the unfamiliar world of Whitehall.

The other element that helped engage a broad audience during those first few minutes was the playfulness and precision of the dialogue. No lines were wasted, all of them made some kind of point (informing us about the individual characters, shedding light on the situation or setting up the plot), and almost all of them elicited a laugh. The exchange between Jim, sitting twitchily sipping his tea, and Annie, fussing tetchily over the furniture, typified the seemingly effortless pertinence of this opening scene:

> JIM: I wish people wouldn't keep ringing me up to
>   congratulate me. Don't they realise I'm waiting for the
>   *call*?
>
> ANNIE: You sound as if you're about to enter the Ministry.

JIM:	Yes, but *which* Ministry? That's the whole point!
ANNIE:	It was a *joke*!
JIM:	Oh! *[He suddenly notices his wife is constantly fidgeting with the furniture]* You're very tense.
ANNIE:	*[Sarcastically]* Oh, no, I'm not *tense*. I'm just a politician's wife. I'm not allowed to have *feelings*! A happy, carefree, politician's *wife*!

The abrupt arrival into their home of Hacker's boorishly intense special adviser, Frank Weisel, not only pushed up the pace but also amplified the interplay of personal and professional themes, with Annie speaking for the audience as the two party men obsess over political matters:

WEISEL:	Did you know Martin's got the Foreign Office—
HACKER:	Has he?
WEISEL:	Jack's got Health, and Fred's got Energy?
ANNIE:	Has anyone got brains?
HACKER:	You mean Education?
ANNIE:	No, I know what I mean.
HACKER:	*[Too preoccupied to notice her sarcasm]* Well, what's left? I mean, what have *I* got?
ANNIE:	Rhythm?

Once Hacker has finally heard the word from the Prime Minister – he is to head the Department for Administrative Affairs – the action moves swiftly away from the traditional sitcom milieu and takes the viewer instead into an environment that, at the time, had only been glimpsed in programmes associated with current affairs. Guided by a formal-sounding voiceover, we follow Hacker's journey from private man to public servant. We see a black London cab glide up outside the black-bricked exterior of Number Ten Downing Street, where the MP emerges to stride purposefully past the posse of pressmen and the two posted policemen and enter the building, then he reappears outside as a freshly anointed Minister. He then gets back into the cab, where he is greeted by his grinning special adviser and is driven off to the site of his new Ministry in Whitehall.

It is at this point we watch as, symbolically, Hacker is further absorbed into the Establishment when he is met at the doors of Whitehall by the insiders: Frank Woolley, the Principal Private Secretary, and Lloyd Pritchard, the Assistant Private Secretary. Although Hacker has arrived in the company of his special adviser, it only takes one length of a grey-tiled corridor before the shades of bureaucracy begin to close upon the politician, as Pritchard ushers Frank Weisel away in one direction while Woolley guides Hacker off in another.

Now separated not only physically but also figuratively from his Westminster colleague ('The Minister now has a whole Department to advise him,' his no longer quite so special adviser is told), Hacker finds himself in unnervingly unfamiliar territory right in the heart of Whitehall, where, inside his grand new office, the solitary politician is introduced to a mass of mandarins. First, in the manner of a jaw-jarring, left-handed jab, he is slightly disorientated by his Principal Private Secretary's ability to appear deferential while dictating the terms of departmental etiquette, dismissing an invitation to call his master 'Jim' ('I'd prefer to call you "Minister", Minister') while requesting that *he* be addressed as 'Bernard'. Then, as if hit by a full-blooded right hook, Hacker is profoundly perplexed by his first official encounter with his Permanent Secretary, Sir Humphrey Appleby:

WOOLLEY:	I believe you know each other?
SIR HUMPHREY:	Yes, we did cross swords when the Minister gave me a grilling over the estimates in the Public Accounts Committee.
HACKER:	*[Sounding flattered]* Oh, I wouldn't say that.
SIR HUMPHREY:	Well, you came up with all the questions I'd hoped nobody would ask.
HACKER:	Well, Opposition is all about asking awkward questions.
SIR HUMPHREY:	And Government is about not answering them.
HACKER:	Well, you answered all mine, anyway.
SIR HUMPHREY:	I'm glad you thought so, Minister. *[Raising his glass of sherry]* Good luck.

[Hacker raises his glass in response]

HACKER: Now, who else is in this department?

SIR HUMPHREY: Well, briefly, sir, I am the Permanent Under-
                Secretary of State, known as the Permanent
                Secretary. Woolley here is your Principal
                Private Secretary. I, too, have a Principal
                Private Secretary, and he is the Principal Private
                Secretary to the Permanent Secretary. Directly
                responsible to me are 10 Deputy Secretaries, 87
                Under-Secretaries and 219 Assistant Secretaries.
                Directly responsible to the Principal Private
                Secretaries are plain Private Secretaries, and
                the Prime Minister will be appointing two
                Parliamentary Under-Secretaries and you will
                be appointing your own Parliamentary Private
                Secretary.

HACKER: [Laughing nervously] Do they all type?

SIR HUMPHREY: None of us can type, Minister. Mrs MacKay
                types. She's the secretary.

It does not take long for the comic dynamic of this relationship between
the elected and the unelected to show itself in all its vivid clarity. Hacker,
the man with a mandate, is all bustle and bluster ('You'll have to forgive
me if I'm a bit blunt, but that's the sort of chap I am'), talking boldly about
abstract generalities ('The Nation'; 'The Public'; 'The Truth') and throwing out clichés like campaign leaflets ('We want a new broom'; 'We're
going to throw open the windows, let in a bit of fresh air'; 'Cut through
all the red tape'; 'Streamline this creaking old bureaucratic machine'; 'A
clean sweep'). Sir Humphrey, on the other hand, is the devil in the details,
always ready to startle Hacker, after listening patiently to the Minister's
latest huff and puff of hot air, by demonstrating, decorously but tellingly,
how much real power can be had from solid knowledge:

HACKER: Open Government! That's what my Party
                believes in! That was the main plank of our
                manifesto – 'Taking the nation into our
                confidence'! Now, how does *that* strike you?

SIR HUMPHREY: In fact, just as you said in the House on May
                  the 2nd last year, and again on November the
                  23rd, and in your *Observer* article, and in your
                  Daily Mail interview, and as your manifesto
                  made clear—

HACKER: Y-You *know* about that?

[He ignores the question and hands Hacker a thick file of papers]

SIR HUMPHREY: I'd like you to have a look at these proposals,
                  Minister. They outline the ways in which this
                  policy could be implemented and contain
                  draft proposals for a White Paper for your
                  approval. We thought that the White Paper
                  might be *called* 'Open Government'.

HACKER: Y-You mean . . . it . . . it's—

SIR HUMPHREY: It's all been taken care of, Minister.

HACKER: Huh? Who . . . who *did* all this?

SIR HUMPHREY: The creaking old bureaucratic machine!

Bernard Woolley, as the humble intermediary between these two high-placed officials, soon reveals that he is enough of a mandarin to have ingested most of the prejudices associated with his institution, but also enough of a secretary to sympathise with the needs of his Minister, with the consequence that he usually ends up satisfying neither. When, for example, Hacker declares that he would like a new chair, Woolley is quick to promise that one will be found, but, instinctively rather than vindictively, cannot resist also volunteering an anecdote: 'It used to be said there were two kinds of chairs to go with two kinds of Minister: one sort folds up instantly, the other sort goes round and round in circles.' This faux pas – the first of many – manages to rattle both of his bosses: Hacker because it is impudent and Sir Humphrey because it is indiscreet.

It is Woolley's strange hybridity – part cynic, part idealist – that looks set to condemn him to a career of bouncing back and forth between his two rival bosses. Take, for example, his reaction to the first of Hacker's 'Big Ideas' – Open Government. Whereas Hacker believes in it without understanding it, and Sir Humphrey dismisses it because he understands it only too well, Woolley only starts to establish a coherent position on the subject after both men have bullied him about it. 'What's *wrong* with open government?' he asks innocently of his Civil Service superiors after Hacker has done his best to convince him of its logic. 'Why *shouldn't* the public know more about what's going on?' The answer, when it comes, shakes the fragile foundations of his freshly formed opinion: 'My dear boy, it's a contradiction in *terms* – you can be *open* or you can have *government!*' Woolley tries to stand his ground ('But surely the citizens of a democracy have a *right* to know?'), but Sir Humphrey's intimidating show of certainty ('No. They have a right to be *ignorant*. Knowledge only means complicity and guilt. Ignorance has a certain dignity') soon grinds him down. 'My dear fellow,' Sir Humphrey concludes, 'you will not be serving your Minister by helping him to make a *fool* of himself. Look at the Ministers we've had: every one of them would have been a laughing stock in three months had it not been for the most rigid and impenetrable secrecy about what they were up to!'

It is evident right from the start, however, that Sir Humphrey and Woolley will always be as linked as Hacker will be alone, because, as two of the 'permanent residents of the house of power', their very presence, their inviolable devotion to the bureaucratic routine, will always prompt in Hacker, as in Crossman and all of the other recently promoted politicians, the sobering intimations of his own evanescence. No sooner is he behind his desk as the new Head of the Department, the well-meaning words of his civil servants summon up the ghosts of Ministers past and future, and Hacker realises how transient his tenure might be:

> HACKER: *[Closing his file and rising as if to go]* Well, I
> think that's it then!
>
> SIR HUMPHREY: Oh, there *are* one or two *more* things,
> Minister . . .
>
> HACKER: Eh? *What* things?
>
> WOOLLEY: Er, yes, if you would just like to check your
> diary for next week, Minister.
>
> HACKER: My *diary*? You didn't know *I* was coming! You
> didn't even know who'd win the election!
>
> WOOLLEY: Er, we knew there would be a *Minister*,
> Minister.

HACKER:	Don't start *that* again!
WOOLLEY:	I'm sorry; even though we didn't know it would be you.
SIR HUMPHREY:	Yes, you see, Her Majesty *does* like the business of Government to continue even when there are no *politicians* around.
HACKER:	*[Chuckling awkwardly]* A bit difficult, surely?
SIR HUMPHREY:	Yes . . . And no.

Hacker's fast-diminishing sense of triumphalism is further depleted when Woolley lists a dauntingly long list of departmental engagements and Sir Humphrey reminds him that, from now on, as a temporary resident of Whitehall, he will not even be able to dodge compromises when it comes to his Westminster commitments:

HACKER:	What about all the *other* things I have to do?
WOOLLEY:	What other things, Minister?
HACKER:	Well, I'm on four policy committees for the Party for a start!
SIR HUMPHREY:	Well, I'm sure you won't want to be putting Party before Country, Minister?
HACKER:	I . . . er . . . N-No, *no*, of course!

Having established the characters and their key interrelationships, the rest of the episode concentrated on the first real tussle between Hacker and Sir Humphrey. When Sir Humphrey hears from his senior colleague, the Cabinet Secretary, that the Prime Minister is keen to close a major defence trade agreement with the United States (it therefore being essential that no one endangers the deal by undermining Anglo-American relations), he hatches a plan to give Hacker a sobering scare ('We'll have him house-trained in no time').

Noting that his Minister continues to be urged on to action by his seemingly indefatigable special adviser, Sir Humphrey arranges for the two of them to 'discover' a secret invoice for £10 million worth of American computer equipment set to be used by the Civil Service. Outraged that a British manufacturer has not been handed such a lucrative commission, they demand that the 'scandalous' contract, if it cannot now be cancelled, should at least be made public as proof that the principle of 'open government' is now being put into practice. Sir Humphrey, after putting up a faux show of resistance, suggests that, if the Minister's mind is set on this course of action, he should reveal all in a speech and then – via Sir Humphrey – release the damning details to the press.

Hacker and Weisel are thrilled to think that they have asserted their authority – 'There,' squeals Weisel to Sir Humphrey triumphantly, 'who's running the country *now*, eh?' – but it does not take long before their victory is revealed to be pyrrhic. Hacker is sitting in his Department browsing through some documents when Woolley arrives brandishing a minute from the Prime Minister's Office, informing him that 'the PM is planning a visit to Washington next month, and is anxious that the visit will result in a valuable Anglo-American defence trade agreement. The importance of obtaining this agreement cannot be overestimated'. Hacker, distracted by his documents, mutters 'Fine,' but then the significance of the message sinks in: 'Oh my God – has my speech gone to the press?' His sense of panic only increases when Sir Humphrey bursts in to report that 'all hell has just broken loose at Number Ten' after they have seen a copy of Hacker's inflammatory speech.

Concealing his obvious delight in his Minister's distress, Sir Humphrey explains that, when questioned by the PM's people as to why the speech had not been sent to them in advance for clearance, he told them that 'We believe in open government'. Affecting mock regret, he adds that this only 'seemed to make things worse'. Ominously, he then tells Hacker: 'The PM wants to see you in the House, right away.'

A quivering Hacker, his face now as pale as his own White Paper, asks Sir Humphrey, in the pathetic tone of a small child who has been caught doing something naughty: 'What's going to happen?' Sir Humphrey sighs and replies sadly, 'The Prime Minister giveth, and the Prime Minister taketh away.' Hacker, now more anxious than ever, scuttles off to face the music.

In the waiting room outside the Prime Minister's Office, Hacker fears the worst. When he spots the big, bossy, beetle-browed Chief Whip emerging from the inner sanctum, his desperate attempt at a friendly greeting gets brusquely rebuffed: 'You really are a pain in the *arse*, aren't you!' Frank

Weisel, hovering as usual by Hacker's side, gets a similarly rude response when he tries to remind the Chief Whip about the party's commitment to open government: 'Oh shut up, *Weasel* – who's asking you?'

After delivering his parting shot to Hacker – 'In politics you have to learn to say things with tact and finesse, you berk!' – the Chief Whip strides off in search of his next victim. Next to emerge is the Cabinet Secretary, who is just as angry as his predecessor, snapping at Sir Humphrey for allowing his Minister to make such a provocative speech and asking if its contents have definitely been sent to the press. 'Well, the Minister gave express instructions before noon,' Sir Humphrey explains, relishing Hacker's discomfort. 'The Minister and I believe in open government,' he adds, eagerly exacerbating the offence, 'we want to throw open the windows and let in a bit of fresh air – isn't that *right,* Minister?' Hacker looks distinctly queasy at the very mention of his own cliché. Sir Humphrey then leans in to his Minister and, lowering his voice, asks him if he would like to give thought to drafting a letter of resignation – 'Just in case'.

Hacker, fearing for his future, elects to get his hands dirty. 'Could we hush it up?' he asks Sir Humphrey. His Permanent Secretary bristles with mock indignation: '*Hush it up*? You mean *suppress* it?' Hacker, embarrassed, mumbles his agreement. Sir Humphrey tries to look thoughtful and concerned: 'I see . . . You mean that within the framework of the guidelines for open government that you've laid down, you are suggesting we adopt a more flexible posture?' Hacker is so flustered he can barely compose a response: 'Do I? Er . . . Y-Yes, yes!'

At this point Woolley rushes in, announcing breathlessly yet loquaciously: 'There appears to have been a development which could precipitate a reappraisal of our position!' A bemused Hacker listens carefully. 'Apparently we failed to rescind the interdepartmental clearance procedure. The supplementary stop order came into effect!' Hacker is still puzzled but suddenly vaguely hopeful. 'So it's all right, Minister, your speech hasn't gone to the press!' Hacker gasps with relief as Woolley completes his explanation. 'It's only gone to the Prime Minister's Private Office, and the Duty Officer had no instructions to pass it out without clearance from the PM and the Foreign Office – it's the American reference, you see!'

Hacker can barely believe his luck: 'But how come?' he exclaims. Sir Humphrey, now looking simultaneously smug and contrite, places a hand on his heart and 'confesses': 'The fault is entirely mine, Minister. The procedure for holding up press releases dates back to before the era of "Open Government" and I unaccountably omitted to rescind it. I do hope you'll forgive this lapse.' Hacker, with similar insincerity, pretends to be generous with his forgiveness. 'That's quite all right, Humphrey, quite all right,' he says. 'After all, we all make mistakes!' Sir Humphrey looks at him with knowing eyes: 'Yes, Minister.'

This opening episode thus ended with all of its aims fulfilled. It had introduced the situation not only with impressive clarity but also (in the writing if not the direction) an admirable lightness of touch, established all of the characters with colour and care, and had also sown the seeds of most of its recurring themes, such as the unending tension between politicians and bureaucrats, the inevitable disparity between abstract ideals and practical reality, the perennial conflict between personal ambition and political prudence, the increasingly dire dangers of dealing with the media and, last but by no means least, the universally profound problem of 'dirty hands'. It had all been handled with consummate care: beautifully written, cleverly and delicately acted and presented in such a way as to maintain a fine balance between comedy and truth.

The critical response to the debut generally followed the traditional pattern for the opening episodes of new sitcoms, with some reviewers preferring to wait a while longer before volunteering a judgement, and a few of the others committing their comments to print insulated by so many nervy doubts and reservations as to render their real opinions more or less opaque. Peter Fiddick, for example, wrote in the *Guardian* that 'the look of the thing is good', and said that the show deserved praise for 'aiming admirably higher than knockabout gags', but then qualified this positive-sounding welcome by complaining that a fleeting comment that used the wrong citation style for Hansard undermined the sitcom's verisimilitude – a complaint which, seeing as only the tiniest proportion of the audience would have been in a position to spot such a minor inaccuracy, seemed patently pedantic.[4]

Probably the most positive evaluation came from David Sinclair in *The Times*, who hailed the originality of the show and predicted that it was set to mollify all of those viewers who felt that the sitcom genre had recently been stuck in the doldrums:

In this series, the kitchen sink and the bedroom, the office and
the factory, the husband/wife/lover/children/aunt/dog/vicar/
undertaker permutations, and the other standard scenarios of
sitcom have been cast aside. But what on earth is left? you scream,
nerves at breaking point. Why the government, of course – and
what could be funnier than that? [. . .] Such topics as the EEC,
official secrets and quangos may seem unpromising raw material,
but just think about them for a moment and you'll see the rib-
tickling potentialities.[5]

The size of the audience for the first episode had been a somewhat
disappointing 1.8 million,[6] which was not particularly unusual for that
time and slot on BBC2 (it had long been one of the curiosities of British
broadcasting that a large part of the viewing public would not watch a
programme on BBC2 – perhaps because of some lingering sense of it
having started out as the nation's 'highbrow' channel – even though they
would happily watch the very same thing if it was repeated on BBC1), but
it was still a source of frustration to those involved with the show. Word of
mouth helped build the audience a little for the next episode, but it would
not be until after the third instalment that the series finally started getting
the kind of viewing figures that were commensurate with its quality.

One reason for this upturn in its fortunes was the publication of a substantial review in *The Listener* magazine. Written by the prominent Labour
politician and former Cabinet Minister Roy Hattersley, it represented an
insider's stamp of approval, and, as a consequence, it commanded a considerable amount of attention. Praising Jay and Lynn for wanting 'to portray
more than the small change of political life', Hattersley went on to link them
with the grand tradition of literate political satire: 'Like Anthony Trollope
[. . .], they aspire to write fiction that is about politics, not just politicians.
And, like him, they achieve some remarkable successes'. After noting the
accuracy and insightfulness of the episodes so far, as well as the sophisticated
nature of the humour, he predicted a bright future for the sitcom:

There are funny things to be said and written about the
profession of politics and enormous entertainment to be provided
by recounting the political ways in which politicians are risible

and ridiculous. Mr Jay and Mr Lynn may, on the evidence of the earliest episodes, be able to entertain us by saying them.[7]

There were also several other positive mentions of the show in the press, which helped to increase the interest. A number of reports, for example, noted how both politicians and civil servants were beginning to speculate as to who might be the models for the characters of Hacker and Sir Humphrey. The *Daily Mail*, for example, gossiped that 'order papers are being waved in the direction of Labour's former Industry Secretary, Eric Varley,' and even quoted the man himself moaning that 'if they'd wanted to use me in the programme I would have charged a pretty big fee'. The paper also related a rumour that Sir Humphrey had been inspired by Sir Douglas Wass, the Permanent Secretary to the Treasury since 1974.[8]

The guesses were, of course, to put it mildly, wide of the mark. Eric Varley, for example, was a serious, complex, disarmingly honest but rather dour figure (a miner's son who had risen quietly but fairly rapidly up through the party ranks) who, although he had made the odd gaffe in his past (such as the time in 1976 when he decided to shut down the loss-making Chrysler car factory, only for his Cabinet colleagues to force him into an embarrassing U-turn), and was once privately chastised by Harold Wilson for being 'too much in the hands' of his officials,[9] was nothing like the kind of ditherer that Hacker personified. The smooth-tongued, discreet and quietly crafty Sir Douglas Wass was a much better bet for Sir Humphrey, but then most Permanent Secretaries, by the very fact that they possessed precisely the kind of personality to be made Permanent Secretaries, would have reminded one of Sir Humphrey – his inclusiveness was partly the point.

The wildest piece of speculation at this stage connected Frank Field with Frank Weisel. Field, the London-born MP for Birkenhead, had never been a political adviser, and (rather like a Labour equivalent of the Tory Party's 'mad monk' Sir Keith Joseph) was a quirky and twitchily earnest operator whose pronouncements were often as complex (sometimes bordering on the gnomic) as Weisel's were risibly simplistic.

It did not matter, however, that the guesses were inaccurate. What mattered was that they were being made at all, and that the show was being talked about. More and more people were starting to be drawn into its cultured, insightful and intriguingly believable netherworld.

The real depth to the series was provided by the power of its ever-present themes, which kept connecting each isolated plot to a richer, regular texture. Whereas most sitcoms flitted skittishly from one self-contained storyline to the next, *Yes Minister*, while never skimping on local detail, touch or colour, never lost sight of the bigger picture.

There were, for example, some deftly delivered satirical observations about the various tensions between bureaucracy and politics. In episode three, Sir Humphrey explained to Woolley how Whitehall is naturally inclined to evaluate itself:

> There has to be some way to measure success in the Civil Service. British Leyland measure their success by the size of their profits. Or, to be more accurate, they measure their failure by the size of their losses. But we don't have profits and losses. We have to measure our success by the size of our staff and our budget. By definition, Bernard, a big department is more successful than a small one.[10]

Similarly, in a later episode, Hacker let slip how Westminster approaches the same process:

HACKER:	You must realise that there is a real desire for radical reform in the air. The All-Party Select Committee on Administrative Affairs, which I founded, is a case in point. It's a *great* success.
SIR HUMPHREY:	Oh, indeed. What has it *achieved*?
HACKER:	Um . . . nothing, *yet*, but the Party's *very* pleased with it.
SIR HUMPHREY:	Ah. Why?
HACKER:	Ten column inches in last Monday's *Daily Mail* for a start!
SIR HUMPHREY:	Oh, I see, the Government is going to measure its success in *column inches*, is it?
HACKER:	Yes . . . No . . . Yes *and* no![11]

Later on in the series, Sir Humphrey, with uncharacteristic directness, serves as the mouthpiece for another bitingly sardonic summary of the Civil Service's take on the relationship between a Permanent Secretary and his Minister:

SIR HUMPHREY:	You are *not* here to run this Department.
HACKER:	I beg your pardon?
SIR HUMPHREY:	You are *not* here to run this Department.
HACKER:	I think I *am*! The *people* think I am, too!
SIR HUMPHREY:	With respect, Minister, you are – they are – wrong.
HACKER:	And who *does* run this Department?
SIR HUMPHREY:	I do.
HACKER:	Oh! I see! And what am *I* supposed to do?
SIR HUMPHREY:	We've been through all this before: make policy, get legislation enacted and, above all, secure the Department's budget in Cabinet.
HACKER:	I sometimes think that the budget is all you ever really care about.
SIR HUMPHREY:	Well, it *is* rather important, Minister. If nobody cared about the budget, we might end up with a department so *small* that even a *Minister* could run it.[12]

This relationship is explained in even more brilliantly damning detail in another exchange – this time between Sir Humphrey, Woolley and another Permanent Secretary, the gloriously orgulous Sir Frederick 'Jumbo' Stewart:

SIR HUMPHREY:	Is something the matter, Bernard?
WOOLLEY:	Er, well, it's just that, er, I've been increasingly worried about, er, keeping things back from the Minister.
SIR HUMPHREY:	What do you mean?
WOOLLEY:	Well, er, why *shouldn't* he be allowed to know things . . . if he wants to?
SIR FREDERICK:	*Silly* boy!

SIR HUMPHREY:	Bernard, this country is governed by Ministers making decisions from the various alternative proposals that we offer them, is it not?
WOOLLEY:	Well, yes, of course.
SIR HUMPHREY:	Well, don't you see? If they had all the *facts* they'd see all sorts of *other* possibilities. They might even formulate their *own* plans instead of choosing between the two or three that *we* put up.
WOOLLEY:	Would that matter?
SIR FREDERICK:	*Would it matter?!?*
WOOLLEY:	But why?
SIR HUMPHREY:	Well, as long as *we* can formulate our *own* proposals, we can *guide* them to the *correct* decision.
WOOLLEY:	Can we? How?
SIR FREDERICK:	It's like a conjurer. The Three-Card Trick. You know: 'Take any card . . .' Then make sure they pick the one that you intend. Ours is the Four-Word Trick.
SIR HUMPHREY:	There are four words you have to work into a proposal if you want a Minister to accept it.
SIR FREDERICK:	Quick. Simple. Popular. Cheap. And, equally, there are four words to be included in a proposal if you want it thrown out.
SIR HUMPHREY:	Complicated. Lengthy. Expensive. Controversial. And if you want to be *really* sure that the Minister doesn't accept it you must say the decision is 'courageous'.
WOOLLEY:	And that's worse than 'controversial'?
SIR HUMPHREY:	Oh! 'Controversial' only means: 'This will lose you votes'. 'Courageous' means: 'This will lose you the election'!

SIR FREDERICK:	You see, if they have all the *facts* instead of just the *options*, they might start thinking for *themselves*.
SIR HUMPHREY:	Mmmm.
WOOLLEY:	And the system works?
SIR HUMPHREY:	*Works*? It's made Britain what she is today![13]

Another impressively effective recurring theme was that concerning the 'cheat of words' – the various uses and abuses of rhetoric. Both Sir Humphrey and Hacker, for example, demonstrated in certain circumstances that they were well versed in the dark arts of 'anti-speak', whereby civil servants and politicians alike conspire to eviscerate language and then use the limp remains as a sort of protective lagging.

In Sir Humphrey's case, of course, such questionable skills are in evidence almost every time he opens his mouth (e.g. 'The traditional allocation of executive responsibilities has always been so determined as to liberate the ministerial incumbent from the administrative minutiae by devolving the managerial functions to those whose experience and qualifications have better formed them for the performance of such humble offices, thereby releasing their political overlords for the more onerous duties and profound deliberations which are the inevitable concomitant of their exalted position'[14]). Even Hacker, however, when he finds himself squirming in such an uncomfortable situation as, say, a probing television interview, shows that he, too, can waffle with the worst of them ('D'you know? I'm *glad* you asked me that question! Because . . . it's a question a lot of people are asking. And why? Because a lot of people want to know the *answer* to it. And let's be quite *clear* about this without beating about the bush: the plain *fact* of the matter is . . . is that it's a *very* important question indeed! And people have a *right* to know!'[15]).

In a more specific analysis of the pros and cons of trying to communicate, and manipulate, through the means of the modern media, the series captured on numerous occasions how dangerous it can be when a politician, rashly unsheathing the simple sword of truth, sets out to carve his or her name with pride in the press. One such instance occurred in an episode in which Hacker's cynical bid to gain favourable personal coverage – by launching an ill-conceived but headline-hunting economy drive ('HACKER SETS AN EXAMPLE!' 'SAVE IT, SAYS JIM!') – sees him resort to such clumsy publicity stunts as eschewing the use of his drinks cabinet, cutting down on staff in his private office and shunning his chauffeur-driven ministerial car, only to end up being photographed looking somewhat tired and emotional one wet and miserable evening as he sinks to his knees in the gutter and struggles to retrieve his car keys from a drain.

The same episode shows how these media misfortunes are often explained away through the devious powers of spin. Sir Humphrey, noting that Hacker's ham-fisted attempt at cutting bureaucracy will only lead to the creation of *more* bureaucracy (with at least four hundred new jobs in the offing if his new administrative 'watchdog' is established), proposes abandoning the policy, scrapping all the yet-to-be-filled vacancies and then issuing an immediate press announcement to the effect that the Minister has done precisely what he promised. 'That's *phoney*,' Hacker complains as he contemplates how much the truth is being twisted. 'It-it's *cheating*, it's *dishonest*, it's just . . . cheating with *figures*, pulling the wool over people's eyes!' Sir Humphrey responds with a knowing grin: 'A Government press release, in fact.'[16]

Another issue within the media theme was addressed later on in the series when the hazards of a politician having a free-willed family was brought briefly into focus, with Hacker's left-leaning student daughter threatening to ruin one of his policies by making the political personal, and vice versa. The Minister, having been persuaded by Sir Humphrey to support proposed legislation that will see certain areas of the countryside lose their protected status ('It's only the urban middle class who worry about the preservation of the countryside – because *they* don't have to *live* in it'), is then horrified to discover that his own faux-radical daughter is one of those planning to stage a front-page-friendly nude protest at an endangered badger colony. 'What about the police?' asks Hacker, desperately. '"MINISTER SETS POLICE ON NUDE DAUGHTER" – I'm not sure that *completely* kills the story, Minister,' replies Sir Humphrey drily. Once again, it is the Permanent Secretary's penchant for spin that saves the public face of the politician, first assuring the daughter that the only extant local animals are rats, and then assuring the Minister that there is no need for him to have such 'facts' confirmed.

It is the ancient problem of 'dirty hands', however, that runs throughout the series like a thread. Although Hacker, decent but driven, arrives in the Department determined always to do the right thing, it does not take long before he finds himself pressured into sometimes doing some of the wrong things in order to achieve it. After considering 'hushing' something up in the opening episode, Hacker, his moral compass now sent spinning by the sheer complexity of practical politics, soon shows himself open to a bit of bribery to seal a deal with a shady foreign leader ('Everyone has his price'[17]), as well as, on occasion, misleading his fellow MPs ('I don't want the *truth* – I want something I can tell *Parliament!*'[18]).

By the final episode of the series, Hacker is clearly a much more morally compromised creature from the one who arrived in Whitehall preaching the pure ideals of openness, honesty and unquestionable integrity, and now – although remaining essentially well intentioned – he appears to be very much at home in a world in which practically everyone is open to at least some degree of corruption. Working in tandem with Sir Humphrey, he saves an important Government-sponsored building project by using his powers of patronage to buy the compliance of a banker, tame a trade unionist and even shut up and shut out his own noisily principled political adviser. Time and again he brushes his own objections aside as he pursues his ultimate objectives.

Although he refrains from saying so himself, he would, one suspects, applaud the ingenuity, rather than condemn the insincerity, of Sir Humphrey's sly redefinition of a cover-up as 'responsible discretion exercised in the national interest to prevent unnecessary disclosure of eminently justifiable procedures in which untimely revelation could severely impair public confidence'.[19] The Minister, at this stage, has hands that are as dirty as any others inside his Department.

As if the sustained and intelligent treatment of this and the other recurring themes was not impressive enough for the short and populist form of the sitcom, the series also managed to find sufficient room and wit to touch on a number of more specific topical issues, ranging from current ecological concerns to the burgeoning use of quangos. Probably the most evocative and provocative of such issues, and the one that was treated with the most clinical satirical swipe, was that pertaining to the chronically vexed question of Britain's role in Europe:

SIR HUMPHREY: Britain has had the same foreign policy
                  objective for at least the last five hundred years:
                  to create a disunited Europe. In that cause, we
                  have fought with the Dutch against the Spanish,
                  with the Germans against the French, with the
                  French and Italians against the Germans and
                  with the French against the Germans and the
                  Italians. Divide and rule, you see? Why should
                  we change now, when it's worked so *well*?

HACKER: That's all ancient history, surely?

SIR HUMPHREY: Yes. *And* current policy. We *had* to break the
                  whole thing up so we *had* to get inside. We
                  tried to break it up from the outside but that
                  wouldn't work. Now that we're *inside* we can
                  make a complete pig's breakfast of the whole
                  thing! Set the Germans against the French,
                  the French against the Italians, the Italians
                  against the Dutch . . . The Foreign Office is
                  terribly pleased – it's just like old times!

HACKER: But surely we're all committed to the
                  European ideal?

SIR HUMPHREY: *Really*, Minister!

HACKER: If not, why are we pressing for an *increase* in
                  the membership?

SIR HUMPHREY: Well, for the same reason. It's just like the
                  United Nations, in fact: the more members
                  it has, the more arguments it can stir up. The
                  more futile and impotent it becomes.

HACKER: What appalling cynicism!

SIR HUMPHREY: Yes. *We* call it *diplomacy*, Minister.[20]

The one aspect of life that was largely missing from the first series was private life, but that absence, understandably, was a reflection of an absence in real life. This was, after all, the story of how a Minister becomes increasingly immersed in the business of government, and, as a consequence, it also had to be, implicitly, the story of how a Minister becomes

progressively alienated from ordinary civilian activities. Like some poor
soul who has followed the footsteps leading into Virgil's dark cave of
Polyphemus, there is only one direction that Hacker is heading, and that
is deeper and deeper into the abyss. In dramatic terms, therefore, there
was probably precious little to show of the typical senior bureaucratic or
political official's life beyond the day-to-day exigencies of government.

True, in theory, and in keeping with a much more conventional sitcom
style, we could probably have seen more of Sir Humphrey off duty than
one fleeting scene of him sharing a shadowy bed with his wife (totalling a
mere fifty-five seconds), and more of Hacker spending some time domes-
tically with his own wife (only six scenes in seven episodes, totalling a
modest sixteen minutes), or his daughter (just one scene, totalling just
four minutes), but, to be fair, the concision had more to do with fact than
fiction. Apart from a few isolated moments when Hacker's wife acted as
his confidante-cum-conscience, such as when she shamed and cajoled him
into finally standing up for himself ('And while you're at it, why not just
sign your letters with a rubber stamp, or get an Assistant Principal to sign
them for you? They *write* them, anyway!'), there was little opportunity for
his family to interact with him genuinely without distracting viewers from
each complicated plot.

The real message conveyed by the peripheral nature of his personal life
was that, whether he likes it or not, the Department of Administrative
Affairs is now Jim Hacker's de facto home, and Sir Humphrey and Woolley
are now his surrogate family. He might have started out on that balcony,
arm in arm with his wife with his party rosette proudly on display on his
overcoat, but gradually, as the red boxes pile up and the problems prolif-
erate, he becomes more and more rooted in his job, and, eventually, this
Westminster man becomes wedded to Whitehall.

This gradual process was charted by means of an effective dialectic. In
three well-paced stages, the transformation was traced.

The first three episodes provided the thesis: Whitehall rules over
Westminster. Sir Humphrey, with his cobra-cool eyes, would listen
patiently to his mouse of a Minister, and then, when the moment was
right, he would pounce, wrapping his words around his prey until all
resistance had been suffocated. Hacker, time and again, would react with
the kind of dazed and dazzled awe that had caused Charles Pooter, in *The*

Diary of a Nobody, to remark that the pronouncements of the similarly verbose and 'very clever' Hardfur Huttle seemed 'absolutely powerful'.[21]

The fourth episode, however, provided the antithesis: Westminster fights back. Jim Hacker, realising that he is being consistently outwitted by his Permanent Secretary, resolves to claw back some authority by acting just as slyly as his tormentor. Spurred on by the combined efforts of his special adviser and his wife, Hacker starts mimicking the master's own brand of deviousness, unnerving Sir Humphrey by waking him up in the early hours of the morning with a speciously complicated query ('I didn't interrupt you in the middle of *dinner* or anything, did I?'), confounding him with his sudden addiction to secrecy ('Humphrey, my lips are sealed!'), anticipating and dismissing all of his procrastinating tactics ('Right: well, we can go ahead, then!'), and then using the media to bypass and bully the bureaucracy ('. . . And I'm happy to announce that we're now ready to put our proposals into publication'), leaving a furious Sir Humphrey facing a fait accompli ('I think,' the discreetly impressed Woolley tells him, 'it's checkmate'). Even though the sheer amount of effort Hacker expends to win this particular battle seems unlikely to be repeated all that often – one already senses that Hacker, compared to Sir Humphrey, is, essentially, lazier as well as slower-witted – the victory does at least show his Permanent Secretary that, from this point on, the Minister is quite capable, on his day, of putting him back in his place.

The fifth episode, as a consequence, provided the series with its synthesis: the start of a tense but tolerable working relationship between Whitehall and Westminster. It was this crucial episode that saw both men realise that, although they would remain rivals for power within the Department that they shared, they also needed each other in order to legitimate the world in which both of them lived.

Entitled 'The Writing on the Wall', the episode began with Hacker once again railing against the resistance he faced from his own group of civil servants, complaining that they always contrive to manipulate whatever policy he attempts to shape no matter how many redrafts he demands ('It *still* won't say what I want it to say. It'll say what *you* want it to say! And *I* want it to say what *I* want it to say!), and Sir Humphrey once again protesting his innocence ('*We* want it to say what *you* want it to say, Minister'). On this particular occasion, Hacker is convinced that his civil servants are trying to sabotage his attempt to trim the size of the bureaucracy by around two hundred thousand members of staff, while Sir Humphrey insists that he and his underlings are actually doing all that they can to accede to their own reduction. Close to the end of his tether, Hacker pleads with Sir Humphrey for one bright and precious moment of candour:

HACKER:	Will you give me a straight answer to a straight question?
SIR HUMPHREY:	Oh, well, Minister, as long as you're not asking me to resort to crude generalisations and vulgar oversimplifications, such as a simple 'yes' or 'no', I will do my upmost to oblige.
HACKER:	*[Puzzled]* Is that 'Yes'?
SIR HUMPHREY:	*[After a long hesitation]* . . . Y-Yes.
HACKER:	Well, here's the straight question—
SIR HUMPHREY:	Oh, I thought *that* was it!
HACKER:	*[Trying hard to brush aside the sarcasm]* When you give your evidence to the think tank, are you going to *support* my view that the Civil Service is overmanned and feather-bedded, or not?
SIR HUMPHREY:	I, ah—
HACKER:	Yes or no – straight answer!
SIR HUMPHREY:	Well, Minister, if you ask me for a *straight* answer, then I shall say that, as far as we can *see*, looking at it by and large, taking one time with another, in terms of the average of departments, then, in the final analysis, it is probably true to say that, at the end of the day, in general terms, you would probably find that, not to put *too* fine a point on it, there probably wasn't very much in it one way or the other.
HACKER:	Er . . .
SIR HUMPHREY:	As far as one can see. At this stage.
HACKER:	Is that 'Yes'? Or 'No'?

SIR HUMPHREY:	*[Thinking hard]* Yes *and* No.
HACKER:	*[Exasperated]* Suppose you weren't asked for a *straight* answer?
SIR HUMPHREY:	Oh, *then* I should play for time, Minister.

Hacker holds the palm of his hand over his furrowed brow, convinced that, yet again, he is going to see his authority undermined in the most subtle but incisive of ways. Sir Humphrey, however, is soon left just as disturbed when he discovers that Hacker is planning to redraft his report one more time and then submit it before it can be amended.

Just when it seems that civil war is about to break out within the Department of Administrative Affairs, fate intervenes with a rumour that will change the perspective of both parties. The Prime Minister, Sir Humphrey hears on the Whitehall grapevine, has decided that being perceived by the public as the man who triumphed over the mandarins is far too politically profitable to be gifted to one of his colleagues (and potential rivals), so he has decided to assume sole responsibility for the policy himself (while shunting the hapless Hacker upstairs as a sort of 'Lord Hacker of Kamikaze'), and is now considering the complete abolition of none other than the DAA ('In one fell swoop: approbation, elevation and castration') as a suitably bold symbol of his anti-bureaucratic intent.

Once Sir Humphrey reports back to Hacker, there is, for once, a consensus:

HACKER:	I'm appalled.
SIR HUMPHREY:	*You're* appalled? *I'm* appalled!
HACKER:	I just can't believe it. I'm appalled! What do *you* make of it, Bernard?
WOOLLEY:	I'm appalled.
HACKER:	So am I! Appalled!
SIR HUMPHREY:	It's *appalling*!
HACKER:	*Appalling*! I-I-I just don't know how to describe it!
WOOLLEY:	Appalling?
HACKER:	Appalling! But I mean . . . is it *true*? Are you sure they weren't having you on?

Once Sir Humphrey has assured his Minister that the plan is deadly serious, the two of them shudder as they contemplate where they might end up once their present abode has been abolished: Hacker, if not sent up to the Lords, then quite possibly shunted sideways to serve as Minister with General Responsibility for Industrial Harmony ('You know what that means?' he exclaims. 'That means *strikes*! From now on every strike in Great Britain will be *my* fault!'), while Sir Humphrey is dispatched to Ag & Fish ('The rest of my career dedicated to arguing about the cod quota'). Woolley's wry little smile at the thought of all this is soon wiped off his face when Sir Humphrey points out that *he* will most probably be relegated to shuffling papers in the Vehicle Licensing Centre in Swansea.

Suddenly, and quite unexpectedly, Sir Humphrey and Hacker find themselves united against a common foe:

SIR HUMPHREY:	Minister, I really *do* mean that we should work together. I *need* you!
HACKER:	Do you *mean* that, Humphrey?
SIR HUMPHREY:	*Yes*, Minister!
HACKER:	Humphrey! How very *nice* of you!
SIR HUMPHREY:	Minister, if the Prime Minister is behind a scheme, Whitehall on its own cannot block it. Now, Cabinet Ministers' schemes are easily blocked *[Checking himself]* Er, redrafted. But the Prime Minister is another matter. We need to fight this in Westminster as well as in Whitehall.

Together, they come up with a way to retaliate. Inspired by the fact that the last piece of legislation due to be supervised by the DAA concerns the introduction of the controversial 'Euro Pass' – an EEC-wide compulsory identity card – they set out to hit the PM where it hurts most by undermining his precious amour propre.

It turns out that the Prime Minister would prefer to keep the contentious Euro Pass plans under wraps until after he has secured a prestigious personal prize – the Napoleon Award, which is bestowed only on those deemed to have made an outstanding contribution to the promotion of

European unity. Once that particular bauble is safely in his hands, it is thought, he will be content to let the identity card idea go the way of most other Brussels-originated proposals and end up being shelved after much internecine debate. Hacker, therefore, lets it be whispered around Westminster that he is considering planting a question in the Commons – via a pliable backbencher – that will force the Prime Minister to commit himself prematurely and publicly to the Euro Pass policy and thus spark a Eurosceptic reaction that would be highly embarrassing 'Napoleon Prize-wise'.

The suggestion gets the desired reaction within the Prime Minister's Office: panic. Hacker, knowing that he now has his opponent on the ropes, proposes to avert such a distressing turn of events by persuading the backbencher to table a different question, this time inviting the PM to quash the rumours regarding the imminent closure of the DAA. When Daniel Hughes, the Prime Minister's senior policy adviser, hears this idea, he tries to mask his sense of relief by pretending that the DAA's rumoured demise never really had any foundation in fact: 'The whole idea was ridiculous,' he splutters. 'Laughable. Out of the question. Joke: ha ha ha!' Sir Humphrey, relishing the moment, takes over the baton to conclude the deal by pressing Hughes to ensure that a minute from the Prime Minister's Office confirming this position will be circulated to all Departments within twenty-four hours – 'So that we can all share it. Joke-wise, I mean'.

As a queasy-looking Hughes rushes off to brief his leader, Hacker and Sir Humphrey sit back and relax together, glorying in the victory that they share:

> HACKER: As President Nixon's henchman once said:
>   'When you've got them by the balls, their
>   hearts and minds will follow.' Am I right,
>   Humphrey?
> SIR HUMPHREY: Yes, Minister!

As all great sitcoms are about trapped relationships (Harold Steptoe is stuck with his father Albert, Captain Mainwaring with second-in-command Sergeant Wilson, Basil Fawlty with wife Sybil), so *Yes Minister* is founded on the fact that, in spite of all their differences, Jim Hacker and Sir Humphrey simply cannot do without each other. As the credits rolled at the end of the final episode of the series, there was no doubt remaining that, regardless of any future political vicissitudes, Hacker and Sir Humphrey were now stuck with each other for good – and bad. There was also little doubt that all of those who had watched and enjoyed each clash between these two characters relished the prospect of them returning as soon as possible to resume their awkward alliance.

Averaging an audience of approximately two million per episode (with an appreciation rating of just over 74 per cent),[22] and, by this stage, warmly praised by the critics, the first series of *Yes Minister* had proved itself to be a more or less instant success. Apart from being rewarded promptly with a guaranteed second series, it also went on to win the Best Comedy award at that year's BAFTAs (the first of several of such honours[23]), and was then given a repeat run, over on BBC1, a few months later, starting in September, when a far more high-profile slot (8.30 p.m. on Thursdays, straight after the hugely popular game show *Blankety Blank*) brought the show a much bigger and broader following, peaking this time at a very healthy 12.2 million viewers.

The wait really had been worth it. More by luck than by design, the show had arrived at just the right time, and its excellence had been appreciated. Its future seemed assured.

Mr Wilson Changes on Trains

One of the aspects of the show that was quick to attract positive comment was its air of authenticity. Some of the sitcom's earliest and most avid fans turned out to be politicians and bureaucrats, who were drawn to its mirror-like characters and storylines. Indeed, the most common question that could be heard, the morning after each episode, around the water coolers in Westminster and Whitehall was: 'How on earth did they know *that*?'

There had been numerous examples that had raised eyebrows among officials during the first series. In the very first episode, for example, the sight of Jim Hacker sitting fidgeting inside his home, staring at the telephone in the hope of a call from Number Ten, caused a frisson of recognition with countless politicians right across the party political spectrum.

Then there was the blatantly dismissive treatment by Sir Humphrey of Jim Hacker's special adviser, Frank Weisel, which once again had a basis in fact. 'I remember saying to a Permanent Secretary in the Ministry of Defence that I thought that was a bit far-fetched,' Sir Robin Butler, who would go on to serve as Cabinet Secretary during the late 1980s and 1990s, would recall, 'but he said that they tried to put one of *their* special advisers in the Adelphi or somewhere miles from the central building!'[24]

Even some of the details that seemed, at the time, too farcical to believe would soon turn out, rather alarmingly, to be all too true. In one episode, for example, Hacker startles the Foreign Secretary with news about a foreign country:

HACKER:	There's been a coup d'état!
FOREIGN SECRETARY:	How do you know?
HACKER:	Well, it was on the news. Didn't you *see*? Don't you *know*? You're *Foreign Secretary*, for God's sake!
FOREIGN SECRETARY:	Yes, but my TV set is on the blink.
HACKER:	Your *TV set*? Don't you get Foreign Office telegrams?
FOREIGN SECRETARY:	Oh, they always come in later. I get all the foreign news from TV.[25]

An actual official in the Foreign Office would later admit, privately and sheepishly, that a fair amount of the Foreign Secretary's information about matters beyond Britain's shores was indeed, at least in that pre-Internet era, gleaned initially from studying the news on the TV.[26]

'We could never have made that up,' Jonathan Lynn later confirmed. 'Of course, the Foreign Office cables eventually arrived, a couple of days later, with somewhat fuller information than you got from ITN, but if there was a coup d'état, or a diplomatic kidnapping or hijacking, the Foreign Secretary learned it from the telly just like the rest of us.'[27]

Such specific insights ensured that the governing class remained glued, rather nervously, to the screen throughout the series, now convinced that the programme they were watching was not so much a sitcom as 'a sort of political "whodunit?"'.[28] Each Monday night they would try to figure out who, on this occasion, had spilled some more of their own trade secrets.

'While other viewers recognised [*Yes Minister*] instantly as a brilliant satire,' Roy Hattersley, the then Shadow Home Secretary and already a prominent fan, would reflect, 'we saw it as an only slightly distorted representation of our daily lives.'[29] Kenneth Clarke, who was a Junior Transport Minister when the first series was broadcast, was quick to concur: 'I've always said that [*Yes Minister*] is far too close to life to be safely shown to the public.'[30]

It was with just this kind of heightened curiosity that such insiders analysed a scene in episode two, 'The Official Visit', that featured an incident that struck some of them (especially those of the Labour persuasion) as yet another tale tweaked from the truth. The scene saw Hacker, travelling up by train to Scotland for an important meeting with the new president of a politically volatile African country, ending up being packed like a sardine inside his own first-class sleeping compartment after a succession of aides and associates intrude to discuss an urgent crisis.

Hacker is in the process of removing his trousers when Bernard Woolley bursts in with an advance copy of the President's forthcoming speech. 'I've underlined the important bits in red ink,' Woolley says, before racing off to distribute copies to other members of their entourage. Now sans trousers, Hacker reluctantly starts reading the speech and is soon horrified to find how controversial it really is. Sir Humphrey, in pyjamas and dressing gown, then enters the cramped compartment, closely followed by the Foreign Secretary (also dressed ready for bed), the Press Officer, Bernard Woolley, and, finally, the very large and sweaty Permanent Under-Secretary of the Foreign Office. 'Welcome to the Standing Committee,' says Sir Humphrey drolly as they all compete to breathe the same air.

Whereas most casual viewers might well have assumed that this scene was no more than a bit of comic business, some insiders, searching through their own memories, suspected that the real inspiration had come from a similarly comical incident when Harold Wilson, who was Prime Minister at the time, had suffered much the same undignified fate as Hacker while on his way back to Number Ten from a Labour Party Conference in Blackpool.

Wilson had always been a famous train enthusiast (as an undergraduate at Oxford, he had written a prize-winning essay on aspects of the Victorian railway system), and travelled regularly by rail down to London from his constituency at Huyton in Liverpool. Often exasperating political colleagues and civil servants alike by being 'lost' somewhere or other between stations when they urgently needed to pass him some information, he had even staged a television interview on a train to celebrate winning the 1966 General Election (and, peevishly, he gave it to ITV, rather than the BBC, on the somewhat bizarre grounds that one of the many ways in which the BBC's supposed pro-Tory bias had shown itself in recent years was in its frequent shots of him merely 'leaving a train or getting on a train'[31]).

The nature of his means of transportation caused innumerable complications as he prepared for major speeches. On one occasion, for example, prior to the 1975 Labour Party Conference in Blackpool, a near-farcical sequence of activity ensued after his secretary, Marcia Williams – later Baroness Falkender – announced (following one of her periodic tantrums) that she was staying behind in London.

As she always insisted, no matter what, on seeing and 'correcting' the drafts of her leader's speeches, her young female assistant was dispatched to take her version up on Friday's overnight train to Blackpool so that her amendments could be incorporated into the finished script. By the time she arrived early on Saturday morning, however, Wilson's other advisers had made further revisions, thus necessitating that the assistant be put back on the train to take the latest draft down to Williams in London, who, after hurriedly making a new set of changes, sent the assistant straight back up to Blackpool on the overnight sleeper.

The same thing then happened again: upon arriving back at the Labour Party's temporary Blackpool base at the Imperial Hotel early on Sunday morning, she was sent straight back to London with the next amended draft, and was then ordered by Williams to return on yet another overnight sleeper with her latest scribbled corrections. When, shortly after arriving in Blackpool on Monday morning, she learned that Williams wanted her sent back down to London again, the exhausted and visibly distraught assistant said that enough was enough and refused to comply. Wilson, anxious as usual to avoid incurring the wrath of Williams, cruelly sacked the secretary on the spot.[32]

There were also countless cases when his advisers, crawling groggily out of their sleeping compartments in the early hours of the morning and then entering a closed car where Wilson was waiting impatiently to resume work on a speech, came close to gagging as the great plumes of smoke from the PM's pipe first hit the back of their noses and throats. 'Oh, Harold,' his long-suffering wife, Mary, would exclaim, 'do stop *kippering* us!'[33] ('Legend had it,' Gerald Kaufman – a regular victim of the fumes produced by that 'uniquely noxious tobacco' – would say ruefully, 'that Harold Wilson only smoked a pipe for public display, in private reverting solely to cigars. If only this had been true.'[34])

It was some of Wilson's former aides who saw the scene in the *Yes Minister* episode and concluded that Jay and Lynn must have based it on yet another one of these incidents. They felt sure that the scene referred back to the tense political time in the autumn of 1965 shortly before the moment when Ian Smith, the Prime Minister of what was then Rhodesia, illegally severed his country's links with the British Crown and issued a Unilateral Declaration of Independence (UDI).

It seems that, after being briefed by Britain's High Commissioner for Rhodesia towards the end of their week in Blackpool, Wilson and his entourage hurriedly boarded a train back to London, where Ian Smith was waiting for make-or-break talks about his country's future behind closed doors at Number Ten. Due to the rapid pace at which various advisers were repeatedly revising his strategy for the meeting, Wilson, in various stages of déshabillé, kept on being invaded by countless officials and aides as he tried in vain to wash, change his clothes and regain some much-needed composure for the diplomatic travails that lay ahead.

The summit with Smith ultimately failed to solve any problems, and Rhodesia went ahead with UDI, but the memory of that chaotic train ride would remain in the minds of those who had squeezed themselves inside the Prime Minister's smoke-filled compartment. It was then, fifteen years later, abruptly rekindled as they saw that episode of *Yes Minister*, arousing the suspicion that the writers had employed yet another crafty copy.

The irony was that, for once, the link was mainly accidental. The real inspiration for the scene, Jonathan Lynn would later reveal, came from the classic ship's cabin routine from the Marx Brothers' movie *A Night at the Opera* (1935), in which Groucho, Chico and Harpo are joined by four stewards, two chambermaids, one cleaner, one manicurist, one engineer and engineer's assistant and one stray passenger ('Say,' says Groucho, 'is it my imagination or is it getting crowded in here?'). 'We didn't hear about a similar scene occurring in Harold Wilson's career until after we had written the episode,' Lynn later explained. 'I think, but I don't remember for sure, that it was Marcia Williams who said to us: "This scene actually happened".'[35]

This isolated anomaly, however, only served to underline the impact that the accumulation of accuracies was having on the audience. *Yes Minister* was so scrupulously well researched, so rooted in real life, that insiders were moved to assume that even the most fanciful scenes must have been drawn straight from the facts.

6

Series Two

We say that someone occupies an official position,
whereas it is the official position that occupies him.

On 26 March 1981, midway through its second series, *Yes Minister* would receive what was, in a sense, its finest accolade. During a debate in the House of Commons, Barney Hayhoe, the Minister for the Civil Service Department, rose to his feet and declared: 'There are occasions when civil servants can help to improve the understanding of the way in which government works. Indeed, those who watch *Yes Minister* may well think that only the Sir Humphreys of this world actually know how it works.'[1] The sitcom about the governing class was now being cited by the governing class. If anyone associated with the show still needed proof of how influential it had so rapidly become, this was surely it.

Indeed, on the eve of the programme's return, a leading political commentator observed that 'a fair proportion of the nation's Right Honourables, KCBs, Ministers of State and humble Assistant Secretaries will risk letting the country run itself for half an hour on Monday evening. They'll all be watching BBC2 – because *Yes Minister* is back'.[2] It was hardly much of an exaggeration: not only had the show struck a chord with the governed, it had also become an obsession with the governors.

The Prime Minister herself had requested a complete set of videotapes of the first series, and declared herself a huge fan of the show (calling it a 'splendid series', she would tell the BBC's Director-General that the tapes had given 'me and my family such a funny and absorbing Christmas'[3]). Many other politicians, from all the major parties, had been similarly effusive in their praise, and it was rumoured that the sitcom had been discussed during scholarly seminars in Whitehall, and that more than one senior civil servant had, on occasion, been heard to say: 'Now, what would Sir Humphrey do about that . . .?'[4]

Some of this, of course, was down to vanity. There is no breed of human being that believes more passionately than politicians in Oscar Wilde's dictum: 'There is only one thing in the world worse than being talked about, and that is not being talked about',[5] and even some civil servants – in spite, or perhaps because of, their traditional culture of secrecy – are not entirely impervious to the siren song of celebrity.

Some of it was also down to self-protective obtuseness. Like people sporting T-shirts bearing the legend 'I'm With Stupid', there was a fair proportion of bureaucrats who regarded the show simply as a satire on politicians, and a similar number of politicians who regarded the show simply as a satire on bureaucrats.

Yes Minister, in this sense, served as a Rorschach test for the inhabitants of Westminster and Whitehall, whose responses would reveal more about them than they ever would about the show. There was, however, far more than this to the programme's popularity within the political class.

While its more self-obsessed and superficial members were plainly pleased to think that their profession was getting some extra attention, there were many others who were not only impressed but also somewhat unsettled by the accuracy of the sitcom's stories, and, in some cases, a little shaken by its satire. This did indeed feel as though daylight was being let in upon magic, and, to those better-bred politicians and bureaucrats who knew their Bagehot, that did not seem an entirely good thing. The burgeoning *Yes Minister* phenomenon, to these more discerning souls, was almost as unnerving as it was entertaining.

To the broader population, though, the show had quickly come to seem like the best politics teacher that they had ever had. In contrast to the frequently smug obscurantism of academia, the partial complicity of the broadsheet commentators and the shameless tub-thumping bias of the tabloid pundits, this sitcom seemed to be speaking directly to the ordinary voter, showing, refreshingly clearly and accessibly, the kinds of things that actually went on inside the corridors, and offices, of power.

The second series, in this sense, would prove to be even more engagingly revealing than the first, because, thanks to the popularity that the show had already achieved, more and more insiders were now prepared to come forward and, strictly off the record, share their secrets with the writers. Politicians especially started queuing up to volunteer anecdotes of their own, usually at the expense of bureaucrats, but sometimes also acknowledging a few of the mishaps that had beset themselves and their colleagues in the Commons.

The enthusiasm that Margaret Thatcher had displayed for the show was particularly helpful in this sense, because up until this point the clandestine input of such Labour Party insiders as Marcia Falkender and Bernard Donoughue (backed up by the recent publication of Barbara Castle's Crossman-style diaries[6]), though invaluable, had left the sitcom undernourished in terms of right-of-centre insight. The growing number of Conservative MPs, therefore, who (reasoning that there was less chance than before of incurring retribution from the whips) were now coming forward to offer their own distinctive perspective, was welcomed warmly by the writers. The picture, already realistic, was getting richer and richer.

There were even some civil servants who, more discreetly, started getting in touch. Although in public many still bristled a little at the mention of the show – the impact of which, through stiff lips, they described as 'healthy' ('Like cod liver oil, presumably,' Jonathan Lynn observed[7]) – and the Head of the Home Civil Service, Sir Ian Bancroft, said sniffily that, although he found the show 'rather funny', he much preferred to watch *Mastermind* and *Call My Bluff*,[8] it was a different matter in private. 'After the programmes were on air,' Antony Jay later confirmed, 'it was much easier and they then wanted to talk to us. We even got summoned to permanent secretaries' offices, but such high-level interest was rare and only happened when they wished to put forward their side of the case. We eventually established a vaguely cooperative relationship with the Civil Service. For instance, Patrick Nairne, who was Permanent Secretary at the Department of Health, let us wander through the private office and he showed us what was in the minister's diary to give us factual background, which was very helpful.'[9]

'Our great strength,' Jay would say, 'was that we were not journalists who had to pretend not to be writing fiction. The people we talked to knew we were writing fiction, and they knew that we would not reveal our sources, which is necessary for a good journalist. They also knew that we would change the story so that it was not traceable back to them.'[10]

This increasingly well-sourced attention to detail would not just attract plaudits. It would also provoke one or two veiled threats.

During the run of the first series, for example, Jay and Lynn had received a call, quite out of the blue, from Sir Lawrence Airey, then Chairman of the Inland Revenue and, technically, a man who was ranked as a Permanent Secretary. He told them how much he was enjoying the show and invited them to lunch. Flattered, and feeling appropriately intrigued at the thought of meeting with their first real-life Sir Humphrey, they accepted.

The two writers arrived at the headquarters of the Inland Revenue, which in those days was at Somerset House beside Waterloo Bridge, and were escorted through a succession of locked iron gates and long, stone-floored corridors until, once they had climbed up some stairs, they found themselves in the boardroom, where they were greeted by all eleven directors. Clearly this was not going to be the relaxed and convivial little lunch they had been expecting.

Following a thimbleful each of sherry, they all sat down to a stilted, chilly, school dinner-style meal of cold cuts with lettuce, cucumber and Heinz salad dressing. There were a few complimentary remarks as the two writers tried to swallow the rubbery ham and the stringy leaves, but, as the lunch went on, more and more of the questions began to revolve around the matter of where they were getting their information from for the shows. The best part of two hours passed, with the two writers politely dead-batting the queries and declining to reveal their sources, and then, to their great relief, it was deemed time for everyone to go.

Sir Lawrence shook their hands as they headed off to the door, muttering to them, 'Let me know what you hear. I'd love to help. I can tell you if what you're hearing is right or wrong.'[11] Both Jay and Lynn thanked him and then made their way through the strange labyrinth back to the world outside, deeply puzzled by what they had just endured.

It did not take long for the mystery to be solved. They had another meeting arranged for that afternoon with their regular political source Marcia Falkender, and, upon hearing where they had just been, she looked at them as if they were mad. 'Oh, God!' she exclaimed, her huge eyes even wider than usual. 'You didn't fall for *that*?' Embarrassed, without quite knowing why, they explained what had happened. She listened attentively, shook her head, sighed a pitying sigh and then told them what had *really* happened.

'The Revenue,' she said, 'is Whitehall's police force. Didn't you know? They were trying to find out what you know and where you're getting your information.'[12] Lynn, bemused, countered by pointing out that Sir Lawrence had actually been quite helpful: 'He offered to check our information out for us.' She shook her head and sighed again. 'Of course he did,' she groaned. 'Then he'd know where you were getting it.'[13]

Antony Jay, who was hardly naive when it came to Whitehall's ways, tried to defuse the situation, stressing that neither he nor his partner had surrendered any secrets. 'I'm sure they could see that we're no threat to national security,' he exclaimed. 'They were probably trying to discover if we are just a couple of harmless funny people or seriously subversive.' At this, Lynn could not resist interjecting: 'Seriously subversive? That's ridiculous! We went to Cambridge.' Falkender narrowed her eyes knowingly and replied: 'As did Philby, Burgess and Maclean.'[14]

Lynn was curious. 'Why,' he asked, 'does the Revenue function as Whitehall's police force?' Falkender replied: 'It's because they have so much information about everyone. They know everything about you and everyone: how much you earn, how much you spend, what you spend it on, where you go, what you do – they can work most of it out from the receipts. And they have the most comprehensive press-clippings service in the country.'[15]

Lynn was still curious, so Falkender acted out how a tax inspector might behave: 'Mr Lynn, look at this clipping. This is you in this photograph, isn't it? It shows you outside Tramps, getting into a chauffeur-driven Rolls-Royce. Look, here's another picture: there you are, driving a Porsche. And here you are at the Cannes Film Festival, drinking the finest champagne – four bottles of Dom, according to your receipt, which I have here. And look, here's a photo of you coming out of the Hotel du Cap. Tell me, Mr Lynn, how do you do all this on fifty-one thousand a year?'[16]

Both Jay and Lynn left their meeting with Marcia Falkender thinking that she was being, even by the old standards of the Wilson-era Labour Government, far too paranoid. It was only a few weeks later that Lynn had cause to think again. He was audited by the Inland Revenue. The investigation, in fact, would go on for three whole years.

'It would have been disastrous for the credibility of *Yes Minister* if I had been fiddling my taxes,' Lynn would remark. 'Whether it was a fishing expedition, an attempt to intimidate me or just a coincidence, I shall never know. But every December, including the three years I was being audited, I received a card from Sir Lawrence Airey and the Board of the Inland Revenue wishing me a Merry Christmas and a Happy New Year.'[17]

Such incidents reminded everyone involved with *Yes Minister* that they were making fun of the State, not some humble subsidiary institution, and, no matter how great the acclamation might be as the key figures played to the gallery, there would always be some who resented the precision of the intrusion. Both Jay and Lynn would wear that thought as a badge of honour. It was all the proof they would ever need. They were hitting their target. Their message was getting through.

The actors were similarly encouraged by the impact the show was having. As they reassembled to rehearse the second series, there was a palpable sense of optimism in the air. Anticipating another set of high-quality, supremely literate scripts, the performers could hardly wait to resume their roles in what already seemed like a very special sitcom.

It certainly helped that, like the writers (who were now due £1,000 each per script), they all were benefiting from a modest but still very welcome pay rise. Paul Eddington was now set to receive £1,000 per episode, while Nigel Hawthorne would be getting £800 and Derek Fowlds £400, with smaller increases for the rest of the regular performers.[18]

The camaraderie between all the members of the cast was good. 'Paul, Derek and I got on very well,' Nigel Hawthorne would say, 'and I don't remember a harsh word from start to finish.'[19] Paul Eddington's recollection would be much the same, with his remarking that the only problems they encountered involved sometimes calling each other by their real names when they were in character.[20]

There were, however, a few very minor tensions that would always lurk beneath the surface. Most of these stemmed from the fact that Hawthorne and Eddington possessed such different personalities.

At heart, the former was an introvert, while the latter was an extrovert. Although Hawthorne's homosexuality had long been common knowledge in theatrical circles, and certainly caused no problems among any of his colleagues, the reluctance to make such a matter public (he would only be 'outed', much to his hurt and irritation, by the media in 1995) meant that he tended to be very protective of the life he shared offstage with his partner, the screenwriter Trevor Bentham, and, by his own admission, he was 'not a social bird'[21] ('I don't want to be part of the hustle and noise of being in the swim of things'[22]). Eddington, by contrast, was a far more relaxed and outgoing sort of character, and had a confidence about him that Hawthorne found at once impressive and irksome.

Hawthorne would describe his co-star as 'touchingly vain', observing that 'he loved being seen in public and was very proud of his membership of the Garrick Club'. Whenever there was a need to promote *Yes Minister* abroad, Hawthorne added, Eddington was usually the one to put himself forward to do it, and, while he was away on such trips, 'he'd be treated as if he were the real thing and revelled in it'.[23] Hawthorne would describe himself, on the other hand, as a man who preferred to lead 'a far more mundane life, growing to love the countryside, having a circle of friends who, more often than not, had nothing to do with things theatrical – and certainly not matters political – becoming more and more insular because of my deep involvement with Trevor, preferring above everything to be in his company'.[24]

The consequence was, he said, that the relationship between him and Eddington would be 'very friendly' without them ever becoming 'great friends'.[25] There was, however, a little more to it than that.

Hawthorne was also unsure, and would remain unsure, of whether the great respect and admiration that he always felt for his co-star was ever fully reciprocated. 'I used to get the feeling,' he later confessed, 'that he never thought that either Derek or I were quite up to it. I'm not suggesting that he thought he was better, just that his support could have been more classy.'[26]

Such insecurities tended to be assuaged by the consistently sunny disposition of Derek Fowlds, who could always be relied on to keep the rehearsal periods bright and cheerful, although, according to Hawthorne, Eddington also 'disapproved of Derek's light-hearted approach, particularly where his work was concerned', in spite of the fact that 'as a pair they got on extremely well'.[27] Such differences, however, remained, in a typically English way, unacknowledged and unexamined throughout the sitcom's run, and certainly never threatened to undermine the general feeling of positivity within the team.

'I didn't even know that Nigel felt like that,' Derek Fowlds would later remark. 'He hid it very well. I certainly can't agree with him about Paul. I always felt that we all got on brilliantly, and I loved them both dearly. It was just a joy to be with the two of them and watch them work together. Paul used to say to me, "This must be a *masterclass* for you, isn't it?" I'd say, "What are you talking about?" He'd say, "Well, you know, standing between Nigel and me every week – it must be *wonderful* for you!" There was that kind of banter between us, and we had an awful lot of fun.'[28] When all three of the main actors returned to work on the second series, therefore, they did so firmly looking forward to reigniting their on-screen rapport.

There was no danger, though, of the team just settling for more of the same. Sydney Lotterby, the producer/director, came back determined to see the show reach new heights.

Speaking to a journalist shortly before work on the sitcom was due to resume, he sounded a note of keen ambition tinged with a healthy degree of humility, stressing how important it was that the series continued to strive for accuracy and realism, not just in its coverage of the political system but also in its portrayal of the main characters. Hacker, especially, needed to be prevented from lapsing into caricature by now being shown to have grown during his time in office.

'We have to get rid of the gaucheness of the Minister,' Lotterby said. 'The process has begun already and the authors have their finger on that – and then we must see the real expertise of the man. He is an expert in politics and we have to see how he becomes a bigger power. I don't mean becoming Prime Minister, but how he gets total control – or doesn't.'[29]

The two writers themselves, while agreeing with Lotterby about the characters, also wanted to explore broader political themes. Both men, for different reasons and to different degrees, now wanted to engage with many of the issues that were being amplified by Margaret Thatcher's Government.

Jay, in particular, had come to feel an elective affinity with the outlook that was being termed 'Thatcherism', and was by this time an active supporter: 'I started advising the Conservatives in 1977,' he would later confirm, 'and went on right through the 1980s.'[30] He had already gone on the same kind of ideological journey as Thatcher, taking in Friedrich Hayek's economic scepticism (with its stress on the complexity and inherent unpredictability of markets, and its doubt that policymakers could master these complexities well enough to guide the economy in the right direction),[31] moving on to Milton Friedman's economic liber-tarianism (a brand of neoclassical liberalism – favouring free trade, open markets, privatisation, deregulation and the reduction in the size of the public sector – which Jay had recently helped popularise in Britain via Friedman's Video Arts-produced television series, *Free to Choose*[32]), and then assimilating James Buchanan's version of public choice theory (an approach which viewed government decisions mainly through the vested interests of the bureaucrats and elected leaders who make them).[33]

The product of this blend of theories was an outlook that, to put it in simple terms, made one an enemy of bureaucratic meddling in poli-tics, political meddling in the economy and moral meddling in society. It also made Jay's perspective on the second series of *Yes Minister* – in stark contrast to a first series that had been created during an era still character-ised by the post-war consensus – very much in touch with the zeitgeist of British politics.

'I was very much an approver,' Jay would say, 'not of the Conservative Party, but of Margaret Thatcher, who was probably more of a Free Trade Liberal in the nineteenth-century mould than a twentieth-century Macmillan/Heath type of Conservative. If a large part of the audience had come to feel after watching the programmes that letting government intervene, interfere, and take over more aspects of life was not the best way to solve the nation's problems, and that the contraction of government activities was probably more desirable than an expansion, then I, person-ally, would have been very happy.'[34]

The left-leaning Jonathan Lynn, however, was relatively sceptical about this new ideological era, but he, too, could see some points of connection. 'Between 1977, when we wrote the pilot, and 1979, when we started film-ing the first episode, unless you were a Marxist you knew that everything had to change,' he would reflect. The first series, as a consequence, 'was definitely critical of the way that the country was governed under the later years of Wilson and Callaghan. We both were opponents of the kind of Marxism that was then current.'[35]

Unlike Jay, however, he never approached the second series, or any of the subsequent ones, with any intention of popularising some of the concerns, let alone complementing any of the convictions, associated with Thatcherism. As far as he saw it, they were producing a comical critique of the system as a whole, rather than a particular part of it, and there was certainly still a strong belief that the Government of the moment was just as deserving a satirical target as the previous one had been.

Nonetheless, there remained a few aspects of their fictional political world that needed updating to make it match the facts of the early 1980s. Both Jay and Lynn had come to the conclusion, for example, that the character of Hacker's special adviser, Frank Weisel, was now too redolent of an earlier era.

The inexhaustibly eristic Weisel had been inspired by the kind of arm-patched, red-tied, union-friendly types who had flitted around the senior Labour figures of the 1970s, and thus no longer seemed to belong, in terms either of temperament or style, to the way that the new Conservative Government was operating. Rather than serving primarily as each Minister's personal ally against the civil servants, special advisers were now starting to be seen more as a mechanism for providing the Prime Minister with expert independent input to counter her own departmental Ministers. Wanting to seem more 'current', but wary of mirroring this new trend too obviously and thus inviting the suspicion that they were commenting on a particular Government, Jay and Lynn elected to do away with the special adviser completely and leave Hacker to take on Sir Humphrey alone.

There were a few more instances of fine-tuning before the scripts for the second series were ready. The impact of the media on politics and politicians, for example, was clearly growing more pervasive and intense (not only in terms of content but also, as Margaret Thatcher's own continuing vocal and sartorial transformation underlined, in terms of form, too), and so image would be made even more of an issue in the show this time around.

There was also the phenomenon of the new departmental select committees to consider. Set up in 1979, these cross-party groups now scrutinised, among other things, the policy and performance of each Whitehall department, and thus represented another potential challenge for both Hacker and Sir Humphrey to face.

Jay and Lynn would make sure that they were fully up to speed on these and countless other developments by spending around three weeks having lunches and meetings with various new, anonymous sources, followed by more in-depth sessions with Marcia Falkender and Bernard Donoughue (Nelson Polsby, by this time, was back teaching in the US). 'We'd meet fairly regularly before each series,' Donoughue would recall of his own sessions, 'mainly in a fish restaurant in the City, and we'd discuss themes and ideas. I would tell them about my experiences. They would let me ramble on. And then, every so often, one of them – especially Jonathan – would say: "*That's* the story!"'[36]

After sketching out some basic plots, they would seek out specific experts in each subject, talk to journalists who had covered such areas and issues in the past, and also work their way through relevant cuttings libraries and archives. Only then, when they really felt they understood a topic inside and out, and could link it intimately to real life, would they retire to write the script.

Piece by piece, Jay and Lynn wove the new elements in with the old, the fresh facts with the familiar fiction, and worked hard to keep the focus firmly on the broadest theme – beyond parties, beyond personalities, beyond topicalities – of the business of how government is actually conducted. There would be some new scenes, and some novel plots, but the basic story would be the same, and the basic story was going to continue.

The writers could barely wait to push on, but, as was always the case, they were not prepared to cut corners when it came to preparation. Everything had to be just right, every detail had to be in place, before they would pick up a notepad and pen.

Even when something was finally written, their drive for perfection was rarely at rest. Bernard Donoughue would recall how they always returned to him for one final expert critique:

> They would send me the scripts, particularly to try and make
> sure that nothing was in any way inaccurate or just plain wrong.
> They knew what they presented had to be authentic; it always
> had to ring true. So if top civil servants were watching it they
> would respect it. So I would go through the scripts and say things
> like, 'Well, look, that room isn't there in relation to that', or 'He
> wouldn't say that', or 'That isn't how it would happen'. It was
> that kind of advice. Then we would meet up again, and I would

go through it all, explaining how to correct certain things. But normally they knew what they were doing. They were brilliant people.[37]

The complete set of scripts for this second series, like all the later ones, was written well in advance of the first recording session (in this case during the late summer and early autumn of 1980). About six weeks prior to production, they met up with Sydney Lotterby and all of the principal members of the cast for a read-through of all seven episodes over the course of two consecutive days. At the read-through there was an opportunity for the actors to suggest any changes or clarifications, and for any other improvements to be considered.

Once the rehearsal period began, the words in the scripts were treated as if they were set in stone. As well as being insisted on by the writers, this was welcomed by the actors, too.

Nigel Hawthorne, especially, was adamant that, in spite of the long and elaborate speeches he always had to deliver, he would never resort to an autocue or cribs, so he made the writers promise never to change a single line within three weeks of the actors starting work on any episode. Employing a mnemonic system that associated a series of key phrases with a sequence of images, he needed to study great blocks of text and commit everything to memory as quickly as possible. Paul Eddington, in contrast, was more pragmatic, and was always happy to hide numerous crib sheets inside Hacker's various official papers, but he, too, wanted to know that he could rely on every page remaining the same.

Derek Fowlds, meanwhile, was often left to listen carefully for long periods of time before timing his brief, but sometimes crucial, response:

Acting, to me, is listening, anyway, and with them it was a joy. I mean, I had long, long scenes with Paul and Nigel with just me listening. During rehearsals I used to pretend to nod off and then I'd yawn and say, 'Are you going to do it like that on the night? Can't you quicken it up?' But they would sometimes play a ten-minute scene between them, and then Bernard had a line at the end which took the scene. And they used to look at me and say, 'Derek, you know, we let you get away with murder!'[38]

One late change came when the always-in-demand Sydney Lotterby found himself dealing with so many other projects that, reluctantly, he arranged for his colleague Peter Whitmore to assume responsibility for filming the series. A versatile producer and director in his own right, Whitmore had worked on programmes ranging from *Dave Allen at Large* to *Terry and June*, and was trusted implicitly by Lotterby to maintain the established style of the show.

The recordings – which were usually held in Studio 8 at Television Centre (with an audience of about three hundred) – did indeed run smoothly, and, as a sign of the show's popularity, the authenticity of the external scenes was further enhanced by the intervention of none other than the Prime Minister herself. When Margaret Thatcher heard that Hacker, in a brief scene in the seventh and final episode ('A Question of Loyalty'), would be seen visiting the fictional PM, she gave her personal permission for the action to be filmed in Downing Street, and – in an unprecedented move – even allowed Hacker to be shown walking right inside Number Ten.[39] Such insider support, now visual as well as verbal, made everyone in the team feel confident that they were making something that was going to be believable on every level.

When the second series was finally ready to be broadcast, its imminent arrival on the screen was heralded with considerably more publicity and optimism than its predecessor had commanded. There was a picture of the three main actors in character on the front cover of the *Radio Times*, a few interviews and plenty of positive previews in the papers. The sitcom that had practically crept into view the year before was now being hailed on its return as a significant televisual event.

The *Observer* called it the medium's 'most sophisticated comedy',[40] while the *Daily Express* dubbed it one of 'the wittiest and best' sitcoms in years.[41] There were numerous other similarly admiring and enticing descriptions, from the tabloids to the broadsheets, which encouraged viewers to look out for the show.

The first episode aired at 9 p.m. on Monday, 23 February 1981, once again on BBC2. The competition that night was not particularly strong – ITV had scheduled against it a repeat edition of its popular police drama *The Sweeney*, while BBC1 offered the *Nine O'Clock News* – and *Yes Minister* came with by far the warmest recommendation of the night.

Entitled 'The Compassionate Society', the opening instalment expertly reintroduced the main characters and their shared situation to viewers. There once again was the Minister, inquisitive and eager, and there was the Permanent Secretary, calm and cautious, and there too was the Principal Private Secretary, willing but often confused. The ties that bound them were as tight as ever, and the dynamism just the same.

In this cleverly crafted and entertaining episode, Hacker begins more or less where he left off at the end of the last series: alarmed to discover that even his driver appears to be better briefed then he is, infuriated to find that his plans – at least the ones that his civil servants dislike – keep being leaked to the media ('This isn't a Department – it's a colander!') and still reliant on the fox-fast mind of Sir Humphrey to get him out of trouble. Having been bullied by backbenchers into launching a full independent inquiry into his Department's half-hearted attempts to streamline National Health Service bureaucracy, he then finds out that a new hospital, built fifteen months ago, is now staffed by 342 administrators and 170 ancillary workers – but has yet to accommodate any patients.

What follows is a classic *Yes Minister* scenario with a second-series spin on it. Hacker, fearing multiple personal setbacks, cannot resist daring to dirty his hands, asking Sir Humphrey if they could ensure that the Department is exonerated by rigging the 'independent' inquiry, and do something about the empty hospital before the press finds out about it.

Sir Humphrey, in his usual Jeeves-like way, responds by suggesting that they appoint a peerage-hunting retired civil servant to chair it, and, unbeknown to his Minister, he also plots to push the hospital's ancillary workers into strike action to save their – and by implication the administrative staff's – jobs. The attempt to rig the inquiry, however, goes awry when it turns out that the 'sound' chairman of their inquiry is also responsible for the Joint Committee for the Resettlement of Refugees, and, after calculating that he has more chance of gaining a peerage by pleasing the latter rather than the former, he threatens to come down against the DAA unless the UK agrees to admit and house a thousand new refugees.

With Sir Humphrey flustered, it is Hacker, rather than his Permanent Secretary, who finds a solution to this particular conundrum by proposing that they use the refugees to fill up their hospital. Triumphant, he then dictates a press release to Woolley, depicting himself as the principled defender of the 'compassionate society'.

Watched by an audience estimated at three million,[42] it was a splendid start to the series, reaffirming all that was intelligent, impressive and attractive about its predecessor, but also suggesting, as Sydney Lotterby had demanded, that some things had changed. The character of Hacker, especially, appeared slightly more complex, with his old insecurity and vanity balanced more steadily by a slightly sharper mind and a much more cynical soul. Viewers had thus been given what they wanted, but even better than they had expected.

Subsequent episodes would build on this achievement and fulfil its promise. Many of the themes that were covered, for example, seemed intriguingly topical, even though the scripts had been written about a half a year before.

At a time when Margaret Thatcher's notoriously irascible, beetle-browed press Secretary, Bernard Ingham, was mastering the dark arts of spin, and some of her Ministers were beginning to obsess about whether their worst publicity was originating from inside or outside of Westminster, Jim Hacker was depicted on a weekly basis getting similarly paranoid. He was pictured poring over the pages of *Private Eye* in case he had been compromised, leaking against colleagues in the House of Commons bar ('The first law of political indiscretion: always have a drink before you leak'[43]), and desperately trying to use the media before it could abuse him.

There were also some scrupulously researched and smartly insightful stories about dealing with the dreaded new nosy select committees (SIR HUMPHREY: 'This is the first and only brief containing possible questions from the Committee with the appropriate answers, all carefully presented to give the Department's position.' HACKER: 'Is it absolutely accurate?' SIR HUMPHREY: 'They're all carefully presented to give the Department's position'[44]); Cabinet reshuffles (anticipating Margaret Thatcher's imminent purge of the 'wets' in her Government, Hacker was seen panicking that he was about to be exiled by his leader to the Lords or, worse still, Europe[45]); the publication of a Leslie Chapman/*Your Disobedient Servant*-style whistle-blower memoir ('It was a *tiny* mistake,' Sir Humphrey protests when Hacker quotes one of the damning examples of bureaucratic waste. 'Give me an example of a *big* mistake!' snaps the Minister. 'Letting people find out about it!' replies his Permanent Secretary[46]); the increasingly brazen attempts by Ministers to stage media stunts ('SIR FRANK: 'Saw your chap on the television last night, cuddling a rabbit.' SIR HUMPHREY: 'Mmm, the St Francis of Tower Hamlets.' SIR FRANK: 'What was it supposed to be in aid of?' SIR HUMPHREY: 'After the rodent vote I imagine'[47]); and even the recent increase in over-seas student fees (SIR HUMPHREY: 'But why don't you fill up your vacancies with *British* undergraduates?' OXFORD MASTER: 'I don't think that's awfully *funny*, Humphrey.' SIR HUMPHREY: 'I wasn't try-ing to be funny.' OXFORD MASTER: 'My dear fellow – anything but *home* students!' SIR HUMPHREY: 'Why?' BURSAR: 'We only get five hundred a *head* for UK students! We'd have to take four *hundred* to replace a mere *fifty* foreigners, and the staff–student ratio would go from one to ten to one to *thirty-four*!' OXFORD MASTER: 'We'd have classrooms, dormitories – it would be like Wormwood Scrubs . . . or the University of Sussex!'[48]).

There were also plenty of the now expected sparklingly incisive anal-yses and parodies. In episode two, for example, there was another classic piece of Civil Service circumlocution:

SIR HUMPHREY: I am fully seized of your aims and of course I will do my utmost to see that they are put into practice. To that end, I recommend that we set up an interdepartmental committee with fairly broad terms of reference so that at the end of the day we will be in a position to think through the various implications and arrive at a decision based on long-term considerations, rather than rush prematurely into precipitate and possibly ill-conceived actions which might well have unforeseen repercussions.

The details of the Faustian deal awaiting every new Minister were explained in episode six:

SIR HUMPHREY: There's an implicit pact offered to every Minister by his senior officials. If the Minister will help us to implement the opposite policy to the one that he's pledged to, which – once he's in office – he will see as obviously incorrect, we will help him to pretend that he is in fact doing what he said he was going to do in his manifesto.

The same episode also offered another insight into the means by which civil servants maintained control over their Minister:

SIR HUMPHREY: Any document which removes the power of decision-making from Ministers and gives it to us is important.

WOOLLEY: Why?

SIR HUMPHREY: Oh, Bernard, don't be obtuse, please. It helps us to take government out of politics. It's Britain's only chance of survival!

WOOLLEY: But even so, couldn't it have waited until he wasn't in such a hurry?

SIR HUMPHREY: Oh, Bernard! When we want Ministers to sign something without asking too many questions we *have* to wait until they're in a hurry – that's when their concentration is at its weakest. They're nice and *vulnerable*. That's why we keep them on the go.

The civil servant's view of the Minister's most useful skills was outlined in the seventh episode:

SIR HUMPHREY: Blurring the issue is one of the basic Ministerial skills.

HACKER: Oh. What are the others?

SIR HUMPHREY: Delaying decisions, dodging questions, juggling figures, bending facts and concealing errors.

The most recurrent of all the underlying themes was, once again, that of political 'dirty hands', with Jim Hacker, now a fully fledged graduate from the school of realpolitik, sullying them so often it seemed he had given up trying to wash them clean. In episode two, for example, he eagerly abandons plans to clean up the honours system once he himself is offered an honorary Oxford doctorate; in episode three (in a sly reprise of the Sir Frank Soskice volte-face), he vetoes his own petition to stop covert electronic surveillance after he discovers that it might help protect him from a death threat;[49] in episode four (the one that most obviously reflected Antony Jay's enthusiasm for the teachings of public choice theory), he decides to drop his support for a lucrative new chemical manufacturing contract, that would create masses of new jobs on Merseyside, purely on the grounds that erroneous reports of health hazards might end up damaging his standing with the electorate:

HACKER:	Something has just struck me.
SIR HUMPHREY:	So I noticed.
HACKER:	D'you know? There could be arguments against this scheme.
SIR HUMPHREY:	Minister, you have already *agreed*—
HACKER:	Yes, but it – it could lead to a loss of . . . public confidence.
SIR HUMPHREY:	You mean votes!
HACKER:	No, no, no, no, no, no! Not *votes*, no, no! No, it's, er, not that *votes* are a consideration! Good heavens, no! Not at *all*! No, but you see, it's the Public Will. This is a *democracy*. And the People don't *like* it!
SIR HUMPHREY:	The People are ignorant and misguided.
HACKER:	Humphrey! It was the People who elected *me*!

In the same episode, when he hears that the Prime Minister is similarly concerned about the bad publicity that the scare stories are causing the Government, Hacker does not even try to hide where his real loyalties lie:

SIR HUMPHREY: It could be said that you're putting Party before Country.

HACKER: Oh, those *hoary* old clichés! Can't you think of a new one?

SIR HUMPHREY: Well, I think, Minister, that a 'new' cliché could perhaps be said to be a contradiction in terms.

HACKER: Humphrey, you know *nothing* because you lead a sheltered life! *I* intend to *survive*! And I'm *not* crossing the PM!

SIR HUMPHREY: Oh, Minister, why must you always be *so* concerned with climbing the greasy pole?

HACKER: The greasy pole is *important*! I *have* to climb it!

SIR HUMPHREY: *Why?*

HACKER: Because it's *there*!

Later on in the episode, after brushing aside all the protests from those who know that he is putting popularity before probity ('It's *politics*!'), he tries to justify removing a dissident head of a chemical corps simply because it suits his personal ambitions:

SIR HUMPHREY: How do you expect the Department of Industry to find a decent replacement when we *forced* his predecessor to resign for taking a *sound* commercial decision which *we* blocked for *political* reasons?

HACKER: Oh, don't bring *that* up again! I have no choice!

SIR HUMPHREY: Minister, a Minister can do what he *likes*!

HACKER: It's the People's Will! I am their leader! I must follow them!

[Sir Humphrey looks bemused.]

HACKER: I have a clear conscience! My hands are clean!

SIR HUMPHREY: Well, I should have thought it was frightfully difficult to keep one's hands clean while climbing the greasy pole!

By the final episode in the series, Hacker, having committed so many dirty deeds that he has just received a congratulatory letter from the Prime Minister ('It's paid off!'), is now clearly so at home in this amoral world that even that arch-Machiavellian Sir Humphrey seems alarmed:

HACKER:	Do you realise, Humphrey, how much this is *worth*?
SIR HUMPHREY:	I believe the going rate is thirty pieces of silver, Minister!
HACKER:	No, Humphrey, loyalty and integrity have received their just reward.
SIR HUMPHREY:	*Loyalty*?!?
HACKER:	I have backed *you* up, Humphrey, in just the same way that *you* have always backed *me* up – isn't that so?
SIR HUMPHREY:	*[Furious but confused]* Er, ah—
HACKER:	I'm sorry? Did you say something?
WOOLLEY:	Ah, I think he said, 'Yes, Minister'.

It was this darkening of Hacker's personality, this further weakening of the whisky priest, which made his survival as a Minister more believable, and was also the most effective piece of character evolution during the second series. Not all of the other figures in the sitcom, however, went so far on such a journey.

The whole point of Sir Humphrey was that, as Permanent Secretary, he was a constant presence, and, as such, he did not have to change – he just had to be. Fully formed and firmly set in his ways long before Hacker had even set a suede-shod foot inside his Department, his rock-solid instrumentality, his shameless amorality meant that he could not be dragged down any deeper.

Woolley, on the other hand, needed to remain torn between Sir Humphrey and Hacker, staying apprenticed to both sorcerers in order to maintain the comic triangle, and so, once again, there was little leeway for further development. What he did show, during this series, was that he was learning a little, but not enough, from each of his mentors, which left him stuck more or less where he was.

On one occasion, for example, he is canny enough to allow Sir Humphrey to bet him a pound that the first thing their media-conscious Minister would say upon entering his office would be: 'Any press reports on my Washington speech?' After shaking on it, a smug-looking Woolley announces: 'He won't, because he's already asked in the car on the way back from Heathrow.' Sir Humphrey is impressed by such deviousness: 'You're learning, Bernard!' Like all of Woolley's rare victories, alas, this one is soon proven pyrrhic, because, when Hacker does arrive in his office, the first thing he says is: 'Bernard, didn't you say there were some press cuttings of my Washington speech somewhere?' Crestfallen, Woolley slips the pound back into Sir Humphrey's hand.[50]

The one character who arguably should have changed but stayed the same was Jim Hacker's wife, Annie. Only glimpsed here and there during the first series, in the second she was, if anything, even more peripheral, and not even quite as coherent as a character. Popping up a couple of times in the third episode, and once in the fifth, she sometimes sounded very politically engaged and interested in her husband's career (reminiscing cheerfully about the first time they discussed 'the effect of velocity of circulation on the net growth of money supply'[51]), and yet at other moments she seemed completely detached and uninterested ('Sometimes I think we deserve a bit of failure!'[52]) – as if Eleanor Roosevelt had suddenly morphed into Mary Wilson. While her limited screen time was entirely understandable – this was not, after all, a domestic sitcom, but rather a professional one – this imprecision was a rare minor blemish in what was otherwise an admirably well-realised world.

Probably the best episode of the second series in terms of plot, pace and depth was the fifth: 'The Devil You Know'. As Jay and Lynn had done in the first series with 'The Writing on the Wall', they used this episode to give both Hacker and Sir Humphrey a brief, tantalising glimpse of an escape from the other, only to conspire, under the pressure of events, to remain within the trapped relationship.

It began with Hacker moaning about interference from Europe. Having managed to persuade all of his Cabinet colleagues to let his own Department of Administrative Affairs take charge of a combined order for new word processors – thus boosting investment in Britain's technology industry (and hopefully prompting such headlines as: 'HACKER'S

MASSIVE INVESTMENT IN MODERN TECHNOLOGY' and 'JIM'S VOTE OF CONFIDENCE IN BRITISH INDUSTRY') – he has been blocked from completing the deal, thanks to an EEC directive from Brussels. It obliges him instead to attend a forthcoming European conference to agree on a common policy.

This intrusion invites Hacker and Sir Humphrey to compare notes on what they most dislike about the European Community. Sir Humphrey starts by reasserting his conviction that the whole thing is a self-serving scam:

SIR HUMPHREY:	It is a game played for national interests, and always was. Why do you suppose we went into it?
HACKER:	To strengthen the brotherhood of free Western nations.
SIR HUMPHREY:	Oh really! We went in to screw the French by splitting them off from the Germans.
HACKER:	Well, why did the French go into it, then?
SIR HUMPHREY:	Well, to protect their inefficient farmers from commercial competition.
HACKER:	Well, that certainly doesn't apply to the Germans!
SIR HUMPHREY:	No, *they* went in to cleanse themselves of genocide and apply for readmission to the human race.
HACKER:	I've never heard such *appalling* cynicism! Well, at least the small nations didn't go into it for selfish reasons.
SIR HUMPHREY:	Oh, really? Luxembourg is in it for the perks. The capital of the EEC – all that foreign money in, hmm?
HACKER:	It's a very sensible central location.
SIR HUMPHREY:	With the administration in Brussels and the Parliament in Strasbourg? Minister, it's like having the House of Commons in Swindon and the Civil Service in Kettering!

Hacker then responds with his own critique, preferring, just as predictably, to shift the blame onto the bureaucracy:

> HACKER: Brussels is a shambles. You know what they say about the average Common Market official?
> He has the organising ability of the Italians, the flexibility of the Germans and the modesty of the French. And that's topped up by the imagination of the Belgians, the generosity of the Dutch and the intelligence of the Irish. It's all a great big gravy train!
>
> SIR HUMPHREY: What do you mean?
>
> HACKER: They live on champagne and caviar, chauffeur-driven Mercedes, private aeroplanes – every one of those officials has got his snout in the trough. And most of them have got their two front trotters in as well!
>
> SIR HUMPHREY: Oh, Minister, I beg to differ. Brussels is full of busy, hard-working public servants who have to endure a lot of exhausting travel and tedious entertainment.
>
> HACKER: Oh, *terribly* tedious, working their way through all that smoked salmon, forcing back all of that champagne!

The real concern, however, turns out to be much closer to home: Sir Humphrey reveals that it was actually one of Hacker's own Cabinet colleagues who tipped off Brussels about his plans to bulk-buy British merchandise: the Secretary of State for Trade and Industry, Basil Corbett. 'Bloody *Corbett* again!' spits Hacker. 'When I think of Basil Corbett I really warm to Judas Iscariot!'

Bernard Woolley has a clue as to what prompted Corbett's latest bit of back-stabbing. There is a rumour that a Cabinet reshuffle is being planned.

Hacker is horrified:

above left: 'Yes, Minister! No, Minister! If you wish it, Minister!' Richard Crossman, whose diaries were such a source of insight for the sitcom.
© *Getty Images*

above right: 'Fact is funnier than fiction.' Sir Frank Soskice, the Home Secretary who snubbed his own petition.
© *Getty Images*

'Dear lady.' Prime Minister Harold Wilson at work in the 1970s with his personal and political secretary, Marcia Williams. © *Mirrorpix*

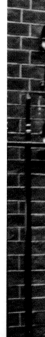

top left: A subtle subversive Antony Jay in the mid-1970s. © *UPP/TopFoto*

bottom left: 'Not a laughing matter.' Leslie Chapman, the ex-civil servant who blew the whistle on bureaucratic incompetence. © *Getty Images*

right: Filming the show in October 1982. The Welsh Office served as the Department of Administrative Affairs, and, thanks to Margaret Thatcher, Number 10 served as Number 10. © *Mirrorpix*

Whitehall's comic triangle; Hacker, Sir Humphrey and Woolley. © *BBC*

'It's the way she tells 'em.' Hawthorne and Eddington sharing the stage with the real Prime Minister in January 1984. © *Mirrorpix*

'Events, dear boy, events.' The unexpected exit of Frank Weisel, Hacker's special advisor, is about to be facilitated. © *BBC*

above left: 'He will see in the life much which is not in the books.' Antony Jay receives his Knighthood in 1988. © *TopFoto*

above right: Parity, at last, with Sir Humphrey as Nigel Hawthorne is knighted in 1999. © *Getty Images*

below: The multi-talented Jonathan Lynn, pictured in 2008 at the Hungarian publication of the *Yes Minister* scripts. © *AFP/Getty Images*

above left: Bernard Donoughue, the show's invaluable advisor, in 2009. © *Getty Images*

right: 'Every Prime Minister needs a Woolley.' Derek Fowlds attends the Gala Night of the stage version of the show, *Yes, Prime Minister* in 2010. © *UK Press via Getty Images*

Going to the country. Simon Williams as Sir Humphrey and Richard McCabe as Hacker in the touring version of *Yes, Prime Minister*. © *REX/Bettina Strenske/LNP*

'What mankind really wishes to economise is thought.' Hacker causes alarm by forming an idea of his own in the 2013 TV revival.
© Geraint Lewis/Alamy

HACKER:	A Cabinet reshuffle!?! I mean I-I've hardly started to do the things that I, er, that we—
SIR HUMPHREY:	Well, perhaps *you* won't be moved, Minister.
HACKER:	Ah . . . Yes . . . But if I'm *not*, it means that my career isn't moving forward as it ought to be!
SIR HUMPHREY:	Well, at least it wouldn't be moving *backwards*.
HACKER:	*BACKWARDS*?? You don't mean . . . Good God . . . But I, I have . . . But it's not . . . I-I-I've been doing all right, *haven't* I? Hu-Humphrey? *We've* done all right?
SIR HUMPHREY:	Yes. *You've* done all right.
HACKER:	*We've* done all right, haven't we, Bernard?
WOOLLEY:	Er, yes, Minister.
HACKER:	I mean, I may not have been the outstanding *success* of this administration, but I haven't exactly been a *failure*. Have I?
WOOLLEY:	No, Minister. You've done all right.
HACKER:	And in some ways I've been quite *successful*. And if Martin were moved to the Treasury . . . there's an outside chance I could get the Foreign Office!
SIR HUMPHREY:	*[Looking uncomfortable]* Er, y-y-yes, perhaps you might.
HACKER:	You don't sound very certain.
SIR HUMPHREY:	I'm *not* certain, Minister.
HACKER:	Why not? What have you heard??
SIR HUMPHREY:	Oh, no, nothing, nothing, I assure you. That's why I'm not certain.
HACKER:	Well, how does *Corbett* know when we don't?
SIR HUMPHREY:	Well, perhaps he has the PM's ear.
HACKER:	Yes . . . And he *is* in the PM's pocket.
WOOLLEY:	Er, then the PM must have rather a large ear.

Visibly flustered but desperate to fight off his fears, Hacker laughs weakly and declares that there is probably nothing to worry about. He is not, however, keen to agree with Sir Humphrey that they should commit to attending the conference in Brussels before they know when the reshuffle is going to happen: 'I've known this sort of thing happening before: one day you're out of your office, next day you're out of office!'

While Hacker rushes off to obsess about his future, Sir Humphrey wanders over to his club to have a brandy or two with the Cabinet Secretary, Sir Arnold Robinson, in the hope of getting some pertinent gossip. Sure enough, as the eyebrows arch and the heads nod, valuable information is exchanged.

The PM, Sir Arnold reveals, thinks that Hacker has done 'all right'. There has, however, been an interesting development: Brussels has enquired as to his availability, as a 'good European', for the next Commissionership. Sir Humphrey's ears prick up at this: 'So you think,' he asks excitedly, 'that he might be gently eased out?' Sir Arnold gives him a knowing look. Sir Humphrey gives him a knowing look in return. At this point, Bernard Woolley comes in to join them.

Assuring him that they are 'merely conjecturing', they ask how he would feel about having a new Minister. Woolley is taken aback. 'I'd be very sorry,' he says, sincerely. Sir Humphrey and Sir Bernard exchange bemused looks. Woolley, in turn, cannot understand their apparent lack of concern for poor Hacker's plight, even if they are only conjecturing. 'But the Minister,' he protests, is 'just starting to get a *grip* on the job.'

SIR ARNOLD: Ministers with a grip on the job *are* a bit of a
                nuisance, you know.
SIR HUMPHREY: They argue.
WOOLLEY: But *all* Ministers argue.
SIR HUMPHREY: Yes, but if they've got a *grip* on the job there's a
                real danger that they might be *right*! One tells
                them that something is *impossible* and they dig
                out an old paper in which one had said it was
                easy. Very tedious!
SIR ARNOLD: But the moment they've gone one can wipe
                the slate clean and start again with the new
                boy. Wonderful things, reshuffles. And Prime
                Ministers like them, too. Fresh. Decisive. Keeps
                everyone on the hop. It's only Ministers who
                panic about them.

WOOLLEY: *[Chuckling at the thought]* Wouldn't it be
                interesting if Ministers were fixed, and
                Permanent Secretaries were shuffled
                around?

[Sir Humphrey and Sir Arnold look at Woolley as if he has gone mad]

SIR HUMPHREY: That, Bernard, would strike at the very heart
                of the system that has made Britain what she is
                today.
SIR ARNOLD: Power goes with permanence.
SIR HUMPHREY: Impermanence is impotence.
SIR ARNOLD: And rotation is castration. It's time they all had
                a little spin.
WOOLLEY: Er, yes, but, surely, in a *democracy*—
SIR HUMPHREY: Thank you, Bernard, that'll be all!

It is only after Woolley leaves that Sir Arnold warns Sir Humphrey that
he would be wise to keep the champagne on ice. The talk about Hacker's
possible successor, he confides, suggests that it could well be none other
than Basil Corbett.

Hacker, meanwhile, has retreated to the security of his home, sitting
with his wife, Annie, mulling over what might be his fate. Still fishing for
reassuring compliments, he fails to hook an encouraging word even from
Annie:

HACKER: I don't even know whether I've been a success or
          a failure. What do *you* think?
ANNIE: I think you've done all right.
HACKER: Hmm, but is that good *enough*?
ANNIE: I don't know. Is it?
HACKER: I don't know. *Is* it?
ANNIE: I don't know.
HACKER: It's so difficult to tell, you see? The PM *might*
          think I've been too *much* of a success. You know
          – a challenge to the leadership.
ANNIE: *[Startled]* YOU???

HACKER: *[Slightly hurt]* No, not me. Martin, with my
            support. And, you see, if the PM *is* standing by
            to repel boarders, then Martin can't be got rid of
            safely – which he can't, not the Foreign Secretary
            – well, I'm the obvious one for demotion. You
            see: isolate Martin.

ANNIE: Where would you be sent?

HACKER: Oh, there's no shortage of useless non-jobs: Lord
            President, Lord Privy Seal, Minister for Sport,
            with Special Responsibility for Droughts and
            Floods . . .

Eating away inside of him throughout this time is the knowledge
that he is being undermined and outmanoeuvred by his bête noire, Basil
Corbett – a rival politician who clearly knows how to dirty his hands and
do bad things better than *he* does:

HACKER: He's a smooth-tongued, hard-nosed, cold-eyed,
            two-faced creep!

ANNIE: Why's he so successful?

HACKER: Because he's a smooth-tongued, hard-nosed,
            cold-eyed, two-faced creep!

Hacker acknowledges that he will have to elbow Corbett out of the
way before Corbett elbows him. 'Elbows,' he reflects, 'the most important
weapon in a politician's armoury.' Annie looks a little disappointed, and
replies: 'Other than *integrity*.' Hacker looks at her as if she has just slipped
into insanity, and rocks back with laughter at the thought of something
so naive. He has, by this stage, long accepted Machiavelli's dictum that a
politician must be willing to 'act like a beast' and know how to 'be a fox to
recognise traps, and a lion to frighten away wolves'.[53]

It is at that moment, however, that he gets a phone call informing him
that he is wanted as one of Britain's new Commissioners for the EEC.
Suddenly some of the appetite for the dirty domestic fight fades away, and
he allows himself to contemplate hopping on board the Brussels gravy
train, leaving all the party infighting far behind as he and Annie embrace

a new, exceptionally well-remunerated, life of leisure and luxury. 'I think we ought to go over and have a *look*,' he suggests dreamily, trying hard not to sound excited.

Sir Humphrey, when he hears about the plan for this trip, starts to panic. Faced with the prospect of having to contend with Corbett rather than Hacker, he realises that he would much prefer the devil he already knows – and the one he can better control – so he starts searching for a solution.

Realising that he has been a tad overzealous in his attempts at frustrating his Minister's ambitions, blocking him not unwisely but too much, he resolves to conjure up an eye-catching personal triumph to convince Hacker, and the Prime Minister, that the right man is in the right place. He thus advises Hacker to ignore the EEC and publicise his original plan to bulk-buy British goods, creating more jobs, more investment, more export orders and, last but by no means least, more votes.

Hacker, upon hearing this tailor-made strategy, is excited. It would indeed get him good publicity, and more votes, and it would prove that he has a good pair of elbows.

As the two men chuckle at the thought of what, between them, they are going to achieve, they also acknowledge the nature of the relationship that they share:

> SIR HUMPHREY: When it comes down to it, Minister, one's own country must come first.
> HACKER: How true.
> SIR HUMPHREY: And although, strictly, this isn't a Government matter, Minister, I personally would be *deeply* sorry to lose you.
> HACKER: Oh, *really*, Humphrey? Is that true?
> SIR HUMPHREY: Yes, and I *mean* that, Minister, *most* sincerely.
> HACKER: That's awfully *nice*, Humphrey. Yes, I suppose we *have* got rather fond of one another, ha ha, in a way!
> SIR HUMPHREY: Ha ha, in a way, yes!

>   HACKER: More like a terrorist and his hostage!
>   WOOLLEY: Er, which one of you is the terrorist?
>   SIR HUMPHREY/HACKER: *He is*!

The awkward bonhomie is broken up rather brusquely when Woolley lets slip who would have taken over at the DAA had the reshuffle actually taken place. 'Basil Corbett?' snaps Hacker. 'Yes, Minister,' Sir Humphrey admits.

This fine episode, like all the others, demonstrated the exceptional quality of a series that was even more insightful and confident than its predecessor, and it would come as no surprise, that, as a consequence, *Yes Minister* would once again be showered with praise and weighed down with awards.

With audiences ranging from 2.8 million to 4.2 million – again, very healthy for BBC2 – with an average of 3.2 million (which ensured that the show was regularly among the channel's top performers in the weekly ratings), the response from those questioned about the series by the BBC's own researchers was exceptionally positive, with the Reaction Index (RI) estimated at 81 per cent for the seven-week run, which was a 7 per cent increase on the performance of the previous series.[54] More encouraging still were the many positive comments from those asked about the show, with those employed as civil servants actually being more positive than anyone else who was polled, giving the series an RI of 85 per cent. 'It was generally considered,' said the report, 'true to life (especially by those with experience of working for the Civil Service)'.[55]

The critics also lauded the sitcom, and, in particular, saluted the partnership between Eddington and Hawthorne, with one hailing them as 'the best double act since Morecambe and Wise'.[56] The most common theme of all, of course, was how funny the series was, with many seasoned sitcom specialists acknowledging its status as one of the classics. Such judgements were soon reaffirmed by the likes of BAFTA, which honoured the show with awards for Best Comedy Series and Nigel Hawthorne for Best Light Entertainment Performance.

Repeated on BBC1 towards the end of 1981, the series continued to attract attention and praise, while whetting the appetite for another set of episodes. Arguably the most inclusive and accessible means of access to contemporary political discourse, the show had become something more than just another sitcom. It had come to seem like a natural part of British life.

'Does that mean that *Yes Minister* has won again?' the notoriously belligerent left-wing Labour MP Dennis Skinner shouted out in the House of Commons during the latest debate about the Civil Service.[57] The reference, in a sense, provided its own answer: *Yes Minister* was now rooted so soundly in the public – and political – consciousness that the governors appeared just as keen as the governed to see what it would say, and show, next.

From the Government of People to the Administration of Things

Probably the most talked-about episode in the second series of *Yes Minister* concerned the story about the hospital without any patients. Rather like the classic *Bilko* episode, 'The Empty Store',[58] and the *Monty Python* sketch about a cheese shop 'uncontaminated by cheese',[59] it was a high-concept premise whose comic simplicity was irresistibly engaging.

It begins with Hacker discovering that, although there are some five hundred or more administrative personnel currently employed at the hospital, there are no patients. Bernard Woolley explains that the building was finished fifteen months ago, and was fully staffed, but then, thanks to Government cuts, no money was left over to recruit any medical services. Hacker is astonished, but Woolley is quick to reassure him that there is, in fact, one sick person in situ: 'The Deputy Chief Administrator fell over a piece of scaffolding and broke his leg'.

The civil servants are bemused as to why Hacker seems so concerned about the case. Sir Humphrey, for example, is questioned on the topic by Sir Ian Whitchurch, the Permanent Secretary of the DHSS:

> SIR IAN: So why is your Minister interested in St Edward's Hospital?
>
> SIR HUMPHREY: Well, he's apparently greatly concerned that it has no patients.

SIR IAN:	Takes all sorts.
SIR HUMPHREY:	Yes.
SIR IAN:	How can there be *patients* when it has no *nursing* staff?
SIR HUMPHREY:	Well, quite.
SIR IAN:	We've found at the DHSS that it takes *time* to get things going.
SIR HUMPHREY:	Yes.
SIR IAN:	First of all, you have to sort out the smooth running of the hospital. Having *patients* around would be no help at all.
SIR HUMPHREY:	No. They'd just be in the way.

Hacker, however, refuses to let the matter drop, regarding it as symbolic of the malaise that is afflicting this area of public policy. 'The National Health Service, Humphrey, is an advanced case of galloping bureaucracy!' Sir Humphrey tries to calm his Minister down – 'Oh, certainly not galloping. A gentle *canter* at the most!' – and explains that there is plenty to do at a hospital even when it is uncontaminated with sick people: 'First there is the Contingency Department, for fire, strikes, air raids, nuclear war, epidemics, food or water poisoning'; 'Then there is the Data and Research Department, who at this moment are conducting a full-scale demographic survey of the catchment area'; 'Then, thirdly, there's Finance, of course – projected accounts, balance sheets and cash flow budgets'; 'Then there's the Purchasing Department, for purchasing medical and other equipment'; 'Fifth, there's the Technical Department, for evaluating equipment'; 'Sixth, there's the Building Department, which deals with the Phase Three building plans, costing and so forth for the final phase of the hospital'; 'And then there's Maintenance, Cleaning and Catering, Personnel in charge of leave, National Health Insurance, salaries, as well as some Staff Welfare Officers, to look after the over five hundred employees'; 'And, finally, Administration'.

Hacker, nonetheless, has the bit between his teeth and is adamant that this embarrassing anomaly will be rectified. He wants this hospital filled with doctors, nurses and patients.

He only gets even more enraged and amazed when, upon visiting the empty hospital, he encounters its Chief Administrator, Mrs Rodgers, who, as she proudly takes him on a tour of all the empty wards and crowded offices, appears just as happy as Sir Humphrey is with the current state of the place:

MRS RODGERS: And this is J Theatre.

HACKER: And how much does all *this* cost?

MRS RODGERS: Together with radiotherapy and intensive care, two and a quarter million.

HACKER: Doesn't it appall you that it's not being used?

MRS RODGERS: Oh, no, it's a very *good* thing in some ways. It prolongs its life. Cuts down running costs.

HACKER: But there are no *patients*!

MRS RODGERS: *No-o-o*, but the essential work of the hospital still has to go on.

HACKER: Aren't *patients* the essential work of the hospital??

MRS RODGERS: Oh, running an organisation of five hundred people is a *big* job, Minister.

HACKER: But if *they* weren't here they wouldn't *be* here!

MRS RODGERS: What?

HACKER: No, this is *wrong*! It *won't* do! Either you must get some patients into this hospital, or I shall close it!

MRS RODGERS: Yes, well, Minister, in the course of time—

HACKER: No, no, no! *Not* in the course of time, Mrs Rodgers. *Now*! Get rid of three hundred of your people, get some doctors and nurses and get some *patients*!

UNION REP: Now, look here, without those three hundred people, this hospital just wouldn't function!

HACKER: You think it is functioning now?

MRS RODGERS: Minister, it is one of the best-run hospitals in the country! It is up for the Florence Nightingale Award!

HACKER: And what, pray, is *that*?

MRS RODGERS: It is won by the most hygienic hospital in the area.

The whole scenario sounded unusually implausible and exaggerated for a *Yes Minister* script, but, once again, it was actually rooted in truth. Antony Jay and Jonathan Lynn had researched the topic as carefully as they always did, and had found plenty of real-life cases that inspired them to write the story.

In January 1976, for example, a new geriatric hospital in Coventry was declared ready to be filled, but six months later it was still vacant, causing the Minister for Health to explain in the House of Commons: 'It has not yet been brought into use because discussions over the allocation of beds between geriatrics and psychogeriatrics have not been completed.'[60] More recently, in 1980, it was revealed in the Commons that the number of new hospitals in the UK that were either not fully utilised or completely empty was fourteen.[61]

Jonathan Lynn was particularly amused to read a newspaper report, a little later, of one newly constructed hospital in Cambridgeshire, which contained only one solitary patient. It was the Matron, who had tripped over some scaffolding and broken her leg.[62]

By the time the episode reached the screen, the phenomenon was actually getting worse. A further report, this time made by the Public Accounts Committee in 1981, would bemoan the spread of bureaucracy within the NHS and criticise it for failing to coordinate the building of new hospitals with the preparation of proper plans to staff and populate them.[63]

The impact of the episode was so great that it would end up being used as an unofficial Video Arts-style training film for some civil servants. David Blunkett, when he was Secretary of State for Education and Employment from 1997 to 2001, used to show a tape of it to officials during 'strategy awaydays' as a gentle reminder that they should be more concerned about outcomes rather than defending their Department at all costs. 'I feared,' he would say of the storyline, 'that that's what might happen if we didn't connect the Civil Service with delivery on the ground. Not with policy development – which they're very good at. Not with preparation for legislation and carrying it through the House – which they're very good at. But actually the delivery of something out there in the community.'[64]

As happened so often with a Jay and Lynn script, the episode not only imitated actual cases but would also anticipate future ones. In this latter sense, there would be a curious coda to this comic tale.

The exterior scenes were shot outside the Medical School in the Reynolds Building at Charing Cross Hospital in St Dunstan's Road, west London. The more significant interior scenes, however, were filmed in the Lancaster Ward of Putney Hospital in Lower Common, Putney, south-west London. It would be this hospital that would end up as a sad case of fact imitating fiction.

It would not happen immediately. Indeed, in the few years after serving as the site of the fictional St Edwards, Putney Hospital (which had opened its doors in 1912) would remain busy and relatively well regarded. It was the source of a 'good news' story in 1983, when it admitted fourteen-year-old Sandy Walker, who was suffering from diabetes, as a patient, even though Walker happened to be a dog; apart from receiving insulin injections, he also had an operation to remove some kidney stones, all on the NHS.[65] Jonathan Lynn would also return to the hospital at the end of the decade to shoot some scenes for his movie, *Nuns on the Run* (which was released in 1990).

In the next few years that followed, however, the good news dried up dramatically, to be replaced by dark tales of bad management, swingeing budget cuts and a 'surplus of beds'; the place went into a sharp decline. The curse of Jim Hacker had struck.

Ironically, Putney Hospital ended up closing in 1998, and then remained vacant, with most of the equipment still in situ from the day of the closure, doing nothing but gathering dust.[66] In 2009, it was revealed that NHS Wandsworth had spent £2.6 million in eight years on securing the now dilapidated site and, supposedly, planning its future. Two years later, the South West London Community NHS Trust blocked the proposed sale of the site because it wanted to further explore the possibility of moving a GP practice or primary care group into the building. No decision was forthcoming.

Then, in 2012, Wandsworth Council finally purchased the site for £4.4 million and announced plans to demolish most of the building in order to make way for a new primary school and some flats (although a local community group immediately went to the High Court to challenge the plan).[67] In February 2013 an internal wall, within the vacant nurses' accommodation block at the rear of the site, finally crumbled and collapsed as the debate over the former hospital's future continued.

Echoes of Jim Hacker's exasperation, therefore, could still be heard more than three decades after his gasps and groans first reached the screen. Time and again, as the various news stories appeared, people would shake their heads and sigh, muttering: 'It's just like *Yes Minister*'. This was recognition humour of the highest order, and it came with a real and enduring political point.

7

Series Three

He who fights with monsters should be careful lest he thereby become a monster. And if thou gaze long enough into an abyss, the abyss will also gaze into thee.

There was only one major aim for the third series of *Yes Minister*. It had to be the best one yet.

There had been no doubt that the show would return for another run. Everyone involved with *Yes Minister* felt that the series still had plenty of creative potential, and it was clear that the demand was there. Apart from the burgeoning viewing figures, there was also some evidence that fans wanted to find other ways to feel that they 'owned' the sitcom. Although this was an era long before DVD box sets, let alone endless repeats and cable and internet streaming services – even home video was still very much in its infancy – the BBC was already looking to exploit the popularity of the show, and its commercial wing was thus encouraging the writers to consider potential spin-offs.

Shortly after completing the second set of scripts, therefore, Jonathan Lynn had been persuaded to start work on adapting all of the episodes for the printed page. 'We were approached by BBC Publications to allow some rip-off novelisations of the sort that are generally done, and we were not interested,' Lynn later explained. After further discussions (and an exasperating amount of procrastination by the BBC[1]), it was decided instead to write something 'in-house' that would really do justice to the sitcom: 'I realised that the only way to do a book of the series was to do it in the style of the *Crossman Diaries*, as Hacker's memoirs, recorded each day on his tape recorder, usually a little drunk, blissfully unaware of what Sir Humphrey was doing behind his back.'[2]

Entitled *Yes Minister: The Diaries of a Cabinet Minister by the Rt Hon. James Hacker MP*, the text was published by BBC Books in 1981, and would be followed by two more volumes in 1982 and 1983. 'It was a very difficult format to write,' Lynn would reflect, 'because many scenes in *Yes Minister* [. . .] do not have Hacker present. So it became necessary to introduce Sir Humphrey's papers, interviews with Bernard Woolley and extracts from other people's memoirs. I felt that the books should have real quality in their own right. Antony was too busy with his company, Video Arts, and I was occupied directing plays; but I was able to find time, intermittently, to do these books. Each volume had a Foreword by the "editors" (us), there were lots of editorial comments and footnotes, and other ways of getting in jokes.'[3]

One eminent recipient of a copy of the first volume was Sir Robert Armstrong, who was Cabinet Secretary at the time. He was both pleased and relieved to find inside what he took to be confirmation that the occasional rumours within Whitehall, that he had been the model for Sir Humphrey, were actually wide of the mark. 'Antony Jay gave me a copy of the book of the first series of the programme and he'd written in the front of it: "To ~~Sir Arnold Robins~~ Sir Robert Armstrong". So I knew I was not Sir Humphrey Appleby!'[4]

Apart from the tie-in books (and a forthcoming series of vinyl and audio cassette releases[5]), there was also growing interest in the show itself from various overseas markets. Sales had already been made in numerous parts of Europe, Australasia and elsewhere (totalling thirty-one countries so far[6]), but now there were plans to start screening *Yes Minister* in America on its latest pay cable service, The Entertainment Channel, and the format rights to the sitcom had also just been sold to a US television producer. Its remarkable ability to make politics seem entertaining was now being noticed on a global scale.

Most importantly of all, as far as the next series was concerned, the show's two writers knew that there was still so much more for them to explore. Every news bulletin, every current affairs programme, every report on proceedings in Parliament, provided them with more ideas for episodes. Another selection of potential plotlines landed on the mat each morning with the delivery of the daily papers.

They also continued to get inspiration from their regular Whitehall and Westminster sources, as well as from new contacts who had been prompted to get in touch out of admiration, or irritation, following previous instalments of the programme. This show was no tired old domestic sitcom, but was still an exceptionally rich and fascinating affair.

The actors saw it almost as clearly as the writers. Each of them, by this stage, felt that they understood their respective characters inside out, and was relishing the chance to take them into a new set of situations.

Paul Eddington, for example, had clearly mastered Hacker's twitchy mix of vulnerability and hardness, often allowing the character to hide behind a carapace of authority but still showing, through those wide, spaniel-like eyes and that gaping mouth, the mounting panic that lurked inside. Eddington did not just show an idea entering into Hacker's head; he also showed it bouncing about inside his skull. 'He was,' Derek Fowlds would say, 'the absolute master of the triple take.'[7] Few performers could oscillate so swiftly yet believably between composure and distress, and, in doing so, instantly remind one of countless other, real-life politicians of the time. He did not so much hold up a mirror to MPs as a magnifying glass.

Nigel Hawthorne was, if anything, even more mesmerising as Sir Humphrey. He was one of those actors who was as fascinating to watch for *how* he was doing something as he was for *what* he was doing. Lesser actors, blessed with such long, elaborate and elegant monologues, would simply have let the lines roll out, like motionless word dispensers, but Hawthorne always thought, and felt, as he spoke, and made the sound of the words give a sense of the workings of the brain from whence they came.

Though Derek Fowlds, as Bernard Woolley, was given far less to say or do, he had equally found a fine way to convey what was distinctive about his character, projecting a charmingly gauche and realistic personality during the brief scenes and exchanges in which he featured. While the other two main characters talked to, and at, each other, Fowlds, subtly, cleverly and effectively, showed Woolley listening, thinking and reacting to the content of their conversations, like an umpire at a Wimbledon final. He later recalled: 'Syd Lotterby had always said to me about my role: "*Pivotal*, Derek, *pivotal*." I liked that. I said, "What does that mean – they can't do it without me?"'[8]

There was similar enthusiasm, and expertise, shown by the team on the other side of the cameras as the third series was planned. More sets were made, with even greater attention to detail, and Peter Whitmore, who was returning to oversee the production in Sydney Lotterby's continuing absence, developed a few subtle changes to the filming of the new episodes, including more – and more pertinent – close-ups for Bernard Woolley, more varied lighting to match the mood of certain scenes and a little more dynamism inside Hacker's office.

Jonathan Lynn, in spite of his own expertise as a theatre director, was not yet tempted to try his hand at shaping the sitcom in the studio, but he and Jay certainly made sure that their opinions were always heard: 'I never wanted to direct [the show] myself, as I had never directed multi-camera shows in front of a live audience, and both Sydney and Peter were expert at it. But Tony and I attended many rehearsals and were unhesitating about giving our notes, comments and suggestions to the cast. We fulfilled the role that is played today by writer/executive producers in American TV.'[9]

'They used to come in at the end of the week,' Derek Fowlds would recall of the two writers, 'and Paul, Nigel and me – because dear Johnny is quite short and Tony is very tall – we'd mutter to each other: "Watch out – here comes Little and Large!" They'd watch us rehearse this stuff that had been amusing us all week, and Paul, under his breath, used to say, "Have they laughed yet? Have they laughed yet?" And then Nigel would whisper, "I think they've *smiled.*" Happy days, they were.'[10]

Jay and Lynn were, as usual, in complete control of their words, although, on a few isolated occasions, they did accept suggestions from the actors. Paul Eddington, for example, was strong-willed enough, as he looked through the new scripts, to stand up to the writers when one passage that seemed to 'make a bit of a mock' of the idea of nuclear-free zones (in the episode called 'The Challenge') offended his pacifist sensibilities ('I said to them, "Look, this is going a bit far, isn't it? I don't mind saying this, but it doesn't sound quite as impartial as you usually are." And they did tone it down a tiny little bit'[11]). There were also times when the writers, knowing how much meaning the actors could convey with merely an expression, gave them the licence to omit the odd line if they thought just a nuanced look would suffice. The sense of mutual respect, and admiration, had never been so strong.

Even the BBC's publicity specialists – never, in truth, the most active and imaginative operators up until that point in time – approached the third series with a greater sense of vigour and thoroughness. They knew, regardless of how high the quality of the next set of shows might be, that the competition for viewers would be more intense than ever.

This was the beginning of a new age of televisual hype. A fourth channel, the imaginatively named Channel Four, would be launched on 2 November 1982, in part as a consequence of recommendations from the Annan Committee of which Antony Jay had been a member. The third series of *Yes Minister* was scheduled to start at 9 p.m. on BBC2, nine days later, on Thursday 11 November, just when many viewers might be most distracted by the novelty of a brand new channel. Thus it would need a bigger push than in the past.

It was clear soon enough in the production process, however, that the publicists would have plenty of positive things to say. This was an award-winning sitcom that was not going to rest on its laurels.

The third series would run more risks. There would be a restlessness about the show, an edgy drive to thrive, with the team spinning more plates in the air. The overall effect, as a consequence, would be more impressive than ever, even though the odd little item might crash and smash.

Themes would blend in with each other and build up from week to week. The battle lines between Whitehall and Westminster would be drawn more obliquely as internal factions on both sides formed and faded in response to each issue and debate. Personalities would be probed a little deeper, and some relationships placed under greater stress. Boosted by a slightly bigger budget, there would also be a broader view inside the DAA, with Sir Humphrey being seen chairing various committee meetings, Hacker exploring different offices and areas and one or two other civil servants playing a more prominent role in certain plots.

Once the series started – screened opposite the news on BBC1, the *Dallas*-style drama *Falcon Crest* on ITV and Nadine Gordimer's post-apartheid parable *Six Feet of the Country* on Channel Four – it soon resumed its old appeal for viewers and critics alike, and attracted even more enthusiastic reactions than ever. Peaking at 4.45 million viewers during its run, and averaging about 3.70 million per episode, it was still well behind the most crowd-pleasing output on ITV (*Coronation Street*, which was pulling in around 15 million) and the most popular sitcom currently on BBC1 (*Hi-de-Hi!*, which was watched by about 11 million viewers per week), but it was consistently close to the top of BBC2's highest-rated shows (the channel's average weekly peak was 7 million) and regularly eclipsed all of Channel Four's latest offerings.[12]

Sometimes the series, straining a little too hard to cover challenging new ground, would misfire and fall slightly below its usual high standards. The final episode, for example, entitled 'The Middle-Class Rip-Off', tried to explore the issue of government subsidies for the arts, but ended up seeming more like a party political broadcast on behalf of the Conservative Party.

Lazily parroting Thatcherism's patronising depiction of working-class people as a bunch of crude Benthamite sybarites who were far too happy playing pushpin in the pubs to ever bother with poetry, it seemed to imply that the state could and should stand aside and allow the market to maintain the existing cultural elites. The old T.H. Green-style liberal desire to help the systematically underprivileged to broaden and better themselves culturally was lampooned via the cartoonishly snobbish Sir Humphrey – 'Subsidy is for *art*, for *culture*. It is not to be given to what the people *want*. It is for what the people *don't* want but *ought* to *have*!' – while Hacker, like Thatcher, sneered at anyone who dared to doubt the dogma of speciously populist cultural relativism ('Let us *choose* what we subsidise by the extent of popular *demand*!').

As a clumsy piece of public choice theory propaganda (screened on the public service BBC, to boot), the episode represented a rare error of judgement for a programme that usually operated above, rather than on one or other side of, any particular ideological debate. It misfired not because it ultimately favoured one position over another, but rather because, on this one occasion, it seemed so disinclined even to challenge such a position, and, pandering to certain popular prejudices, thus sounded more like a hectoring monologue than the usual calm, confident and inclusive dialogue.

Most of what preceded it in the series, however, displayed, in stark contrast, the kind of subtlety and Socratic rigour that had made the show so absorbing, thought-provoking and admirable – regardless of where any viewer happened to be located on the political spectrum. The flaws in logic, along with those in character, would thus be distributed widely and impressively fairly.

There were, for example, many more sparklingly apposite satirical lines about bureaucratic inertia (SIR HUMPHREY: 'Minister, it takes *time* to do things *now!*'[13]); and institutionalised irrationality (HACKER: 'The three articles of Civil Service faith: it takes longer to do things quickly; it's more expensive to do them cheaply; and it's more democratic to do them in secret'[14]); and administrative aimlessness (SIR HUMPHREY: 'There are no ends in administration, Minister, except loose ends. Administration is eternal'. WOOLLEY: 'For ever and ever . . .' WOOLLEY/SIR HUMPHREY: '. . . amen'[15]). There were also plenty of equally effective digs at political spin and elision (INTERVIEWER: 'Figures that I have here say that your Department's staff has risen by ten per cent.' HACKER: 'Certainly not.' INTERVIEWER: 'Well, what figure do *you* have?' HACKER: 'I believe the figure is much more like 9.97'[16]) and government pragmatism (HACKER: 'Are you saying that winking at corruption is government policy?' SIR HUMPHREY: 'No, no, Minister. It could never be government *policy*. That is unthinkable. Only government *practice*'[17]).

There was also a classic explanation by Sir Humphrey of why civil servants needed to remain aloof and scrupulously neutral when advising their Ministers on political policies:

> I have served eleven governments in the past thirty years. If I'd believed in all their policies, I would have been passionately committed to keeping out of the Common Market, and passionately committed to going into it. I would have been utterly convinced of the rightness of nationalising steel, and of denationalising it, and renationalising it. Of capital punishment, I'd have been a fervent retentionist, and an ardent abolitionist. I would have been a Keynesian and a Friedmanite. A grammar school preserver and destroyer. A nationalisation freak and a privatisation maniac. But above all, I would have been a stark staring raving schizophrenic.[18]

There were also more telling observations about the distinctive personalities of those who comprised the show's key comic triangle. The chronically ambivalent Woolley, for example, was weighed up carefully by Sir Humphrey, who still could not quite decide whether he was really a 'high-flyer', or just 'a low-flyer supported by occasional gusts of wind'.[19] Sir Humphrey himself was put down, from a safe distance, by Hacker (HACKER: 'Let me make one thing perfectly clear: Humphrey is *not* God, okay?' WOOLLEY: 'Will you tell him, or shall I?'). Hacker, in turn, received the usual caustic barbs from Sir Humphrey ('But I didn't expect you to *do* anything. I mean, you've never done anything *before*').

There were also several more well-researched and amusingly insightful glimpses into the kinds of ways in which Whitehall strives to spirit away compromising information, such as when Sir Humphrey shows Hacker how to 'tidy up' an historic file:

SIR HUMPHREY: Well *[opening a file]* this is what we normally do *[hands Hacker a document]* in circumstances like these . . .

HACKER: 'This file contains the complete set of papers except for a number of secret documents, a few others which are part of still active files, some correspondence lost in the floods of 1967' – was 1967 a particularly *bad* winter?

SIR HUMPHREY: No, a *marvellous* winter. We lost no end of embarrassing files.

HACKER: 'Some records that went astray in the move to London, and others when the War Office was incorporated in the Ministry of Defence, and the normal withdrawal of papers whose publication could give grounds for an action for libel or breach of confidence or cause embarrassment to friendly governments'. Well, that's pretty comprehensive. And how many does that normally leave for them to look at?

[Sir Humphrey, silent, looks coy]

HACKER: How many does that *actually* leave? About a hundred?

[Sir Humphrey remains silent as Hacker keeps guessing]

HACKER: *Fifty? Ten? Five?* Four? *Three?* Two? *One??* ...
                Zero???
SIR HUMPHREY: *Yes*, Minister.[20]

One of the ways that the series tried to appear fresh and different was in its use of guest actors in unusually noteworthy roles. Two in particular – Eleanor Bron and Ian Lavender – would make key contributions to certain instalments of this set of shows.

This had been one aspect of the sitcom that had, behind the scenes, failed to take off during the previous series. Time and again, during the planning of the second set of episodes, one well-known actor after another had passed on a cameo role. Mel Smith, for example, had turned down the admittedly very small role of the militant union rep in 'The Compassionate Society' (it was taken over by Stephen Tate); Eleanor Bron had similarly passed on the offer of playing the tenacious select committee member Mrs Phillips in 'The Quality of Life' (Zulema Dene appeared in her place); and Billie Whitelaw had done the same when offered the part of Betty Oldham in 'A Question of Loyalty' (which was played by Judy Parfitt instead).[21]

Times, however, had changed, and the reputation of the sitcom had risen. The show, by this time, was much more of a talking point, as well as a more prestigious (and slightly better-paid) production, and, perhaps most importantly, the cameo roles were stronger and more appealing.

Eleanor Bron appeared in the opening episode, entitled 'Equal Opportunities', playing a strong, intelligent, charismatic woman who would end up seeming like the *Yes Minister* equivalent of *Sherlock Holmes'* Irene Adler. Conan Doyle's unusually memorable female creation only appeared in one short story – 'A Scandal in Bohemia' – but her alluringly independent personality left a profound impression on both Holmes and Watson, with his friend and chronicler recalling how her refulgent presence had threatened to be 'a distracting factor which might throw a doubt upon all [Holmes'] mental results'.[22] Similarly, Jay and Lynn's character for Eleanor Bron, an up-and-coming Under-Secretary named Sarah Harrison, manages to intrigue and unnerve both Hacker and Sir Humphrey.

Hacker spots her working in his Department and is immediately struck by her beguiling combination of charm and expertise. Even Sir Humphrey, whose general awareness of the female sex has only normally amounted to the admission that his wife happens to be a woman, has definitely noticed Ms Harrison, and, as a self-confessed 'great supporter', admits that she is 'very able, for a woman, er, for a person'.

Hacker – who is keen to promote gender equality (quite a topical issue given that the 1979 election had returned the lowest number of female MPs for nearly thirty years, amounting to a mere 3 per cent of the Commons, and only one woman – Baroness Young – had joined Margaret Thatcher in her Cabinet[23]) – sees Harrison as the ideal figurehead for his drive to establish a 25 per cent quota of women in senior administrative positions within the next four years, and thus plans to promote her to Deputy Secretary in his Department. Sir Humphrey, although he was responsible for her previous promotion, is opposed to this further rapid elevation on the grounds that 'it's not her *turn* yet', but can see why his Minister is so keen on fast-tracking her rise to the top.

Both men, however, are in for a huge surprise when they summon her to impart the news of her imminent promotion. She listens, smiles and then politely turns them down, revealing that she is actually about to resign from the Civil Service to become a director at a merchant bank:

> HACKER: *[Stunned]* You were to be my, so to speak, Trojan horse.
>
> HARRISON: Well, quite honestly, Minister, I want a job where I don't spend endless hours circulating information that isn't relevant about subjects that don't matter to people who aren't interested. I want a job where there's achievement rather than merely activity. I'm *tired* of pushing paper. I want to be able to point at something and say: '*I* did that'.
>
> SIR HUMPHREY: I don't understand.
>
> HARRISON: I know. That's why I'm leaving.

Hacker is dumbfounded. Surely, he asks her, the government of Britain is an extraordinarily important and worthwhile thing? She smiles and agrees. The problem, she explains, is that she has not encountered anyone who appears to be *doing* it. She is also, she adds, tired of all the 'pointless intrigue', which, most recently, has seen him use her as just another pawn in the endless chess game.

He looks at her with a hurt expression:

> HACKER: Sarah, you probably don't realise this but I
>   fought quite a battle for you.
> HARRISON: *[Suddenly turning angry]* Oh, have you? I didn't
>   *ask* you to fight a *battle* for me. I'm not *pleased*
>   at being part of a twenty-five per cent quota.
>   Women are *not* inferior beings and *I* don't
>   enjoy being patronised! I'm afraid you're just as
>   paternalist and chauvinist as the rest of them.
>   I'm going somewhere where I shall be accepted
>   on my own merits, as an equal, as a *person*.

> *[As she leaves, Hacker, shaken and confused, looks over*
> *at a similarly bemused Sir Humphrey]*

> HACKER: You can't win, can you?

Sarah Harrison was, by a long way, the most coherent and fully formed female character that Jay and Lynn had written so far, which was particularly welcome seeing as Jim Hacker's wife, Annie, remained a maddeningly inchoate figure (sometimes seeming pushy and principled, sometimes dazzled by shiny objects, and, in this episode, an outspoken advocate of positive gender discrimination until she discovers that her husband finds Sarah Harrison attractive, after which she turns her back on the whole idea).[24] The presence of this character also served to highlight how insular and immature both the Minister and his Permanent Secretary remained, with both of them acting like overgrown schoolboys – one co-educational, one single-sex – when contemplating the issue of gender.

Ian Lavender was equally significant playing a figure who was obviously modelled on the real-life Civil Service whistle-blower Leslie Chapman. Called Dr Cartwright, an Under-Secretary with special but neglected expertise in local government, he, just like Chapman, is desperately hoping that an untamed politician will read his cost-cutting proposals and change departmental policies accordingly. Featured in two consecutive episodes – the first entitled 'The Challenge' and the second 'The Skeleton in the Cupboard' – Dr Cartwright represented the enemy within as far as Sir Humphrey was concerned, slipping his Minister dangerously practical advice on the sly ('brown envelope jobs').

Hacker, on the other hand, can hardly believe his luck. Cartwright hands him a thick file full of information that can be used to shape a new policy and thus win him plenty of praise:

CARTWRIGHT: It's all in here.
HACKER: What's this all about?
CARTWRIGHT: Controlling expenditure. I'm proposing that all council officials responsible for a new project would have to list their criteria for failure before they were given the go-ahead.
HACKER: What do you mean?
CARTWRIGHT: It's a basic scientific approach. You must first establish a method of measuring the success or failure of an experiment. Then when it's completed you can tell whether it's succeeded or failed. A proposal would have to state: 'This scheme would be a failure if it lasts longer than *this*, or costs more than *that*, if it employs more staff than *these*, or fails to meet these pre-set performance standards'.
HACKER: That's fantastic, but you could never make it work.
CARTWRIGHT: Of course you can! *[Pointing at the file]* It's all in there.
HACKER: Bernard, this is my *top* priority reading for the weekend!

Cartwright is not only a threat to Sir Humphrey's authority, but also, and more importantly, a threat to his relationship with Hacker, and so, after causing a suitable frisson within the Department, it is inevitable that this rogue agent will be removed:

HACKER:	I have learned some *very* interesting facts.
SIR HUMPHREY:	Well, I sincerely hope it does not happen again!
HACKER:	I beg your pardon?
SIR HUMPHREY:	You simply cannot go round speaking to people in the Department!
HACKER:	Why not?
SIR HUMPHREY:	Minister, how can I advise you properly if I don't know who is saying what to whom? I *must* know what is going on! You simply cannot have completely private conversations. Now, supposing you're told things that are not true—
HACKER:	Well, if they're *not* true you can put me right.
SIR HUMPHREY:	But they *may* be true. Now that is not *entirely* false, but misleading, open to misinterpretation . . .
HACKER:	I believe you're trying to keep things from me, Humphrey!
SIR HUMPHREY:	Absolutely not, Minister! Minutes *must* be taken, records *must* be kept. You won't be here for ever, you know, nor will we. In years to come, it may be vital to know what you were told. If Cartwright were moved tomorrow, how could we check on your information?
HACKER:	Cartwright *won't* be moved tomorrow.
SIR HUMPHREY:	Oh, *really?*

The darkest and most interesting moments in the series, however, revolved around Hacker's spasm of morality. Throughout the previous two series, and the first three episodes of this one, Hacker had been seen leaping through each one of the circles of Hell with all the mounting enthusiasm of an Olympic hurdler in sight of a gold medal, showing fewer and fewer qualms about diving into political problems and getting his hands completely dirty.

In the opening episode, for example, he only gets serious about promoting gender equality when he thinks it might suit his own personal ambitions, hoping that such a supposedly 'principled' policy will improve his reputation as a Minister and do some good at the polls. The same thing happens in the next episode, when he hears that something else might prove a vote winner. 'A *vote* winner?' he exclaims, his principles once again popping like punctured bubbles as he contemplates lending his name to a policy about which he is utterly unconvinced.[25] In the third episode, he is at his most cynical and cruel so far, relishing the prospect of completely destroying the career of his Permanent Secretary for a thirty-year-old mistake, and only relenting after he has watched Sir Humphrey crumble in front of his eyes and agree to bend the rules for the sake of Hacker's own party.

It comes as quite a surprise, therefore, when, rather implausibly, he suddenly teeters on the brink of the abyss and starts trying to pull back, lecturing everyone else on the need to do the right thing and generally behaving as though he now thinks he has a halo hovering above his head. He is full of self-righteous indignation in episode four, when, for example, he realises that a Government trade agreement has been secured through bribery (Sir Humphrey prefers to call it 'creative negotiation'), and bristles at Sir Humphrey's self-serving claim that 'a cynic is what an idealist calls a realist'.[26]

This belated intrusion of scruples reaches a climax in the penultimate episode, 'The Whisky Priest' (which was partly inspired by *Oilgate* – a recent study about the 1960s sanctions scandal[27]), when Hacker, at his most self-deluded, attempts to act as moral arbiter for the whole of Whitehall and Westminster. Upon hearing some disturbing information from an army officer, the morally motivated Major Saunders, he marches into his Department determined to fight the good fight:

> HACKER: Last night a confidential source disclosed to me that British arms are being sold to Italian red terrorist groups.
>
> SIR HUMPHREY: I see. May I ask who this confidential source was?
>
> HACKER: Humphrey, I just said it was confidential.
>
> SIR HUMPHREY: Oh, I'm sorry, I naturally assumed that meant you were going to tell me.
>
> HACKER: You don't seem to be very *worried* by this information.

SIR HUMPHREY:	Well, these things happen all the time. It's not our problem.
HACKER:	So does robbery with violence. Doesn't *that* worry you?
SIR HUMPHREY:	No, Minister – Home Office problem.
HACKER:	Humphrey: we're letting *terrorists* get hold of *murderous* weapons!
SIR HUMPHREY:	*We're* not.
HACKER:	Well, who *is*?
SIR HUMPHREY:	Who knows? The Department of Trade, Ministry of Defence, Foreign Office . . .
HACKER:	*We*, Humphrey. The British Government. Innocent lives are being set at risk by *British* arms in the hands of *terrorists*.
SIR HUMPHREY:	Only Italian lives. Not *British* lives.
HACKER:	Well, then, the British tourists abroad.
SIR HUMPHREY:	Tourists? Foreign Office problem.

The Permanent Secretary warns his Minister that the sale of arms abroad is not a topic that rewards close scrutiny. 'A basic rule of government,' he notes, 'is never look into anything you don't have to, and never set up an inquiry unless you know in advance what its findings will be.' Hacker is insistent: 'We're talking about good and evil!' 'Ah,' says Sir Humphrey brightly, 'a Church of England problem.'

The Minister, suddenly wanting to keep his hands clean, protests that they should only be thinking about right and wrong, so Sir Humphrey decides to remind him of how the real world works. 'Either you sell arms or you don't,' he points out. 'If you sell them, they will inevitably end up with people who have the cash to buy them.' Hacker, like a man who has just discovered soap, is still horrified by the grubbiness of all, and so, once again, Sir Humphrey feels obliged to give him a refresher lesson in deontological ethics: 'May I point out to you that something is either morally wrong or it isn't. It can't be *slightly* morally wrong.'

Hacker, however, is having none of it. Displaying breathtaking hypocrisy, bearing in mind all of the dubious decisions he has happily made – in a spirit more akin to cant than Kant – since he came to office, he now seems to think of himself as a beacon of political virtue in a murky administrative world:

HACKER:	For the first time I fully understand that you are purely committed to means and not to ends.
SIR HUMPHREY:	Well, as far as *I'm* concerned, Minister, and all of my colleagues, there is no difference between means and ends.
HACKER:	*[Sombrely]* If you believe that, Humphrey, you will go to hell.
SIR HUMPHREY:	*[Smiling facetiously]* Minister, I had no idea you had a theological bent.
HACKER:	You are a moral vacuum.
SIR HUMPHREY:	If you say so, Minister.

Hacker, supremely pleased with his new self-delusion as the shining white knight of Westminster, strides off to alert the Prime Minister. Sir Humphrey, meanwhile, fears another Watergate, with an inquiry into this isolated issue leading 'to one ghastly revelation after another'.

Hacker, however, never gets to see the PM. He is headed off by the Chief Whip, who has no time for this kind of ill-conceived crusade, endangering the signing of an international anti-terrorist agreement in 'a fit of moral self-indulgence'. Just in case he has not scared Hacker enough by barking at him about Cabinet responsibility and party loyalty, the Chief Whip then hints that the Minister might also be on the brink of wrecking his own prospects of taking over the Foreign Office. This is quite enough to slap Hacker back into amorality.

He now has to silence Major Saunders, who still expects him to expose the dirty deal, but Sir Humphrey knows what will overcome this problem: 'the Rhodesia Solution'. Back when there were oil sanctions against the country, a member of the British Government was informed that certain companies were flouting those sanctions, but, in order to avoid undermining such covert trading deals, he elected to tell the Prime Minister in such a way as to ensure that he failed to know that he had been told.

'You write a note which is susceptible to misinterpretation,' Sir Humphrey explains. Dictating to Woolley, he starts drafting the appropriate style of report: 'My attention has been drawn, on a personal basis, to information which suggests the possibility of certain irregularities . . .' Getting Woolley to insert a reference to the relevant piece of legislation ('Section One of the Import, Export and Customs Powers [Defence] Act 1939'), he moves on to suggest that somebody else should do something about it – 'Prima facie evidence suggests that there could be a case for further investigation to establish whether or not an inquiry should be put in hand' – and then he smudges it all over – 'Nevertheless, it should be stressed that available information is limited, and relevant facts could be difficult to establish with any degree of certainty'.

'That's *most* unclear,' Hacker observes. 'Thank you, Minister!' Sir Humphrey replies. Once the Permanent Secretary has added his finishing touches to the trick, arranging for it to arrive at Number Ten on the day that the Prime Minister is due to fly off for an overseas summit (thus making it harder for anyone to tell whether it was the PM or the acting PM who actually saw the letter), Hacker knows that he, too, is well on his way to Hell.

Back at home, he lies on the couch, drunk on whisky, and whines to his wife:

HACKER:	I'm a moral vacuum.
ANNIE:	Cheer up, darling. Nothing good ever comes out of Whitehall. You did what you could.
HACKER:	You don't really mean that.
ANNIE:	I do.
HACKER:	Nah, I'm just like Humphrey and all the rest of them.
ANNIE:	Now that's *certainly* not true. He's *lost* his sense of right and wrong. You've still got yours.
HACKER:	*Have* I?
ANNIE:	It's just that you don't use it much. You're a sort of whisky priest. You do at least know when you've done the wrong thing.
HACKER:	Whisky priest?
ANNIE:	That's right.
HACKER:	*[Thinking it over]* Good . . . Let's open another bottle.
ANNIE:	We haven't got one.

HACKER: That's what *you* think!

[He opens up one of his red boxes and produces a new bottle.]

HACKER: Who said nothing good ever came out of
            Whitehall?

            [He unscrews it]

            Do you want one?

ANNIE: Yes, Minister.

It might not have made complete dramatic sense in the broader context of the sitcom as a whole, but as an episode it was certainly one of the
highlights of an uneven third series. Far more effectively rendered than Sir
Humphrey's own personal crisis in 'The Skeleton in the Cupboard' (which
had seen Nigel Hawthorne overact so wildly – by his own supremely high
standards – that he had the preternaturally self-controlled Permanent
Secretary contort his face like a gargoyle and stuff a handkerchief inside
his mouth), 'The Whisky Priest' was a classic *Yes Minister* comical critique. Perceptive, precise and pertinent, it did what the sitcom did best
and made people think at the same time that it made them laugh.

Even the small, partial failures of the third series, however, had been noble
failures, because they were the result of the team's being bold and brave enough
to eschew the line of least resistance and try instead to surprise, enlighten
and delight. Watched by an enthusiastic audience each week (which would
expand dramatically once the show was repeated on BBC1 in the summer of
the following year), the run was as well received as its predecessors had been,
and won several more awards, including BAFTAs for Best Comedy Series
and, for Nigel Hawthorne, Best Light Entertainment Performance.

By way of a coda, a brief extra scene was recorded for a special seasonal
show, *The Funny Side of Christmas*, which was broadcast on BBC1 on
27 December. Set on the day before the Minister escaped from Whitehall
for the festive break, it had a flustered-looking Sir Humphrey rush into
Hacker's office to deliver an urgent message to the startled Minister:

SIR HUMPHREY: I wonder if I might crave your momentary
                indulgence in order to discharge a by no means

disagreeable obligation which has over the years become more or less established practice, within Government circles, as we approach the terminal period of the year – calendar, of course, not financial – in fact, not to put too fine a point on it, week fifty-one – and submit to you with all appropriate deference, for your consideration at a convenient juncture, a sincere and sanguine expectation, indeed confidence, indeed one might go so far as to say *hope*, that the aforementioned period may be, at the end of the day, when all relevant factors have been taken into consideration, susceptible of being deemed to be such as to merit a final verdict of having been by no means unsatisfactory in its overall outcome and, in the final analysis, to give grounds for being judged, on mature reflection, to have been conducive to generating a degree of gratification which will be seen in retrospect to have been significantly higher than the general average.

HACKER: What's he *talking* about??

WOOLLEY: Well, Minister, *I* think Sir Humphrey just wanted to crave your momentary indulgence in order to discharge a by no means disagreeable—

HACKER: All – All right, Bernard! Humphrey?

SIR HUMPHREY: At the end of the day, Minister, all things—

HACKER: No, no, just . . .

SIR HUMPHREY: Yes, Minister?

HACKER: Are you saying 'Happy Christmas'?

SIR HUMPHREY: *Yes*, Minister!

It was a charming way to finish off an eventful year – the third in the lifetime of *Yes Minister*. The show had come a long way for a popular sitcom. It had established itself, it had polished itself and now it had pushed itself. The question now was: where, if anywhere, could and should it go from here?

Whisky Galore

In terms of pure comedic charm, the most satisfying episode in the third series had been 'The Moral Dimension'. It had featured dubious diplomatic deals, surreptitious religious slights and clumsy cupidity, and once again – far more than viewers realised – most of the fiction had been formed by fact.

Unusually for the show, a considerable amount of the action took place outside of the DAA offices in Whitehall, because Jim and Annie Hacker, along with Sir Humphrey, Woolley and the rest of a large delegation, fly off to the oil sheikdom of Qumran in order to finalise one of Britain's biggest-ever export orders. The prospect of returning triumphant fills all concerned with a sense of excitement, but, inevitably, one or two problems are encountered along the way.

This episode was inspired by two real-life incidents, one already widely reported and the other still very much a secret. The former involved a coffee pot, the latter some bottles of Scotch.

The coffee pot in question had belonged to the Labour MP and former Cabinet Minister Anthony Crosland. He had been given the item, donated by the architect John Poulson, when opening a school in Bradford in January 1966 in his capacity as the then Secretary of State for Education and Science. The gift had gone unreported and largely unnoticed until 1973, when, in the course of investigating the extent of the now disgraced and bankrupt Poulson's bribery of senior political figures in order to facilitate his business ambitions, court officials discovered that Crosland had not only accepted the coffee pot, but had also written a gushing letter of thanks to Poulson, saying: 'I tremble to think how much it cost. I shall treasure it as a memory of a very beautiful building'.[28]

By the end of a month of intense media and political pressure, a 'profoundly embarrassed' Crosland told the House of Commons that he 'had no recollection' of receiving the pot, which, once 'traced' inside his house by his wife, had been shown to have 'never been used' and was actually suspected of being a cheap reproduction. Vowing to send it on 'to the trustee in bankruptcy for his benefit', Crosland moaned: 'All I want is to get rid of the bloody thing. It has never been used. I was unaware of its existence'.[29]

Having read all about the incident and remembered it, both Antony Jay and Jonathan Lynn had always kept it in mind as a potential anecdote to be exploited, and the right time for it had now arrived. 'In that episode,' Antony Jay would reveal, 'we mixed in the Anthony Crosland coffee pot story, only we changed it to a vase.'[30]

While at the reception in Qumran, Hacker is presented with a seventeenth-century rose water vase as a gift from one government to another. Annie Hacker is delighted with the item, so she is greatly disappointed when Woolley explains to her that it will be classified as government property, and that the only way that she would be allowed to keep it – rather than see it put 'in a basement somewhere in Whitehall' – is if it were to be valued at less than fifty pounds.

Taking pity on the Minister's wife, Woolley sidles off to see if he can find someone able and willing to solve the problem discreetly. Sure enough, one of the Qumrani officials proves only too happy to certify that this 'very valuable' rose water vase is actually a mere copy worth just a very convenient £49.95. Delighted, Hacker takes charge of the gift and brings it back home with her.

Some time later, however, a journalist friend visits Annie, sees the vase on display and, unconvinced that it is a mere replica, calls the Qumrani embassy to enquire as to its real value. The officials there are incensed to hear it suggested that they would have passed off a cheap copy as a precious antique, and the Foreign Office fears that this little matter is in danger of becoming one of the biggest diplomatic incidents in recent years. Jim Hacker, as a consequence, is left to lie his way out of the controversy.

The other parallel with real life, involving the bottles of scotch, occurred when the team was preparing to touch down in Qumran. Alarmed when

Sir Humphrey reminds him that, as alcohol is banned in the country under Islamic law, they are facing hours of sipping nothing more potent than warm orange juice, Hacker is determined to find a way to bypass the ban.

He first suggests hip flasks, but Sir Humphrey dismisses the idea as far too risky. Undeterred, he then comes up with the idea of setting up a special 'communications room' next door to the reception: 'You know, emergency telephones, telex lines to Downing Street, all that sort of thing. Then we could fill it with cases of booze brought in from the agency'. Sir Humphrey hails the proposal as a 'stroke of genius' and pledges his 'enthusiastic support'.

Once inside, at the reception, chatting politely to the Qumrani officials, the plan is put into action:

> WOOLLEY: Excuse me, sir, there's an urgent call for you in
>   the communications room. A 'Mr Haig'.
> HACKER: *[Bemused]* General Haig??
> WOOLLEY: Er, no, 'Mr Haig'. You know – with the dimples.
> HACKER: *[The penny drops]* Ah yes! Do excuse me – most
>   important!

Hacker then rushes off to the special room, where a junior official opens up a red despatch box to reveal a full bottle of Haig whisky. The Minister, once his glass of orange juice has been 'improved' with several measures of the hard stuff, returns to the reception eager to keep the plan going:

> HACKER: Ah, Bernard, you're wanted in the
>   communications room: a 'Mr John Walker'.
> WOOLLEY: Johnny Walker?
> HACKER: Yes, from the Scotch Office – *Scottish* Office.
> ANNIE: Isn't there a message for me, darling?
> HACKER: Yes, of course, there is. Bernard'll get it for you if
>   you give him your glass – er, if you give him your
>   glass, he'll get you some more orange juice as well!

It does not take long before another call comes in:

> HACKER: Ah, Bernard, any, er, messages in the
>   communications room?
> WOOLLEY: Oh, well, there is one for Sir Humphrey,
>   Minister. Yes, the Soviet Embassy is on the line,
>   Sir Humphrey: a 'Mr Smirnoff'.
> HACKER: Are you sure there isn't one for me?
> WOOLLEY: Oh, well, there *was* a message from the British
>   Embassy compound, the school – a delegation of
>   Teachers.
> HACKER: Ah! I must go and greet the teachers. Before the
>   Bell's goes – er, *bell* goes!

Hacker, upon his return, is now swaying slowly from side to side, but still the ruse goes on:

> WOOLLEY: Oh, there was a message for you in the
>   communications room, er, er, the VAT Man –
>   your 69 returns.
> HACKER: What??
> WOOLLEY: VAT 69.
> HACKER: Oh? *Ah*! Yes, thanks!

As he staggers off, spilling 'orange juice' as he goes, Sir Humphrey looks concerned: 'I'm rapidly coming to the conclusion, Bernard, that the Minister has had *almost* as many urgent messages as he can take!'

Baroness Symons, who was a middle-ranking civil servant at the time when the episode was first broadcast (but who would become a Foreign Office Minister in Tony Blair's Government), would later recall her reaction to the scene: 'I didn't know the Foreign Office as well as I do today. At the time, I thought it was extremely funny, but I thought it was fanciful. I'm pained to say that, having now been in the Foreign Office/Ministry of Defence for the best part of eight years, I don't think that was *quite* as fanciful as all that. I think there was a good deal of an echo of the way in which things are handled.'[31]

Indeed, as far-fetched as this aspect of the episode might have seemed in those days, something remarkably like it had actually happened. Jay and

Lynn learned about it, secretly at the time, from the closest of their own special advisers, Bernard Donoughue.

In January 1978, in his capacity as Head of the Number Ten Policy Unit, he had accompanied a delegation led by the then Prime Minister, James Callaghan, on a ten-day tour of the subcontinent, taking in India, Bangladesh and Pakistan. The two-fold aim was to stimulate various trade links with Britain and strengthen diplomatic relations. It was close to the end of the trip, as they headed into Pakistan, that an ingenious clandestine operation, devised and led by Donoughue, took place:

> We were facing a very long evening there, with a very long reception followed by a two-hour after-dinner speech from the President, with only water or orange juice to drink. So I – along with Tom McNally, who was then Callaghan's Political Secretary – plotted ahead of it, working out how we could deal with this and get ourselves something stronger, such as whisky, to drink. And I came up with this story about how we'd need to be in urgent touch with Downing Street, so we'd have to have our desk with a telephone very close to the huge reception room and the dinner room, so that we could be in immediate contact with Number Ten in case there was a crisis. And hidden in the desk drawers were several bottles of whisky. And it worked out very well. Every now and again, some of us would go out to this desk with our glasses half full of orange juice, and top them up from the desk drawers with very good whisky. You could tell who our 'inner team' were by the fact that they were going around with these glasses full of suspiciously brown orange juice! Callaghan wasn't part of the inner team, I should point out. He didn't drink. A very fine Prime Minister, but he was a puritan, and Tom and I were cavaliers, so he wouldn't have approved of what we were up to![32]

The show, once again, had demonstrated its dictum that truth was funnier than fiction. While most people just laughed at a very entertaining episode, the few who were in the know wondered what would be the next secret to be screened.

8

Interregnum

If we want things to stay as they are, things will have to change.

After the third series of *Yes Minister*, there was a pause for thought. For the first time since the sitcom started, there was a degree of doubt about its future.

The BBC in those days had a wise and relaxed 'wait and see' attitude when it came to recommissioning many of its most successful shows. Preferring to let its best sitcoms progress at a pace that suited the programme-makers rather than the channel controllers, the message to the writers was always to wait until they felt that they had something worthwhile to say, and then pick up the telephone and let an executive know. It was only at this point that the wheels would be set in motion for another series to be made.

John Howard Davies had recently been promoted to Head of Light Entertainment, while Gareth Gwenlan, another seasoned supporter of sitcoms, had replaced him as Head of Comedy, so *Yes Minister* still had the right friends in the right places. There was no real prospect, therefore, of the BBC suddenly losing interest in the show.

There were also still plenty of influential fans who were eager for further instalments. In June 1983, for example, shortly after the General Election, Jonathan Lynn was pleased to find that Margaret Thatcher remained a fervent admirer of the show. He had written to her, somewhat surprisingly considering his left-of-centre reputation, to congratulate her on her 'magnificent and excellent election victory',[1] which prompted a predictably warm response. She wrote back quickly, by hand, not only to thank him for the sentiment but also to reaffirm her affection for the sitcom:

I love your programmes. Every one a winner. The dialogue and timing are superb. And the insight into the thought processes of politicians and civil servants is supremely perceptive.[2]

There was just as deep an appreciation for the show over at the Labour Party's HQ in Walworth Road, where, ironically, its Leader, Neil Kinnock, and his then Press Secretary, Patricia Hewitt, had recently written and performed an unofficial *Yes Minister* sketch attacking Thatcher's handling of the Falklands conflict:

INTRO: And now a word from one of the more alert, far-seeing of the present Government's ministers. The Minister for Bureaucratic Indifference, Mr Jim Hacker.

HACKER: Hello everyone. Some of our critics are saying that my colleagues and I are too easily manipulated by our civil servants. But this is just rubbish! As I intend now to demonstrate to you. I've just sent for my new Permanent Secretary (the one who replaced Sir Humphrey), Dame Patricia.

HEWITT: You wanted to see me, Minister?

HACKER: Ah yes, Dame Patricia. There's something about the Government's loan to Argentina that I just can't understand.

HEWITT: *That* doesn't really surprise me, Minister.

HACKER: What?

HEWITT: Nothing, Minister.

HACKER: Well, the thing is, since they're still threatening us, why in God's name are we lending them money?

HEWITT: Well, isn't it quite obvious, Minister?

HACKER: No.

HEWITT: Well, if we forced them to repay it, it would completely destroy Argentina's economy.

HACKER: Well, what's wrong with that? It's a pity someone didn't think of that last April, it could have saved us a war!

HEWITT: Ah, but we *did* think of it last April, Minister.

HACKER: What?! So why didn't we blow the whistle on the Argies *then* and stop the killing?

HEWITT: Minister, it's really all *quite* simple. The fact is that such a course would have ensured an *inauspicious* prognosis for the liquidity of our fiscal institutions.

HACKER: What does *that* mean?

HEWITT: The banks would have lost money.

HACKER: Why?

HEWITT: *[Sighs as if with a stupid child]* Oh dear, let me put it this way, Minister. If we asked for our money back the Argentines would be declared bankrupt and they wouldn't have to pay us anything at all.

HACKER: Just let me get this right . . . are you trying to tell me that we sent thousands of troops pissing all over the South Atlantic rather than write off a few quid on a bad debt?

HEWITT: Oh, not a 'few' quid, Minister, several millions actually.

HACKER: But why so much money?

HEWITT: Because, Minister, Argentina is like us, and has to pay for life's little necessities . . . like fighter planes, Exocets, artillery, that sort of thing.

HACKER: What – so they can then use them on British soldiers?

HEWITT: Well, *technically* that is correct, Minister. They *may* do that from time to time, but you have to remember, Minister, they *are* our friends.

HACKER: *Friends*?!

HEWITT: Quite so, Minister, *and* an essential bulwark against the Communists.

HACKER: Oh, are they? I see! Well, it's a good thing we aren't lending money to the Communists.

HEWITT: Well, that's not strictly true either, Minister. There *are* one or two outstanding financial arrangements with the Eastern Bloc, especially with Poland.

HACKER: Poland? Dame Patricia, I've just had a brilliant idea!

HEWITT: I was afraid of that. [I should have used more long words.]

HACKER: Why don't we tell General Jaruzelski that unless he ends repression against Solidarity we will bankrupt his country?

HEWITT: Because, Minister, if repression ends, there'll be more civil unrest, the Polish economy will destabilise, fiscal controls will evaporate and the banks . . .

HACKER: I see: will lose money. So, let me get this straight, Dame Patricia. It is the policy of this Government to go to war with its friends, to connive at the repressive policies of its enemies . . . and to lend money to both.

HEWITT: I couldn't have put it better myself.

HACKER: You know, Dame Patricia, sometimes I think the country is being run by complete idiots.

HEWITT: Yes, Minister.[3]

On this one topic, therefore, even the Government and its Opposition were united. All of the country's politicians wanted *Yes Minister* to come back.

Neither Jay nor Lynn, however, was sure about writing any more episodes. For one thing, the research involved for each and every script was extraordinarily time-consuming and also extremely tiring. In those days, without the option of a few easy clicks on a computer, the writers had to travel and consult all of the relevant libraries and archives in person, as well as devote hours and hours to wining and dining their increasingly wide range of political and bureaucratic moles. The consequence was that they had become the willing victims of their own remarkably meticulous attention to detail.

They were also the victims of their own success. The growing popularity of the show had gradually increased the pressure on them to keep topping their own triumphs, and this did not just drain their creative energy but also distracted them from their various solo projects.

Although the general public probably regarded them simply as 'the *Yes Minister* writers', the sitcom remained, in truth, a relatively low-paid, part-time project, as Jay continued to oversee the very busy Video Arts and Lynn carried on with his theatrical and other media interests. It was getting harder and harder for them to find the spare time to collaborate on the show.

Finally, they were caught in two minds as to whether continuing would be wise for the long-term reputation of the sitcom. They loved it, and were very proud of what they, and all of their colleagues, had so far achieved, and thus were loath, at this stage, to risk devaluing its reputation by allowing it to outstay its welcome.

The main creative issue was that Hacker had been in charge of the DAA now for three years, and such longevity was becoming less and less believable. Most Ministers, in real life, stayed for no more than two-thirds of that time in any one Department before being demoted, promoted or shifted sideways. Richard Crossman, for example, had spent a mere twenty-two months as Minister of Housing and Local Government, and then just nineteen months as Secretary of State for Health and Social Services.

Jay and Lynn could, of course, have moved him to another Department via a reshuffle, but the whole point of inventing the all-purpose DAA had been to avoid him being identified with a specific, limited area, and so, dramatically, he seemed destined to be stuck where he was. While the writers were confident about keeping the stories plausible, they were less sure about how to keep their Minister's career sufficiently convincing. It was thus tempting to call time on his, and the show's, tenure.

The actors, meanwhile, were too distracted by other projects to reflect for very long on what if anything might happen next with their sitcom. 'As far as we knew,' Derek Fowlds would recall, 'they were thinking of ways to change it while keeping us all together.'[4] They trusted the writers to reach a decision that would be in the best interests of the show, but, in the meantime, as the arch pragmatists that their profession tends to nurture, they immersed themselves in other work.

Paul Eddington rarely seemed to have a blank page in his diary. He appeared on television alongside Nanette Newman in another sitcom, *Let There Be Love* (BBC2, 1983), which he later dismissed as 'rather depressing' because the standard of the scripts fell far below those of *Yes Minister*.[5] In the theatre, he moved swiftly from one production to another, starring in the autumn of 1983 in two plays at Bristol Old Vic (Terence Rattigan's *The Browning Version* and Peter Shaffer's *Black Comedy*) and then in the West End in Charles Dyer's *Lovers Dancing* at the Albery, before moving on to Chichester in the summer of 1984 to star in a revival of Alan Bennett's *Forty Years On*. He also worked on several radio shows, recorded innumerable voiceovers, appeared in commercials and even managed to squeeze in a few more promotional trips abroad.

Nigel Hawthorne was not quite as active, preferring to keep some time free to relax out of the spotlight with his partner Trevor Bentham, but he still selected a series of interesting stage projects during this period, appearing during the summer of 1983 at The Pit in two prestigious RSC productions: Ibsen's *Peer Gynt* and Molière's *Tartuffe*, supporting Antony Sher. There were also a few radio and television plays, including a memorable version of André Brink's *A Dry White Season* for BBC Radio 4 in February 1983.

Derek Fowlds worked just as steadily. He appeared in February 1983 at the Redgrave Theatre, Farnham in Robin Hawdon's frenetic new farce *The Birthday Suite*, and then toured in several other productions. There was also a starring role in the pilot of an unusual ITV sitcom called *Affairs of the Heart* (focusing on a man recovering from a heart attack, it would eventually reappear as a series a couple of years later).

As the months went by, the BBC was certainly still very interested in seeing the show continue, but it had failed to realise how undervalued the two writers had come to feel. *Yes Minister* was, after all, their idea, based on their research and built on their beautifully crafted scripts, but, whenever the show had been honoured for its success, the writers had been left neglected.

For example, every time the most prestigious award ceremonies came around, in spite of the fact that *Yes Minister* had always figured prominently on the list of nominations, Jay and Lynn, the writers, were notably not only overlooked but not even in attendance. 'Each time Nigel [Hawthorne] and Sydney Lotterby or Peter Whitmore won BAFTA awards for our show,' Jonathan Lynn would remember, 'and each time we were not invited. We won the Broadcasting Press Guild Award twice, and we didn't even know about it until Paul [Eddington], who was always gracious, rang my front-door bell, handed me the certificate and said, "I think this really belongs to you and Tony"'.[6]

As snubs go, this was probably the worst. There were, however, quite a few others.

Jay and Lynn had a similar experience with the people responsible for the recently established Public Lending Right programme, when they applied for royalties for their *Yes Minister* tie-in books. The letter they received in response pointed out that, as the author appeared to be 'the Rt Hon. James Hacker MP', neither Jay nor Lynn was entitled to any payments unless they could provide proof that they had made a significant contribution to the books.

It was no better closer to home. Jonathan Lynn's wife used to shop at the same butcher's, in Muswell Hill, as Paul Eddington's wife, and on one occasion, when both of them were there, the butcher congratulated Eddington's wife on her husband's great success in *Yes Minister*, and then turned to Lynn's wife and asked: 'How's your old man, Rita? Haven't seen him on the telly much recently. Does he get any work now?'[7]

The lack of fame came as something of a relief. Both writers preferred their work, rather than themselves, to be well known. They did hope, nonetheless, that their efforts had at least been fully appreciated by the people behind the scenes at the BBC, and so they decided to see how much they were really esteemed by the powers that be.

Talks about another series were initiated, but the writers were in an uncompromising mood. 'We asked for a lot more money,' Lynn would recall, 'and we didn't hide our view that writers were disrespected by the BBC hierarchy, who had it in their power to change the perception of the writer's pre-eminent contribution to television programmes.' Naming their price, they asked for ten thousand pounds (between them) per script – very little by today's media standards, and a relatively modest sum even in those days as far as commercial television was concerned, but still much more than the BBC, up to that point, had paid to a couple of sitcom writers. Somewhat surprised and shaken, the executives tried to reassure the pair, but failed to do enough. 'The BBC wanted us to continue,' said Lynn, 'but it was not willing to step up financially.'[8]

The talks collapsed and the writers declared that they would move on to other projects. Their supporters at the BBC were saddened, but the pair did not seem to have any regrets. 'As the BBC wouldn't give us a pay rise of any consequence,' Jonathan Lynn would say, 'we were more than happy to move on. We both were busy with other work.'[9]

It came, in a way, as a relief. There was so much more, so much else, that both men wanted to do.

Antony Jay had plenty of other interests, both in politics and business, to occupy his time and was very much in the mood for pastures new. 'We really did think that series three was the end,' he later explained. 'Anyway, I was pretty busy as chairman and script writer/editor of Video Arts.'[10]

Jonathan Lynn was excited at the prospect of taking on new challenges, not only back in the theatre but also now in films. He had received an offer from Hollywood.

John Landis, the director of such popular movies as *Animal House* (1978), *The Blues Brothers* (1980), *An American Werewolf in London* (1981) and *Trading Places* (1983), as well as the groundbreaking promotional video for Michael Jackson's *Thriller* (1983), was planning to make his next movie a comedy-mystery inspired by the board game *Cluedo*, and he wanted Lynn to write the screenplay. Lynn agreed, but, by the time he had completed it, Landis had become distracted by other projects, and so, exploiting the fact that he was a major player, he pulled some strings so that Lynn could direct it instead. Released as *Clue* (1985), it would mark the start of a second career for Lynn as a Hollywood writer/director.

Back in Britain, he continued to work in the theatre, directing a prestigious revival of Joe Orton's black comedy *Loot* at the Ambassadors Theatre in London during the first half of 1984, and then transferring it to the Lyric for the rest of the year. The imaginative production, though extremely well received, was blighted by the tragic death of its star, Leonard Rossiter, who suffered a fatal heart attack in his dressing room on the evening of 5 October.

Lynn also found the time, between the two runs of *Loot*, to direct another high-profile play – an adaptation for the National Theatre by John Mortimer of the classic Georges Feydeau farce *A Little Hotel on the Side* – as well as work on another screenplay and, in collaboration with Monty Norman, a musical. As much as he loved *Yes Minister*, like Antony Jay, he was far too busy to miss it.

The BBC, in their absence, was still trying to find a way to bring the show back. Caught, typically, between a rock and a hard place, it was wary of finding the extra funds for the writers, as the tabloids could be trusted to use such a move as an excuse to condemn the Corporation for its supposed profligacy, and it was even more fearful of losing the sitcom for good, as, in that case, the tabloids would exploit the failure to come up with the extra cash as a reason to judge the Corporation for its excessive frugality. John Howard Davies, however, was determined to find a way to resolve the situation – 'There was no way on my watch that we were going to let it just fade away'[11] – and, as a stopgap measure that would at least keep the show in circulation, he and his colleagues persuaded Jay and Lynn to allow the BBC to reuse some of the existing scripts for radio.

Produced and adapted by Pete Atkin (yet another former member of the Cambridge Footlights and an occasional collaborator with Clive James), the first series was recorded at the Paris Theatre, Lower Regent Street, London in April and May of 1983 and broadcast on BBC Radio 4 during October and November, with a second run being transmitted the following year.[12] Featuring most of the original cast (with Eddington and Hawthorne, on modest radio rates, finally achieving parity with £125 each per episode, and Fowlds lower, as usual, on £80[13]), with the one notable addition of Bill Nighy replacing Neil Fitzwiliam as Frank Weisel (for £65 per episode[14]), the recording sessions were very happy affairs and the finished programmes were, in their own way, as polished as their television equivalents.[15] Attracting more media coverage than was expected for a radio series, let alone for what was basically a set of edited repeats of old television shows, the success of the venture helped John Howard Davies and others in their campaign to persuade their colleagues that the return of the show to the screen would merit the extra expense involved.

Something else happened, however, at the start of the following year, that would suddenly bring *Yes Minister* right back into the public consciousness. Its most powerful fan demanded that it return.

The cue came at the start of 1984 courtesy of Mary Whitehouse, when her noisy mouthpiece, The National Viewers' and Listeners' Association, announced its intention to honour *Yes Minister* at its annual awards ceremony for exemplifying 'wholesome television' (a previous recipient had been *Jim'll Fix It*). As if this was not a big enough 'treat' in itself, Whitehouse also took it upon herself to invite none other than the Prime Minister, Margaret Thatcher, to present the award to the team. (There is no doubt that Whitehouse, as a staunch Tory, saw the party political capital to be generated from such an event, as her letter assured the Prime Minister that, while she would not be required to make a formal speech, 'you would, needless to say, be more than welcome to use the occasion as you saw fit'.[16])

Inside Number Ten, Thatcher accepted the invitation enthusiastically, and then discussed with her Press Officer, Bernard Ingham, how best to exploit the occasion. It was Ingham who hit upon the idea that she should perform a special *Yes Minister* sketch alongside Paul Eddington and Nigel Hawthorne (Derek Fowlds was on tour at the time in *The Norman Conquests* and was thus unavailable).[17] Rather than ask Jay and Lynn to write it, Thatcher asked Ingham himself to conjure something up.

'I wrote the script,' he later confirmed. 'Number Ten honed it. We rehearsed it endlessly in Mrs Thatcher's study. She played herself, of course. Sir Robin Butler [her Principal Private Secretary] played Jim Hacker, not I fear to Mr Eddington's standards, and myself a pathetic Sir Humphrey. Mrs Thatcher was determined to get every inflection right. It was like writing a speech for her, an endless operation.'[18] The aim, he would say, was 'to demonstrate that perhaps she was not devoid of a sense of humour after all'.[19]

All of this was going on without the knowledge of either of the *real* writers, or any of the real actors. The first that Jay and Lynn knew of the award was a few weeks before the event was due to happen. While neither of them was particularly pleased to hear that their show would be receiving the Mary Whitehouse stamp of approval, they thought it would be petty to protest, so they greeted the news as graciously as they could manage.

It was only a little later that they were informed that Margaret Thatcher was going to present the award, and that the ceremony would be broadcast live on BBC Radio 4's *The World at One* programme. Then, a mere two days before it was set to take place, the call came from Number Ten revealing that Thatcher would be joining Eddington and Hawthorne to perform a short sketch that, it was said, she had written.

Both writers were shocked. For Antony Jay it came as a pleasant surprise: 'I was delighted,' he later admitted. 'To actually get the accolade of the Prime Minister being keen enough on the programme to show the world that she would like to be in it! As far as I was concerned it kind of put the crown on the programme as far as public political acceptance was concerned.'[20] Jonathan Lynn, in contrast, was (in spite of his earlier fan letter to Thatcher) horrified, regarding it as nothing more than a cynical PR stunt by Number Ten's Press Office ('My first thought was: "What the hell is she doing writing sketches when she ought to be running the country – somewhat better than she's running it at the moment!"'[21]).

The two actors, who were the last of all to know, were even more alarmed and appalled. During the evening before the ceremony, Paul Eddington was resting in his dressing room at the Albery Theatre when he received a call from the BBC bearing the news that Mary Whitehouse would not be presenting the award. Having dreaded being pictured with her in public, he sank back in his chair and breathed a huge sigh of relief. He was then told that Margaret Thatcher would be doing it instead, causing him to leap up and gasp with distress. Then came the additional news that she would also be 'acting' alongside him and Nigel Hawthorne.

Now he was apoplectic. This, he shouted, was an outrage. This was going to turn a tribute to *Yes Minister* into a cheap photo opportunity for Number Ten. Worse still, after all the efforts, over the years, to keep the sitcom clear of associations with any particular political party, here would be the Leader of the Conservative Party practically pinning a big blue rosette on the show.

He immediately picked up the telephone and called his co-star, who was relaxing that evening at his home at Burnt Farm Ride in Enfield, and spluttered his indignation at this cynical imposition, telling Hawthorne that, 'as a matter of principle', he must refuse to do it.[22] Hawthorne, however, while feeling similarly shocked and queasy about the imminent event (the news of which he had, at first, taken to be a hoax), understandably questioned why Eddington expected *him* to do the dirty work, and

– in a classic bit of theatrical buck-passing – suggested that it was really Eddington's responsibility to refuse, as it was his name that came first in the credits.

Panicking, each man called Jonathan Lynn, and begged him to help extricate them from this embarrassment. Lynn, however, pointed out that neither he nor Jay had been consulted about any of this, and, as it was the actors who had been invited, it was up to the actors to say 'yea' or 'nay'.

Neither Eddington nor Hawthorne, when push came to shove, felt brave enough to snub the Prime Minister publicly, feeling that it would cause more trouble than it would be worth, and so, with great reluctance, they received their scripts the following morning, gazed aghast at the clumsy, tin-eared dialogue, bit their lips hard and then set off grimly to face their ordeal. 'A mixture of nervousness and vanity,' Eddington would say, 'eventually won the day.'[23]

It was thus at lunchtime on Friday, 20 January 1984, in the chilly crypt of All Souls Church in Langham Place, beside Broadcasting House, that *Yes Minister* met the Prime Minister. Jay and Lynn joined Eddington and Hawthorne at the event, and it was immediately obvious, upon their arrival, how expertly Bernard Ingham had choreographed the whole occasion, timing it perfectly not only for live radio coverage but also for inclusion in London's *Evening Standard*, the forthcoming television news bulletins and the following morning's papers.

Inside, as an acutely awkward-looking Eddington and Hawthorne sat clutching their scripts on a couple of fold-up wooden chairs, Margaret Thatcher (who by this time had rehearsed the sketch no fewer than twenty-three times with her staff, and had then gone over it once again in the car on the way to the location) made her rapid, pigeon-toed way over to the assembled wall of lights, microphones and cameras and announced brightly that this was 'the world premiere of *Yes, Prime Minister*'.[24] Then, taking her place beside the two actors, the sketch commenced:

> THATCHER: Ah, good morning, Jim, Sir Humphrey. Do come in and sit down. How's your wife? Is she well?
>
> HACKER: *[Puzzled]* Oh yes, fine, Prime Minister. Fine. Thank you. Yes, fine.

THATCHER:	Good. *So* pleased. I've been meaning to have a word with you for some time. I've got an idea.
HACKER:	*[Brightening visibly]* An idea, Prime Minister? Oh good.
SIR HUMPHREY:	*[Guardedly]* An *idea*, Prime Minister?
THATCHER:	Well, not really an idea. It's gone beyond that, actually. I've given it quite a bit of thought and I'm sure you, Jim, are the right man to carry it out. It's got to do with a kind of institution and you are sort of responsible for institutions, aren't you?
SIR HUMPHREY:	*[Cautiously]* Institutions, Prime Minister?
HACKER:	*[Decisively]* Oh yes, institutions fall to me. Most definitely. And you want me to set one up, I suppose?
THATCHER:	Set one up? Certainly not! I want you to get *rid* of one.
HACKER:	*[Astonished]* Get *rid* of one, Prime Minister?
THATCHER:	Yes. It's all very simple. I want you to abolish economists.
HACKER:	*[Mouth open]* Abolish *economists*, Prime Minister?
THATCHER:	Yes, abolish economists . . . and quickly.
SIR HUMPHREY:	*[Silkily]* All of them, Prime Minister?
THATCHER:	Yes, all of them. They never agree on anything. They just fill the heads of politicians with all sorts of curious notions, like the more you spend, the richer you get.
HACKER:	*[Coming around to the idea]* I see your point, Prime Minister. Can't have the nation's time wasted on curious notions, can we? No.
SIR HUMPHREY:	*[Sternly]* Minister!
THATCHER:	Quite right, Jim. Absolute waste of time. Simply got to go.
HACKER:	*[Uncertain]* Simply *got* to go?
THATCHER:	*[Motherly]* Yes, Jim. Don't worry. If it all goes wrong I shall get the blame. But if it goes right – as it will – then you'll get the credit for

redeploying a lot of underused and misapplied resources. Probably get promotion, too.

SIR HUMPHREY: *[Indignantly]* Resources? Resources, Prime Minister? We're talking about *economists*!

THATCHER: *Were*, Sir Humphrey. *Were*.

HACKER: *[Decisively]* Yes Humphrey, *were*. We're going to get rid of them.

THATCHER: Well, it's all settled, then. I'll look forward to receiving your plan for abolition soon. Tomorrow, shall we say? I'd like you to announce it before it all leaks.

HACKER: *[Brightly]* Tomorrow then, Prime Minister.

THATCHER: Yes. Well, go and sort it out. Now, Sir Humphrey . . . what did you say your *degree* was?

SIR HUMPHREY: *[Innocently]* Degree, Prime Minister?

THATCHER: *[Firmly]* Yes, Sir Humphrey, degree. *Your* degree. You have one, I take it – most Permanent Secretaries do, or perhaps two?

SIR HUMPHREY: *[Modestly]* Er, well actually, Prime Minister, a Double First.

THATCHER: Congratulations, Sir Humphrey, but what *in*?

SIR HUMPHREY: *[Weakly]* Politics . . . er . . . and, er . . . Economics.

THATCHER: *[Soothingly]* Capital, my dear Sir Humphrey, capital. You'll know *exactly* where to start!

SIR HUMPHREY: *[Bleakly]* Yes, Prime Minister.

[Exit Jim Hacker and Sir Humphrey]

More *Hi-de-Hayek* than *Yes Minister*, it was comical only in its awkwardness, with Thatcher, far from demonstrating a hitherto well-hidden sense of humour, actually looking and sounding more robotic than ever. So eerily reminiscent of Dame Edith Evans as Lady Bracknell that one half expected her to screech 'A *handbag*?' at Hacker, she slowly over-enunciated her way through her lines while Eddington and Hawthorne, pale-faced and anxious, resembled hostages being forced to record an 'all's well' message to their families.

When it was over, Thatcher acknowledged the forced applause, and then Jonathan Lynn was presented with the award. Sensing that this was the only chance he and the team would have to leave a scratch or two on the Government's gleaming PR machine, he stepped up to the microphone and said: 'I'd like to thank Mrs Mary Whitehouse for this award, and I should also like to thank Mrs Thatcher for finally taking her rightful place in the field of situation comedy.'[25]

There followed, he would say, 'a brief but audible gasp' from the assembled reporters, and then 'a volcanic eruption, one of the biggest laughs I ever got in my career'.[26] There was only one person in the room who was not laughing. It was Margaret Thatcher.

The slight failed to spoil the stunt, as the subsequent coverage was more or less what Bernard Ingham had expected: broad, fawning and favourable (it was even shown, in full, on that evening's TV news). It did, nonetheless, make the *Yes Minister* team feel a little less aggrieved about having had to endure the whole sorry affair.

Eddington and Hawthorne were then teased remorselessly about their involvement by the otherwise engaged Derek Fowlds. 'I found it hilarious,' he later recalled, 'because they were clearly *so* uncomfortable. They were both very left wing, so of course I called them up, shouting, "*Hypocrites!* You two – acting with *Maggie Thatcher*? How *dare* you?" I would have loved to have been there. I think Paul and Nigel missed me propping them up!'[27]

What would come to seem most ironic about the experience was the fact that, as everyone reflected on the encounter during the months that followed, the sense of irritation that it engendered started to reignite the old passion for the show. Paul Eddington summed up the feeling when he said: 'When we started, we set out to annoy absolutely everybody. Then Mrs Whitehouse gave us an award – presumably for the cleanest show on the air – and Mrs Thatcher insisted on making the presentation. So clearly we had failed'.[28]

That feeling, that niggling sense of frustration, planted a seed. Fail again, fail better. Maybe they did have unfinished business, after all, with *Yes Minister*.

It was around this time, serendipitously, that Bill Cotton, the BBC's newly appointed Director of Television, greatly encouraged by all of the fresh media coverage of the sitcom, decided to make Jay and Lynn a new and improved offer. 'I loved the show,' he would say, 'and as soon as I took over I made bringing it back one of my top priorities.'[29]

Inviting the two writers to a meeting in his office at Television Centre, they talked through what was desirable and what was practicable, acknowledged not only market forces but also the limited size of the Light Entertainment department's budget and eventually agreed on a compromise: Cotton would pay them the full sum they had demanded, but, in return, they would have to commit to writing sixteen more episodes, broken up into two series, and also a Christmas special.[30]

Jay and Lynn had one more condition. They agreed they could and would go back, but only by going forward. Hacker would have to be moved, and Sir Humphrey and Woolley would have to move with him. Cotton agreed, they shook hands and the show was recommissioned.

It would be, Jay and Lynn still felt, quite a big artistic gamble. They could not be sure that it would work, or that the audience would welcome it, and believe in it, so they concentrated on writing the Christmas special. If that elicited the right reaction, and everyone involved was happy, then they could look forward with confidence to creating another couple of series.

The usual in-depth research began, exploring themes and issues and individual cases. Contacts were sounded out, discreet briefings were held and the careful plotting commenced.

When they were finished, at the end of November, they brought the actors back and had them read through the script. The response was uniformly positive. It worked, everyone agreed; it was clever and coherent and funny. There was a logic to the changes, and a renewed sense of life in the characters, as well as a precision and an acidity about the wit. On every level this script represented real progress.

There was only one problem: the actors said that they wanted to make it without the presence of a studio audience. Paul Eddington, in particular, felt that some programmes in the past had been spoiled by the need for him and, especially, Nigel Hawthorne to keep pausing during very complicated exchanges in order to ensure that their lines were not drowned out by the great waves of audience laughter. It had also rattled him that some people seemed to think, completely erroneously, that the laughs were so loud they must be 'canned'. The time was right, he argued, for the show to rise above the old sitcom traditions and trust the viewers at home to respond appropriately without any audible prompts.

Jay and Lynn were having none of it. If that was what the actors wanted, they declared, then they would not be writing any more shows.

The actors, taken aback by such an uncompromising reaction, listened carefully to the writers' reasons for resisting such a proposal. They needed a studio audience, Jay and Lynn said, to undermine unfriendly attacks. Without the sound of laughter, they argued, any senior politician or bureaucrat with an axe to grind could claim that the show was just unfunny and biased political troublemaking, and thus pressurise the BBC into dropping it as soon as possible. 'Three hundred people, randomly selected, watching in the studio and laughing their heads off,' said Lynn, 'was our insurance policy.'[31]

There was also something warm and welcoming about the sound of laughter in the studio. *Yes Minister* could easily have ended up as a sort of treat for the middle-class elite, and one reason why it had avoided such a fate was the fact that it used the reassuring appeal of the traditional sitcom to attract a much broader audience. It would thus seem perverse, after dodging the line of least resistance for so long, all of a sudden to repackage the show as something self-consciously worthy and lofty. *Yes Minister* was, and would always be, a satire for the nation, not for the niche.

The actors saw the writers' point and dropped their demands just as suddenly as they had raised them. The show would go ahead as planned, and be recorded in front of a studio audience.

Produced and directed once again by Peter Whitmore, the one-hour seasonal special, entitled 'Party Games', was broadcast on Monday, 17 December 1984 at 8.30 p.m. on BBC2. Set, appropriately enough, during the run-up to Christmas in Whitehall, the story quickly reacquainted viewers with Jim Hacker, who was now not only Minister at the DAA but also his party's new Chairman.

Seated in his office, Hacker is preoccupied with two pressing matters. One concerns the huge piles of Christmas cards that Woolley has divided up depending on the importance of the recipient and the style of signature required (an onerous annual chore that the then Chancellor, Nigel Lawson, had told the writers about[32]), and the other concerns the EEC directive to standardise the 'Euro-sausage' (re-categorising all home-grown sausages as 'the emulsified high-fat offal tube'), which he knows is bound to anger and alienate British voters.

Sir Humphrey, meanwhile, has rushed off for an urgent meeting with Sir Arnold Robinson, the Cabinet Secretary. Sir Arnold confides to Sir Humphrey that he has decided to retire early in the New Year, and will soon have to let the Prime Minister know his recommendation for his successor. Sir Humphrey takes his cue and asks Sir Arnold what he plans to do in his retirement ('It's just that there might be jobs you could pick up, where you could serve the country, which your successor, whoever he might be, could put your way – er, persuade you to undertake . . .'). Sir Arnold mentions a few ideas – the chairmanship of the Opera House Trust, the Chancellorship of Oxford, the Deputy Chairmanship of the Bank of England, Head of the Security Commission, the Presidency of the Anglo-Caribbean Association – while Sir Humphrey casually takes a few notes. 'Well,' says Sir Humphrey, 'I'm sure that any successor worth his salt would be able to arrange these, Arnold.' After being further reassured that such a successor – 'the *right* successor' – would also ensure that the odd past error of judgement was kept under wraps, Sir Arnold assures Sir Humphrey that his name is now heading his one-name list of candidates.

Back in Hacker's office, Sir Humphrey breaks the news to his Minister:

> The relationship, which I might tentatively venture to aver has
> been not without some degree of reciprocal utility and perhaps
> even occasional gratification, is approaching a point of irreversible
> bifurcation, and, to be brief, is in the propinquity of its ultimate
> regrettable termination.

Hacker, once he thinks he has deciphered this announcement, fears that Sir Humphrey must have some kind of terrible disease, until Sir Humphrey assures him that they will still be seeing each other regularly, 'once a week at least'. Upon realising that he is now in the presence of the Cabinet Secretary designate, Hacker is both relieved and fearful, noting not only that the Prime Minister will have to suffer what he has been suffering, but also that Sir Humphrey, ominously, will soon be advising the PM on the respective merits of his various Ministers.

The news is made public at the staff Christmas drinks party, where a well-oiled Hacker toasts his old tormentor's future. Driving home very slowly, he is stopped by the police, who advise him to let his wife take over the wheel. The following day he is chastised by Sir Humphrey, in his new capacity as Cabinet Secretary, for being involved in such an incident. Fortunately for Hacker, however, the Home Secretary has also been caught driving while drunk, which is all the more embarrassing seeing as he is responsible for the latest 'Don't Drink and Drive' campaign, and, unlike Hacker's error of judgement, the misdemeanour has made the front page of the papers.

Soon after, it is announced that the Prime Minister is going to retire early in the New Year. Hacker, putting two and two together, concludes that the PM has been hanging on until he is sure that the now disgraced Home Secretary, whom he has always disliked, will not have a chance of succeeding him.

When asked by his wife whom he thinks are the main candidates to take over, he replies that they will probably be Eric, the current Chancellor, or Duncan, the Foreign Secretary. Mulling over their respective prospects, he is torn as to which one he should support. 'If I support Eric and Duncan gets it, well, that's it. And if I support Duncan and Eric gets it, well, that's it, too.' Annie suggests that it might be best if he supports neither of them. 'Then whichever of them gets it,' he protests, 'that's it!'

When pressed, he makes a typical Hackeresque decision. He will be backing 'Duncan . . . Or Eric'.

Both candidates proceed to solicit his support. Eric confides that, if elected, he will make Jim Foreign Secretary. Duncan, on the other hand, hints that, if *he* is elected, Jim will be made the next Chancellor. He duly pledges his support to each of them.

Sir Humphrey and Sir Arnold, meanwhile, have also been running the rule over Eric and Duncan's chances, and both candidates have come up wanting. 'It's like asking which lunatic should run the asylum,' mutters Sir Arnold. 'The trouble is,' moans Sir Humphrey, 'they're both interventionists. They both have foolish notions about running the country themselves if they become Prime Minister.' Another danger is that each of them represents an internal faction, so the triumph of either will soon divide the Government.

What is needed, the two grandees agree, is a compromise candidate: someone who is 'malleable . . . flexible . . . likeable . . . no firm opinions . . . no bright ideas . . . not intellectually committed . . . without the strength of purpose to change anything . . . someone who you know can be manipulated, er, "professionally guided", leaving the business of government in the hands of the experts . . .'. Both Sir Humphrey and Sir Arnold, after reflecting separately on such a portfolio of personal qualities, come to the same conclusion, and start sniggering to themselves.

When Woolley arrives and joins them, they cannot resist sounding him out about their new plan:

SIR HUMPHREY: What would you say to your present master as the next Prime Minister?

WOOLLEY: *[Dumbfounded]* The *Minister*?

SIR HUMPHREY: Yes.

WOOLLEY: *Mr Hacker*?

SIR HUMPHREY: Yes.

WOOLLEY: As *Prime Minister*?

SIR HUMPHREY: Yes.

[Woolley pulls back a shirt cuff and checks his watch]

SIR HUMPHREY: Are you in a hurry?

WOOLLEY: Er, no. I'm just checking to see it wasn't April the First.

SIR ARNOLD: Are you suggesting that your Minister is not up to the job of Prime Minister?

WOOLLEY: Oh, *no*, Sir Arnold. It's not for me to, ah, well, I mean, of course I'm sure he's, er . . . oh *gosh*!

SIR ARNOLD: There is a considerable body of opinion that can see many *advantages* in the appointment.

SIR HUMPHREY: For Britain.

SIR ARNOLD: For *Britain*.

WOOLLEY: Er, yes, well . . . er, yes . . .

SIR HUMPHREY: So we trust you to ensure that your Minister does nothing *incisive*, or *divisive*, over the next few weeks?

SIR ARNOLD: Avoids anything *controversial*.

SIR HUMPHREY: Expresses no firm opinion about anything at all. Now, is that quite clear?

WOOLLEY: Er, yes, well, I think that's probably what he was
             planning to do anyway.

It is agreed that the two main candidates will have to step aside for
such a compromise figure to emerge as the new favourite, but Sir Arnold
is confident that, once Sir Humphrey has taken a look at their MI5 files,
such an occurrence will start to seem surprisingly likely. Sure enough,
there is enough dirt in there to cause Sir Humphrey to push ahead with
the plan.

Summoning Hacker to the Chief Whip's office, Sir Humphrey proceeds to manoeuvre him into position:

SIR HUMPHREY: There are certain items of confidential
                 information which, whilst in theory might
                 be susceptible to innocent interpretation, do
                 nevertheless contain a sufficient element of,
                 shall we say, ambiguity, so that were they to be
                 presented in a less than generous manner to an
                 uncharitable mind, they might be a source of
                 considerable embarrassment, even conceivably a
                 hazard, were they to impinge on the deliberations
                 of an office of more than usual sensitivity.

HACKER: I'm *sorry*?

CHIEF WHIP: He is talking about security question marks!

HACKER: *Security*? What do you mean?

CHIEF WHIP: Secrets.

HACKER: Yes, I know what *security* means! But what do
                 you *mean*?

CHIEF WHIP: *I'm* not allowed to know.

HACKER: Why not??

CHIEF WHIP: Security.

SIR HUMPHREY: So you see, Minister, since in the PM's absence
                 you are deputising on Party matters, perhaps I
                 can show you this . . .

[He hands Hacker a file]

SIR HUMPHREY: It's the security file on the Chancellor of the
                 Exchequer . . .

Hacker, reaching hurriedly for his glasses, tries hard not to seem excited as
he scans the lurid contents: 'The dirty old . . . You wouldn't have thought he'd
have the *time*, would you?!' Sir Humphrey then hands Hacker the security
file on the Foreign Secretary. 'Astounding!' gasps the Minister. Prodded by
the Chief Whip into the realisation that all of these scandals waiting to happen must rule both figures out of the running for the top job in Government,
Hacker agrees that there is an urgent need to find another candidate – one
who is 'sound, likeable, flexible, normal, solvent and acceptable to both
wings of the Party'. Sir Humphrey cannot resist adding one more thing to
this list: 'And someone who understands how to take *advice*, Minister'.

Hacker, struggling to conceal his own ambition, is shaken and excited
when both the Chief Whip and Sir Humphrey suggest that he puts himself up for the position. Slowly shedding his affectation of modesty like
an unusually coy cabaret artiste, he eventually accepts the invitation, and
asks for some advice:

HACKER: Wouldn't it be enough to start campaigning, just
               let people know that I want the job?
CHIEF WHIP: Quite the reverse, I think. Better to let people
               know you *don't* want it.
HACKER: Would *that* be enough?
SIR HUMPHREY: Well, as long as you tell *everybody* you don't want it, yes.
CHIEF WHIP: Leave the campaigning to me. If anybody asks you,
               simply say you have no ambitions in that direction.
HACKER: Yes, of course, but supposing somebody was to
               say, 'Does that mean you refuse to stand?' You
               know how these media people try to trap you.
SIR HUMPHREY: Well, Minister, it's not my place, but on previous
               occasions the generally acceptable answer has
               been: 'While one does not *seek* the office, one
               has *pledged* oneself to the service of one's *country*,
               and if one's friends were to *persuade* one that
               that was the best way one could *serve*, one *might*

reluctantly have to accept the responsibility whatever one's own private wishes might be'.

HACKER: *[Hurriedly scribbling in his notebook]* '. . . private wishes might be'. Yes, I think I've got that!

He is then told that there are two more things for him to do. First, he needs, as Party Chairman, to advise Eric ('the pervert') and Duncan ('the swindler') privately to stand down, and then he needs to stage-manage some kind of sudden public success to raise his profile.

The first task is discharged with remarkably little fuss, once Hacker has resolved to get his hands nice and dirty again. Rather than be seen to want to ruin his two colleagues, he convinces them both, discreetly, that he is desperate to save them from scandal. Grateful for his protection, they duly drop out of the race.

Hacker is less confident about completing the other task satisfactorily, as he complains that he is already 'up to my neck in the Euro-sausage' and is running out of time. It is at this point that Sir Humphrey, once again, arrives, Jeeves-like, to find a swift solution.

He arranges for Hacker to have a word – or rather to sit quietly while *he* has a word – with the European Commissioner about 'our little sausage problem'. It does not take long for Sir Humphrey to convince the Commissioner, in the interests of harmony, to rename the Euro-sausage 'the British sausage' – thus handing Hacker his timely public triumph.

All of the remaining pieces of the plot fall neatly into place, and The Rt Hon. James Hacker ends up in Sir Humphrey's office, waiting anxiously for the news that he has been elected unopposed as the new leader of his party. With Woolley eagerly accepting his invitation to remain his Principal Private Secretary ('Gosh!'), all that is left is for Hacker to receive confirmation of the internal election result. When the telephone finally rings, a poker-faced Sir Humphrey takes the call and then, as the agitated Hacker points at himself hopefully and asks, 'Is it . . .??' Sir Humphrey replies calmly: 'Yes . . . Prime Minister.'

For an instant, Hacker looks astonished, and then, his expression suddenly becalmed, he slowly slides his right hand inside his jacket in the manner of Napoleon. He has won. He has made it to Number Ten.

Jay and Lynn had made it, too. They had gone back and moved on.

'Party Games', watched by 8.2 million viewers (BBC2's biggest audience of the Christmas period),[33] was an unqualified triumph. Without losing any of its trademark accuracy, comic elegance or keen intelligence, and while staying true to the characters and the context, the extended special had simultaneously reinvigorated the old show and brought about its reinvention.

Yes Minister had come to a natural conclusion. *Yes Prime Minister* was now set to take its place.

PART THREE

*The greatest teacher of all in Parliament, the head-master of the nation,
the great elevator of the country – so far as Parliament elevates it – must be the
Prime Minister; he has an influence, an authority, a facility in giving a great tone to
discussion, or a mean tone, which no other man has.*
Walter Bagehot

*Our most obvious defects spring from the constitutional position of Civil Servants.
They are at all times answerable to some Minister who will get the praise
and blame for what they do, and this determines many of their
actions and reactions.*
Sir Edward Bridges

9

Yes, Prime Minister

What do we do now?

There was something rather apt about Jay and Lynn having to make Jim Hacker seem like a real Prime Minister. After all, real-life politicians had been trying to seem like a real Prime Minister ever since the latter part of the eighteenth century.

Far from having been born in broad daylight and framed by a clear constitutional definition, the role had emerged through the murkiness of Parliamentary convention, and only then as a term of derogation rather than approbation. Sir Robert Walpole, who was the first in a succession of First Lords of the Treasury to be associated with the term, never recognised it as a title, let alone embraced it as an office, and even when, eventually, the title did start being treated as if it was something positive and semi-official, no one really bothered to outline the proper parameters of its powers.[1]

In stark contrast, then, to the American Presidency, which has always been rooted in rules and comes to each incumbent with the equivalent of a set of detailed stage directions, the British Premiership has only been animated through a volatile mixture of imitation, imagination and improvisation. The consequence has been that all modern Prime Ministers have been left to re-envision the role according to their own personal strengths and political circumstances. From Disraeli to Cameron, from Churchill to Thatcher, from Lloyd George to Blair, the only reliable test of the legitimacy of the interpretation has been whether or not they can get away with it.

Antony Jay knew all of this very well indeed, having immersed himself in the biographies of British leaders during his preparation for the mid-1970s series *A Prime Minister on Prime Ministers*. He had also picked up the odd tip from the 'star' of that series, Harold Wilson himself ('I remember one occasion [in 'Party Games']. We had Jim ask if he wanted to be Prime Minister, and had him reply, "I have no ambitions in that direction, but I suppose if my colleagues pressed me I might have to consent." Harold said that was the correct reply'[2]). Jay was thus eminently well placed and primed to judge how plausible, or not, it would be to elevate Jim Hacker to this ill-defined but historically exalted position.

'How on earth could we make him Prime Minister?' he had asked out loud as he and Lynn were discussing the switch. 'You know, he's such a bumbling fool.' He already knew, however, how to answer such a question: 'Well, it's not *impossible* for bumbling fools to be Prime Minister, if the right things happen . . .'[3]

While the number of bona fide bumbling fools to have actually presided from within Number Ten remains a matter of some contention, Jay certainly knew of countless stories in which even quite sensible leaders had sometimes appeared, behind that big black door, as fairly bumbling, and very human, figures. Thanks to the private input of Bernard Donoughue, for example, he had assimilated numerous additional anecdotes about Harold Wilson, during his final term in power, and James Callaghan, during his only term in power, in which they seemed to suffer, Hacker-style, from various degrees of distress, despair and befuddlement.

There were even a few first-hand admissions to be found in past Prime Ministerial memoirs. Alec Douglas-Home had famously claimed that he required the use of a box of matches to help him 'simplify' the sums that were cited in important economic documents, and also quoted a memorably curt conversation he had with a make-up artist to explain why he had never mastered the medium of television:

> Q. Can you not make me look better than I do on television?
> A. No.
> Q. Why not?
> A. Because you have a head like a skull.
> Q. Does not everyone have a head like a skull?
> A. No.[4]

The more Jay and Lynn thought about it, the less odd it seemed for them to picture Jim Hacker ensconced inside Number Ten. He would probably not even have been the worst, they reasoned, and so they set about making it happen.

Before production began on 'Party Games', the two writers met Paul Eddington in the BBC Club at Television Centre and broke the news to him about his character's imminent elevation. 'We said, "You're going to be Prime Minister in the next series",' Lynn would recall, 'and you could see him change before our very eyes.'[5] The head tilted slightly to one side, the eyebrows arched elegantly and the nose rose just a fraction higher than normal, as Eddington contemplated playing a person deemed primus inter pares.

They also told Nigel Hawthorne about his own character's promotion to Cabinet Secretary, but he realised that it would have little impact on Sir Humphrey other than providing him with the licence to seem even more supercilious than before. While a politician is more like an actor in rep, bouncing breathlessly from one characterisation to the next as he or she tries to keep impressing the audience while climbing up the greasy pole, the civil servant is more like an actor in a high-class version of a soap, never really changing but slowly maturing like (as Sir Humphrey would put it) 'an old port' or (as Hacker would put it) 'Grimsby'.[6]

There would still be the same basic dynamic between Sir Humphrey and Hacker, as the tension between Number Ten and the Cabinet Office next door was like that between a Minister and his or her Department, but now writ large. There was, for example, the same contrast in terms of longevity: at the time the first series of *Yes, Prime Minister* was being written, there had been just six Cabinet Secretaries (with an average of 11.2 years each in office) since Sir Maurice Hankey became the first person to hold the position back in 1916, whereas, during the same period of time, there had been fourteen different Prime Ministers (with an average shelf life, per term, of a little over three years each).[7]

There was also the same disparity between them in terms of the power that comes from knowledge. The Cabinet Secretary, unlike the Prime Minister, is allowed to see all the papers of previous governments, and so, in this sense, he will always have his political counterpart at a significant disadvantage. By sitting next to each successive Prime Minister at all of the meetings of the Cabinet and its major subsidiary committees, and acting as his or her chief policy adviser, editor and father confessor, he also accumulates an incomparable fund of insights into what makes each leader tick, triumph, trip up and tumble.

With Hacker relocated to Number Ten, therefore, and Sir Humphrey to 70 Whitehall, connected to each other via the famous internal corridor, the same kind of clashes could take place as before, only now the stakes would be so much higher. Their relationship, as a result, was set to evolve into something that seemed more intense and intertwined than ever.

The people who were most excited about all the changes were actually the two writers themselves, because they could now look down from the Prime Minister's lofty perch and survey the entire political landscape, swooping whenever and wherever they saw something that could be captured and consumed in a comedy plot. 'Defence, foreign policy and other things that were way out of Jim Hacker's area of government,' Lynn later remarked, 'these were the subjects we hadn't [until now] been able to touch.'[8]

It was not just an opportunity for them to explore a wider range of issues. It was also a chance for them to mirror the Prime Minister's broader concerns, and more dogged commitments, and run certain themes from one episode to the next. With so many Prime Ministers coming to office complete with a ready-made 'Big Idea' (always aimed at making their name but usually doomed to fail) tucked under their arm, the writers wanted to show what happened to that bold ambition from one episode to the next.

They also recognised that it would do the new version of the show no harm now that, thanks mainly to Margaret Thatcher's increasingly Führerprinzip interpretation of what a Prime Minister should be, the very nature of the institution itself was currently the subject of regular debate. Ever since overseeing Britain's role in the Falklands War in 1982, followed not entirely coincidentally by her landslide victory in the General Election of 1983 (the most decisive election triumph since 1945[9]), Thatcher's ever-confident style of leadership had been growing progressively autocratic and imperial, symbolised by her habit of referring to herself as 'we' and her obsession with ascertaining whether or not certain people were 'one of us'. As one disaffected former Cabinet Minister after another started making public their doubts about her managerial skills (such as the newly sacked Francis Pym's complaint that 'any dissent, or even admittance of doubt, is [treated as] treachery and treason'[10]), and even one of her distinguished Conservative predecessors in Number Ten, Harold Macmillan, was moved to describe her as a 'brilliant tyrant',[11] the implicit contrast with the cautious and consensually minded Hacker would add another dimension to the satire.

The writers, however, remained just as resistant as they had ever been to the temptation to make the individual episodes appear overtly timely and topical, because, as they always insisted, far less changed in politics than any particular generation of politicians preferred to admit. When they were planning the first set of stories for *Yes, Prime Minister*, therefore, they sought out that day's edition of the *Daily Telegraph*, placed it alongside one published on the same day and date from thirty years before, and compared the political stories on each of the two front pages. It came as no surprise to either writer that they were, in essence, more or less identical.

Jonathan Lynn summarised the similarities: 'Should we or shouldn't we be in Europe? Why don't we trust the French, or like the Germans (or vice versa)? Is the Franco-German alliance dominating Europe at our expense? Why should we give so much money to the Common Agricultural Policy, just to support French farmers? How will Europe affect our special relationship with America? What do we do about an impending war in the Middle East? What about the environment? Is there a risk of inflation/deflation (delete where applicable)? Is the NHS getting even worse and are the waiting lists getting longer? Why are house prices rising again? What's wrong with the Honours list? How do we get defence spending under control? Why don't we have a national transport policy?'[12]

Even the respective inside pages, with their small talk of such things as leak inquiries, bureaucratic inertia, potential leadership challenges, party conferences, diplomatic issues and local government concerns seemed remarkably alike. The names might have changed and the prices inflated, but otherwise the political news of the mid-1980s looked basically the same as that of the mid-1950s.

The conclusion was that 'topicality' mattered far less than believable characters, enduring themes and the general truths that emerged from the attention to particular details. *Yes, Prime Minister*, therefore, would not strive to be a satirical snapshot of the Thatcher years, but rather would aim, just like *Yes Minister* had done before it, to engage with the broad and basic system through which any particular figure, from any point in the modern era, came and went and eventually disappeared.

The research thus focused once again on linking together a variety of anecdotes and case studies in order to discern the most significant patterns and principles. Marcia Falkender and Bernard Donoughue remained available for consultation, and the writers also now had access to a wider than ever range of other well-placed Westminster and Whitehall sources, as well as all of the usual archives and libraries. Their conversations now revolved around figures (past and present) at the very top of the political and bureaucratic hierarchies, and, as a consequence, they were conducted even more discreetly than before, but the insights were just as forthcoming. Gradually, as Jay and Lynn sifted through all of the fascinating details, a series of stories started to appear.

For all of the previous instances when Jay, especially, had drawn on ideas that were also associated with the intellectual hinterland of the Thatcher Government, both of the writers (perhaps still somewhat stung by the recent attempt by Number Ten to co-opt the sitcom for the purposes of political publicity) were more determined than ever to cause Conservatives to feel just as bruised as Liberals or Labourites by their show's satirical blows: 'I would consider *Yes, Prime Minister* to be much less Thatcherite,' Jonathan Lynn would later claim, 'because [. . .] as time wore on much of what we wrote was critical of the Conservative Government. Moreover, I should stress that whether we were pro- or anti-Thatcherite is not significant. The two series [*Yes Minister* and *Yes, Prime Minister*] were essentially about the relationship between politicians and civil servants, and that focus [. . .] never changed.'[13]

If these new shows did contain a conscious message, it concerned, as Lynn observed, a critique of the current claims that the Civil Service was being 'tamed' by the 'tough' Conservative Government:

> Towards the end of the 1980s it became an accepted truth –
> it was in all the newspapers, which should make one deeply
> suspicious of its accuracy – that Margaret Thatcher had been
> successful in politicising the Civil Service; that the Civil Service
> was now right wing and Tory; and that it represented the

Conservative Government. Why did the Civil Service never deny that it had become politicised by Thatcher? The answer is: why should it? The senior members of the Civil Service want the Government and the media to think that they are house-trained, compliant and under Government control: that is the joke of the series. It is much easier for a Civil Service department to pursue its own agenda if everyone thinks it is pursing the Government's agenda.[14]

Jay and Lynn thus believed that, contrary to the many current popular reports and editorials, the view of the system that had been summarised back in 1973 by the MP Nicholas Ridley, and reaffirmed some time later by the rebellious bureaucrat Leslie Chapman, remained, in essence, as true in the mid-1980s as it had been many years before. As Ridley had written:

> The British Civil Service is sometimes compared to a fly-wheel;
> to slow it down or speed it up immense effort is necessary; it
> has a vast inbuilt momentum of its own. Rather, I think, it is
> like an enormous steel spring; it can be pulled out of its natural
> position by great exertion but it eventually pulls you back by
> its sheer persistence. Thus, towards the middle and end years
> of each government some of the same policies begin to appear
> whatever the reforming, even crusading nature of the incoming
> government. Undermined by the system, exhausted by the
> workload, battered by events, they relax their pull upon the
> spring and are pulled back, themselves, to the position the Civil
> Service always wanted.[15]

The point was not to depict this phenomenon by siding systematically with either Hacker or Sir Humphrey, because, as Antony Jay emphasised at the time, both of them were symptoms rather than causes of the malaise at the heart of British government. 'The reason there isn't any malice in the series [. . .] is that we think if we were in the position of either of them, as the system created them, we would be doing pretty well the sort of things that they do. When you get Jim Hacker in a spot, knowing what you do about the pressures on him and what his real motives are – and we admit he is a pretty power-seeking, achievement-oriented politician, but nevertheless not off the end of the spectrum – we think, well, what would *we* do? And Sir Humphrey the same: what would you do if this Minister came along with this lunatic idea?'[16]

It was not, in truth, the most morally demanding or rigorous of perspectives. After all, if Jay and Lynn's own Video Arts training films had been so fatalistic and indulgent (and they were partly inspired by the fact that so much traditional corporate and commercial training *was* so fatalistic and indulgent) they would never have made a difference, and such a deterministic view could surely be used as an all-purpose, off-the-peg excuse for any and every weak-willed and/or cynical political or bureaucratic official around (as Disraeli put it, 'Circumstances are beyond the control of man; but his conduct is in his own power'[17]).

It was certainly, nonetheless, a well-meaning and balanced approach which would at least help to keep the main critical focus, as in the previous shows, on the process as a whole. The real, trapped relationship between Prime Minister and Cabinet Secretary would be mirrored by the fictional one between Hacker and Sir Humphrey.

All of this, Jay and Lynn were confident, would be clear and accessible so long as the scripts covered the right range of topics with the right degree of accuracy. The satire should not be imposed on the stories; it should emerge quite naturally from out of the truth of the situations.

It was not just the writers, however, who needed to refresh their approach to engage with the change from *Yes Minister* to *Yes, Prime Minister*. The team responsible for the sets (led by Valerie Warrender, an experienced and very versatile production designer who had previously worked on programmes ranging from *Monty Python's Flying Circus* to *Doctor Who*) also needed to create a new physical environment for Hacker and Sir Humphrey, and in this they too showed an admirable attention to detail.

They were helped in this ambition by no less a figure than Sir Robin Butler, Margaret Thatcher's Principal Private Secretary, who (having been authorised by the Prime Minister to do so, and reassured by Bernard Donoughue that they could be trusted) took the team on a guided tour of 10 Downing Street, explaining who did what and who sat where as they moved through the building. Valerie Warrender would remember the occasion vividly:

This was when Mrs Thatcher was not in residence. Although we were permitted to take notes about the layouts and décor details, photography was forbidden. It was possible to visit the Cabinet Room, the Cabinet Office, the Private Office of the Prime Minister, the Pillared Room, the Small Dining Room, the Entrance Hall, the connecting corridors and the White Drawing Room. The Cabinet Room was of particular interest because of the large lozenge-shaped table, the top covered with brown felt to protect the polished surface and the leather blotters laid in front of each chair ready for the meetings. One of the most impressive interiors was the Pillared Room with the large paintings, huge flower displays echoing the rich colour of the wallpaper and a Tabriz carpet. In the studio the carpet was actually a painted replica on scenic canvas.[18]

The only demand that came from Downing Street was that, in return for this privileged access, the team would slightly alter the internal geography of the building to comply with security concerns. With this agreement in place, the work began on bringing Whitehall to White City.

The extremely detailed notes and sketches that had been taken during the tour formed the basis of the designs, but these were further enhanced, where needed, with descriptions from special reference books, historic portraits and film stills. The whole construction process was an unusually elaborate practical enterprise – 'Obviously some of the sets were large,' Valerie Warrender would recall, 'so the production was set in two adjacent studios at TV Centre with the audience in one of them'[19] – but, eventually, everything was in place.

The result was that the finished sets were actually far closer to the reality than most outsiders would ever realise. Indeed, when Paul Eddington first ventured onto the floor of what now passed as the Cabinet Room, he could not quite believe how precisely the set reflected the real thing. Brian Jones, the floor manager, came over to him and proudly held up a photograph of the actual room, and Eddington, innocently, looked at it, assuming it was merely an assemblage aide-memoire for the production team, and said, 'Yes, I know, I'm standing in it!' 'No, no,' replied Jones. 'This is a picture of the *real* one.'[20]

Eddington was astonished. Glancing backwards and forwards between the photograph and the set, he was open-mouthed in admiration for what the team had done. 'I went round examining the ornaments, the design of the chairs, the moulding round the fireplace and so on. It was hardly distinguishable from the original, and this was true of all the interiors: the Permanent Secretary's office, the Cabinet Secretary's, the Whips' and so on. Only two things were deliberately inaccurate: the views out of the windows and the labels on the doors.'[21]

Even Sir Robin Butler himself, when he saw the reproduction, was taken aback by the accuracy, to the extent that, when Nigel Hawthorne later had occasion to visit him in the real Cabinet Room (to record a brief interview for the BBC radio show *Down Your Way*[22]), he felt distinctly disoriented, wondering who was visiting whom. 'I had an identity crisis,' he would recall. 'I wasn't really quite sure whether he was the real thing or I was!'[23]

The same urge to verisimilitude informed the costume designs by Richard Winter, with plenty of research done on everything from the appropriate weight of cloth to the style of design for the suits that the actors were to wear. In an environment in which everyone, politicians and bureaucrats alike, would be formally suited and booted, it would have to be the small details – such as Sir Humphrey's darker and more classically tailored two-button woollen suits adorned with college- or club-crested ties (sporting tasteful half-Windsor knots), or Hacker's slightly lighter, slightly flashier, more 'lived-in' sets of clothes (including a few 'trying too hard' double-breasted numbers, with a semiotically confused selection of schoolboy knotted ties), and Woolley's plainer, less noteworthy choices – that highlighted the differences in the characters.

Sir Humphrey, it was reasoned, was an extremely self-assured man with traditional tastes whose job kept him based mainly in one particular place and well out of the public eye, and so his wardrobe would be tasteful, predictable and reserved (while reflecting, very subtly, the recent increase in his salary), whereas Hacker, who was much more insecure and eager to please and impress, would be constantly rushing between the theatre of the House of Commons, the forensic stare and glare of the television studios and the businesslike milieu of Number Ten, and so he would require a wider and more eclectic range of clothes, reflecting the need of a Prime Minister to be part authority figure, part working politician, part celebrity and part (in a very awkward and unwilling way) national fashion icon. Woolley, meanwhile, would simply need to remain smart but bland, ensuring that he could step into and out of the background as each scene required.

Such care, on all levels, was encouraged by Sydney Lotterby, who, in the autumn of 1985, was finally free to return to the show as producer/director. Two of his other most time-consuming commitments, the very popular sitcoms *Ever Decreasing Circles* and *Open All Hours*, had now finished (the former in 1984 and the latter in 1985), while a new project, another sitcom called *Brush Strokes*, would not be ready for broadcast until the autumn of 1986, so he was able to immerse himself in the planning of *Yes, Prime Minister*.

His first task was to cast the two new characters, who would, every now and then, be seen to be assisting Prime Minister Hacker. The first was his new Press Secretary, Malcolm Warren, and the second was his new political adviser, Dorothy Wainwright.

Jay and Lynn felt the time was right to introduce a Press Secretary partly because such a figure had been lurking around the position of Prime Minister for years (with the hard-boiled, sharp-tongued, fiercely loyal ex-tabloid hack Joe Haines, who served Harold Wilson in that capacity from 1969 to 1976, setting the standard for subsequent practitioners), and partly because the incumbent, Bernard Ingham, had made the role even more of a talking point.

Although the term 'spin doctor' was still not quite in common parlance at the time, the intimidatingly aggressive Ingham, through his increasingly notorious 'off the record' press lobby briefings (which, reported only as emanating from 'Whitehall sources' or 'sources close to the Prime Minister', tended to undermine anyone in the Cabinet whom Margaret Thatcher happened to regard at the time as 'not one of us'[24]) and his quick and forceful 'corrections' of potentially embarrassing facts, figures or phrases, was certainly one of the people who helped inspire the use of the term. A former Labour Party candidate, he was a career civil servant who (at least in the eyes of many outsiders) had now seemingly 'gone native' and committed himself to the Tory – or more accurately the Thatcher – cause. As the parliamentary sketchwriter Simon Hoggart put it: 'Bernard was Margaret Thatcher when being Margaret Thatcher 24/7 was just too much for her.'[25]

The Press Secretary in *Yes, Prime Minister* – so as to help keep a healthy distance between the Hacker and Thatcher Governments – would be as equable and inoffensive as Ingham was belligerent and brusque, thus, ironically, conforming much more to the traditional template of the job than any of the latest real-life practitioners had done. Warren would be more obviously an ordinary civil servant rather than a special political henchman, exuding a beige-like personality that suggested he was more likely to place a friendly arm around a troublesome journalist than hold a knife to their throat.

Lotterby chose Barry Stanton for the role. A regular small-screen presence since the early 1960s, Stanton had appeared in most of the popular police and crime shows of the past couple of decades, dividing his time fairly evenly between playing down-to-earth coppers and run-of-the-mill thieves, but Lotterby had also liked his more recent performances in the John Esmonde/Bob Larbey sitcom *Now and Then* (which ran for two series between 1983 and 1984), in which he had played 'Uncle Gordon', the avuncular owner of a surgical appliances shop.

The on-screen blandness of the character would not give Stanton any real chance to shine, but Lotterby trusted him to flesh it out and make the figure seem believable. Resembling a pleasantly attentive GP, the bearded, rounded Stanton's Malcolm Warren would serve Hacker dutifully and with quiet efficiency, while leaving all of the dark arts to Sir Humphrey.

Hacker's new political adviser, on the other hand, was set to be a much stronger and more significant sort of character. The real-life Prime Minister was now using several informal advisers to strengthen her independence from, and power over, her Ministers, with the likes of Tim Bell (an advertising and PR executive who not only masterminded successive Conservative election campaigns but also coached the leader on how best to alter and control her image) and Alan Walters (an economist who helped her challenge the authority of more than one Chancellor of the Exchequer) rattling Cabinet cages.

By giving Hacker his own special adviser, in the form of Dorothy Wainwright, the writers were therefore not only reflecting a genuine trend but also ensuring that the intellectual battle between the Prime Minister and his Cabinet Secretary would not be too imbalanced in favour of the latter. Rather than make it seem as though Hacker had suddenly acquired a better brain and greater guile, they gave him some much-needed expert backup.

Building on the impact that Eleanor Bron's bright female character, Sarah Harrison, had made at the start of the third series of *Yes Minister*, Dorothy Wainwright would provide *Yes, Prime Minister* with a welcome new female regular, unsettling the men on both sides of the Whitehall–Westminster divide with her willingness to pit her wits against them. Cleverly adding the pressure of gender to the dynamic of the show without inviting direct comparisons with Margaret Thatcher, she was probably, aside from the obvious elevations, the shrewdest revision of the new series.

Sydney Lotterby deliberated for a while on the possible options for the role, but eventually decided on Deborah Norton to play the part. Strongly and aptly reminiscent of a young Marcia Falkender (and especially of Bernard Donoughue's version of a young Marcia Falkender), with piercing eyes and a powerful voice, she had worked steadily on the stage and in television for more than fifteen years, and was well suited to animating a part that involved snapping out lines with upper-middle-class self-assurance while maintaining a suitably haughty expression.

With these two castings in place, the rest of the preparations continued at a rapid pace. More illustrations were commissioned from Gerald Scarfe for the opening title sequence, with special story-themed sketches added to introduce each new episode; the preferred studios were booked (once again, usually TC4 or sometimes TC8); and the stars were briefed as to the schedule for rehearsing, location shooting and recordings.

Always someone who relished working closely with the best actors, Sydney Lotterby was especially delighted to resume his association with Eddington, Hawthorne and Fowlds when rehearsals began in the last few weeks of the year, and the actors, in turn, were happy to be reunited with him. 'It felt so right to have him back,' Derek Fowlds would say of Lotterby. 'He'd started it all off, after the pilot, with the series proper. Peter Whitmore had come in and taken over the reins for a while, and he was a delightful man, too, but I think you always like to go back to the beginning if you can. We always had a soft spot for Syd. He was part of the family.'[26] With everyone greatly impressed both with how the scripts had been written and how the staging was progressing, the rehearsal sessions were very positive and high-spirited occasions, with Lotterby ensuring that every minute was put to good use.

As he looked forward to recording the episodes, there was really only one thing that caused him concern. Paul Eddington seemed to be in increasingly poor health.

Eddington had been burdened by health problems of varying degrees of severity for most of his life. He had suffered during his early teens from tuberculosis, which necessitated his spending six months away from school and left him anxious about contracting any further infections. Although he eventually recovered fully and went on to establish himself as an actor, he started experiencing problems again in his early thirties, when he was diagnosed as suffering from ankylosing spondylitis, a progressively painful and debilitating type of chronic arthritis that affects parts of the spine including bones, muscles and ligaments. The treatment that he was obliged to undergo for this affliction caused occasional bouts of radiation sickness. Then he started suffering from ulcerative colitis, as well as a skin condition that would soon be discovered to be a rare form of cancer (Mycosis fungoides, a type of cutaneous T-cell lymphoma).

He bore all of these many problems privately and quietly with remarkable fortitude, good humour and grace, but, inevitably, they placed a great physical (and mental) strain on him as, driven on by the ordinary actor's paranoia about the bookings one day drying up, he continued to work hard not only on one production after another but also, sometimes, on more than one project at a time. During the preparations for *Yes, Prime Minister*, for instance, he continued appearing onstage in a production of Tom Stoppard's *Jumpers* at the Aldwych, as well as working on numerous voiceovers, radio projects and commercials, and there were occasions when he arrived at the North Acton rehearsal rooms feeling very drained and uncomfortable.

He decided, as a consequence, to put in a request to the BBC for a chauffeured car to transport him to and from rehearsals, but, much to his and his friends' irritation, the request was rejected. It seems that the relevant people at the BBC, who do not appear to have been aware of the extent of Eddington's health problems, reasoned that agreeing to such an arrangement would create a precedent that, potentially, would lead to the Corporation being bombarded by star demands for similar privileges.

It angered Eddington, and did not go down well with his colleagues (Jonathan Lynn would complain that it was 'cheap' and 'ungenerous', and, responding to the point about creating a precedent, he reminded people of the classic *Yes Minister* line: 'You mean, you can't do the right thing now because it might mean you have to do the right thing next time?'[27]), but the actor accepted it and carried on stoically with the work.

Indeed, it energised him to come back as Hacker. From starting out as the actor most sceptical of the show's potential, he was now as proud as anyone about what it had achieved, not only at home but also abroad (it had recently been sold to its forty-fifth country, China, where, aptly enough, it was set to be dubbed into Mandarin[28]), and was fully committed to its reinvention. Surrounded by his fellow actors and well looked after by Lotterby (as well as the writers, who made sure that he was seated in as many scenes as possible), he loved playing Hacker again, and could not wait to portray him as Prime Minister.

The time would soon come. Following a quick break for Christmas, the team reassembled at Television Centre at the start of 1986 to start recording the series.

10

Series One

In political activity, then, men sail a boundless and bottomless sea; there is neither harbour for shelter nor floor for anchorage, neither starting-place nor appointed destination.

The first series of *Yes, Prime Minister* received a very warm welcome. Nothing on television, during the three years since *Yes Minister* had last been seen, had come close to matching the show's remarkable combination of intelligence, realism, knowledge and wit. Its return, in revised form, represented a reassuring move at a time when accusations were in circulation that British television was in the process of being 'dumbed down'.[1]

There were numerous admiring profiles and respectful interviews in the newspapers and several television promotional features, and a picture of all three stars (photographed outside a mock-up of Number Ten) adorned the cover of the *Radio Times*. It was, by the relatively restrained standards of the time, an unusually broad and enthusiastic response to the revival of a sitcom that dared to go against the trend for safe, inoffensive and formulaic fare.

The opening episode – which was broadcast at 9 p.m. on BBC2 on Thursday 9 January 1986 – made it clear from the start that this series, now that Jim Hacker had become Prime Minister, was going to be the most ambitious one yet in terms of the nature and treatment of its themes. Within the first two minutes it had Hacker hovering over the button that could trigger a nuclear war.

In what followed, every major aspect of the country's Cold War nuclear policy was sliced up and satirised, while the dangerous opportunism of those responsible for managing it was subjected to a suitably excoriating comic critique. In one scene, Hacker's Chief Scientific Adviser dismisses the concept of Britain having its own nuclear deterrent because (as an attack would either be direct and immediate or, more likely, indirect and gradual) the time to press the button would either be too late or too soon, and thus proposes cancelling the purchase of any more nuclear weapons and using the £15 billion saved to build a large conventional army enhanced with high-tech weaponry.

This gives Hacker what a worried-looking Woolley describes as a 'courageous' idea. If he did indeed decide to cancel the missiles, use the money to build a large conventional army *and* reintroduce conscription (which would also provide the idle youth of the nation with 'a comprehensive education to make up for their comprehensive education'), he would solve Britain's defence, unemployment and education problems in one dramatic stroke.

Feeling the hand of history upon his shoulder, his voice takes on a Churchillian burr as he decides to name this new policy 'Hacker's Grand Design'. Sir Humphrey, of course, is not at all enthusiastic about such an idea and urges the Prime Minister to try 'masterly inactivity' instead, but Hacker is adamant.

Sir Humphrey is aghast: 'You can't just reorganise the entire defence of the realm just like that!' Hacker, however, points out that he is the Prime Minister: 'I have the power'. Sir Humphrey asks, hopefully, if the plan is merely to stop buying Trident nuclear weapons and start buying Cruise missiles instead, but Hacker insists that he intends to stop buying any such type of the means of mass destruction.

Sir Humphrey tries to make his Prime Minister see sense:

SIR HUMPHREY:	With Trident we could obliterate the whole of Eastern Europe.
HACKER:	I don't *want* to obliterate the whole of Eastern Europe.
SIR HUMPHREY:	It's a *deterrent*!
HACKER:	It's *a bluff*. I probably wouldn't use it.
SIR HUMPHREY:	Yes, but they don't *know* that you probably wouldn't.
HACKER:	They probably *do*.
SIR HUMPHREY:	Yes, they *probably* know that you probably wouldn't. But they can't *certainly* know!

HACKER:	They probably certainly know that I probably wouldn't!
SIR HUMPHREY:	Yes, but even though they probably certainly know that you probably *wouldn't*, they don't certainly know that, although you probably wouldn't, there is no probability that you certainly *would*!

Hacker, however, vows to press on. He sounds out the Chief of the General Staff, General Howard, about his plan and, much to his surprise, finds that the Army man is very much in favour of such a move, but doubts that the Royal Navy and the RAF would support it. A solution, he says, would be to appoint someone to the soon-to-be vacant post of Chief of the Defence Staff who has an Army background – someone very much, in fact, like himself – to push the policy through.

The General then bumps into Sir Humphrey, who shocks him with the news that Hacker is not only going to abandon nuclear weapons but is also planning on bringing back conscription. 'We can't bring in a mob of punks, and freaks, and junkies and riff-raff!' the old soldier protests. 'We must stop him!'

Sir Humphrey assures him that they only need to slow Hacker down. 'After a few months, most new Prime Ministers have more or less ground to a halt anyway.'

The Cabinet Secretary achieves this aim by warning the Prime Minister that the Americans will be most displeased if Britain stops buying its Trident missiles and fails to replace them with another American-made nuclear weapon. Worse still, as far as Hacker's own amour propre is concerned, this displeasure would manifest itself initially via the downgrading of his first official trip as Prime Minister to the White House. 'Your meeting would not be with the President,' Sir Humphrey informs him. 'You would be entertained by the Vice-President.'

Hacker is horrified. 'The *Vice*-President?' he gasps. 'But even *Botswana* was met by the President – I saw it on the news!' Sir Humphrey, quietly delighted to see that he can still make Hacker squirm, points out that Botswana had not just cancelled a £15 billion order for Trident. When Hacker admits that the meeting with the President 'is vital for PR', Sir

Humphrey tells him that he will have to postpone his 'Grand Design' and the morally compromised Prime Minister, reluctantly, agrees.

The episode – which, with delicious irony, was broadcast only hours after the real Defence Secretary, Michael Heseltine, had stormed out of Number Ten after resigning over a difference of opinion on investment issues[2] – struck just the right tone. It not only underlined the wider range of subjects that would now be addressed (with some of the more sobering insights eliciting an audible gasp as well as a laugh from the studio audience), but it also, very swiftly and smoothly, updated the audience on the evolution of the relationship between Hacker and Sir Humphrey.

Hacker, as the new Prime Minister, was now shown to be not only more powerful but also more isolated than ever. He seems to have struck a Faustian deal, dirtying his hands to achieve an exalted office but at the expense of an atrophied life. Inside what his unhappy wife calls the 'goldfish bowl' of Number Ten, hemmed in by the ever-present nosy journalists and gawking tourists, and with blank-faced security men patrolling the corridors and intruding into the rooms, he only really has his job, and it is obvious that, like all of his predecessors, he is still not quite sure what that is.

Sir Humphrey, on the other hand, is like the pedigree cat that now has all of the best-quality cream. Having always seemed far more wedded to Whitehall than to his wife, he is simply delighted to have reached the pinnacle of his chosen profession, the master of all he surveys.

Hacker, unnerved by being the highest head above the parapet, keeps talking about how powerful he is in order to distract himself from his own nagging feelings of impotence. Sir Humphrey, calm and safe inside his carapace of conservatism, has no need to boast about his own great power because he is far too busy making full use of it.

Hacker is still painfully aware that he could lose everything by committing one bad mistake. Sir Humphrey, secure in the permanence of his own position, is happily aware that, if he so wished it, he could ensure that Hacker would lose everything by allowing him to go ahead and make that one mistake.

This contrast in the two men's moods and means would continue until midway through the series, with the arrival of the episode entitled 'The Key'. This would be the moment when, just like in earlier series, the contest between them was, to some extent, evened up.

The plot of 'The Key' concerned the intrusion into Hacker and Sir Humphrey's closeted shared environment by the political adviser Dorothy Wainwright. The Cabinet Secretary has decided that she is an 'impossible woman' who might 'confuse' the Prime Minister, so he has taken the necessary steps to move her office as far away as possible from the centre of power – to the front of the building, three floors up, along the corridor, down two steps, around the corner and four doors along to the right, next to the photocopier.

When Hacker discovers what was so special about the location of her previous office – it is in *the* key strategic position, opposite the gents' loo, where she was able to eavesdrop on every potential plan to plot against the PM – he snaps into action and orders Woolley to put her back where she once belonged. Sir Humphrey, once he hears about this, is outraged, and tries to reassure Hacker that there is no need for any outsider to be allowed so far inside:

> HACKER: I need someone who's on *my* side.
> SIR HUMPHREY: But *I'm* on your side. The whole *Civil Service* is on your side. Six hundred and eighty thousand of us – surely that's enough to be going on with?
> HACKER: Yes, but they all give me the same advice.
> SIR HUMPHREY: Which proves that it must be correct!

Wainwright, however, proves to be just as cynical and crafty as Sir Humphrey, and convinces Hacker that he needs to clip Sir Humphrey's wings. If, she suggests, he were to take away Sir Humphrey's other role as Head of the Home Civil Service, and hand over all of its powers to the Permanent Head of the Treasury, his influence would be greatly diminished. Hacker, upon hearing this, and contemplating a 'divide and conquer' strategy for the bureaucracy, is excited: this seems to be his best chance to tame his chief tormentor.

Bernard Woolley, bending weakly whichever way the wind blows, is used to block Sir Humphrey from straying from the Cabinet Office and wandering into Number Ten. Spurred on by the ferociously determined Dorothy Wainwright, he does as he is told and tells Security to change all the locks so as to stop Sir Humphrey from entering.

Sir Humphrey, upon realising that his key no longer fits, marches off to the front door of Number Ten and tries to enter there, only to be stopped by the resident policeman. He is then driven to leaping out of a back window from his office in Whitehall, racing through the garden and triggering security alarms by trying to force open the windows to the Cabinet Room.

After finally bursting in to where Hacker, Wainwright and Woolley are huddled, he complains about his situation:

SIR HUMPHREY: Prime Minister, I must protest in the strongest possible terms my profound opposition to a newly instituted practice which imposes severe and intolerable restrictions upon the ingress and egress of senior members of the hierarchy and which will, in all probability, should the current deplorable innovation be perpetuated, precipitate a constriction of the channels of communication, and culminate in a condition of organisational atrophy and administrative paralysis which will render effectively impossible the coherent and coordinated discharge of the functions of government within Her Majesty's United Kingdom of Great Britain and Northern Ireland.

HACKER: You mean you've lost your key?

It was actually one of the least convincingly realistic episodes in this or any of the previous series – not only would it have been highly improbable (though not impossible) that any mere Principal Private Secretary would have dared to side with a transient Prime Minister (and a here today, gone tomorrow special adviser) over a permanent and hugely powerful Cabinet Secretary, but it would also have been completely out of character for the hyper-cautious Bernard Woolley to defy Sir Humphrey Appleby (who, in any case, was usually far too wily to be outwitted in such a way). It was, nonetheless, actually based on a real-life scenario ('The then Cabinet Secretary, John Hunt, was desperate to get a key to get into Number Ten,' Bernard Donoughue later revealed. 'And the Principal Private Secretary,

Robert Armstrong, was keen to see that he didn't have one. It wasn't true he climbed in, but, as soon as I talked about it, Jonathan spotted that immediately as the basis for an episode'[3]), and, more importantly, it did provide Hacker with a collaborator, however cartoon-like, to defend Westminster against Whitehall.

Dorothy Wainwright's attitude towards Jim Hacker would echo that of Marcia Falkender towards Harold Wilson. Bernard Donoughue, who witnessed it at first hand during his own time inside Number Ten, would write about Falkender's wildly volatile mixture of positivity ('Instinctively [she] goes like a knife to the heart of matters'[4]) and negativity (she 'frightens everyone', and 'behaves appallingly when she is removed from the centre of things'[5]), and how she would constantly boss the Prime Minister around (doing everything from withholding the 'reward' of a sandwich until the ravenous PM had dutifully signed the required number of documents and telling him when to go to bed, to arguing with him about the right time to call an election[6]), while also noting how Wilson 'loves it when she shouts at him, corrects him, opposes him'.[7]

Wainwright would behave in a similar, if slightly toned down, manner towards Hacker.[8] Brisk, brusque and belligerent, she would often address the Prime Minister as if he was a dim little schoolboy, and, though a little shaken, he would never seem to object. Although no more democratically representative, and hardly any more accountable, than Sir Humphrey himself, she would, nonetheless, act with the air of someone who thinks that she has far more legitimacy than a mere civil servant, and it was this brazen (albeit misplaced) self-confidence and brutal directness that would make her such a striking contrast to the Cabinet Secretary as they competed for Hacker's attention.

Hacker's dealings with Sir Humphrey, as a consequence, would seem rather more complex, and complicated, than before. Distracted by the many other duties and schemes that now came with his broader brief, Sir Humphrey would sometimes learn a little later than he used to about possible crises and concerns, and would thus be more worried about who might be influencing the Prime Minister in his absence. Hacker, meanwhile, would appear both relieved and unnerved by the slight increase in freedom that he has in Number Ten to seek out alternative sources of advice.

In the sharp-brained and seemingly fearless Wainwright, who craves change at any cost, he has a potentially vital political accomplice to help him battle against the bureaucrats, but he also realises that in Sir Humphrey, who values stability above anything else, he has an indispensable ally to help him overcome his own failings – a man who knows more, has experienced more and has solved far more problems than any transient special adviser would either have the wish or the will to do. When push comes to shove, therefore, it remains highly likely that Hacker will trust Sir Humphrey more than Wainwright to keep him in power.

The relationship between Hacker and Sir Humphrey, though, would take second place, for most of this series, to the issues that bothered them both. More prominently than before, ideas would drive this sitcom on, dictating its structure and scenes.

Along with the already firmly established themes of administration versus government, public duty versus party loyalty, open and honest communication versus cynical political spin and the moral problem of dirty hands, many new preoccupations were added, including the proper and improper form of foreign policy, the nature of a modern defence strategy, the tension between the pursuit of wealth and the promotion of virtue, security and surveillance, the use and abuse of patronage, the concept of the United Nations and the supposed 'special relationship' between Britain and North America.

In the second episode, for example, the theme of smugly specious democratic responsiveness is satirised with striking accuracy when Sir Humphrey explains to Woolley how parties and governments manage to manipulate public opinion:

SIR HUMPHREY: You know what happens: nice young lady comes up to you. Obviously you want to create a good impression, you don't want to look a *fool*, do you? So she starts asking you some questions: 'Mr Woolley, are you worried about the number of young people without jobs?'

WOOLLEY: Yes.

SIR HUMPHREY: 'Are you worried about the rise in crime among teenagers?'

WOOLLEY: Yes.

SIR HUMPHREY:	'Do you think there is a lack of discipline in our comprehensive schools?'
WOOLLEY:	Yes.
SIR HUMPHREY:	'Do you think young people welcome some authority and leadership in their lives?'
WOOLLEY:	Yes.
SIR HUMPHREY:	'Do you think they respond to a challenge?'
WOOLLEY:	Yes.
SIR HUMPHREY:	'Would you be in favour of reintroducing National Service?'
WOOLLEY:	Oh . . . well, I suppose I *might* be.
SIR HUMPHREY:	'Yes or no?'
WOOLLEY:	Yes.
SIR HUMPHREY:	Of course you would, Bernard. After all you've said you *can't* say no to that. So they don't mention the first five questions and they publish the last one.
WOOLLEY:	Is that really what they do?
SIR HUMPHREY:	Well, not the reputable ones, no, but there aren't many of those. So, alternatively, the young lady can get the opposite result.
WOOLLEY:	How?
SIR HUMPHREY:	'Mr Woolley, are you worried about the danger of war?'
WOOLLEY:	Yes.
SIR HUMPHREY:	'Are you worried about the growth of armaments?'
WOOLLEY:	Yes.
SIR HUMPHREY:	'Do you think there is a danger in giving young people guns and teaching them how to kill?'
WOOLLEY:	Yes.
SIR HUMPHREY:	'Do you think it is wrong to force people to take up arms against their will?'
WOOLLEY:	Yes.
SIR HUMPHREY:	'Would you oppose the reintroduction of National Service?'

WOOLLEY: Yes.

SIR HUMPHREY: There you are, you see, Bernard. The perfect
              balanced sample.

The new theme that ran from start to finish, providing a sense of
continuity within and between episodes, concerned the Prime Minister's
determination to define his time in power, to stamp his signature on the
Premiership, with the implementation of a Big Idea. This, again, was
reflecting a real political tradition.

Machiavelli had encouraged it when he remarked: 'Nothing enables
a ruler to gain more prestige than undertaking great campaigns and performing unusual deeds'.[9] It would be a lesson that all leaders, including
British Prime Ministers, were extremely keen to learn.

Sometimes the attempt has been bold and practically precise, such as
Lord Grey's Reform Bill in the early 1830s, and sometimes it has been
bold but practically imprecise, such as Harold Wilson's promise to harness
'the white heat of technology' in the early 1960s, and sometimes – many
times – it has been craven and incoherent, but, in some shape or form, it
has usually been there, hovering over the new Prime Minister like a home-
made halo as he or she enters Number Ten, prompting civil servants to
find ways to make it happen or contrive ways to make it fail and fade away.

In Hacker's case it is his 'Grand Design', with which, in spite of Sir
Humphrey's succession of stalling tactics, he doggedly persists from one
episode to the next all the way to the end of the series. There are times,
such as in 'The Ministerial Broadcast', when it is right at the centre of the
story, and other times, such as in 'The Smoke Screen', when it lurks out
on the periphery, but it is always there, serving as a symbol of Hacker's
tenuous but tenacious hold on the sense that he is still the master of his
own destiny.

In a series that was consistently thought-provoking and entertaining,
there were arguably two instalments that, for different reasons, stood out.
For sheer intellectual and satirical audacity, 'A Victory for Democracy'
was exceptional, and, as a model of classic sitcom structure, plotting and
pacing, 'The Bishop's Gambit' was a gem of the genre.

'A Victory for Democracy' represented *Yes, Prime Minister* at its most
uncompromisingly ambitious. Inspired partly by the Falklands War of

1982 and partly by the US invasion of Grenada in 1983,[10] the story concerned a clash between Number Ten and the Foreign Office, with the Prime Minister eager to ingratiate himself with another country, and his foreign policy specialists anxious to avoid Britain being dragged into another country's dubious military venture.

The Anglo-American alliance has been undermined by the news of Hacker's Grand Design, so when Hacker hears about plans for America to interfere in the Commonwealth realm of St George's Island to prevent a potential communist coup d'état, his self-protecting political instincts tell him to pledge Britain's support to the campaign.

Sir Richard Wharton, however, in his capacity of Permanent Secretary to the Foreign Office, is disturbed to hear of such a move, reasoning that the situation in St George's – which is a modest little island in the Indian Ocean – is very messy, with Soviet and Libyan-backed guerrillas lurking up in the mountains and a set of front-line African states ready to take offence at any meddling emanating from elsewhere, while Britain has a lucrative contract in place to build a new airport and harbour installation on the island provided it avoids backing the wrong side. The FO, therefore, would prefer it if Number Ten kept its snout out of the whole sorry business.

'He must understand,' Sir Richard tells Sir Humphrey about the Prime Minister, 'that once you start interfering in the internal squabbles of other countries you're on a very slippery slope. Even the Foreign Secretary's grasped that.'

There is, however, a further tension. It seems that Hacker also thinks it would play well with the White House if Britain was to abstain when the UN comes to vote on a forthcoming motion by the Arabs that condemns the recent actions of Israel. Sir Richard, on the other hand, dismisses the suggestion as just one more example of Number Ten 'sucking up to the Americans', notes that both sides in the Middle East are almost as bad as each other and, on this occasion, is in favour of backing the Arabs (and their oil supplies).

With these two rival interpretations of realpolitik thus determining the intentions of two different branches of the same Government, an internal struggle ensues. Number Ten is ready to dirty British hands for America, while the Foreign Office is ready to dirty British hands mainly for money.

It falls to the well-meaning Woolley to try to end the stalemate by sounding out Sir Richard and Sir Humphrey about finding a possible compromise, but all he receives for his troubles is an explanation of why this kind of division exists ('Diplomacy is about surviving until the next century. Politics is about surviving until Friday afternoon') and a classic lesson in how British foreign policy forms and functions:

SIR RICHARD:	The problem is that the interests of Britain nearly always involve doing deals with people that the public think are the baddies.
SIR HUMPHREY:	And not helping the goodies occasionally when it doesn't help us.
SIR RICHARD:	So we avoid discussion of foreign affairs. Or rather, we keep all discussion inside the Foreign Office, and then we produce one policy for the Foreign Secretary – which represents our considered view – and he can act upon it.
WOOLLEY:	What, no options?
SIR RICHARD:	None.
WOOLLEY:	No alternatives?
SIR RICHARD:	None.
WOOLLEY:	What if he's not satisfied?
SIR RICHARD:	Well, if *pressed*, we look at it again.
WOOLLEY:	And come up with a different view?
SIR RICHARD:	Of course not! We come up with the *same* view!
WOOLLEY:	But what if he *demands* options?
SIR HUMPHREY:	Well, it's obvious, Bernard: the Foreign Office will happily present him with three options, two of which are, on close inspection, exactly the same.
SIR RICHARD:	Plus a third, which is totally unacceptable.
SIR HUMPHREY:	Like bombing Warsaw or invading France.
SIR RICHARD:	And better still, we occasionally encourage the Foreign Secretary to produce his *own* policy, then we tell him that it would inevitably lead to World War Three, perhaps within forty-eight hours.

WOOLLEY:	I see. Er, I'm sorry to appear stupid—
SIR HUMPHREY:	Oh, perish the thought, Bernard!
WOOLLEY:	But in my experience, Ministers are somewhat concerned about the effect of policy on domestic political opinion. Now, *our* system doesn't seem to allow for that.
SIR RICHARD:	Well, of course not. We take the *global* view. We ask what's best for the *world*.
WOOLLEY:	Well, most Ministers would rather you ask: 'What's the *Daily Mail* leader going to say?'
SIR HUMPHREY:	Oh, Bernard, we can't have foreign policy made by *yobbos* like Fleet Street editors or backbench MPs!
SIR RICHARD:	Or Cabinet Ministers.
SIR HUMPHREY:	Or Cabinet Ministers! We take the right decisions and let them sort out the politics later!

Woolley's mind is whirling at this, but he still manages to ask his superiors how the Foreign Office will respond if, as the Prime Minister thinks likely, the people of St George's end up appealing to Britain for support. In a charitable mood, Sir Richard avers that the FO will 'give them every support, short of help'. Exasperated, Woolley then asks them what they will do if the Prime Minister insists on serious action. This prompts them to summarise 'The Four Stage Strategy' – the standard Foreign Office response in a time of crisis:

SIR RICHARD:	In Stage One, we say: 'Nothing is going to happen'.
SIR HUMPHREY:	In Stage Two, we say: 'Something *may* be going to happen but *we* should do nothing about it'.
SIR RICHARD:	In Stage Three, we say: 'Maybe we *should* do something about it but there's nothing we *can* do'.
SIR HUMPHREY:	In Stage Four, we say: 'Maybe there was something we *could* have done but it's too late now'.

With Woolley failing to broker a mutually satisfactory deal, the internecine fighting breaks out once again. The Foreign Office quietly overrules Number Ten about abstaining from the UN vote ('The White House will do its nut!' Hacker exclaims upon discovering the deception), and so Number Ten bypasses the Foreign Office to send a British airborne battalion to St George's on 'a goodwill visit'.

As in fact, so in fiction, there is no neat and tidy resolution to this struggle for power and influence. The Prime Minister might have won this particular battle on points (by doing just enough to placate his American friends), but the war, it is clear, will go on, and on.

While 'A Victory for Democracy' thus exemplified the quality of the show's content, 'The Bishop's Gambit' did the same for its form. It was sometimes overlooked, thanks to the dazzling dialogue and the sharp satirical insights, that Antony Jay and Jonathan Lynn were also brilliant masters of the *craft* of creating a thirty-minute sitcom story, and this particular instalment was a fine demonstration of that skill.

'The Bishop's Gambit' sets up three seemingly unrelated storylines. First, a British nurse has been detained in the Islamic state of Qumran for possession of a bottle of whisky and is facing ten years in prison as well as forty lashes; second, the Prime Minister is due to consider the two candidates put forward by the Church of England for the vacant diocese of Bury St Edmunds; and third, Sir Humphrey is sounded out by the Master of his Oxford alma mater, Baillie College, about succeeding him when he eventually retires.

The episode then proceeds to twist these three disparate strands together. Sir Humphrey discovers that the only obstacle to him becoming the next Master is the current Dean, who dislikes him intensely, so he starts plotting to persuade the Prime Minister to appoint the Dean as the new Bishop of Bury St Edmunds; and, realising that there are already two candidates for the post, he contrives to provide the Dean with the possibility of a game-changing personal triumph by packing him off as an emissary to Qumran to negotiate the release of the nurse. It is thus with a delightfully swift and subtle structural sleight of hand that Jay and Lynn, within the first two-thirds of the show, have all three storylines running smoothly towards their shared denouement.

They also suffused each subsection with more, and better, comic lines than many other sitcoms of the period managed in three times the amount of minutes available. There were barbs, for example, aimed at academics (MASTER: 'He never reads a new book, never thinks a new thought.' SIR HUMPHREY: 'I see. So being an Oxford don is the perfect job for him'); bishops ('Bishops tend to have long lives – apparently the Lord isn't all that keen for them to join him'); religious modernists (SIR HUMPHREY: 'The word "modernist" is code for non-believer.' HACKER: 'You mean an *atheist?*' SIR HUMPHREY: 'No, Prime Minister, an atheist clergyman couldn't continue to draw his stipend, so, when they stop believing in God, they call themselves "modernists"'); theologians ('Theology is a device for enabling agnostics to stay within the Church'); Church versus State ('It's interesting, isn't it, that nowadays politicians want to talk about moral issues and bishops want to talk politics?'); and the Civil Service versus the Government ('The Foreign Office never expect the Cabinet to agree to any of their policies – that's why they never fully explain them').

The resolution itself is just as assured as what has gone before. The Dean does indeed help free the nurse, coming home in a blaze of personal glory, and all that is left is for Sir Humphrey to pave the way to the diocese for him by depicting his only rival as a dangerous radical:

SIR HUMPHREY: He tends to raise issues that often governments would prefer not to have been raised. He's a trenchant critic of abortion, contraception for the under-sixteens, sex education, pornography, Sunday trading, easy divorce and bad language on television. He would be likely to challenge the Government policy on all those subjects.

HACKER: But these are subjects on which the Government is hoping to have *no* policy. Our policy is not to have a policy!

SIR HUMPHREY: Well, quite. He's against your no-policy policy.

WOOLLEY: You see, he'll demand that you ban abortions, Sunday trading, contraception for the under-sixteens—

HACKER: Yes, yes, thank you, Bernard, yes, I get the picture.

SIR HUMPHREY: And he's also against repression and persecution in Africa.

HACKER: *[Puzzled]* So are we.

SIR HUMPHREY: Yes, but he's against it when practised by black governments as well as white ones.

HACKER: Oh! You mean he's a racist?

SIR HUMPHREY: *[Smiling sweetly]* But you can choose him if you like.

Now convinced ('on mature consideration') that the lazy, eccentric but harmless Dean is the right man for the job (as well as the right man in the news to lend Number Ten some good publicity), Hacker is pleased to think that all of this has happened just because Sir Humphrey, for once, has put aside all thought of professional or personal gain and actually done the decent thing, even though, by his own admission, he and the Dean cannot abide each other. 'Well done,' Hacker says warmly. 'Helpful, impartial advice: the best traditions of the Civil Service!' Sir Humphrey bows his head slightly and, trying for a shy smile, replies: 'Yes, Prime Minister.'

The series, after impressing in all of these ways, came to an end on 27 February with an episode – 'One of Us' – that explored the subject of espionage. Once more, without the writers trying too hard, it reached the screen seeming topical.

In 1979, Margaret Thatcher had responded to rumours about a clandestine security scandal by naming Sir Anthony Blunt, a former officer in British intelligence and personal adviser on art to the Queen, as the 'fourth man' in the infamous Cambridge spy ring of the 1950s, which had also included Guy Burgess, Donald Maclean and Kim Philby. Although he had privately confessed his involvement back in 1964, gaining immunity from prosecution in return for agreeing to reveal to MI5 all that he knew about the Soviets, Thatcher decided, fifteen years later, to make his guilt a matter of public knowledge. 'I believe she did it because she didn't see why the system should cover things up,' her Press Secretary, Bernard Ingham, later claimed. 'This was early in her Prime Ministership. I think she wanted to tell the Civil Service that the politicians decide policy, not the system. She wanted them to know who was boss.'[11]

Public interest in espionage issues was further heightened six years later, in September 1985, when the Attorney General began proceedings in New South Wales to prevent Peter Wright, a former assistant director of MI5, from publishing his book *Spycatcher*, which contained an account of alleged irregularities and illegalities by members of the security service.[12] Reports of the continuing legal battle would rumble on for three years,[13] and were thus very much in the minds of many viewers when *Yes, Prime Minister* turned its attention to the matter.

'One of Us' saw Hacker receive a visit from Sir Geoffrey Hastings, the Director General of MI5, who has some top-secret and disturbing security news. Echoing the real-life case of Sir Roger Hollis (whom Peter Wright had recently accused in *Spycatcher* of having been a Soviet mole), Sir Geoffrey confides that his predecessor, the late Sir John Halstead, has now been revealed – thanks to the confession he bequeathed to the Government – as a Russian spy. Although an earlier inquiry into suspicions about his activities had cleared him, Sir Geoffrey points out that it had not been as rigorous as the matter had actually required:

SIR GEOFFREY: They missed some rather obvious questions and checks so obvious that, well, one wonders . . .

HACKER: *[Knowingly]* Yes . . . *[Puzzled]* Er, *what* does one wonder?

SIR GEOFFREY: Well, one wonders about the chaps who cleared him. Whether they were . . . you know . . .

HACKER: I see . . . er, whether they were stupid, you mean?

SIR GEOFFREY: No, Prime Minister. Whether they were also, um . . .

HACKER: *Spies*? My God! Who headed that inquiry?

SIR GEOFFREY: Oh, Lord McIver, but he was ill most of the time.

HACKER: Ill?

SIR GEOFFREY: Well, er, gaga. So effectively it was the Secretary who conducted it.

HACKER: Well, who was the Secretary?

SIR GEOFFREY: Er, Humphrey Appleby.

Hacker's eyes light up at this news. The prospect of seeing Sir Humphrey squirm never fails to excite his imagination. Sir Geoffrey, however, is quick to reassure him that there is no evidence that Sir Humphrey, who after all is clearly 'one of us', had ever been tempted to cover up for 'one of them'.

Hacker suggests that, in that case, they might as well forget all about it, but Sir Geoffrey points out that, if they did nothing about it, and then at some later stage it was found that Sir Humphrey, who is now the Cabinet Secretary and the ultimate keeper of secrets, did indeed do something wrong, then it would not look at all good for the Prime Minister.

Hacker agrees, and decides to broach the subject, privately, with the man himself. Sir Humphrey laughs off the suggestion that Halstead was a spy, only for Hacker to shock him with the news that MI5 now has his posthumous confession. 'Well,' gasps Sir Humphrey, 'this certainly leaves a lot of questions to be asked.' Hacker glares at him and says: 'Yes, and I'm asking you the first of them: why didn't *you* ask him a lot of *questions?*'

Sir Humphrey is stunned and rather hurt at what is being implied. He was, for one thing, very busy at the time, and for another, 'the whole object of internal security inquiries is to find no evidence', so he simply cannot see, as a good civil servant, what he did wrong.

Hacker, however, is clear on this. He has a real problem: it has to be incompetence or collusion.

There is a certain steeliness about the Prime Minister as he scrutinises the anxious reaction of his Cabinet Secretary. It seems as if Hacker senses – like Ingham said of Thatcher at the start of the Anthony Blunt affair – that this might be an ideal opportunity for a new Prime Minister to show 'the Civil Service that the politicians decide policy, not the system'.[14]

Sir Humphrey rushes off to seek advice from his predecessor, Sir Arnold Robinson, who, from his position of leisure, is able to give a calm and sober analysis of the situation. If Sir Humphrey is proved to be innocent, he will still be viewed as incompetent, and, as the Prime Minister could quite easily have swept the matter under the carpet by blaming the 'gaga' peer, it seems that the real intention is to remove Sir Humphrey from his position, after which all of his subordinates in the Civil Service would be exposed to the PM's sweeping scythe.

Sir Arnold's solution is simple. Sir Humphrey must make himself appear so valuable to the Prime Minister that there is no way he can be sacrificed.

Sir Humphrey knows exactly what to do. For some time now, he knows, Hacker has been fussing over opinion polls that suggest that his personal standing with voters is on the decline, and, in the last day or so, he has been complaining that the evening news bulletins have been more interested in reporting on the plight of an eight-year-old girl's sheepdog (which has strayed onto the artillery range on Salisbury Plain) than they have been in noting his latest performance at Prime Minister's Questions. What thus needs to be done is to have Number Ten intervene to save the dog, let Hacker lap up the subsequent good publicity and accept his own thanks in private.

Hacker, as always more interested in personal popularity than principles, accepts Sir Humphrey's plan and then settles back on his sofa to watch the suitably sentimental news reports. 'Say no more about it,' he beams at Sir Humphrey the next morning, as he brushes aside any calls for a new inquiry and concentrates instead on all the favourable front-page headlines. 'Completely forgotten!'

There is only one matter left to be dealt with, says Sir Humphrey, with a glint in his eye. He then proceeds to discuss Hacker's favoured defence cuts, and lets it be known that the cost of rescuing the dog was the huge sum, for that period, of £310,000. Such a disproportionate expense, at a time of supposed swingeing cost-cutting, will not look good in Parliament, let alone the papers, and Hacker knows it only too well.

'I think I may have been a little hasty,' he says, disguising the start of a shiver. 'Yes, Prime Minister,' replies Sir Humphrey, disguising the start of a smirk.

Once again, the power dynamic between Hacker and Sir Humphrey had taken another tip. It left viewers eager to see what would happen to the relationship in the next set of episodes to be screened.

Consistently topping the ratings for BBC2, this first series of *Yes, Prime Minister* had averaged an audience of 6.8 million, with a high of 7.5 million,[15] receiving the usual positive reviews. Nigel Hawthorne won yet another Best Light Entertainment Performance BAFTA – his third for this role – and the series was named Best Entertainment Series by the Broadcasting Press Guild.

The show was also honoured by the organisers of the Campaign for Freedom of Information. They presented both Antony Jay and Jonathan Lynn with a special award in recognition of their 'unique and unparalleled contribution to wittily exposing the cynicism of Whitehall secrecy'.[16]

The return had been a genuine triumph on every level. Artistically, critically and commercially, it had matched, and arguably even surpassed, all of the high expectations that news of its revival had encouraged.

More popular, relevant and influential than ever, it reminded all those who were bemoaning the dumbing down of British television of what the medium could, and should, do when it respected the intelligence of a broad audience. It lifted standards as well as spirits, and, for its many admirers, another series could not come too soon.

Case Study 4

Thank You for Not Smoking

The ability of the show to turn old facts into new fictions had been evident right from the start, but, increasingly, the sitcom also demonstrated an equally remarkable gift for anticipating future incidents, issues and trends. In 'The Smoke Screen', for example, we can now see a fiction that later became a fact.

The episode focused on a radical plan, proposed by Dr Thorne, the Minister of State for the Department of Health and Social Security, to eliminate smoking. The phased plan to achieve this involved, first, a complete ban on all forms of tobacco sponsorship and advertising, even at the point of sale; second, Government investment in anti-smoking publicity; third, a ban on smoking in all public spaces; and, fourth, a series of progressive, deterrent tax rises over the course of the next five years until a packet of cigarettes cost about as much as a bottle of whisky.

Hacker is stunned by this proposal. Although he assures his Minister that he is sympathetic to the intention, he urges him to be realistic. The Treasury would only say that smoking brings in about £4 billion in revenue every year – roughly a third of the NHS' funds – and so the Government cannot manage without it. 'You can't beat the Treasury,' says Hacker solemnly.

Then he has an idea. It is a devious idea, rather than a noble one, but it excites him. He will let his idealistic Health Minister press on with his campaign, because, he reasons, it will make the Treasury come to see his own unpopular plan – to use some of the savings from his 'Grand Design' for a £1.5 billion tax cut (which will win Hacker 'masses of votes') – as far less unpalatable than the prospect of throwing away £4 billion a year by abandoning the tobacco industry.

Sir Humphrey, when he hears of Hacker's supposed willingness to back the Health Minister's demands, is greatly distressed. 'No man in his right mind could possibly contemplate such a proposal,' he exclaims. The Prime Minister, however, cites the estimated one hundred thousand deaths each year that stem from smoking, and insists that he is right behind the plan:

HACKER: Smoking-related diseases cost the NHS 165 million pounds a year!

SIR HUMPHREY: Yes, but we've been into that. It has been shown that if those extra one hundred thousand people had lived to a ripe old age, they would have cost us even more in pensions and social security than they did in medical treatment! So *financially* speaking, it's unquestionably better that they continue to die at about the present rate!

HACKER: When cholera killed thirty thousand people in 1833, we got the Public Health Act. When smog killed two and a half thousand people in 1952, we got the Clean Air Act. A commercial drug kills half a dozen people and we get it withdrawn from sale. Cigarettes kill a hundred thousand people a year. And what do we get?

SIR HUMPHREY: Four billion pounds a year. And twenty-five thousand jobs in the tobacco industry, a flourishing cigarette export business helping our balance of trade, two hundred and fifty thousand jobs related to tobacco in newsagents, packaging, transport—

HACKER: Oh, these figures are just guesses!

SIR HUMPHREY: No, they're Government statis . . . They're *facts*!

HACKER: Oh, I see. So your statistics are facts and my facts are merely statistics!

SIR HUMPHREY: Prime Minister, I'm on your *side*! I'm merely giving you some of the arguments that you will encounter!

HACKER:	Thank you, Humphrey, I'm so glad to know we will have support such as yours!
SIR HUMPHREY:	But Prime Minister, it will be pointed out that the tobacco companies are great sponsors of sport. Now, where would the BBC sports programmes be if cigarette companies couldn't advertise – er, couldn't *sponsor* – the events that they televise?
HACKER:	Humphrey, we are talking about *one hundred thousand* deaths a *year*!
SIR HUMPHREY:	Yes, but cigarette taxes pay for a third of the cost of the National Health Service. We're saving many more lives than we otherwise could because of those smokers who voluntarily lay down their lives for their friends. Smokers are national *benefactors*!

Having endured Sir Humphrey's predictable protestations, Hacker then has to put up with an unsolicited intervention from his Minister for Sport, a chronically coughing member of the tobacco lobby, who warns the Prime Minister that this plan will not only damage sporting events but will also affect voting at many marginal seats that are stuffed full of workers in the tobacco industry. Hacker, however, who is impatient to pursue his own deviously dirty-handed scheme, brushes all such complaints aside and presses on with the pose.

Sir Humphrey, meanwhile, is frustrated to find that nothing looks likely to stop what he believes is a moral campaign. He could try the old 'we don't want a Nanny State' conceit, he notes, but then rejects that on the grounds that it could just as easily be used for legalising the sale of marijuana, heroin, cocaine, arsenic and gelignite. He does try to embarrass Hacker by reminding him that, in the past, he has been the willing recipient of a great amount of VIP hospitality at tobacco company-sponsored sporting and cultural events, but even this fails to deflect the PM from his apparent course of action. 'I've had drinks at the Soviet embassy,' he observes calmly, 'that doesn't make me a Russian spy!'

It is at this point that Hacker, sensing that Sir Humphrey has, for once, run out of ways to frustrate him, seizes his moment and cuts to the chase. Reminding Sir Humphrey that the Treasury is not only blocking the Health Minister's calamitously expensive plan but also his own far more modest one-off tax cut, the Cabinet Secretary takes the hint and departs to make some calls and pull some strings.

It does not take long for Sir Humphrey to return from the Treasury with the good news that, with the proviso that the anti-smoking policy is shelved, the tax cut can go through. The ruse has worked.

The only problem now is to find a way to stop the Health Minister from resigning in protest at this cynical betrayal, but Hacker solves that by promising him that his plans have only been temporarily postponed, and then promotes him away from trouble to a vacancy in the Treasury. He then selects the one person who can be trusted to take over as Minister for Health and drop the plans for good: the tobacco-addicted Sports Minister.

Antony Jay had drawn some inspiration for the theme by talking informally to Kenneth Clarke, who at the time was nearing the end of his very eventful spell as Minister of State for Health (he would soon be made both Paymaster General and Employment Minister).[17] Clarke, notoriously, was an improbable-looking champion of issues relating to health, not only because of his tabloid image as a doughty trencherman with a fondness for cigars, beer and spirits, but also because of his increasingly close ties with the tobacco industry (he would become Deputy Chairman of British American Tobacco in 1997). 'I can't remember whether I gave him any brilliant ideas,' he would say of his meeting with Jay, but he did admit that, after this episode had been broadcast, many people asked him if he was the model for the wheezing, chain-smoking Sports Minister, and he acknowledged that some of the on-screen conversations 'were remarkably similar to the exchanges I was having with my own officials'.[18]

It was this mischievous association that aroused most interest at the time, causing plenty of amusement within Westminster, but it would be the broader theme itself that, with the benefit of hindsight, would seem more intriguing to those who watched the episode again in later years. Back in 1986, the sense that the idealistic Health Minister's plan was doomed to failure was hard to resist, because, as the story suggested, the tobacco lobby was very strong and the revenue the industry generated continued to dazzle the Treasury (indeed, just one day after the episode was broadcast, an MP commented in the Commons: 'Anyone who watched *Yes, Prime Minister* last night will have seen a programme which, in jest but also in all seriousness, showed the difficulty of introducing anti-smoking legislation, bearing in mind vested interests, electoral consequences, loss of taxation revenue and other issues'[19]). Eventually, however, the mood began to change, and, slowly but surely, the fictional plan started to be imitated by the facts.

The Health Minister in the sitcom had demanded a complete ban on all forms of tobacco sponsorship and advertising, even at the point of sale. In reality, following the passing of the Tobacco Advertising and Promotion Act (2002), advertising in the press and on billboards was outlawed from February 2003, followed later the same year by a ban on sponsorship of UK sporting events. Further bans, on certain adverts in tobacconists and large adverts in pubs, clubs and shops, followed in 2004. The Health Act of 2009, together with regulations made under the Act, enabled further restrictions on tobacco sales and advertising. The Department of Health then announced that cigarettes and other products would have to be kept under the counter from 2012 for large stores and 2015 for small shops.

The second demand in the sitcom was for Government investment in anti-smoking publicity. In 2003, the British Government committed itself to investing £31 million in a succession of national anti-smoking campaigns. The European Commission followed this in 2005 with the launch of its Help campaign, targeting all Europeans between the ages of fifteen and thirty-four through national media, television and web-based campaigns.

The third demand was for a ban on smoking in all public spaces. Just nine months after the episode was first broadcast, a Private Member's Bill, sponsored by Joe Ashton MP, aimed at creating no-smoking areas in pubs, received its first reading in Parliament.[20] Several more Private Members' Bills on more or less the same subject were launched and debated over the course of the next few years. 'Choosing Health', a Government White Paper proposing a smoking ban in almost all public places in England and Wales, was published in 2004, and, in July 2007, a formal ban finally came into force.[21]

The fourth demand was for a series of progressive, deterrent tax rises. Between 1991 and 2001, the proportion of tax in the retail price of cigarettes rose from 73 per cent to 80 per cent, thanks in part to the introduction of a tobacco duty 'escalator' in the autumn 1993 Budget, whereby the Government committed itself to raising tobacco duties by at least 3 per cent per year in real terms.[22]

There was one sign of stubborn resistance: the price of a packet of cigarettes would continue to be considerably cheaper than that of a bottle of whisky. In every other way, however, the proposals made in a British sitcom had been turned into a reality, during the course of a couple of decades or so, by the British Government.

It is a strangely ironic experience, therefore, to witness, with the benefit of hindsight, the moment when Sir Humphrey first hears of these plans in the episode back in January 1986:

SIR HUMPHREY: I was just wondering if you had an interesting chat with Dr Thorne?

HACKER: Yes. He proposed the elimination of smoking.

SIR HUMPHREY: *[Erupts with laughter]* By a campaign of mass hypnosis perhaps?

The studio audience joined Sir Humphrey in his loudly incredulous laughter. The whole proposal seemed absurd. Things, however, have changed, and that response, from this distance, now sounds quite hollow.

11

Series Two

There are three classes which need sanctuary more than others – birds, wild flowers, and Prime Ministers.

The pressure on Antony Jay and Jonathan Lynn was immense as they worked on their next set of scripts. It was clear that, by this time, they were not just writing a sitcom. They were writing something that had become a genuine national institution.

The references to *Yes, Prime Minister*, during and after its first series, were striking in their ubiquity. MPs, the vast majority of whom watched the show religiously, were instinctively associating all kinds of real-life issues and events with the stories playing out on screen: 'We are in danger of being overtaken by events in the form of the popular television programme *Yes, Prime Minister*' (Robert Key)[1]; 'That seems to have been written by a scriptwriter for *Yes, Prime Minister*' (Lord Morton of Shuna)[2]; 'There are of course some civil servants who want to have things all their own way, on the pattern of *Yes, Prime Minister*' (Lord Cledwyn of Penrhos)[3]; 'This is a matter for a connoisseur of *Yes, Prime Minister*' (Denis Healey)[4]; 'My honourable friend does not seriously imagine, does he, that Ministers write regulations? If so, he has not watched *Yes, Prime Minister* with sufficient perspicacity' (Sir Nicholas Fairbairn)[5]; 'I suspect that the whole elaborate bureaucratic farce would do credit to the authors of *Yes, Prime Minister* (John Home Robertson)[6]; 'I cannot help but recall the series *Yes, Prime Minister*, which many of your Lordships will have seen on television' (The Earl of Perth)[7]; and 'I was wondering whether, if the BBC, which produces the programme *Yes, Prime Minister*, were to come along and ask you whether it could have a copy of the script of today's events you would feel that it was a little over the top?'(Dennis Skinner).[8]

It was much the same in various countries overseas. When, for example, Margaret Thatcher arrived in Israel in May 1986 for an official visit, it was reported that the President, Chaim Herzog, joked that her arrival had finally convinced the Israeli people, who were avid viewers of *Yes, Prime Minister*, that 'the name is not Hacker, but Thatcher'.[9] The following year, when Paul Eddington was working in Australia shortly before the Federal Election, the incumbent Prime Minister, Bob Hawke (who had already staged a photo stunt in which he was shown wrestling 'Hacker' for possession of his seat in Parliament House), invited him along to a rally and said to the crowd, 'You don't want to listen to me, you want to listen to the *real* Prime Minister', and then left the actor to improvise a Jim Hacker speech.[10]

'They really did treat him like that everywhere he went,' Derek Fowlds would recall. 'I was in Australia with Paul when we were both working there in separate plays, and we often used to go around together and be interviewed about *Yes, Prime Minister* because the show was such a big hit there, and, seeing how they responded to him, I'd always walk behind him on those occasions, just like Bernard, and open doors for him. I think he liked that!'[11]

Paul Eddington was, indeed, by this time getting so used to being welcomed to other countries as if he genuinely was a political VIP (such as when he was invited to breakfast with the Prime Minister of Norway and lunch with Denmark's Minister for Culture[12]), that he had grown increasingly sympathetic to, and protective of, his on-screen alter ego. 'I am often asked if I base Hacker on a real person,' he told reporters. 'The answer is I do. That person is myself. He is as vain and greedy and easily swayed as I am. The main difference is that Hacker can bend to his civil servants. I lack his flexibility and for that reason would never make a successful politician.'[13]

It was this sense of personal investment, and professional pride, in his portrayal that had come to cause a certain amount of unacknowledged discomfort for his co-star Nigel Hawthorne. For all of Eddington's brilliance as Hacker, capturing perfectly that deceptively complex and nervy mixture of cloudy idealism and earthbound pragmatism, he had been overlooked for the most prestigious acting awards time and again in favour of his supposed supporting (and thus less handsomely remunerated) colleague.

Eddington himself was far too decent and gracious a man to complain about this, but Hawthorne had come to feel distinctly embarrassed by the 'Hawthorne beats Eddington' reports that greeted the announcement of each new list of BAFTA winners.

Although they remained very different people, with very different interests and dispositions, they had grown into a working relationship together that was not only exceptionally effective but also warm and mutually respectful. It therefore genuinely upset Hawthorne to think that any personal success was coming at his colleague's expense. 'It was unfortunate,' he would say of the BAFTA awards, 'that we should both have been selected for the same category [Best Light Entertainment Performance]; we were a team and should never have been put in competition.'[14]

'Paul *was* upset that Nigel won the BAFTAs and he didn't,' Derek Fowlds would confirm. 'He was totally brilliant as Hacker, and yet he was never acknowledged in the way that Nigel was. He used to say to me, "Why does Nigel always win?" And I just used to say, "Because he's got longer speeches than you!"'[15]

Hawthorne, by this stage, had beaten Eddington to the award on no fewer than three separate occasions, and was destined to do so once again. It was a fact that diminished the pleasure he could, and should, have taken from such public recognition. 'I knew how desperate he was to get the award,' he later reflected, 'so it became increasingly difficult to know what to say to him.'[16]

It therefore came as something of a relief when, for once, they achieved parity in terms of the regalia of fame. In the New Year's Honours List of 1987, both Nigel Hawthorne and Paul Eddington were awarded the CBE for services to drama. The latter was working in Australia at the time, and when he went to Melbourne Airport to greet his wife, who had flown over to celebrate, he was mobbed by the media. It meant a great deal to him, and when, later that day, he joined Nigel Hawthorne 'down the line' for a BBC radio interview back in Britain, there was a palpable sense of camaraderie and real delight in each other's achievement.

Thus the atmosphere was better than ever when the two of them, along with Derek Fowlds, were reunited in the autumn – after being awarded a modest pay rise ('It had always gone up very, very slowly,' Derek Fowlds would recall. 'By the time we finished, the boys were on £3,000

an episode, and I was on £2,000'[17]) – to rehearse the second series of
Yes, Prime Minister. They knew that, in all probability, this was going to
be the final outing for the show. Nothing had been announced publicly,
and internally nothing had been decided definitively, but this series would
complete the deal that Jay and Lynn had agreed with Bill Cotton (who in
any case was about to retire from the BBC), and the writers already felt
that the time was probably right for the sitcom to bow out. It was also
recognised, privately, that Paul Eddington's health was deteriorating (he
would seldom be seen, for this reason, moving from behind his desk),
which only added to the feeling that this was the most prudent moment
to bring things to a close.

Everyone was determined to make these final eight episodes as special
as possible. This was not just a job. It was a precious part of their lives,
something they all loved, something that made them proud, and, as col-
laborators, as friends, on both sides of the camera, they wanted to savour
every moment together, right through to the very end.

The research and the preparation were as detailed and diligent as usual,
but there was an extra little touch here and there as the team looked for
ways to give the production one final polish. Jay and Lynn had packed the
scripts with plenty of pertinent themes (including secrecy, censorship, diplomatic tensions, crises in education and the arts, political leaks, Cabinet
infighting, local government issues and scandals in the City), and Sydney
Lotterby had ensured that everything from the size and accuracy of the
sets to the intensity and quality of the rehearsals was even better than the
previous series (he even had the everyday sounds around Whitehall and
Number Ten, including the chimes of Big Ben, recorded to provide a very
faint ambient soundtrack for when the Cabinet Room was shown).

The new series began on Thursday, 3 December 1987 in its usual slot:
9 p.m. on BBC2. The front-page news that morning had included reports
of a former Prime Minister (Edward Heath) criticising the current Prime
Minister (Margaret Thatcher).[18] It seemed an apt sign. The time was just
right for *Yes, Prime Minister* to make its return.

It would show Hacker to be a more frustrated and disillusioned figure
than before, his dream of realising his 'Grand Design' long since dashed
and his sense of purpose greatly diminished. Gone was the would-be 'head-
master of the nation'; what was left was more of a glorified relief teacher,

always wondering how, in the parlance of past PMs, 'to make angles into curves'.[19] Surrounded by order-paper-waving sycophants in the spotlight of the Commons (including 'the ones hoping to be promoted' and 'the ones afraid of being sacked'[20]) and stalked by rivals in all kinds of shadowy places outside of the lower chamber, he now seems to have realised, belatedly, that he is playing a leading role that has been cruelly underwritten:

> HACKER: When I became Prime Minister I thought I was going to have *power*. And what *have* I got? I've got *influence*, that's all. I've got no power over the police, the rates, EEC directives, the European courts, our courts, the judges, NATO . . . What *have* I got the power to do?[21]

His Cabinet Secretary's answer to that question will be bleak: he should simply be grateful for what he already has, which is 'responsibility without power – the prerogative of the eunuch throughout the ages'.[22] His Party Chairman's answer will, if anything, be even bleaker: 'You have the power to lose us the next election'.[23]

He is the one goldfish in the goldfish bowl, swimming round in circles open-mouthed, occasionally bumping his head on the glass as he seeks an escape from the dull routine. His mind is no longer preoccupied with the pull of destiny; it is, from now on, consumed by the prosaic details that dog him from day to day.

Sir Humphrey, meanwhile, is his usual dominant and Delphic self, moving around Whitehall as he sees fit, as fluid as Hacker is fixed, making sure that he maintains a panoptic view of all that happens within the political system as a whole. 'I need to know everything,' he stresses. 'How else can I judge whether or not I need to know it?'[24]

It is Bernard Woolley who will seem the most different in this series. He is still naive (HACKER: 'Say that it's a pack of lies.' WOOLLEY: 'Yes, but, the thing is, it is, sort of, *true*.' HACKER: 'Oh shut up!'[25]), still pointlessly picky ('I'm sorry to be pedantic, but if you *nail* a leak you make another'[26]), still addicted to childish puns (SIR HUMPHREY: 'It was nicked. By two of last year's pupils.' WOOLLEY: 'A pair of nickers'[27]), and still woolly (WOOLLEY: 'Do you know what my problem is?' SIR

HUMPHREY: 'Your problem, Bernard, is that you don't ever come to the point!'[28]), but, as he bosses around various underlings in the Prime Minister's Office, he is also shown to be busier than ever, a little more confident, slightly more outspoken and even, when the occasion seems to warrant it, more likely to show some real initiative. While Hacker and Sir Humphrey are therefore merely trying to maintain their status at the top, Woolley, at last, is showing signs of being ready to shin further up the greasy pole.

The predicament of Hacker, however, remains the main focus of this series. Suspicious of Whitehall, suspicious of Westminster, he now belongs to no one and everyone, a solitary leader facing up to an uncertain future.

The first episode, called 'Man Overboard', captured this climate of chronic insecurity extremely well by showing Hacker sitting on his own inside the Cabinet Room, worrying about a possible challenge to his leadership. As usual, his anxiety has been artfully exacerbated by Sir Humphrey.

It all stems from a proposal by the Employment Secretary to relocate a proportion of Britain's armed services personnel from the south to the north of England. Hacker thinks that it is a splendidly sensible idea. There is currently little or no logic, he notes, in the concentration of so much of the armed forces – about four hundred thousand personnel – in the south when there are only twenty thousand in the north. 'The Admiralty Ships Division needs a deep-water port,' he says sarcastically, 'so that has to be at Bath – thirty miles inland! The job of the Marines is to defend Norway so we station them at Plymouth! Armoured vehicle trials take place in Scotland so the military engineering establishment clearly has to be in Surrey!'

Even Sir Humphrey, in private, considers it 'a very reasonable plan', but his colleagues at the Ministry of Defence are horrified by it. Besides bossing the Department around and ignoring its own inscrutable 'strategy', it will also, they moan, undermine morale among the top brass: the senior officers and their wives, stuck permanently 'up north', will be denied regular access to such staples of 'civilisation' as Wimbledon, Ascot, Henley, the Army & Navy Club and Harrods. It is all, they insist, quite intolerable.

Sir Humphrey sympathises with his metropolitan-minded associates, but he realises that it would be foolish to attack the plan, so he elects to attack the man instead. The Employment Secretary is the one responsible for the idea, so, if the paranoid Prime Minister was to have reason to question the motives behind it, he might well be inclined abruptly to withdraw his support.

Sir Humphrey duly sets to work. All he needs to do is stand patiently and silently as Hacker defends the plan against whatever objections he imagines Whitehall will make, and then, at the moment the Prime Minister praises the Employment Secretary for suggesting it, pull up a chair, sit down and agree wholeheartedly about what a 'good chap' the Minister is:

SIR HUMPHREY:	He's absolutely *brilliant*. A *superb* intellect. Strong footwork. Excellent elbows. Oh, a *major* figure without a doubt.
HACKER:	*[Sounding slightly jealous]* He's not *that* good!
SIR HUMPHREY:	But he *is* a good chap, wouldn't you say?
HACKER:	Well, yes, I just said so.
SIR HUMPHREY:	Oh, yes, indeed. Very *popular*.
HACKER:	*[Looking slightly concerned]* Is he?
SIR HUMPHREY:	Oh, yes!
HACKER:	Not as popular as *that*, surely?
SIR HUMPHREY:	Oh, yes. In Whitehall. And with the Parliamentary Party, I understand.
HACKER:	Ah, with the Parliamentary Party, I suppose, yes.
SIR HUMPHREY:	And with the grass roots, so I'm told.
HACKER:	Are you?
SIR HUMPHREY:	And he has quite a following in Cabinet, too, doesn't he?
HACKER:	*[His expression growing grim]* Does he?
SIR HUMPHREY:	In fact, people are beginning to talk about him as the next Prime Minister.
HACKER:	Wha-What do you mean??
SIR HUMPHREY:	Oh, I mean when you decide to retire.
HACKER:	I'm not *going* to *retire*! I've only just *got* here!

Sir Humphrey, smiling brightly, rises to his feet and prepares to leave, but Hacker now is hooked:

HACKER:	Why should people be talking about the *next* Prime Minister?
SIR HUMPHREY:	Oh, I'm sure it's just general speculation, Prime Minister.
HACKER:	Does *he* want to be Prime Minister?
SIR HUMPHREY:	Well, even if he *does*, surely you've got no reason to suspect his *loyalty*? I mean, he isn't planning to build up a personal following or anything. Is he?
HACKER:	*Isn't* he?
SIR HUMPHREY:	*Is* he?

Hacker is well and truly rattled. He studies the Employment Secretary's most recent speeches and is angered when he cannot find any positive remarks about his leadership. This, and the amount of time he spends chatting up backbenchers in the tea room, and the number of them he invites to his home for cosy dinner parties, now strikes Hacker as 'bloody suspicious'.

The seed that Sir Humphrey has planted then receives more than enough nourishment with which to grow when Hacker summons his Chief Whip. This supposedly omniscient official, unwilling to admit that he has absolutely no idea what his Prime Minister is talking about, is sucked into the speculation:

HACKER:	*[Coldly]* How are things going, Chief Whip?
CHIEF WHIP:	*[Suspiciously]* Er, quite well, really. Why?
HACKER:	You've *noticed* nothing?
CHIEF WHIP:	Well . . . It's a difficult time . . . bit of unrest on the backbenches. But what, er, did you have in mind, er, precisely?
HACKER:	A plot! A leadership challenge!
CHIEF WHIP:	*[Trying to hide his surprise]* Ah. Yes. Well, actually, I have no real *evidence* of anything.
HACKER:	But you have *suspicions*?
CHIEF WHIP:	Oh, I *always* have suspicions!
HACKER:	How far has it gone?
CHIEF WHIP:	Only a very . . . um . . . ah . . . very . . . um . . . ah . . .

WOOLLEY:	Early stage?
CHIEF WHIP:	Early stage. As far as one can tell.
HACKER:	Do you think you ought to have a *word* with him? Tell him I *know* what's going on? I don't want to lose him from the Cabinet, I just want him under *control*.
CHIEF WHIP:	Perhaps, er, you should have a word with him yourself?
HACKER:	No, no, no, not at this stage. Who else is involved?
CHIEF WHIP:	Apart from . . .?
HACKER:	Apart from Dudley, obviously.
CHIEF WHIP:	*[Startled]* Dudley?? *[Recovers composure]* Yes, of course, apart from Dudley. Well . . . apart from *Dudley*, well, it's, um, it's a bit early to say. I-I mean, there may be nothing in it.
HACKER:	Geoffrey, I'm not taking any risks!
CHIEF WHIP:	No, absolutely *not*! Now I'll go and make a few more enquiries!

Sir Humphrey now cranks up the intensity of the situation by leaking to the press certain 'confidential disinformation' which suggests that the Prime Minister is blocking his Employment Secretary's plan. Upon seeing this on the front page of his newspaper, Hacker is convinced that it has been planted there by his supposed 'rival' to make him look bad, and he retaliates by leaking his own information (conveniently supplied by the MOD via Sir Humphrey) that outlines all of the possible problems with the plan.

The Employment Secretary, confused and angered by this apparent betrayal, promptly resigns from the Government in protest (accusing the Prime Minister of being 'dictatorial' and of running 'a presidential-style Government'). Hacker is thus relieved to have defeated his rival (and rather flattered by the claims that he is 'dictatorial' and 'presidential'), and Sir Humphrey is pleased to have thwarted his plan.

There is, however, one more twist in this tale. Sir Humphrey moves to ensure that Hacker harbours no doubts about his decision by revealing that, as far as he understands it, the Employment Secretary had already been planning to resign, on Budget Day, over a lack of sufficient funds for him to deal with the problem of unemployment. Hacker agrees that, in that case, it was quite right to force him out.

Feeling that his job is done, Sir Humphrey is happy to indulge the Prime Minister, congratulating him on his 'brilliant' and strong leadership. Hacker, however, once he has dictated a suitably triumphant-sounding press release, startles Sir Humphrey by suddenly swerving off-piste:

> HACKER: Hold on, I've got an idea!
>
> SIR HUMPHREY: Prime Minister!
>
> HACKER: Now that the Employment Secretary is gone, we could *reinstate* the plan!
>
> SIR HUMPHREY: *[Stunned]* But . . .
>
> HACKER: Don't you see? I could press *on* with it now! And it won't look like weakness, it'll look like *strength*!
>
> SIR HUMPHREY: But the whole point was—
>
> HACKER: Was what? It wasn't to stop the *plan*, surely?
>
> SIR HUMPHREY: No, no, no . . . It was to, um, establish your authority.
>
> HACKER: Exactly! And I've done that. So if we recreate the plan it will show that I *wasn't* against it and that Dudley's resignation was pointless! Right?
>
> *[Sir Humphrey is so angry and confused he is struggling to speak]*
>
> HACKER: Put it top of the agenda for the next Cabinet. Okay?
>
> SIR HUMPHREY: . . . Yes, Prime Minister.

Having restored the familiar see-sawing struggle between Hacker and Sir Humphrey with this entertaining opening episode, the series could move on to resume its exploration of the system as a whole, keeping sight of the big picture as it delved into the most telling details. The spirit of Richard Crossman, in particular, would seem to haunt many of these episodes, almost as if the writers had returned to their original inspiration in order to refresh the clarity of their critique, cutting through all of the superficial issues to remind people of the most essential dynamics of power.

There was even an early nod and a wink as to how this classic source had first crept into the public consciousness. Just as the news of the plan to publish the first volume of Crossman's diaries had caused consternation in the Cabinet Office during the mid-1970s (with the Cabinet Secretary of the time, Sir John Hunt, warning his colleagues that allowing it to reach the public domain 'would bring the whole system into disrepute', and the Prime Minister, Harold Wilson, raging at the damning depiction of him as a master of tactics with no idea of strategy[29]), so the news (in episode two) that Hacker's predecessor is preparing his own volume of memoirs prompts Sir Humphrey and Hacker to worry about its possible revelations. While the book featured in the sitcom fails to end up in print (thanks to the premature death of its author), many of the insights that did end up being published in Crossman's three volumes are gleefully reprised in this set of storylines.

In both the first and the second episodes, for example, the old Crossman idea of the Civil Service in general, and the Cabinet Secretariat in particular, as the 'keeper of the muniments' was illustrated, more directly and in greater detail than ever before, via a compelling two-part masterclass from Sir Humphrey. Part one of the demonstration occurs during a Cabinet meeting when Hacker's soon-to-be ousted Employment Secretary, furious about the fate of his plan, protests (quite rightly) that the Prime Minister had promised in the previous session that it would be given further discussion.

Sir Humphrey intervenes here to show how much control he has as the master of the minutes:

SIR HUMPHREY: There was *no* such promise, and the Prime Minister did *not* support the proposal. If he *had*, it would appear in the minutes. And it doesn't.

MINISTER: *Doesn't* it? Prime Minister, why was my request for a further discussion, and your reply, not minuted?

HACKER: Er, I . . .

SIR HUMPHREY: It is characteristic of all committee discussions and decisions that every member has a vivid recollection of them and that every member's recollection of them differs violently from every

other member's recollection. Consequently,
we accept the convention that the official
decisions are those, and only those, which
have been officially recorded in the minutes
by the officials, from which it emerges with an
elegant inevitability that any decision which has
been officially reached will have been officially
recorded in the minutes by the officials, and any
decision which is not recorded in the minutes
has not been officially reached – even if one or
more members believe they can recollect it. So,
in this particular case, if the decision had been
officially reached, it would have been officially
recorded in the minutes by the officials. And it
isn't, so it wasn't.

HACKER: Told you so!

The second part of the masterclass takes place in the next episode, when Woolley asks for advice about how best to report what happened at another important meeting:

SIR HUMPHREY: Bernard, the minutes do not record everything that was said at a meeting, do they?

WOOLLEY: Well, no, of course not.

SIR HUMPHREY: And people change their minds during a meeting, don't they?

WOOLLEY: Well, yes.

SIR HUMPHREY: So the actual meeting is a mass of ingredients for you to choose from.

WOOLLEY: Oh. Like cooking?

SIR HUMPHREY: Like – no, *not* like cooking! Better not to use that word in connection with books or minutes. You choose, from a jumble of ill-digested ideas, a version which represents the Prime Minister's views as he would, on *reflection*, have liked them to emerge.

WOOLLEY: But, if it's not a *true* record . . .

SIR HUMPHREY: The purpose of minutes is not to record events, it
                  is to protect people. You do not take notes. If the
                  Prime Minister says something he did not mean to
                  say, particularly if it contradicts something he has
                  said publicly, you try to improve on what has been
                  said. Put it in a better order. You are *tactful*.

WOOLLEY: But how do I justify that?

SIR HUMPHREY: You are his servant.

WOOLLEY: Oh. Yes.

SIR HUMPHREY: A minute is a note for the records, and a
                  statement of action, if any, that was agreed upon.

Another theme that was featured in more than one episode was that of
the increasingly cynical view of, and attitude towards, the modern mass
media. First, for example, there was a summary[30] of how politicians viewed
those newspapers that were still supposed to be one of the means whereby
the governors are monitored by the governed:

SIR HUMPHREY: The only way to understand the press is to
                  remember that they pander to their readers'
                  prejudices.

HACKER: Don't tell *me* about the press. I know exactly
                  who reads the papers: the *Daily Mirror* is read
                  by people who think they run the country;
                  the *Guardian* is read by people who think they
                  ought to run the country; *The Times* is read by
                  people who actually do run the country; the
                  Daily Mail is read by the wives of the people
                  who run the country; the *Financial Times* is read
                  by people who own the country; the *Morning
                  Star* is read by people who think the country
                  ought to be run by another country; and the
                  Daily Telegraph is read by people who think it is.

SIR HUMPHREY: Prime Minister, what about the people who read
                  The Sun?

WOOLLEY: The *Sun* readers don't care who runs the country,
             as long as she's got big tits.[31]

This was followed by a glimpse of how troublesome complexities, rather than being explained and defended, are instead secreted away inside a range of tabloid-friendly clichés:

HACKER: I'm not at all happy about my speech for the
              Party Conference. It contains absolutely no good
              news.
WAINWRIGHT: We couldn't think of any.
HACKER: Well, we have to make the bad news *look* good.
              Now, I'd better say something about the Health
              Service – 'care for the elderly . . . mothers
              and children . . . growing up into a healthy
              nation . . .'
WAINWRIGHT: 'Value for money'?
HACKER: Can't say that. Everybody knows that costs are
              completely out of control.
WAINWRIGHT: Right: 'We are spending more than ever to make
              our Health Service the best in the world'.
HACKER: Good. Now, Defence. I was hoping to say
              something about defence cuts but I haven't been
              able to persuade them to make any yet.
WAINWRIGHT: 'This Government will not put the security
              of the nation in jeopardy by penny-pinching
              and false economies'. Not that we'd really have
              put the security of the nation in jeopardy by
              having *one* service music school instead of three
              separate ones for the Army, Navy and the RAF. I
              mean, there can hardly be a specific Royal Naval
              method of playing the bassoon!
HACKER: You're not going to put that in, are you? *[She
              glowers at him]* Er, no, sorry.
WAINWRIGHT: Is there anything good we can say about the
              economy?

HACKER:	Hmm, the economy, that's a problem. No really good news at all.
WAINWRIGHT:	Oh, we'll find something. Unemployment coming down at all?
HACKER:	No.
WAINWRIGHT:	'We shall make the attack on unemployment our top priority'. Pay?
HACKER:	Rising too fast.
WAINWRIGHT:	'We cannot afford to pay ourselves more than we earn, and the world does not owe us a living'. Interest rates?
HACKER:	Too high.
WAINWRIGHT:	You mean *they* might come down before the Conference? Now *that* would be terrific!
HACKER:	I don't have that kind of luck.
WAINWRIGHT:	Well, if the whole picture's a total disaster we could always wave the Union Jack: 'The nation's great destiny'.
HACKER:	'Unique role on the world stage'.
WAINWRIGHT:	'Devote every effort to building a peaceful and prosperous world for our children, and our children's children'.
HACKER:	That's probably about how long it'll take![32]

Then there was recognition of how, in the age of spin, politicians much prefer to use media interviews to evade rather than engage with the electorate. When, for instance, Sir Humphrey prepares for a rare exchange with an 'outsider' in the media, Hacker is only too happy to give him the benefit of his own expertise:

HACKER:	If he *does* say that lots of people want to know the answer to that question, you say: 'Name *six*!' That'll fix him – he'll never be able to remember more than two!
SIR HUMPHREY:	Oh, excellent, Prime Minister. Any more tricks?
HACKER:	'*Tricks*,' Humphrey? This is *technique*. Attack

> *one* word in the sentence, like, um, 'frequently':
> '"*Frequently*"? What do you *mean*, "frequently"?'
> Or attack the interviewer. Say: 'You clearly have
> never read the White Paper itself, have you!' Or
> else ask your own question, like: 'That was a
> very interesting question. Now let me ask *you* a
> question!' You see?

SIR HUMPHREY: Oh, *thank* you, Prime Minister.[33]

In addition to all of this, there was also another reference to the readiness of contemporary politicians to turn practically any occasion, no matter how ostensibly delicate or dignified, into a self-serving media stunt. When, for example, a state funeral is being planned, Hacker can hardly wait to exploit its PR potential. 'Dignified grief goes down very well with the voters, especially when it's shared by the world's statesmen,' he says, before adding dreamily, 'It's a wonderful thing, death – so *uncontroversial . . .*'[34]

Such a coldly calculating attitude slotted very snugly into the broader theme of the amoral nature that the system tends to cultivate. Time and again, from one episode to the next, the notion of dishonesty, deviousness and dirty hands kept intruding rudely into view:

SIR ARNOLD: I presume the Prime Minister is in favour of the
                 scheme because it will reduce unemployment?
SIR HUMPHREY: Well, it'll *look* as if he's reducing unemployment.
SIR ARNOLD: Or look as if he's *trying* to reduce
                 unemployment.
SIR HUMPHREY: Whereas in reality he's only trying to look as if
                 he's trying to reduce unemployment.
SIR ARNOLD: Yes, because he's worried that it doesn't *look* as
                 if he's trying to look as if he's trying to reduce
                 unemployment.[35]

PRESS OFFICER: Do you want to give any interviews?
HACKER: Certainly not.
PRESS OFFICER: Shall I say why?

HACKER: Oh, make it a quote: 'Insignificant matter of
                   no national importance, typical of the media's
                   trivialisation of politics'.
PRESS OFFICER: And who shall I attribute that quote to?
HACKER: 'Close Cabinet colleagues'.[36]

SIR HUMPHREY: It's up to you, Bernard, what do you want?
WOOLLEY: I want to have a clear conscience.
SIR HUMPHREY: A *clear conscience*?
WOOLLEY: Yes.
SIR HUMPHREY: When did you acquire this taste for luxuries?[37]

The most overtly ideological episodes in the series were the sixth ('The
Patron of the Arts') and the seventh ('The National Education Service'),
both of which seemed heavily influenced by, and inclined towards, the
kind of public choice theory ideas that were still being popularised by
the Conservative Government. Antony Jay, by this time, was not only
well known for his support of such views, but was also (unofficially)
writing some of the witty lines, phrases and passages that defended them
in the speeches of not only Margaret Thatcher herself, but also certain
real-life Cabinet Ministers of the day, including the Chancellor of the
Exchequer, Nigel Lawson.[38] It would therefore be his input, rather than
that of Jonathan Lynn, that would be most noticeable in these particular
storylines.

'The Patron of the Arts' was, in a sense, a reprise of the old *Yes Minister*
episode from 1982, 'The Middle-Class Rip-Off', but, though making the
same basic point, it was at least mercifully less crude in the manner of its
exposition. It concerned the plight of Jim Hacker, who, having accepted
an invitation to be guest of honour at the annual British Theatre Awards
dinner, now knows that the size of next year's grant to the Arts Council is
going to be cut, so he is desperate to avoid being attacked and ridiculed
by angry actors as 'the philistine at Number Ten' at an event that will be
broadcast live on television.

What follows is the same simplistic distinction between an absurdly
snobbish defence of subsidised culture ('We have a great heritage to support,' Sir Humphrey haughtily exclaims. 'Pictures hardly anyone wants

to see, music hardly anyone wants to hear, plays hardly anyone wants to watch. You can't let them die just because nobody's interested!') and a lazy dismissal of it ('There are no votes for me in giving money to the arts,' moans Hacker). The story itself, though, is considerably more interesting and entertaining.

Hacker searches for a solution to his PR problem. Sir Humphrey proves to be of no use when he asks for advice about how to handle the occasion (HACKER: 'It's to be to a hostile audience of posturing, self-righteous, theatrical drunks.' SIR HUMPHREY: 'The House of Commons, you mean?'), but his political adviser Dorothy Wainwright comes up trumps when she suggests that he should call the bluff of the artistic activists by threatening to sell the National Theatre and devolve dramatic productions, thus leaving the company to hire existing theatres around the country and become 'strolling players again instead of . . . civil servants'.

This proposal so scares the Managing Director of the National Theatre that he abandons plans to attack the Prime Minister publicly and instead meekly accepts the reduction in his grant. 'There are many calls on the public purse,' he says contritely, delivering his speech as Hacker sits beside him, gloating. 'Education . . . inner cities . . . health . . . kidney machines . . .'

Jonathan Lynn would later claim that the episode had managed to be so even-handed in the way it covered its subject that it provoked a range of reactions that said more about those who espoused them than it did about the content itself. 'The interesting thing about this programme was that everyone saw in it what they wanted to see,' he said. 'All our socialist friends were convinced that this programme proved that we were socialists. All our Conservative friends felt that this proved that we were Conservatives. This episode appeared to be an attack on Thatcher's policy towards the arts, but it was also, at the same time, critical of the way that arts organisations ran themselves. The arguments set out in the programme were equally hostile to both sides.'[39]

This was surely a little too generous an interpretation. While it is true that the episode did indeed score some strong satirical points against the management of arts organisations (a critique helped by the fact that Lynn, as a director at the National Theatre, knew all about its faults as well as its strengths), in addition to the cynicism of certain aspects of Government policy on the arts, it was still arguably the case that the majority of viewers, left to form a judgement purely on the evidence of the story, would have been far more sympathetic to Hacker's aesthetic incomprehension than they would have been to Sir Humphrey's glib elitism.

A more balanced treatment of the issue would have had someone counter the contemptuous comments with a positive argument for such funding, but the only lines given to the pro-arts representatives were ones that questioned alternative uses of public money: HACKER: 'We'll do what we can, but there are many calls on the public purse, y'know: inner cities, schools, hospitals, kidney machines . . .' ACTORS: '. . . Tanks, rockets, H-bombs . . .' The closest the episode came, therefore, to a positive defence of the arts was that the arts were not as morally dubious a waste of public money as tanks, rockets or H-bombs.

For two writers who were themselves working in the arts, and collaborating on a sitcom that almost certainly would never have found an audience, or at least a broad audience, anywhere else but the publicly funded BBC, the approach seemed, to put it mildly, less than gracious. It was not just biting the hand that fed them. It was also, some might say, punching themselves in the mouth.

A far more ambitious and impressive form of satirical polemic took shape in the subsequent episode, 'The National Education Service'. This saw Hacker, spurred on by Dorothy Wainwright, resolve to revamp his Government's education policy dramatically by dragging schools into the marketplace:

> WAINWRIGHT: Suppose schools were like doctors. I mean, after
>   all, under the National Health Service you can
>   choose whichever doctor you like to go to, can't
>   you?
> HACKER: Yes.
> WAINWRIGHT: And he gets paid per patient. Well, why don't
>   we do the same with schools? Have a National
>   Education Service. The parents could choose the
>   schools they want and the schools get paid per
>   pupil.

There was in fact a real-life backdrop to this idea. Back in 1982, Sir Keith Joseph, the then Secretary of State for Education and an arch-monetarist, wanted to introduce education vouchers. Every parent would receive a voucher and be free to 'cash it in' at a school of his or her choice – the theory being that, under the influence of parental choice operating in a schools market, the efficient would flourish while the inefficient would go to the wall.

Margaret Thatcher (criticised repeatedly by her predecessor Edward Heath for being 'obsessed' with market economics and eager to see people shop for their children's education 'as though they were in Sainsbury's or Marks & Spencer'[40]) was known to have been much in favour of this 'noble concept', but it was not long before Sir Keith was meekly acknowledging (in a paper prepared for him by his civil servants) numerous problems that suggested his own plan would be 'impracticable and costly'. The result was that, after a year or so of internal deliberations, the Government, instead of succeeding in establishing parent power, ended up with even more centralised DES power: in short, the Government got the exact opposite of what it had set out to achieve, while the supposedly 'tamed' Civil Service had delivered precisely what it had wanted.[41]

The topic, therefore, fitted perfectly within *Yes, Prime Minister*'s classic Whitehall versus Westminster battleground, and also provided the writers with an opportunity to revisit the original ideological argument. 'Dorothy Wainwright,' Jonathan Lynn would later acknowledge, 'was arguing pure Friedmanism when she countered Sir Humphrey's claim that it was impossible to rationalise education without centralisation by pointing out that two and a half thousand private schools solve planning problems every day by simply responding to changing circumstances – i.e., to the marketplace'.[42]

Likewise, Sir Humphrey's response to the proposal very much mirrors the Civil Service's actual response to the education voucher plan:

SIR HUMPHREY: With respect, Prime Minister, I think that the
                DES will react with some caution to your rather
                novel proposal.
HACKER: You mean they'll block it?
SIR HUMPHREY: I *mean* they will give it the most serious

and urgent consideration and insist on a
thorough and rigorous examination of all
the proposals, allied to a detailed feasibility
study and budget analysis, before producing a
consultative document for consideration by all
interested bodies and seeking comments and
recommendations to be included in a brief, for
a series of working parties who will produce
individual studies which will provide the
background for a more wide-ranging document,
considering whether or not the proposal should
be taken forward to the next stage.

HACKER: You mean they'll block it?
SIR HUMPHREY: Yup.

The writing, as usual, is on the wall at Whitehall, and Hacker, like Sir Keith before him, knows that his plan is doomed. Jonathan Lynn did not see the episode as the show 'taking sides'; he and Jay saw themselves merely recording how things worked, or failed to work, in the 1980s.[43] Antony Jay, while acknowledging his personal preferences, would make much the same point: 'It might have been that we, not as experts but as outside observers, thought that certain policy options were viable and good, but that was as far as it ever went. We were not trying to abolish the DES, though if it had come as a result of our programme we would not have been shocked or saddened particularly'.[44]

The series concluded by returning its focus to the more personal dimension of the relationship between Hacker and Sir Humphrey. Ever since that first day back in 1980 at the DAA, this trapped relationship between politician and civil servant had given all of the show's ideas and themes their flesh, bones and blood, their human mise en scène, and it was therefore only fitting that the finale should explore this strangely intimate partnership one more time.

Entitled 'The Tangled Web', the story (another strikingly prescient one, bearing in mind later real-life hacking scandals) concerned surveillance, secrecy and survival. It begins with Hacker in an unusually ebullient mood, boasting about his latest performance in the Commons at Prime

Minister's Questions. 'They were on their feet,' he says of his backbenchers, 'cheering, stamping, waving their order papers!'

Unfortunately, it turns out that one of his answers was problematic. When asked if he had authorised the tapping of an MP, Hugh Halifax's, telephone, Hacker had denied any such involvement, dismissing the accusation as 'sheer paranoia'. Sir Humphrey, however, is furious about this response:

SIR HUMPHREY: So, I gather you denied that Mr Halifax's phone had been bugged?

HACKER: Well, obviously, it was the one question today to which I could give a clear, simple, straightforward, honest answer.

SIR HUMPHREY: Yes, unfortunately although the answer was indeed clear, simple and straightforward, there is some difficulty in justifiably assigning to it the fourth of the epithets you applied to the statement, inasmuch as the precise correlation between the information you communicated and the facts insofar as they can be determined and demonstrated is such as to cause epistemological problems of sufficient magnitude as to lay upon the logical and semantic resources of the English language a heavier burden than they can reasonably be expected to bear.

HACKER: *Epistemological?* What are you *talking* about?

SIR HUMPHREY: You told a lie.

HACKER: A *lie??*

SIR HUMPHREY: A lie.

HACKER: What do you *mean* a lie?

SIR HUMPHREY: I mean you . . . lied. Yes, I know, this is a difficult concept to get across to a politician. Um, you, um . . . ah, yes: you did not tell the truth.

It turns out that, up until about seventeen minutes ago, Hugh Halifax's telephone was indeed being tapped. This means that the Prime Minister has, unknowingly but still technically, misled the House of Commons.

Hacker is horrified. Why, he exclaims, was he not told about this? Sir Humphrey tries to explain:

SIR HUMPHREY: It was thought that it was better not to inform
                you. You see, Hugh Halifax is one of your
                Government team and as such it was thought
                that it was better not to create distrust. We only
                tell you when you should be *aware*.

HACKER: And when's that?

SIR HUMPHREY: You should *now* be aware because you've just
                denied it.

HACKER: Well, it would have been rather more helpful if
                I'd been aware *before* I denied it!

SIR HUMPHREY: On the contrary, Prime Minister, if you had been
                aware *before* you denied it, you *wouldn't* have
                denied it.

HACKER: But I needed to *know*!

SIR HUMPHREY: We do not always tell you about bugging when
                you need to know.

WOOLLEY: You see, at times, Prime Minister, we need you
                not to know.

HACKER: *Why* did you decide that I didn't need to know?

SIR HUMPHREY: I didn't.

HACKER: Well, who did?

SIR HUMPHREY: Nobody. It was just that nobody decided to tell
                you.

HACKER: Well, that's the same thing!

SIR HUMPHREY: On the contrary, Prime Minister. To decide to
                conceal information from you is a heavy burden
                for any official to shoulder, but to decide not to
                reveal information to you is routine procedure.

Hacker is none the wiser, but he does know that there has been a terrible 'cock-up' and, as a result, his political future is in peril. Sir Humphrey, however, does not seem very sympathetic, pointing out that the Prime Minister 'should not have denied something about which you did not know', and, crucially, he made that error of judgement because he did not first clear his answers with his officials.

There is worse news to come. Sir Humphrey has been summoned by the House of Commons Privileges Committee to respond to the allegations about the matter. He knows what lies in store – if he tries to dodge the damning questions, they will ask him why he will not give the same clear denial that the Prime Minister has already given the House of Commons – so even he is unsure how best to proceed.

Hacker is shaken badly enough when he first hears of this development, but is left even worse when he encounters Sir Humphrey at his most pompous:

> HACKER: You'll just have to confirm what I said in the House.
> SIR HUMPHREY: But that would be lying.
> HACKER: Well . . . *[whispers conspiratorially]* nobody would *know.*
> SIR HUMPHREY: Oh, what a tangled web we weave!
> HACKER: Humphrey! You must! Otherwise it'll look as though *I* was lying!
>
> *[Sir Humphrey looks unconvinced]*
>
> HACKER: Humphrey – you have a loyalty!
> SIR HUMPHREY: *[Solemnly]* To the truth. I'm sorry, Prime Minister, I cannot become involved in some shabby cover-up.

The Cabinet Secretary then departs to give a rare interview to BBC Radio 3. He is his usual impenetrable self throughout the conversation, but then, once it is over, he relaxes and speaks with dangerous candour on a range of potentially inflammatory topics, including the 'parasites' among the unemployed, entirely unaware that the tape is still running.

Once, back in Whitehall, he receives what appears to be an advance copy of the programme, he is horrified to hear that all of his most indiscreet 'off the record' remarks have been included. 'What am I going to do?' he asks Woolley, looking utterly helpless and despondent.

Luckily for him, Woolley realises that the producer is an old friend of his from their time together at Oxford, so he races off and takes possession of the offending master tape. Before he reassures Sir Humphrey, however, he decides to let the Prime Minister in on the secret, and plays him the tape.

Hacker, realising its significance, is delighted. Parity, in his daily power struggle with Sir Humphrey, is about to be restored.

When Sir Humphrey arrives in the Cabinet Room, Hacker relishes the opportunity to play back the recording and watch his old colleague squirm. Sure enough, the sound of each incriminating word hammers another nail into the coffin of Sir Humphrey's composure, draining the blood from his frightened face. Once the tape has been heard in all of its horror, Hacker – adopting the stock political pose of studied solemnity – warns him of what a disaster it would be if such loose talk should ever reach the papers. Quivering with contrition, Sir Humphrey is pathetically eager to prove his remorse, and is even prepared to lie – or, as he prefers to put it, 'issue a clarification' – in order to explain away the potential embarrassment. 'Clarification,' he tries to explain with a nervously con-spiratorial snigger, 'is not to make oneself *clear*; it is to put oneself *in* the clear'. Hacker, struggling to hide his delight at hearing such a naked offer of deceit, looks at the blanched and bowed Sir Humphrey knowingly and then remarks: 'Oh, what a tangled web we weave!'

The torture over, Hacker assures Sir Humphrey that he has possession of the only existing copies of the recording. He cannot resist, however, withholding them for a while longer, claiming that he needs to ponder the security issues involved: 'I certainly have no intention of joining in some shabby cover-up . . .'

Then, as if apropos of nothing in particular, he asks Sir Humphrey if he has decided yet what he will tell the Privileges Committee:

SIR HUMPHREY: Ah, yes, Prime Minister, I have decided that in the interests of, ah, national security, that, um, the only honourable course is to support your statement in the House.

HACKER: And say that Hugh Halifax's telephone has never been bugged?

SIR HUMPHREY: And say that I have no evidence—
HACKER: *No*, Humphrey! And say the Government
has never authorised the bugging of MPs'
telephones!
SIR HUMPHREY: And say the Government has never authorised
the . . . *[He shivers with discomfort]* Supposing
they find out the truth?
HACKER: You'll just have to say that nobody told you.
Because you didn't need to know. Agreed?

[Sir Humphrey sighs dejectedly]

HACKER: Splendid. Well, that's settled, then!

[Sir Humphrey rises, and holds out his hands]

SIR HUMPHREY: May one have one's tapes back?

[Hacker moves to hand them over, hesitates, then thinks better of it]

HACKER: Tomorrow. After the Committee on Privileges.
All right, Humphrey?
SIR HUMPHREY: *[Glumly]* Yes, Prime Minister.

This time, Sir Humphrey had been thwarted. The next time, one suspected, Hacker would probably be the one to lose out. That was how it had always been. That was how it would always be. That was the main message that came from this, and all of the other, episodes.

For that run at least, though, that was the end of it. The music began, the credits rolled, the audience applauded, the programme ended. The series was over.

There was no audible or on-screen announcement about what, if anything, was happening next with *Yes, Prime Minister*. All that was said was that this was the end of the run. The show's most avid fans were left in the dark, hoping that a third series would soon come.

12

The End

Style is an instrument, and is made imperishable only by embodiment in some great use. It is not of itself stuff to last; neither can it have real beauty except when working the substantial effects of thought or vision. Its highest triumph is to hit the meaning; and the pleasure you get from it is not unlike that which you get from the perfect action of skill.

The third series never did come. That final instalment, which went out on 28 January 1988, would be the last. After thirty-eight episodes in eight years, *Yes Minister*, and *Yes, Prime Minister*, was at an end.

It had gone out at the top, as the team had wanted. The last series attracted the usual critical applause (the *Observer*, for example, judged it 'nearly perfect'[1]) and awards (including a fourth BAFTA for Nigel Hawthorne – again, alas, at Paul Eddington's expense – and a richly deserved special writers' award for Antony Jay and Jonathan Lynn).

It was repeated at the end of 1988 on BBC1, and, just like the previous series, brought in a bigger audience. There was still no official confirmation that the sitcom was now over. There would be the occasional comment in the newspapers expressing hope that another series would soon be announced, and critics continued to refer to the show in the present tense as if it remained a going concern. It just never returned.

When asked, twenty-six years later, whether there had been any doubt in the two writers' minds as to the fate of the programme, Antony Jay was inclined, on reflection, to say that the line had indeed been drawn: 'It was fairly clear to me and Johnny that Paul [Eddington] wasn't up to another series. Also, Johnny and I felt we had pretty well exhausted the possibilities – if we went on we'd be in danger of repeating ourselves.'[2] Jonathan Lynn, however, would reply to the same question with a playfully ambiguous answer. 'Yes,' he said. 'And no.'[3]

'We'd had a wrap party,' Derek Fowlds would later recall, 'at which we all got rather merry! And we knew that Johnny and Tony had said that they *probably* weren't doing any more. So we sort of knew that that was it. But we always knew that all of us would stay friends, so that made it easier. The friendships would go on.'[4]

Nothing was ruled out definitively in the years that followed, except for the idea of reuniting just to do more of the same. Everyone was busy doing other things, but there would still be isolated moments, every now and again, when Jay or Lynn would wonder if there was something more that might be done with the show and its main characters.

Lynn even toyed with the idea of taking the satire inside of the House of Commons itself. 'I wanted Paul to stand for Parliament,' he later revealed. 'I wanted him to change his name by deed poll to "Jim Hacker". And in an election he would have won. And I said, "If you become an MP, I promise to write all your speeches, and we can have a tremendous amount of fun." And Paul was a responsible kind of person, he said, "That would bring the whole edifice tumbling down in ruins", and I said, "Well, yes, it might!" So he said: "No, no, I can't do that!"'[5]

It was not only the BBC that remained open to the idea of a return. Every now and again the notion of a stage version would be proposed by some or other impresario, but, as Antony Jay would reveal, 'Paul and Nigel couldn't commit for more than a three-month run, whereas managements would have needed at least six months to recoup their investment, and we felt that no one else could really play it while they were around.'[6] A movie version was mooted as well ('I don't know if we ever got as far as "seriously" discussing a film with the actors,' Lynn would say. 'We would have mentioned that we were thinking about it'[7]), but, once again, it proved too difficult to reassemble all the members of the cast. The team, it seemed, had dispersed for good.

Both of the writers were in many ways rather relieved finally to have their respective solo careers free from further interruption. After being obliged to put so many other interests and ventures on hold while they buried themselves in the research that each *Yes Minister* and *Yes, Prime Minister* script required, they could at last find the time for different ways to work and play.

Antony Jay continued to lead a very contented life, with his wife

Rosemary, at their home in Langport, Somerset (which was also, entirely aptly, the birthplace of that other great analyst of the British Constitution, Walter Bagehot). As the older of the two writers – he was fifty-eight when the sitcom ended – he was now more interested in leisure than labour, but remained open to any new projects that intrigued him.

In 1988, his place within the very Establishment that he had done so much to satirise was well and truly assured when he was awarded a knight-hood for services to broadcasting. 'He really got it,' said Jonathan Lynn, only half jokingly, 'for services to the Conservative Party – something I would never have got and would never have wanted!'[8] He and John Cleese then sold their Video Arts production company in 1989 for the reported sum of £50 million.[9]

Further honours, of the kind that would certainly have pleased Sir Humphrey, would come in the years that followed. In 1992, for example, Jay was made a Fellow of the Royal Society of Arts and a Companion of the Institute of Management; in 1993, he was appointed a Commander of the Royal Victorian Order; and, in 2001, he was made an Honorary Fellow of his alma mater, Magdalene College, Cambridge.

Wealthy and widely respected, he was free to do more or less whatever he wanted, when and where he wanted. He continued working on train-ing films, documentaries (including the BBC's *Elizabeth R* in 1992) and royal broadcasts, and he wrote and edited numerous books (including *The Oxford Dictionary of Political Quotations* in 1996) as well as the occasional pamphlet on business, broadcasting and political issues. He also spent plenty of time sitting in his garden and sampling some of the bottles from his large and very impressive cellar of fine vintage wines.

Jonathan Lynn was by this point living in Pacific Palisades, Los Angeles, with his psychotherapist wife, Rita. Aged just forty-five when the show finished, he was still very ambitious and particularly eager to develop his newly established Hollywood career as a director. Having enjoyed a major commercial hit in 1990 with the comedy *Nuns on the Run* (which starred his fellow Pembroke alumnus, Eric Idle, along with Robbie Coltrane), he went on to work steadily in the industry, making several more noteworthy movies including *My Cousin Vinny* (1992), *The Whole Nine Yards* (2000) and *Wild Target* (2010).

The actors, meanwhile, did what was natural and looked for other work. *Yes, Prime Minister* was a hard show to follow, but at least its extraordinary success meant that its stars were not short of offers.

Paul Eddington found himself in demand not only in Britain but also in a number of countries around the world. In spite of his continuing health problems he was anxious to remain as active as possible, and got on with touring, appearing in commercials, recording voiceovers and continuing to pick and choose his projects for the theatre, television and radio. He also gave his support freely to a fairly wide range of artistic, social and political causes, chairing Equity's International Committee for Artists' Freedom, serving on the Council of the Howard League for Penal Reform and acting as an adviser to the International Shakespeare Globe Centre.

Television, for a while, held the least appeal, because so few of the scripts that were submitted to him came close to matching the quality of the ones crafted by Jay and Lynn, but, after taking a break from the medium, he did accept the odd offer, such as one of the leading roles in Peter Hall's four-part production of Mary Wesley's *The Camomile Lawn* on Channel 4 in 1992. He remained more resistant to the prospect of returning to small-screen comedy, though, and rejected a number of lucrative offers to do so, including a starring part in a BBC comedy drama written by Debbie Horsfield entitled *The Riff Raff Element*.

In the years that followed his farewell to the role of Jim Hacker, it was the theatre that commanded most of his time and energy. In 1988 he starred in a double bill of Terence Rattigan plays, *The Browning Version* and *Harlequinade*; the following year he began appearing as the ageing, self-deceiving fop Sir Harcourt Courtly in what would turn out to be a long-running revival of Boucicault's *London Assurance*; in 1990 he starred as the bumbling Monsieur Jourdain in a new production of Molière's classic *Le Bourgeois Gentilhomme*, and the next year he not only portrayed the uxorious Sir Paul Plyant in a revival of Congreve's *The Double Dealer* (which, much to his pride and pleasure, was directed by one of his four children, his daughter Gemma) but also appeared as the easily duped Orgon in Peter Hall's restaging of Molière's *Tartuffe*.

In 1993, he gave an exceptionally clever and subtle performance (for which he received the Critics' Circle Best Actor Award) as the seedy and starving poet Spooner in Harold Pinter's *No Man's Land*. He seemed, to many, to be at the peak of his powers. Peter Hall, indeed, went so far as to call his acting 'Mozartian'.[10]

It was also in 1993, shortly after completing his run in *No Man's Land*, that *The Sun* newspaper, with its well-known commitment to serving the public interest, decided that the time had come to reveal that Eddington was suffering from skin cancer. He was informed of the 'story' by telephone the night before, and then, once it was published, he and his wife were besieged by a horde of hacks.

'I was horrified by the feeling of persecution,' he would say, 'and became absurdly nervous; we even put up a screen in the hall to prevent reporters peering through the letterbox. If I had to go out for some purpose I would spend minutes peeping out of the window in an effort to see whether the coast was clear before dashing to my car.'[11]

The only thing that the media intrusion did, apart from attract public sympathy for his plight, was to harm his health further through all the stress and to undermine his chances, during his final couple of years, of getting any more work. The BBC would hire him to play Justice Shallow in a new production of *Henry VI*,[12] but other than this the offers dried up. It seems that some prospective employers, now wary about hiring an actor whose publicised poor health and partially scarred and blotchy face (even though it had already been disguised with special make-up for some while) might prove a distraction to a production, passed him over for a number of possible projects, much to his hurt and frustration.

Desperate to keep himself busy by doing what he did best, he was, nonetheless, determined to act again. He managed to do so in 1994, thanks in part to his old friend and *Good Life* co-star Richard Briers, who agreed to act alongside him in a new production of David Storey's play *Home*. A simple but poignant tale about two elderly men who sit together in the sun and chat about their lives while their minds begin to fail, it was a suitably intimate and humane fiction with which a fine actor might bid his farewell.

'Dickie knew how ill Paul was – as did the producer and director,' Eddington's wife, Tricia, later said of Briers' involvement. 'But everyone was very keen to do it. Dickie could just fit it in before he took on yet another project. He very much wanted to do it and Ann, Dickie's wife, backed him up. At times the schedule was very difficult, because Paul had to have his treatment and still carry on with rehearsals. The treatment exhausted him, so Dickie – being Dickie – took away all the stress of the publicity and interviews. "Look, old love," he said, "I'll do it. If they've got one of us they don't need you." That meant Paul could conserve all his energies for the stage.'[13]

The production was well received. One critic praised Eddington as 'bleakly brilliant',[14] another called him 'a master of nuance',[15] while a third applauded him for his portrayal of a man whose eyes, 'even when brimming with tears, suggest he dwells in some private world of his own'.[16] It had been a huge strain, but he had maintained his impeccable standards right through to the end.

Paul Eddington died, at the age of sixty-eight, in 1995. Just a month before he passed away, he made a deeply moving and characteristically defiant appearance on the BBC1 programme *Face to Face*, in which he made light of his increasingly disfiguring illness. 'People are kind enough to say "how brave" and all the rest of it,' he said. 'I'm not brave at all. I do wish, very sincerely, that I hadn't got this problem. But as I have it, there's no alternative but to say, "Yes, I've got it"'. His autobiography appeared a couple of weeks after that appearance. His title for it was *So Far, So Good*.

A journalist had once asked him what he would like his epitaph to be. He suggested: 'He did very little harm.' He added that earning the right to such a claim was not easy: 'Most people seem to me to do a great deal of harm. If I could be remembered as having done very little, that would suit me.'[17]

Probably the sweetest, simplest and most apt of all the many tributes to him came from John Howard Davies, who, all those years ago, had hired him to play Jim Hacker. 'I loved him,' he said. 'I thought he was a smashing man, and I wish there were more of his kind about.'[18]

Nigel Hawthorne sounded a similarly heartfelt note. 'He was the bravest man I ever met,' he said of his former co-star. 'He never seemed to complain about his poor health, and he had been ill for many years, but always bore it with dignity and humour.'[19]

Hawthorne himself had been just as active as Eddington in the years since *Yes, Prime Minister*. Like his old friend, he had found few new television projects that appealed, and preferred to spend much of his time back on the stage.

He did so, however, on his terms, and his terms only. Still scarred by all of the snubs he had endured prior to his success in *Yes Minister*, he regarded the new clamour for his services with more than a small measure of cynicism. 'I was offered the sort of parts by the Royal Shakespeare Company which five years ago I'd have cried with joy to get,' he would reflect. 'But this time I told them, "You have left it too late".'[20]

He was predictably impressive as a spymaster in the Tom Stoppard play *Hapgood* (1988); profoundly moving as C.S. Lewis in William Nicholson's *Shadowlands* (1989); mesmerisingly complex as the porphyria-plagued sovereign in Alan Bennett's *The Madness of George III* (1991); and, directing himself, he also appeared as the vain and rickety Lord Ogleby in *The Clandestine Marriage* (1996). His last, and not particularly satisfying, stage role was the lead in *King Lear* with the RSC at the Barbican, Stratford-upon-Avon, and in Tokyo in 1999 and 2000.

He also enjoyed increasingly high-profile successes with movies. There were times, such as when he appeared with Sylvester Stallone, Wesley Snipes and Sandra Bullock in the sci-fi thriller *Demolition Man* (1993), when the money was far more of an attraction than the art, but he was always searching for roles that would help stretch him in this medium. Taking part, for example, in two new attempts to do justice to Shakespeare on the big screen, he played Clarence in Ian McKellen's modernised *Richard III* (1995), and Malvolio in Trevor Nunn's version of *Twelfth Night* (1996). Steven Spielberg cast him as the pro-slavery President Martin Van Buren in *Amistad* (1997), and he was David Mamet's first and only choice to play the obsessive Arthur Winslow in his adaptation of Terence Rattigan's *The Winslow Boy* (1999).

His biggest international success, however, came in 1994, when he reprised his stage role in the movie *The Madness of King George*. It won him a 'Best Actor' Academy Award nomination, a great wave of critical praise and brought this very private man far more publicity and media attention than he had ever wanted.

In the build-up to his appearance at the Academy Awards ceremony, as part of the seemingly endless succession of promotional interviews that all nominees are obliged to endure, he gave a brief interview to the American gay magazine *Advocate*. 'I didn't know the magazine,' he would say. 'I don't mix in those circles.'[21] Naively, having been told that the publication had a very small circulation in the States, he thought that hardly anyone would ever read it (and even fewer would be interested), and so, once the mainstream media had indeed noticed the piece and 'outed' him in newspapers all over the world, he was horrified. 'It was terrible,' he would say of the moment when (just as they had done to Paul Eddington before him, only now even more aggressively) a swarm of journalists and camera crews descended upon the house that he shared with his partner Trevor Bentham, and started staring through the windows and shouting questions through the letterbox. 'We had to hire four security guards to keep them away from the house.'[22]

He would remain mystified and 'frightened' by the intensity of the interest, and traumatised by the intrusion into his and Bentham's quiet private life. 'We had always treated the press with great courtesy,' he said, 'always made a point of going together to public functions. They had cabinets full of pictures of the two of us arriving at BAFTA, the Olivier and *Evening Standard* awards, which we've done through the years. They knew perfectly well there wasn't a story. There wasn't a sudden revelation.'[23] He resented the 'outing' so much because, he stressed, he had never really been 'in' – he had just been private.

Bentham was by his side when he sat in the audience at the Academy Awards. He did not win – Tom Hanks did for *Forrest Gump* – but, relishing the opportunity to lose himself for a few hours in the sheer unreality of such an exotic event, he enjoyed the occasion greatly. Bentham then accompanied him to Cannes, where, once again, Hawthorne was nominated for an award. He lost out, once again – this time to Jonathan Pryce for *Carrington* – but he was cheered and applauded so enthusiastically that, as he later admitted, he 'broke down a bit'.[24]

Upon the couple's return to England, however, they still feared that people 'would be looking at us with disgust and that our lives had been irrevocably changed'.[25] Hawthorne therefore rather dreaded having to appear so soon afterwards onstage at the Shaftesbury Theatre in order to present an Olivier Award, and was thus both surprised and deeply touched by the warmth of the welcome he received from the audience. It was the same wherever he and Bentham went in the weeks and months that followed: there was only sympathy, affection and respect. The 'fuss', as he put it, was over.[26]

A much happier time was had on New Year's Day in 1999, when it was announced that he was to be knighted for services to theatre, film and television. A KBE, added to a CBE, might not have caused much excitement inside Whitehall, where it takes a more exclusive-sounding set of initials to set the pulse racing (WOOLLEY: 'Of course, in the Service, CMG stands for "Call Me God". And KCMG for "Kindly Call Me God".' HACKER: 'What does GCMG stand for?' WOOLLEY: '"God Calls Me God"'[27]), and it still left him missing Sir Humphrey's flashy GCB, but he was, nonetheless, extremely flattered and touched to accept the honour. Emerging from the ceremony at Buckingham Palace that was held later that year, he smiled as he told reporters, 'The gentlemen in front and behind me were senior civil servants, so I was in good company.'[28]

He died on Boxing Day in 2001, aged seventy-two, from a heart attack. He had been in very poor health for the previous eighteen months, having first been diagnosed with a pulmonary embolism before it was discovered that he also had pancreatic cancer. His autobiography, entitled *Straight Face*, would be published early the following year.

Trevor Bentham, who was with him when he died, would later write of the man he loved: 'To have known him was a joy. To have shared my life with him was exhilarating. I hope that there is an afterlife so he will have been aware of the shock caused by his death and the massive love that came – still comes – to act as comfort for the sadly missing years.'[29]

There was now only one point left of the great comedy triangle: Derek Fowlds was left to mourn his two friends. Interviewed shortly after the news of Paul Eddington's death had been announced, he said: 'He was a great actor and he has shown such strength and courage over the last ten years. He was greatly loved.'[30] Following the memorial service for Nigel Hawthorne, he commented: 'We worked together for eight years and remained very close. He was very supportive. He always made me laugh. We never had a cross word. It was just a joy to be with him. I will miss him very much.'[31]

Fowlds, like the others, had remained busy after *Yes, Prime Minister*. He made one-off appearances in ITV's *Inspector Morse* in 1988,[32] *Boon* in 1990,[33] *Van der Valk* in 1991[34] and *The Darling Buds of May* in 1992[35]; essayed the role of Oliver Davidson, a grey man from the Home Office, in ITV's 1989 six-part Cold War drama *Rules of Engagement*; played a drably sinister MI6 officer called Crombie in the BBC's 1990 six-part political thriller *Die Kinder*; and also appeared as the errant husband John Gutteridge in ITV's 1992 eight-part domestic drama *Firm Friends*.

His most significant and long-lasting success, however, came when he played Oscar Blaketon, a curmudgeonly police sergeant turned pub owner, in the ITV period police drama series *Heartbeat* for its entire run from 1992 to 2010. 'When I finished *Yes, Prime Minister*,' he would later reflect with great amusement, 'I was just fifty. But I was still playing Bernard as thirty-six. And when I started *Heartbeat*, my son, Jeremy, said to me, "Dad, you've gone from juvenile to geriatric overnight!"'[36] A self-consciously cosy and nostalgic show, it would still contrive to offer him a new challenge as an actor ('It was such a different role from Bernard, and a very different character from me, and Blaketon was Northern and I'm from the South, so it was a bit of a stretch in the beginning'[37]), and it also ensured that his amiable face would remain a fixture on British television.

There were still occasions during this period when his old sitcom would intrude into view. In 1997, for example, he gleefully reprised the role of Bernard Woolley to read Antony Jay's *How to Beat Sir Humphrey: Every Citizen's Guide to Beating Officialdom* for BBC Radio 4. He was also very willing to recall the many happy days that he'd spent working with Eddington and Hawthorne whenever there was a new attempt to commemorate and celebrate the show. 'It's always so nice to remember being with them,' he would say.[38]

That was the thing about *Yes Minister* and *Yes, Prime Minister*. The show had ended, but it had never gone away.

There was, for example, the merchandise. In 1989, Jonathan Lynn's series of 'Jim Hacker diaries' was repackaged in two large volumes as *The Complete Yes Minister* and *The Complete Yes, Prime Minister*. Proving to be phenomenally popular with readers and reviewers alike, they would be lodged in the top-ten bestseller lists for more than a hundred weeks, and were translated into numerous other languages. (In 2013, as Li Keqiang became the new Premier of China, it would be revealed that, during the early 1990s, his wife, Cheng Hong, had translated the *Yes Minister* books (as '遵命大臣') into Mandarin. It was said that he was studying the volumes to prepare himself for dealing with his country's own obstructive civil servants.[39])

Along with the books came the home videos (which started intermittently in the mid-1980s but were relaunched early on at the start of the
next decade), and then later the DVDs (starting in 2001), and both radio
series were released on CD (in 2002). There was even an early computer
game (developed by Oxford Digital Enterprises and published by Mosaic
for the ZX Spectrum platform) in 1987.[40]

There were also more repeats of the actual show from the mid-1990s
onwards, thanks to the emergence of cable and satellite channels in the
UK. The TV nostalgia channel UK Gold ensured that both *Yes Minister*
and *Yes, Prime Minister* would remain in circulation not only for those
who had seen them the first time round, but also for a succession of new
generations of viewers.[41]

All of this helped to maintain the interest of the fans, but there was also
something else, something quite profound, going on during this period.
The programme had become part of the culture of the country, a common
frame of reference for anyone who wanted to address and make sense of
the theory and practice of government and politics.

In broadcasting terms, it provided a template, and an expectation, that
could and would be used to inspire a new wave of accessible political satire.
Ranging from the frenzied knockabout comedy of Laurence Marks and
Maurice Gran's *The New Statesman* (1987–94), which featured Rik Mayall
as the ruthless right-wing Tory MP Alan B'Stard, to Michael Dobbs and
Andrew Davies' gloriously mischievous thriller *House of Cards* (1990–5),
which featured Ian Richardson as the sinuously devious Chief Whip
Francis Urquhart, the impact of *Yes Minister* and *Yes, Prime Minister* would
continue to be felt throughout the rest of the century and into the next.

This was by no means limited to domestic popular culture. The original
series were still being shown in more than eighty countries, encouraging
more and more writers, performers and producers that it was both possible and desirable to make political ideas, arguments and insights engaging
and entertaining for a broad audience.

Several countries were encouraged enough to attempt to make their
own versions of the sitcom to suit their own systems. An American
version, entitled *All in Favor*, was put into production in 1987 only to collapse when the studio lost its nerve about how commercially competitive
it might be. 'It's so long ago that I can hardly remember it,' Jonathan Lynn

would later say, 'but I wrote a pilot script. I consulted Tony, of course.'[42] It was not a happy experience: 'They wanted to make it a family show. They wanted to make it like, you know, *Cosby* in the White House.'[43] A number of other countries, however, were much more positive and brought their own adaptations to the screen.

India was first to do so in 2001, followed by Turkey in 2004 and the Netherlands, Israel and Ukraine in 2009. Sweden, Portugal and Canada also bought the rights with the intention of developing their own versions.

These bids to grow the sitcom in foreign soil would witness some intriguing 'modifications'. The Indian manifestation, for example, which was called *Ji, Mantriji*, was produced in Delhi in collaboration with BBC Worldwide, and remained largely faithful to the original scripts, but they were still adapted in certain ways for Indian politics (and audiences), with references to Russia changed to Pakistan, football altered to cricket, badgers replaced by monkeys and the EEC changed to SAARC – the South Asian Association for Regional Cooperation. Jim Hacker, meanwhile, was renamed Suryaprakash Singh (played by the well-known Indian actor Farooque Sheikh) and Sir Humphrey was now called Rajnath Mathur (played by Jayant Kripalani).

The Dutch version took more liberties with the characters. Jim Hacker was renamed Karel Bijl, Sir Humphrey Appleby was transformed into a woman, while Bernard Woolley was made a Moroccan called Mohammed.

Back in Britain, the sense that the sitcom had embedded itself in the popular consciousness was getting stronger rather than weaker. In 1989, for instance, it came as no surprise when it was reported that a stray black and white cat, who had wandered into Number Ten and been made 'Chief Mouser to the Cabinet Office', had been christened 'Humphrey' in honour of the character in the show. The very triviality of the example only served to underline how natural such references now seemed. The show had acquired its own adjectival power: to say that something was 'a *Yes Minister* situation', or that a figure, phrase or stunt was 'straight out of *Yes, Prime Minister*', was sufficient to make perfect sense to the average viewer or voter.

The start of a new century did nothing to diminish its reputation. If anything, the contrary was the case. In 2000, the British Film Institute's prestigious poll to determine the nation's one hundred best-ever television programmes placed *Yes Minister* and *Yes, Prime Minister* ninth.[44] In 2004, a rather less rigorous BBC survey to find 'Britain's Best Sitcom' had the show on the list at sixth.[45] In both 2006 and 2010, MPs, unsurprisingly, voted the show the greatest political comedy of all time.[46] In any discussion of a new political satire, the benchmark was invariably the same: 'How good, or accurate, or believable is it compared with *Yes Minister* and *Yes, Prime Minister*?'

One writer and broadcaster who was even more influenced than most by the sitcom was Armando Iannucci. By this time an accomplished satirist in his own right as the co-creator of the brilliant news and current affairs spoofs *On the Hour* (BBC Radio 4, 1991–2) and *The Day Today* (BBC2, 1994), he acted as the on-screen advocate of the show when the BBC held its 2004 'Best Sitcom' poll.

He argued at the time:

> *Yes Minister* made the driest subject possible – the minutiae
> of politics – into sparkling comedy. No sitcom has been so
> thoroughly researched – it used real Whitehall insider moles to
> spill the beans – and meant that (unlike Richard Curtis, for
> example) the writers were considered a threat to national security!
> *Yes Minister* was more than a sitcom, it was a crash course in
> Contemporary Political Studies – it opened the lid on the way the
> Government really operated. It remains the most quintessentially
> British of the British sitcoms – understatement, embarrassment,
> Masonic secrecy and respect for the rules all in evidence. It had
> the only sitcom title sequence – drawn by Gerald Scarfe – that
> was a genuine work of art. And, perhaps above all else, it is the
> lasting legacy of two of our greatest actors: Paul Eddington and
> Nigel Hawthorne.[47]

Iannucci would freely admit that it was actually due (at least in part) to the preparation he did for his advocacy of this sitcom – which involved watching every single episode all over again – that inspired him to create his own contemporary satire on British politics, *The Thick of It*. Launched in 2005 (initially on BBC Four and later transferring to BBC2), it differed from its predecessor by focusing on politics rather than government, and responded to the even more cynical climate of the time by adopting a colder, harsher tone as it explored the aimless tail-chasings of solipsistic politicians (the kind of callow creatures who go straight from school to study Politics, Philosophy and Economics at Oxford, and then become political researchers before getting elected as MPs) and their equally blinkered advisers, no longer able or interested in pursuing any *grand projet*, and so immersing themselves instead in a culture of micromanagement that too few of them have the intelligence to master let alone transcend.

In place of a Jim Hacker, who had at least experienced something of the world before becoming an MP and continued to hang on, albeit limply, to something that resembled a hinterland, *The Thick of It* pictured spin-manipulated marionettes, not moral enough to know when they risked being immoral, evading words and meanings like the simulated agents bending away from the bullets in *The Matrix*. It was not life as Jim knew it, but the lineage, indisputably, was his.

Iannucci then went on to do what American broadcasters had ultimately failed to do with *All in Favor* and brought some of the spirit of *Yes Minister* to Washington with his US sitcom *Veep*. First broadcast in 2012, it featured the very talented comedy actor Julia Louis-Dreyfus as Selina Meyer, the Vice-President of the US. Strongly reminiscent of Jim Hacker's first phase as a Minister, hindered more than helped by a coterie of officials and advisers, Meyer is vulnerable and weakly well meaning but also fiercely ambitious and quite willing to dirty her hands if she thinks it will keep her close, or preferably even closer, to power.

Neither *The Thick of It* nor *Veep* would display any of the literary elegance and cultural complexity that were such key ingredients in *Yes Minister*, but the absence was more to do with social and cultural rather than artistic trends. The more elaborately educated administrative wing of government was not really the focus of either sitcom (and in that sense both of them actually harked back before *Yes Minister* to an earlier and simpler satirical tradition), and the crudity of thought and language on show over on the political side was only reflecting the change in the reality of the situation. In 1915, for example, the future Prime Minister Harold Macmillan read Aeschylus as he lay wounded in the trenches; whereas in 1998, the recently elected Prime Minister Tony Blair read the modish sociologist Anthony Giddens as he sat back and relaxed in Number Ten. It has been a case of downwards and inwards for quite a while.

Jim Hacker did tend to lapse into cod Churchillian when he was feeling unusually statesmanlike, but even in those days such eloquence (outside of Sir Humphrey's Whitehall) seemed comically out of date. It was hardly a surprise, therefore, when *The Thick of It*'s Malcom Tucker moaned that a certain Minister was 'about as much use as a marzipan dildo',[48] or when *Veep*'s VP responded to a proposal by saying, 'I'd rather set fire to my vulva. So that's a no'.[49]

The mirror might have been bequeathed by *Yes Minister*. What it was now reflecting belonged to another time.

The memory of the original home-grown shows, however, would never look like fading away. For Britain's politicians, for example, it remained, regardless of how many supposed successors it spawned, the one external critique that kept intruding into their world.

Year after year, the citations continued to come. In 1992, for instance: 'The Sir Humphrey Applebys of every country in Europe have got together, and they say, "You cannot do that, Minister"' (Tony Benn);[50] in 1998: 'Does my hon. Friend agree that Sir Humphrey Appleby is alive and well?' (Richard Spring);[51] in 2000: 'The transcript of the interrogation reads like a script from *Yes, Minister*' (Vince Cable);[52] also in 2000: 'As it might have been said in *Yes, Prime Minister*, that is a very courageous decision by my right hon. Friend' (John Major);[53] in 2002: 'That is Sir Humphrey-speak for a complete mess' (George Osborne);[54] in 2004: 'Sir Humphrey does not always get things right' (Peter Hain);[55] in 2008: 'In *Yes Minister*, nothing frightened the politician Jim Hacker more than when his Permanent Secretary, Sir Humphrey, listened to his latest idea and described it as "brave"' (Michael Portillo);[56] and in 2010: 'Where was Sir Humphrey when I needed him?' (Tony Blair).[57]

The show's veteran consultant, Bernard Donoughue, after being ennobled as Lord Donoughue of Ashton and appointed a Junior Minister in the 1997 Labour Government, would actually discern a more profound (and rather ironic) influence on the new generation of Ministers:

> These were young people who had grown up watching the show. And some of them came in, as a consequence, *excessively* primed,. and were out to demonstrate their masculinity by not listening to their civil servants. And I think they went too far. Because

they were young, inexperienced Ministers, and they hadn't a clue what to do. So my view was that, in many cases, it would have been better if the civil servants had done it rather than them. But you could really hear them say this: 'I'm not going to let Sir Humphrey run *me*!' *Yes Minister* really had influenced them that much. For a whole generation, it had been their textbook on how to conduct government. But this crop of young Cabinet Ministers frightened me a bit. You could just tell they were thinking, '*We* don't want to be Jim Hacker!' And the point was they exaggerated the number of Sir Humphreys around. Because Sir Humphrey was brilliant – sometimes to pernicious ends, but he *was* brilliant. And when I came into Government I found that the number of brilliant top civil servants was sadly few. *I* would rather have had *more* Sir Humphreys![58]

There would also be many occasions when seasoned students of the sitcom would point out how some of its storylines still seemed to be acted out in real life. In 2001, for example, when the Conservative Party published its manifesto for the forthcoming General Election, it was evident that a commitment by the then leader William Hague (a self-confessed great fan of the show) to give parents 'their first choice of school for their children', had strong echoes of Jim Hacker's 'National Education Service'.[59]

In the same decade, during the increasingly awkward and tense 'partnership' between the Chancellor Gordon Brown and his Prime Minister Tony Blair, following the apparent collapse of their infamous 'Granita pact',[60] some commentators were equally quick to quote from the 1986 episode of *Yes, Prime Minister* in which Sir Humphrey seemed to anticipate just such an imbroglio: 'The Chancellor will never forgive the Prime Minister for beating him to Number Ten, and the Prime Minister will never trust the Chancellor. After all, one never trusts anyone that one has deceived.'[61]

Thus the sitcom never seemed to date. Current events kept underlining its continuing relevance.

In 2012, the British Prime Minister David Cameron, busy trying to cope with the distinctly 'Hackeresque' situation of running a Coalition Government, acknowledged his own admiration for the sitcom. 'You'll be amazed to know that [when] I was a student in the 1980s, a student of Economics and Politics, I once had to write an essay on "How true to life is *Yes Minister*",' he told his Malaysian counterpart Najib Razak. 'I think I wrote in the essay that it wasn't that true to life. I can tell you, as Prime Minister, it *is* true to life.'[62]

So much time had passed since the original shows had been screened, but the interest, affection and appetite for them were still there. People still watched the repeats, read the books and watched the DVDs. The famous lines and speeches kept on being quoted and recited. The stories continued being related to the present day.

That seemed to be the sum of the sitcom's fate in the twenty-first century. It was more than two decades since *Yes, Prime Minister* had ended, and, although it was still so loved and so keenly missed, no one, any more, expected it to come back in any way, shape or form. Everyone, as a consequence, was in for an extraordinary shock.

PART FOUR

The danger for modern liberty is that, absorbed in the enjoyment of our private independence, and in the pursuit of our particular interests, we should surrender our right to share in political power too easily. The holders of authority are only too anxious to encourage us to do so. They are so ready to spare us all sorts of troubles, except those of obeying and paying!
Benjamin Constant

It is indeed difficult to conceive how men who have entirely given up the habit of self-government should succeed in making a proper choice of those by whom they are to be governed; and no one will ever believe that a liberal, wise, and energetic government can spring from the suffrages of a subservient people.
Alexis de Tocqueville

13

The Revival

I'd like to say thank you on behalf of the group and ourselves and I hope we've passed the audition.

It came like a bolt from the blue. In February 2010, it was announced that *Yes, Prime Minister* was returning as a stage play.

It was the last thing that any admirer of the show was expecting. It was not just that it was twenty-two years after the last episode was seen on the small screen. It was also that it was fifteen years since Paul Eddington, and almost nine years since Nigel Hawthorne, had passed away.

The belated revival of a sitcom, as such, did at least have quite a few precedents. Some of them, indeed, had been successful. Galton and Simpson brought back *Steptoe and Son* after a five-year interlude. Clement and La Frenais revived *The Likely Lads* as the even better *Whatever Happened to the Likely Lads?* after a seven-year hiatus. Eric Sykes reprised *Sykes And A . . .* as *Sykes* following the same seven-year absence. John Sullivan also returned to *Only Fools and Horses* once after a three-year gap, and then again after a five-year gap.

Several other attempts had been considerably less effective. *The Rag Trade*, for example, which had ended on the BBC in 1963, fell flat when it was brought back by ITV after fourteen years in 1977. *Bootsie and Snudge*, which also had its original finale in 1963, met with a similar fate when ITV exhumed it eleven years later in 1974. *Till Death Us Do Part* was brought to a close by the BBC in 1975, then returned briefly on ITV as *Till Death* six years later in 1981, and then was transmogrified (to mixed reviews) back on the BBC as *In Sickness and in Health* in 1985. *Up Pompeii!*, having finished in 1970, was brought back twice, in 1975 and 1991, looking a shadow of its former self. Similarly, in a TV culture that was getting increasingly retrogressive, *The Liver Birds*, which had last been seen in 1978, flopped badly when it returned in 1996, and *To the Manor Born*, which ended in 1991, proved a disappointment when it was brought back as a one-off special in 2007.

The notion of a sitcom coming back not in its original medium of television, but rather in the different form of the theatre, was, however, a much more recent phenomenon. It had happened in 2005, when Ray Galton, thirty-one years after *Steptoe and Son* had disappeared from the screen, collaborated with John Antrobus on a spin-off stage play, *Murder at Oil Drum Lane*. It happened again the following year, when Marks and Gran decided to do much the same with *The New Statesman*.

The *Steptoe* revival, with its two original stars having long since died, featured a new pair of performers, with Jake Nightingale standing in for Harry H. Corbett and Harry Dickman replacing Wilfrid Brambell. *The New Statesman*, in contrast, had been able to call on the services of its old leading man, Rik Mayall, to lend the venture some lustre. Neither production, however, really caught the popular imagination, arousing a certain amount of initial curiosity without going on to attract much critical praise.

The cultural climate did not, therefore, seem particularly clement as far as a *Yes, Minister* stage play was concerned. What mattered, though, was that both Antony Jay and Jonathan Lynn were very keen to write it.

The plan had been hatched about six months earlier, during the summer of 2009, when both of them had been reminded of the fact that it would soon be the thirtieth anniversary of the arrival of *Yes Minister* on the screen. This imminent event did not in itself prompt the two writers to snap back immediately into action, but, as both of them – Jay in England and Lynn in America – reflected on what could and should be done to mark the occasion, they started to consider the idea of returning to the show 'before it was too late'.[1]

Two producers – Mark Goucher and Matthew Byam Shaw – had made contact to express their interest in staging a play. Neither writer, however, was ready yet to commit to such a project, and, while they agreed to negotiate a provisional deal, they refused to take any money in advance in case they failed to come up with something that seemed actually good enough to work.

Lynn then decided to fly over to the UK to visit Jay at his home, an earthy, easy-going organic farm in Langport. It was merely an opportunity for the two men to discuss their options informally while enjoying the chance to be back in each other's company.

There was no pressure, just plenty of pleasure. 'Tony is exceptionally generous,' Lynn later remarked, 'and has a lot of great wine, more than he can drink unless he outlives Methuselah. He opened a case of Château Margaux 1990 and we had a bottle or two every night with dinner.'[2] It was in this relaxed and convivial atmosphere that the two writers started to wonder: had Whitehall really changed as much as some people claimed since the sitcom had ended? What would Hacker and Sir Humphrey be arguing about now? What kind of plot would work in, say, a two-hour play instead of a thirty-minute sitcom? Would the old charm return with the new challenge?

'We were cautious about the [idea of a] play,' Lynn would say. 'We repeatedly reassured each other that we were unlikely to make any pro- gress in the first ten days [which was the length of their stay], and if we managed to hammer out a story, then that would be good progress and it wouldn't matter at all if we found we had lost the knack or had nothing more to say. We started at nine the next morning. By lunchtime we had a rough storyline. Tony, who loves to categorise things, remarked happily that it had "gone from being a problem to being a task". He was right. By the time we left Somerset nine days later, we had a good story and most of Act One was written.'[3]

They were now fully energised by the thought that they were collabo- rating once again, but there was one problem still to be resolved. The new play would only work if a large enough number of people accepted actors other than the much-loved and much-missed Paul Eddington and Nigel Hawthorne as Hacker and Sir Humphrey (as well as, of course, Derek Fowlds, who was now aged seventy-two and well past retirement age for a Principal Private Secretary, as Woolley).

The two writers were probably the only people at that time who would have challenged the view that Eddington and Hawthorne had made the characters of Hacker and Sir Humphrey definitively and eternally their own, but, then again, only the two writers had a bona fide right to do so. As great and as genuine as their respect and admiration for Eddington and Hawthorne remained, Jay and Lynn still saw the characters as *their* creations, speaking *their* words, and thus they did not see why it should be impossible for them to find other talented performers to bring Hacker and Sir Humphrey back to life.

The ultimate concern for the writers, after all, was not the characters: it was the system. They might as well have invented two completely different characters – in fact, it would surely have been so much easier, commercial considerations aside, had they done so – but they were determined to press on with what they had.

Both men were adamant: when asked if they had ever contemplated replacing Hacker, Sir Humphrey and Woolley with a fresh trio of authority figures, Jay would say, 'No, never',[4] while Lynn, just as firmly, said, 'No. It would not have been *Yes, Prime Minister* without them.'[5] Most of the awards might have gone to the actors, and most of the public and critical attention had gone in their direction, too, but as far as the writers were concerned, the characters, like the show as a whole, belonged to them; it was their writing, more than anything else, that had made *Yes, Prime Minister* what it was.

They knew, nevertheless, that the vast majority if not all of the fans might think otherwise, and it unnerved them for a while. Their mood changed, however, once they reflected on other cases. 'I realised,' said Lynn, 'that so many beloved characters have been recast, like Doctor Who, James Bond, Sherlock Holmes – not to mention Hamlet! – and the audience simply accepts a new interpretation by a different actor and treats it on its merits. We hoped that would be the case with our characters.'[6]

Such optimism was no doubt further boosted by the knowledge that the BBC had only just 'updated' *The Fall and Rise of Reginald Perrin* (which ended in 1979) as *Reggie Perrin* in April 2009, with Martin Clunes taking the place of the deceased Leonard Rossiter. Even if that particular much-hyped revival had been met with reactions ranging from the hostile to the ambivalent, the absence of a backlash against Clunes himself at least suggested that the new cast of *Yes, Prime Minister* would be given a reasonably fair chance.

Jay and Lynn (with Bernard Donoughue, once again, acting as expert adviser[7]) were now free to concentrate fully on the script itself. The main question to be addressed in this context was: what needed to be altered, updated or replaced in terms of the political and administrative world that they had last explored twenty-nine years earlier?

The simple answer was: not as much as one might think. 'Nothing really changes in government,' Lynn would insist. 'Progress is a sham and topicality is an illusion. People go into politics thinking they can change the way it works, but it's like wrestling a blancmange. You can do what you want to it, but it comes right back at you . . . just as bad as before.'[8]

The more complex answer was: all kinds of minor details. Information, speculation and gossip, for example, now went into circulation much more quickly, thanks to gadgets such as smartphones and tablets as well as twenty-four-hour news channels, and the role of spin doctors, sound bites and special advisers was more prominent and more public than before. The so-called 'geography of power' had also shifted somewhat, with fewer decisions being made at full Cabinet level and more now being devolved to smaller and more specialised Cabinet committees. Moreover, while political discourse had superficially become less formal, it had, more significantly, become less accessible, with every 'proactive', 'incentivised' and 'pathfinding' politician now schooled in the same smug, jargon-ridden and lazy geek-speak.

Most of the additions and revisions, however, struck Jay and Lynn as relatively trivial compared to the core set of things that had stayed much the same. While they made sure that Sir Humphrey, for example, would face more competition as he tried to influence his Prime Minister, and Hacker would show a much-improved, almost Blair-like mastery of PR as he looked to protect his own position, the writers were content to keep the basic situation, and relationship, that the two characters shared more or less as it was.

What they were still concerned to find, though, was a suitable crisis to use as a device to drive their storyline. In all of the classic *Yes Minister* and *Yes, Prime Minister* episodes, there had always been a 'hideous dilemma' at its heart that seemed plausible enough to send Hacker into a panic and Sir Humphrey into a plot. Now, they felt, the problem was that something *had* changed enough to make their search much harder.

What, they believed, had changed was society itself. Seemingly imbued by a mood of ennui, the British public appeared harder to shock, and, more pertinently, their politicians appeared harder to shame.

'Shame!' was still shouted in Parliament whenever someone wished to register their displeasure, but fewer MPs actually seemed to *feel* it when they were caught doing something that surely deserved it. 'Since we started to write *Yes Minister*,' Jay and Lynn reflected ruefully, 'shame went out of style':

> Politicians, like other celebrities, reflect our society. Remember John Profumo? He had sex with a prostitute, lied to the House, and spent the next 40 years in penance. Twenty years later Cecil Parkinson, a married man, had an affair with his secretary; she went to the newspapers with the story – no shame there, apparently – and nine years later Parkinson accepted a peerage and became chairman of the 'family values' party. Embarrassment, yes. Shame? Not so much. We are not moralists about sexual conduct but all satirical writing involves a moral standard, frequently self-imposed, which is not being met. Our concerns are hypocrisy and dishonesty, because those are usually the funniest. But in looking for subject matter for the play, we looked for things that still shock people. We couldn't find very many.[9]

Probably the most obvious real-life example, at first glance, was the MPs' expenses scandal (which was still playing out as Jay and Lynn were working on the script), but, on closer inspection, the writers found it to be neither particularly new nor especially rich in dramatic potential. 'After all,' they said, 'that system was deliberately designed by the Callaghan Government as a way to get around the pay freeze. MPs were *supposed* to inflate their expenses. They were expected to do it discreetly, however, and weren't expected to commit actual fraud such as claiming for paid-off mortgages, or duck houses, or moat-clearing. But they virtually all did it and no one felt guilty. Shame had been replaced by embarrassment – horror at what you have done replaced by horror at people finding out what you have done.'[10]

It then occurred to the writers that there was one kind of scandal that still had the capacity to shake and shock. This was the scandal that involved foreigners.

While reports of the average domestic scandal rarely seemed to provoke more than a collective shrug of the shoulders, the news of another country's scandal still managed to fascinate a fair proportion of the nation. The multiple alleged financial, political and sexual antics of Italy's then Prime Minister Silvio Berlusconi, in particular, were regularly commanding plenty of space on Britain's front pages, featuring as they did such topics as his decision to appoint a former topless model, Mara Carfagna, as Equal Opportunities Minister in his Government, and the announcement by his wife, Veronica Lario, that she was leaving him because he 'consorted with minors' at what were termed, much to the British tabloids' delight, 'bunga bunga parties'.[11]

It was this kind of 'exotic' ingredient, Jay and Lynn decided, that would spice up the storyline quite nicely. One way or another, they would have something sufficiently 'hideous' to horrify Hacker.

The script, when it was finished, was set in Chequers, the Prime Minister's official country residence, between one Friday afternoon and a Sunday morning in autumn. The atmosphere inside is tense: Europe is in financial meltdown; Britain's Government clings precariously to power after a close election; the Cabinet is divided; and the Prime Minister is in urgent need of help from dubious new allies.

The financial crisis, Sir Humphrey admits, has been caused in part by the kind of computer models on which even the Civil Service now tends to rely:

SIR HUMPHREY: No one knew that those computer models in the City were being given faulty information. Everyone assumed the mortgages were worth their face value.

HACKER: But they were worth nothing! Why didn't anyone know? Why didn't *you* know?

SIR HUMPHREY: [*Sighs, humiliated*] Everyone thought that everyone else understood what was going on and nobody wanted to admit they couldn't make sense of it.

HACKER: Why couldn't they?

SIR HUMPHREY: Because it *didn't* make sense! Everybody thought that all the others knew, and there *were* some who knew, but the ones who didn't know didn't believe that the ones who *did* know knew.

HACKER:	Say that again?
SIR HUMPHREY:	Nobody wanted to rock the boat because everyone was making so much money!

The consequence is that, as Britain currently has the Presidency of the European Council, Hacker (eager to spread the blame and share the strain) has convened a Euro-conference in the hope of finding a solution to the recession. All too predictably, however, the assembled representatives of the member states have so far failed to agree to anything except to disagree with each other.

Salvation suddenly seems to loom on the horizon when the oil-rich central Asian state of Kumranistan comes on board and offers a $10 trillion loan to build a pipeline that will zigzag through the whole of Europe. The deal, however, is thrown into disarray when the country's Foreign Secretary arrives and demands that unless the Government supplies him with an underage girl with whom he can spend the night, the contract will remain unsigned.

This 'hideous dilemma' takes the second half of the satire into the realm of farce – a form of drama at which Jonathan Lynn (who was also set to direct the play) was an acknowledged master, and which also suited the spirit of the fiction, and indeed the real-life contemporary political situation, rather well. Just as farce is all about a world that is fast spinning out of control, so Hacker finds himself plunged into just such a world, encircled by bewildering economic abstractions, ethereal political conventions and wildly unpredictable animal spirits, thus forcing him to contend with a living reality that is vastly more complicated, more confusing, more contradictory and much, much messier than its description on paper.

There would be a few things in the play that acknowledged the changes that had taken place since the sitcom was last shown. Hacker, for example, is now quite addicted to his BlackBerry, while Sir Humphrey has learned how to dismantle and scramble it; the Government now boasts a 'Twitter Tsar' (whose appointment was announced in a tweet); officials and politicians all argue among themselves about the reality of global warming; and administrators and governors alike are increasingly reliant on computers. In place of the sitcom's Dorothy Wainwright, who was forthright but still quite formal, there is a more aggressive, assertive and even more misguided special adviser called Claire Hutton (included, according to Jonathan Lynn, not only to reflect the fashion but also 'because we wanted a younger person in it'[12]), a party-dressed policy wonk who is so at home by the Prime Minister's side that she addresses him as 'Jim' as she tells him what to do.

Much of the story and the material, however, would underline just how many themes and issues had indeed remained basically the same over the past thirty years or more, from the formulaic clichés that are used to swathe and suffocate the media's searching questions, to the sleaze that has either to be smeared or smothered. There are still Oxbridge classicists in the Civil Service, and ambitious amateurs in the Government, and too many people in Westminster and Whitehall who are far too preoccupied with what gets written about them in the *Daily Mail*.

At the heart of the play, as at the heart of the sitcom, there was the archetypal comic relationship between the fallible master and the crafty servant, Jim Hacker and Sir Humphrey. The battle-scarred Hacker, certainly, has grown a little more opinionated and worldly-wise, and much readier to stand up to his Cabinet Secretary and sometimes even lecture him ('Computer models, Humphrey, are no different from fashion models: seductive, unreliable, easily corrupted, and they lead sensible people to make fools of themselves'), while Sir Humphrey – in the manner of Jeeves responding to Bertie Wooster's sudden fondness for strumming the banjolele – has reacted to this unwelcome change by becoming a little more critical and cynical about his boss (WOOLLEY: 'Power abhors a vacuum.' SIR HUMPHREY: 'And we are currently led by one').

In general, though, the dynamic is much as before. Sir Humphrey is still the artful virtuoso of verbosity:

Well, Prime Minister . . . one hesitates to say this but there are
times when circumstances conspire to create an inauspicious
concatenation of events that necessitate a metamorphosis, as
it were, of the situation such that what happened in the first
instance to be of primary import fraught with hazard and menace
can be relegated to a secondary or indeed tertiary position while
a new and hitherto unforeseen or unappreciated element can
and indeed should be introduced to support and supersede those

prior concerns not by confronting them but by subordinating them to the overarching imperatives and increased urgency of the previously unrealised predicament which may in fact now, ceteris paribus, only be susceptible to radical and remedial action such that you might feel forced to consider the currently intractable position in which you find yourself.

Hacker, likewise, is still only just bright enough to know that he is not quite bright enough (repeatedly declaring 'I must *do* something' and then looking hopefully at those who might be able to think of something sensible for him to do), only able to commit to any course of action when he can envision the personally favourable headlines it is likely to engender ('TRIUMPH FOR PRIME MINISTER!') and willing and able to dirty his hands whenever it seems to suit him:

SIR HUMPHREY: Prime Minister, you have always taken a very high moral tone. You're on the record against teenage sex. If you were now to endorse prostitution as an instrument of policy, there's a chance you could be accused of inconsistency.

HACKER: There are exceptions to every rule.

Bernard Woolley, meanwhile, is still the limp link between them: a mimetic mandarin, a sponge that seeks in vain to soak up only the good things that slosh towards him. A pedant without a purpose, he continues to wander unwittingly through conversations like Bambi gambolling across a minefield: WOOLLEY: 'It beats me why anyone would want to be Prime Minister.' SIR HUMPHREY: 'It's the only top job that requires no previous experience, no training, no qualifications and limited intelligence'; WOOLLEY: 'I believe in democracy, Sir Humphrey.' SIR HUMPHREY: 'It does you credit. And if all the voters were as informed and intelligent as – say – me, or even you, it could possibly work. But that's hardly realistic'; WOOLLEY: 'You know, I'm sure Humphrey wouldn't leak.' HACKER: 'Are you?' WOOLLEY: 'No.'

When it came to (re)casting these roles, Jay and Lynn were anxious to avoid those actors who would be inclined merely to imitate their illustrious predecessors. They wanted performers who would bring something fresh to their characters.

They chose David Haig to play Hacker. Well known in his own right as one of Britain's busiest character actors, having caught the eye in numerous productions over the past thirty years, including the movie *Four Weddings and a Funeral* (1994), the sitcom *The Thin Blue Line* (1995–6) and a wide range of stage plays, the balding and moustachioed actor was particularly adept at playing ordinary men unnerved by extraordinary problems.

Henry Goodman was picked to play Sir Humphrey. A tall man whose piercing eyes, sharp cheekbones and hawk-like nose made him vaguely reminiscent of Danny Kaye, he was best known for portraying strong and devious figures, including the eponymous king in *Richard III* at the RSC and the cynical lawyers Billy Flynn in *Chicago* and Roy Cohn in *Angels in America.*

The actor assigned to the part of Bernard Woolley was Jonathan Slinger. Very versatile, with a face that could suggest anything from dreamy placidity to edgy eccentricity, he was a performer who had been steadily making a name for himself in the theatre at the RSC and the National Theatre, as well as appearing occasionally in one-off television dramas.

Jonathan Lynn enjoyed the experience of directing this new version of the old comic triangle, relishing the subtle changes in each interpretation as the actors built up the layers of their respective roles. Without trying too hard to be different from the original characterisations, they found ways to accentuate those elements that suited their own particular strengths. 'They are not doing impressions,' said Lynn approvingly. 'They are playing it differently, and very well.'[13]

The production (which also featured Emily Joyce as Claire Hutton, the only female character now that Annie Hacker had been consigned to the sidelines) opened at the Chichester Festival in the summer of 2010, running from 13 May to 5 June. Following on from the real-life General Election of 6 May, which had resulted in a Coalition Government, the script had been fine-tuned by the writers to include a few extra topical jokes, as Hacker's anxiety over his own wafer-thin majority was made to seem remarkably current and pertinent.

The play was then moved to the Gielgud Theatre, in London's West End, where it would run from 17 September 2010 until 15 January 2011. The response, critically and commercially, was generally very positive, with audiences and reviewers alike appearing to accept (or at least tolerate) the inevitable changes in personnel while embracing the return of the familiar elegance and intelligence that was evident in the script.

Quentin Letts, writing in the *Daily Mail*, rated the play's 'observations on the chicanery of Whitehall as cute as ever',[14] while Michael Billington, in the *Guardian*, expressed his admiration for the way it ventured into 'buoyant farce' and still managed to locate 'its madness in a world we all recognise',[15] and the *Daily Telegraph*'s Charles Spencer enthused that it was 'both hilarious and a telling satire on the unscrupulousness of government'.[16] Some found faults in the acting (one critic, for example, judged Henry Goodman's portrayal of Sir Humphrey 'too heavy-handed in his coy cunning',[17]) while a few felt that too much of the television show's old intimacy had been lost ('subtle it ain't'[18]), but the overwhelming majority regarded the production as a great success.

It would later be taken on a very well attended UK tour, with a new cast (featuring Simon Williams as Sir Humphrey and Richard McCabe as Hacker), before returning for a second run in London's West End, and was also staged, among other places, in Australia and America. The odd new topical line was added for these productions, including a couple of jokes about telephone hacking and one about the debt-ridden Greeks, and (given the publicity surrounding the 'Operation Yewtree' investigations[19]) the reference to sex with an underage girl was eventually altered to mention of multiple adult partners. The reviews were once again predominantly positive, with even the *Hollywood Reporter* (while betraying its unfamiliarity with the original show via its clumsy references to 'common-touch politico Jim Hacker' and his 'fixer-nemesis Sir Humphrey') praising the play for avoiding the 'standard-issue political spoofing to focus more valuably on the foibles of actual policy and governance'.[20]

The experience left Jay and Lynn not only feeling vindicated for their decision to revive their great creation, but also eager to explore the possibility of using the play as the basis for another television series. Spreading out elements of the storyline across a sequence of six interrelated half-hour episodes, with the aim of illustrating how a Prime Minister cannot afford to deal with each crisis in a vacuum but rather has to contend with them in the midst of five or six other crises, they started planning how the scripts might take shape.

They were disappointed, however, to find that the BBC, when given the chance ('out of courtesy') to commission the new series, was cautious, requesting to see a pilot script before making a firm commitment. The writers were greatly offended by this response, arguing (somewhat disingenuously seeing as the old cast was no longer available) that 'there were thirty-eight pilots available on DVD'. The BBC responded by explaining that it was now 'standard policy' to request a pilot. 'So we said our policy was to not write a pilot for them,' Jonathan Lynn would snap. 'I thought it was absolutely extraordinary.'[21]

Curiously enough, there was no similarly furious denunciation of the commercial ITV1, or Channel 4, or Channel Five, none of whom jumped in to snatch the sitcom from under the nose of the Corporation, even though as rival terrestrial broadcasters (presumably with the same access to the thirty-eight 'pilot' episodes on DVD) they could have offered the sitcom roughly the same size of audience the writers surely desired. Jonathan Lynn would say, when asked if there had indeed been any other offers from the main commercial channels, 'I have no idea',[22] while Antony Jay would say, 'No, as I remember it, it was the original [production] company who did it.'[23] (ITV1, it should be noted, did go ahead, just a year later, and commissioned a new series of another former BBC sitcom, the vastly inferior *Birds of a Feather*.)

The revived *Yes, Prime Minister* would end up instead, faute de mieux, on the niche nostalgia cable and satellite channel GOLD (formerly known as UK Gold and now partly owned by the US company Scripps Networks Interactive and partly by BBC Worldwide), where, alas, it was destined to reach a far smaller proportion of the viewing audience.

Jay and Lynn, nonetheless, were simply pleased to have secured the degree of control that they wanted over the series (co-producing it with their old BBC Head of Comedy, Gareth Gwenlan, who was now operating as a freelancer), and proceeded to write each script with the same kind of care and meticulous research that they had lavished on all of the old episodes. David Haig and Henry Goodman agreed to continue in their stage roles, while Chris Larkin (who as a teenager had studied the original shows while working for his A level in Politics and Government) was recruited to take over as Bernard Woolley from Jonathan Slinger (who was preparing to appear as Hamlet for the RSC), and Zoe Telford was brought in to replace Emily Joyce as Claire Hutton.

Jonathan Lynn, who would co-direct with Gareth Gwenlan, took primary responsibility for preparing the cast for the recordings. 'I was a hundred per cent involved with everything,' he later confirmed. 'Tony, who is somewhat older than me and has health issues, came to the read-through and first rehearsal every week, and the dress rehearsal and performance. There was some give and take with regard to lines: essentially the actors would sometimes point out that something they were saying could be clarified in a particular way, and I would sometimes agree to change it. It was a fairly collaborative atmosphere, I think.'[24]

The schedule was basically the same as it had been back in the 1980s. Each episode (now timed at around twenty minutes, due to its being broken up and extended by ten minutes of adverts) would be rehearsed during the week, and then it was recorded in front of a live studio audience – now as before, ironically, at BBC Television Centre – on the Sunday evening.

One thing that had certainly changed since the last time *Yes, Prime Minister* was on the screen was the amount of pre-publicity that any show could expect, and, for a show with the pedigree of this one, the coverage was exceptional for a programme on a minority channel. There were countless interviews and articles in the newspapers and magazines, on radio and television and in various places on the web, all attracting attention to the imminent revival of a classic comedy show. There was also a tie-in documentary, *Yes, Prime Minister: Re-elected*, featuring the two writers and the new cast. Few existing fans of the old sets of series, nor many who had only seen the stage play, would have failed to notice what was due to happen. *Yes, Prime Minister* was coming back.

The first episode, entitled, 'Crisis at the Summit', was broadcast at 9 p.m. on Tuesday 15 January 2013. Featuring a credit sequence that used a new set of caricatures by Gerald Scarfe and an upbeat rerecording of Ronnie Hazlehurst's original theme tune, it was basically an updated version of the first act of the play, introducing the initial elements of the existing plot and also reintroducing the new cast characters.

Again set in Chequers, again over the course of an autumn weekend, Hacker has sought refuge there after enduring a media grilling in London over how badly things have been going:

INTERVIEWER: So, Prime Minister, the pound is falling, the
              Footsie's dropping like a stone, inflation could
              be on the way up, your coalition is divided, and
              now the conference on the Euro crisis looks like
              a dead end. It's all a bit of a disaster, isn't it?
HACKER: You know, I'm glad you asked me that . . .

Tired after trying in vain to guide his fellow European leaders in the
direction of an acceptable consensus ('It's like herding cats!'), he privately
fears the worst about the summit meeting ('Dealing with Europe isn't
about success, it's about concealing failure'), and, in spite of one last gasp
of bravado, is clearly in desperate need of some help:

HACKER: It is time for me to get hands on and give some
                leadership.
SIR HUMPHREY: Oh, good.
HACKER: So, tell me what I should do.
SIR HUMPHREY: Now that's just the kind of leadership we need!
HACKER: Thank you, Humphrey!

The rest of the opening instalment concentrates on establishing the
plotline concerning the rescue offer from Kumranistan, drawing on
many of the best early lines and exchanges from the play. It ends with
the Eurosceptic Hacker, having been enlightened by his special adviser,
demanding that Sir Humphrey admit that the Kumranistani loan will only
reach the UK via the European Central Bank, and will thus be dependent
on the Government abandoning sterling and joining the euro. 'Yes, Prime
Minister,' the Cabinet Secretary reluctantly confirms.

The first episode of the 'new and exclusive' series was watched by an
estimated 283,000 people (which amounted to approximately 1.17 per
cent of the available audience). It easily beat the channel's twelve-month
'slot average' of 114,000 viewers (about 0.47 per cent of the available audience),[25] but it was a poor reward for a sitcom that had always worked so
hard to engage with the biggest and broadest audience possible.

The acting was uneven. The great success was David Haig (now sans
moustache) as Hacker. A tightly coiled ball of nervy frustration, suggesting

a dollop of Harold Wilson, a big drip of John Major and a wee dram of Gordon Brown, he was instantly believable as a Prime Minister weighed down by the woes of the nation while worried about the intrigues and schemes that are afoot within his party. Never able entirely to ignore the nagging feeling that he is not up to a job whose crucial description is still missing, there was a delicate sense of pathos about him that added to the air of authenticity.

Less successful was Henry Goodman as Sir Humphrey, mugging almost as much as he had done in the stage play. In stark contrast to Nigel Hawthorne's portrayal, whose calm visage allowed only the sub-tlest hint at the synaptic acrobatics that were going on behind the bland mandarin's mask, Goodman's characterisation was all show and tell, with squat-thrusting eyebrows, darting eyes and a ready grin that suggested he was more Tigger than Jeeves, more Uriah Heep than Iago, and certainly not the discreetly dangerous, panther-like plotter of the original series.

Chris Larkin's Woolley also lacked the unforced charm and well-schooled dutifulness of Derek Fowlds' interpretation, although his sleepy-haired naivety, if writ a little too large, did at least suit the comedy of his character as it was now written. Zoe Telford, on the other hand, struck a sure tone from the beginning as the driven and doubt-free Claire Hutton.

What was most reassuringly impressive about the episode was the script, which was full of Jay and Lynn's trademark rigour and wit. It was topi-cal (WOOLLEY: 'A Hung Parliament's a bad thing?' SIR HUMPHREY: 'Yes, Bernard. Hanging's too good for them!'), amusingly nerdish ('No Prime Minister or US President has been elected without a full head of hair since Eisenhower and Churchill in the 1950s') and admirably candid (SIR HUMPHREY: 'We will have to pay a premium on the loan, but not for many years to come, when there will be a *different* government.' HACKER: 'Well, that's all right, then!'), and provided viewers with the main reason for staying with the sitcom and watching the rest of the run.

The reaction to the start of the series, however, was mixed. Among the reviews that arrived the following day, the *Independent*'s Tom Sutcliffe felt that the pace of the comedy 'was a beat or two off';[26] the *Daily Telegraph*'s Mark Monahan was much more enthusiastic, praising the 'terrific' cast and claiming that the 'writing is as sharp as ever';[27] while Sam Wollaston, writing in the *Guardian*, delivered the most damning of all the responses, branding the decision to bring back the show 'a mistake' before adding: 'Best forgotten, lest it sully fond memories'.[28]

Over on Twitter, where snap judgements popped up throughout the duration of the programme like fleas hopping on a dog, the comments were too diverse to confirm anything other than the incoherence of the medium of their expression: 'It all feels horribly forced'; 'Absolutely superb, very funny and brilliantly written'; 'Bad casting. No flair'; 'Pretty epic'; 'Slightly disappointing that the first episode of new *Yes, Prime Minister* is a rehash of the stage version. And that it's not very funny'; 'At last some great comic writing back on TV'; 'An outright embarrassment of sub-mediocrity especially after the golden gem that was the original'; 'Pleasantly surprised so far by this remake'; and 'Utterly devoid of charm. Memory sullied'.[29]

Several prominent politicians, who were well known to have been fervent fans of the original series, would aver that they were, alas, so busy attending to affairs of state that they had 'not yet had the opportunity to see' either this or subsequent episodes.[30] This was, in a sense, an encouraging sign, bearing in mind the recent fashion for Prime Ministers and Ministers to down tools in order to publicise their opinions on everything pop cultural from the plight of fictional characters in *Coronation Street*[31] to the carefully choreographed crises of contestants on *The X Factor*,[32] but, given their previously professed strong allegiance to this particular show (and the eager participation of some of them in the pre-publicity for its successor), their seeming failure even to record it for future scrutiny suggested a certain reluctance to welcome the revival.

The sole survivor of the original trio of stars, Derek Fowlds, was another who was left feeling far from satisfied by the new version. 'They were very, very fine actors,' he would say of the cast, 'but, for me, it seemed that they were trying too hard to be funny, and I'm afraid I didn't believe a word of it. It just reminded me of how natural and truthful Paul and Nigel were as those people.'[33]

The rest of the episodes continued to develop the basic storyline covered in the play, while also entwining such other topics as MPs' expenses claims, secrecy, leaks, patronage, Scottish independence, postcolonial diplomacy, the huge debt crisis, the influence of oil-rich countries, the purpose and influence of the BBC (an old hobby horse of Antony Jay's) – and the debate concerning global warming (a more recent hobby horse of Jay's[34]). There was also, in the background, a return to the original series' reflection on the differences between personal and public morality.

One of the highlights was a summary by Sir Humphrey of Whitehall realpolitik:

SIR HUMPHREY: Bernard, there are two worlds. There is the world of high principles, noble ideals and eternal verities. That is the world of philosophers, theologians, academics. And then there is the world of unsavoury realities and squalid practicalities. The world of politics and government. My world, Bernard, and yours. The real world.

WOOLLEY: But Sir Humphrey, this is a matter of black and white.

SIR HUMPHREY: No, no, there's nothing black and white in our world, Bernard. Ours is a world of dirty grey. I appreciate you wish to take the moral course. Well, sometimes it is unclear which course that is. Politicians, they can talk about what is right and what is wrong. We talk about what works, and what doesn't. So we put morality in the pending tray.[35]

The series was brought to a close on 19 February 2013 with an episode ('A Tsar is Born') which sought to tie all of the strands of the story together. Close to collapsing under the strain of such multiple worries as an unproductive European summit, an international financial crisis, a disloyal Cabinet, a critical media, damaging new computer predictions about global warming and the 'Kumranistani pervert' reneging on his country's deal with the UK, Hacker is close to giving up and resigning. Sir Humphrey saves the day by coming up with yet another ingenious plan.

He proposes using the idea of global warming – a concept that he has previously treated with cheerful contempt – to fashion a new policy that will transform the Prime Minister's fortunes at a stroke. After boldly committing the Government to battle climate change, he can introduce a special global warming tax on fuel to generate much-needed revenue in the short term, while 'phasing in' any additional expenditure over the course of the next half-century; he can also be seen to demand that all other major countries agree to review their emissions policies, and then, when they fail to change their ways, he can call for a series of earnest international conferences to reconsider their decisions. 'We can, Prime Minister, under *your* leadership, agree to save the world!' The beauty of the whole initiative, Sir Humphrey points out, is that 'it will be fifty years before anybody can possibly prove you're wrong'. Hacker is thrilled ('The voters will *love* me!'), and not even Woolley's scepticism can spoil his sense of redemption:

> WOOLLEY: There is *one* problem: nothing will have actually
>   been achieved.
> SIR HUMPHREY: It will *sound* as though it has. So people will
>   *think* it has.
> HACKER: That's all that matters!

In terms of critical attention, the series went out with a whimper, with few reviewers pausing to reflect on its run. *The Times* was an exception, judging the finale 'as sharp and funny as all the rest',[36] but, as with the vast majority of the output on the minority channels, the show (after one short and sharp blast of pre-publicity) seemed to have been sent out under the radar of the national press. The viewing figures had remained tiny, ranging from the initial peak of 306,000 down to a mere 109,000 for the sixth and final episode, averaging just 202,000 per programme.[37] It was still a coup for GOLD, which boosted its performance in that time slot quite significantly, but for a sitcom of such stature, and with such a history, it really did not seem right.

It was hard to gauge the general reaction to the revival, other than to conclude that it was underwhelming. With traditional critical sources largely silent, and the views expressed via the new social media far too mixed to be in any sense conclusive, all one could say with any confidence about the new *Yes, Prime Minister* was that it had been neither a complete failure nor an unqualified success.

There had been some good things. David Haig's performance, from start to finish, was extremely well judged, conveying a sense of mounting panic and paranoia with a naturalness that kept the core of the show close to plausibility even when things were becoming rather cartoon-like out on the periphery. His Hacker was nothing like Paul Eddington's Hacker, and was all the better for it.

It was also impossible not to admire, yet again, the cleverness of the scripts, which, while lacking some of the sureness and subtlety of their classic predecessors, still shone in comparison to the majority of what else was on offer in the sitcoms of the time. There were, in addition, a few nice little visual touches, such as Sir Humphrey's grudging nod to calls for sartorial informality by pushing his pocket handkerchief down just out of view.

There had also been some bad things. The studio audience, for example, sounded too eager to laugh, cheer and clap, and it diminished the achievement of those lines that genuinely merited such an explosive response. One of the many remarkable things about the original series was that there would be times when the on-screen insights would be so clear, pertinent and provocative that one could actually 'hear' the studio audience fall silent and think about the issue. In the new version, there seemed to be a kind of compulsion to have every comic line, no matter how simple or slight, boosted by the sound of raucous guffaws, which was certainly in keeping with the fashion in broadcasting to bellow 'give it up' at audiences (as if laughter and applause was some kind of quasi-feudal obligation), but which nonetheless did a disservice to the memory of the old shows.

There was also a loss of tension in the traditional comic triangle between Hacker, Sir Humphrey and Woolley. Sir Humphrey, perhaps partly due to the presence of the fragrant special adviser who seemed forever draped over Hacker's sofa, no longer appeared to have any real rapport with his Prime Minister. While Hacker staggered around his study like a wounded animal, looking at windows, floors and walls more often than he did human beings, the static Sir Humphrey's oddly oleaginous smirks and sneers seemed to be emitted purely for the benefit of the cameras.

Another flaw was the fact that, as Hacker was now so much more aware of Sir Humphrey's scheming, most of the comedy to be had from the

Prime Minister's deluded belief that he was still outwitting his Cabinet Secretary was lost. This was, after all, a political world that had itself been influenced by *Yes Minister* and *Yes, Prime Minister*: the new show was trying to satirise a class of people who had, at least in part, been shaped by the old shows.[38]

Bernard Woolley, meanwhile, no longer glanced back and forth at each of his masters as they competed to control his thoughts, but rather sought each of them out separately in order to express, rather gratuitously, how alarmed he was at what was happening. He was, as a consequence, not so much one-third of a trio but rather a solitary commentator on a duo.

None of this, however, did anything of great significance to affect the reputation of the original series. Some people had sought out the revivals, onstage and on screen, and some of them had been impressed, while some were disappointed. Many more had preferred to stay focused on the repeats, the DVDs and the memories, appreciating a great sitcom at its best.

The reactions, for and against, served to show how much the show still meant. More than thirty years on from its first appearance, it remained lodged in so many hearts and minds, no longer just a television programme, more part of the whole climate of popular political opinion. It was a remarkable achievement by the writers and the actors, and by the original broadcaster that had dared to give their show a home, and it would never be forgotten.

Before *Yes Minister*, sitcoms were valued mainly for the quantity of their laughs. After *Yes Minister*, sitcoms were also valued for the quality of their ideas. That, in terms of a contribution to television, to humour and to politics, was about as great and as good as it could get.

EPILOGUE

I believe that British television rests on specific British traditions, and in the first place, that it rests on the literary and dramatic genius of the British people and, secondly, on the sophistication in constitutional matters which you might expect from a country which has been talking itself in and out of trouble, and on the whole succeeding, for a long time.
Huw Wheldon

The truth is that you cannot be memorably funny without at some point raising topics which the rich, the powerful and the complacent would prefer to see left alone.
George Orwell

Epilogue

Very few television shows change the way one looks at the world. *Yes Minister*, and *Yes, Prime Minister*, did just that.

By combining accuracy with entertainment and information with humour, the sitcom arrived in 1980 to make the basics of an entire political system comprehensible and interesting to a far broader proportion of the population than the majority of expert commentators, up to that point, had thought possible. When it started, most aspects of how the country was governed were treated as though they were far too complicated, or important, to be subjected to widespread public scrutiny. *Yes Minister* challenged that conception, and changed it for good.

Suddenly the average voter could see how government and administration interacted, how responsibilities were divided up and distributed, how policies were developed, how decisions were made and how successes and failures were defined, described and defended. Schools, newspapers and television current affairs programmes, as well as political parties, should have been striving to make all of this clear as a matter of public service, but the very courageous decision to do so, and in a way that was genuinely accessible, was actually taken by the makers of a situation comedy.

Yes Minister and *Yes, Prime Minister* did more to engage and educate the general public about politics, in thirty-eight short episodes, than most of the so-called 'serious' means of enlightenment had done since the age of the great reform acts. Walter Bagehot, writing during that time of cautious and incomplete democratisation, had warned darkly of the dangers of subjecting British politics to the opinions of 'poor ignorant people'.[1]

More than a century later, it was left to a humble television situation comedy to attempt to remedy the matter – not by giving plural votes to the enlightened middle-class elite,[2] or by urging the many to defer to a special few 'of conscience and known ability',[3] but rather by actually having the imagination, talent, integrity and, most importantly of all, the *respect* to educate the masses about how the system really worked.

It made people realise how much more effort went into shutting them out than letting them in. It made them see how much that was wrong was presented as right. It made them appreciate how far short of being their best possible selves so many public servants fall.

It also, of course, made them laugh. It always made them laugh.

It was in large part down to the scripts. There had been some astonishingly gifted writers of sitcoms before Antony Jay and Jonathan Lynn teamed up, but none of them, before this pair came along, had managed to craft scripts that were as well researched, wide-ranging and wonderfully funny as this. All of the intricacies of Whitehall could be covered, all of the anxieties of Westminster acknowledged, all of the ambiguities of a constitution that has intrigued, bemused and enraged historians and commentators for centuries captured and conveyed, and, within the same space of just a few minutes, the audience reduced to helpless laughter.

It was also down to the actors – the original actors – who made three representative men seem so distinctively and remarkably real. Unlike lesser performers, who would merely have hidden behind the clever words and served the screen as static stereotypes, this trio of stars brought sensitivity and subtlety to their portrayals, rooting the interplay of general ideas within the interactions of particular individuals. Crucially, they connected the comedy of the head with the heart.

It also helped the sitcom – even though its two co-creators would not always seem particularly keen on acknowledging the fact – that it was screened and supported by the BBC. A commercial channel would have had the funds, easily, to make a show like *Yes Minister*. Only the BBC, the channel so cynically maligned and undermined by politicians, had the good taste, and the great faith, and the grand purpose, to actually do so.

There were several digs at the Corporation's expense during the show's run (e.g.: SIR HUMPHREY: 'Does he watch television?' HACKER: 'He hasn't even got a set.' SIR HUMPHREY: 'Fine, make him a Governor of the BBC'), but they only served to emphasise what an admirably tolerant, mature and humane home the sitcom had been given. In broadcasting, as in politics, genuine prudence (of the classical kind) seldom begets anything other than cynicism or indifference, but the fact remains that it was a great British public service broadcaster that gave us a great British public service sitcom.

Looking back today on what the programme achieved, there is understandable pride. Antony Jay, when asked what gave him the most satisfaction about the sitcom, said: 'I think it was the fact that people in the political world all accepted the accuracy of it.'[4] Jonathan Lynn, in answer to the same question, remarked similarly but more expansively:

> We exaggerated a bit, sometimes, to enhance the comedy, but
> we told the truth. The public now knows much more about how
> government works. We found that when we invented things, they
> had usually happened, or happened subsequently. Most gratifying
> and astonishing of all, our inventions of 'Sir Humphrey' and 'Yes,
> Minister' seem to have entered the language as shorthand for
> Civil Service obstruction (rightly or wrongly) and absurdity in
> government. No writer could hope for more.[5]

Derek Fowlds, the last surviving member of the show's classic comic triangle, reflected on the sitcom with the same mixture of satisfaction and affection: 'There were great scripts, great times, great laughs, and two wonderful, wonderful actors, who became two of my best friends in the world. So I thank them. And I miss them.'[6]

Sydney Lotterby, the producer, was just as warm in his recollections: 'I feel lucky to be associated with it. I just happened to be around at the right time to do it. And then, with those writers, and those actors – what a delight. It was definitely one of the best shows that I've done, and it made such an extraordinary impact.'[7]

Lord Donoughue, the show's longest-serving and most significant special adviser, celebrated the programme's far-reaching achievement:

> It was a textbook that was put on television and it reached so
> many people. Jonathan and Antony were geniuses. Jonathan

could spot a comic story so quickly, and Antony was brilliant at writing that kind of Sir Humphrey dialogue. And what they created, with its fundamental and timeless themes, remains just as relevant today as it was back then.[8]

So much in British politics has changed since that day in 1980 when *Yes Minister* first appeared on the screen, and yet so much has stayed the same. One of the reasons why we know the latter is that the former happened. As Armando Iannucci put it: 'It's a mark of [the show's] subversive influence that we now cannot trust a politician if he sounds like a character from *Yes, Minister* or deploys the sort of malformed logic for which the programme was famous. If it's depressing that this sort of logic is still used, it's a cause for rejoicing that we now have the means to identify it.'[9]

The show, it is true, did not change politicians very much. It did not expunge the smog of humbug and hypocrisy that still hovers over the Westminster environment.

There are still far too many politicians – supposedly mature adults – who happily act like novelty nodding, bobbing, barking dogs during Prime Minister's Questions, and shamelessly duck, dive and dissemble during perfectly reasonable televisual interrogations, and forget that they are in Parliament for reasons of service rather than self-aggrandisement. There are also, quite probably, still far too many civil servants, still secreted far too safely behind the scenes, who, like Sir Humphrey, have undergone complete 'principlectomies' and will go to any lengths to keep everyone else standing still.

This mere sitcom did, however, change something. What it changed, significantly, was *us*. We see through it all so much more easily now, and are so much better briefed to fight back.

It used to be said that we should meekly accept the 'charmed spectacle' that our supposed superiors choose to parade in front of us.[10] It used to be said that regular public scrutiny of Parliamentary proceedings would 'debase' the great debates and 'trivialise' the serious affairs.[11]

Since the evening of Monday, 25 February 1980, we all have a simple rebuttal – perfectly polite but nonetheless perfectly apposite – to such condescending claims. It should be said in a calm but knowing tone: 'Yes, Minister'.

YES MINISTER (BBC2)

Main regular credits: written by Antony Jay and Jonathan Lynn; drawings by Gerald Scarfe; theme music by Ronnie Hazlehurst.

Main regular cast: Paul Eddington (Jim Hacker), Nigel Hawthorne (Sir Humphrey Appleby), Derek Fowlds (Bernard Woolley).

SERIES 1

Open Government (25.02.1980)
With Diana Hoddinott (Annie Hacker), Neil Fitzwiliam (Frank Weisel), John Nettleton (Sir Arnold Robinson), Fraser Kerr, Edward Jewesbury, Norman Mitchell and David Moran.
Produced and directed by Stuart Allen.

The Official Visit (03.03.1980)
With Tenniel Evans (Foreign Secretary), John Savident (Sir 'Jumbo' Frederick), Thomas Baptiste, Robert Dougall and Antony Carrick.
Produced and directed by Sydney Lotterby.

The Economy Drive (10.03.1980)
With John Savident (Sir 'Jumbo' Frederick), Diana Hoddinott (Annie Hacker), Neil Fitzwiliam (Frank Weisel), Milton Johns, Pat Keen, Patricia Shakesby, William Lawford, Frank Tregear and Norman Tipton.
Produced and directed by Sydney Lotterby.

Big Brother (17.03.1980)
With Diana Hoddinott (Annie Hacker), Neil Fitzwiliam (Frank Weisel), Robert Urquhart, Robert McKenzie, Frederick Jaeger, Andrew Lane, Sheila Ferris and Matthew Roberton.
Produced and directed by Sydney Lotterby.

The Writing on the Wall (24.03.1980)

With Tenniel Evans (Foreign Secretary), John Savident (Sir 'Jumbo' Frederick), Neil Fitzwiliam (Frank Weisel) and Daniel Moynihan.

> Produced and directed by Sydney Lotterby.

The Right to Know (31.03.1980)

With John Savident (Sir 'Jumbo' Frederick), Diana Hoddinott (Annie Hacker), Gerry Cowper, Harriet Reynolds and Roger Elliott.

> Produced and directed by Sydney Lotterby.

Jobs for the Boys (07.04.1980)

With Neil Fitzwiliam (Frank Weisel), Richard Vernon (Sir Desmond Glazebrook), Arthur Cox, Richard Davies, Brian Hawksley, John D. Collins and Charles McKeown.

> Produced and directed by Sydney Lotterby.

SERIES 2

The Compassionate Society (23.02.1981)

With John Barron, Norman Bird, Rosemary Frankau, Stephen Tate, Arthur Cox, Lindy Alexander and Robert Dougall.

> Produced and directed by Peter Whitmore.

Doing the Honours (02.03.1981)

With John Pennington (Peter), John Nettleton, Frank Middlemass, William Fox, Margo Johns and Anne Maxwell.

> Produced and directed by Peter Whitmore.

The Death List (09.03.1981)

With Diana Hoddinott (Annie Hacker), Graeme Garden, Ivor Roberts, Colin McCormack, Michael Keating and Jay Neill.

> Produced and directed by Peter Whitmore.

The Greasy Pole (16.03.1981)

With Brenda Blethyn, Freddie Earlle, Jerome Willis, Sheila Fay, Geoffrey Toone, Maureen Stevens, Lindy Alexander and Robert Dougall.

> Produced and directed by Peter Whitmore.

The Devil You Know (23.03.1981)

With Diana Hoddinott (Annie Hacker) and Arthur Cox.

> Produced and directed by Peter Whitmore.

The Quality of Life (30.03.1981)

With Richard Vernon, Peter Cellier, Antony Carrick, Zulema Dene, Rex Robinson, Roger Martin and Sue Lawley.

> Produced and directed by Peter Whitmore.

A Question of Loyalty (06.04.1981)

With John Pennington (Peter), Judy Parfitt, Nigel Stock, Rosemary Williams, Anthony Dawes and John Rolfe.

> Produced and directed by Peter Whitmore.

SERIES 3

Equal Opportunities (11.11.1982)
With John Nettleton (Sir Arnold Robinson), Diana Hoddinott (Annie), Eleanor Bron, Richard Simpson, Peter Howell, Jeffrey Segal, Donald Pelmear and Talla Hayes.
                                        Produced and directed by Peter Whitmore.

The Challenge (18.11.1982)
With John Nettleton (Sir Arnold Robinson), Ian Lavender, Doug Fisher, Stuart Sherwin, Frank Tregear and Ludovic Kennedy.
                                        Produced and directed by Peter Whitmore.

The Skeleton in the Cupboard (25.11.1982)
With Ian Lavender, Donald Gee, John Pennington and Rosemary Williams.
                                        Produced and directed by Peter Whitmore.

The Moral Dimension (02.12.1982)
With Diana Hoddinott (Annie), Antony Carrick, Vic Tablian, Sam Dastor, Walter Randall and Michael Sharvell-Martin.
                                        Produced and directed by Peter Whitmore.

The Bed of Nails (09.12.1982)
With John Nettleton (Sir Arnold Robinson), David Firth, Nigel Stock, Peter Dennis, Robert East and David Rose.
                                        Produced and directed by Peter Whitmore.

The Whisky Priest (16.12.1982)
With Diana Hoddinott (Annie Hacker), John Fortune and Edward Jewesbury.
                                        Produced and directed by Peter Whitmore.

The Middle-Class Rip-Off (23.12.1982)
With John Nettleton (Sir Arnold Robinson), John Barron, Patrick O'Connell, Derek Benfield and Joanna Henderson.
                                        Produced and directed by Peter Whitmore.

SPECIAL (BBC1)

Untitled two-minute sketch in *The Funny Side of Christmas* (27.12.1982)

SPECIAL (BBC2)

Party Games (17.12.1984)
With John Nettleton (Sir Arnold Robinson), Diana Hoddinott (Annie Hacker), James Grout, Peter Jeffrey, Philip Stone, André Maranne, Ludovic Kennedy, Anthony Pedley, David Warwick, Laura Calland, Roger Davidson, David Howey, Bernard Losh, Roger Ostime, John Pennington, Martyn Read and Rex Robinson.
                                        Produced and directed by Peter Whitmore.

YES, PRIME MINISTER (BBC2)

Main regular credits: written by Antony Jay and Jonathan Lynn; drawings by Gerald Scarfe; theme music by Ronnie Hazlehurst.

Main regular cast: Paul Eddington (Jim Hacker), Nigel Hawthorne (Sir Humphrey Appleby), Derek Fowlds (Bernard Woolley).

SERIES 1

The Grand Design (09.01.1986)
With Diana Hoddinott (Annie Hacker), Barry Stanton (Malcolm Warren), Frederick Treves, Oscar Quitak, Jonathan Stephens and Miranda Forbes.
                          Produced and directed by Sydney Lotterby.

The Ministerial Broadcast (16.01.1986)
With Barry Stanton (Malcolm Warren), John Wells, Brian Gwaspari and Carolyn Lyster.
                          Produced and directed by Sydney Lotterby.

The Smoke Screen (23.01.1986)
With Peter Cellier (Sir Frank), John Barron, Clive Merrison, Bill Wallis and Brian Hawksley.
                          Produced and directed by Sydney Lotterby.

The Key (30.01.1986)
With Deborah Norton (Dorothy Wainwright), Peter Cellier (Sir Frank) and Victor Winding.
                          Produced and directed by Sydney Lotterby.

A Real Partnership (06.02.1986)
With Diana Hoddinott (Annie Hacker), John Nettleton (Sir Arnold), Peter Cellier (Sir Frank) and Deborah Norton (Dorothy Wainwright).
                          Produced and directed by Sydney Lotterby.

A Victory for Democracy (13.02.1986)
With Clive Francis, Ronald Hines, Donald Pickering and David de Keyser.
Produced and directed by Sydney Lotterby.

The Bishop's Gambit (20.02.1986)
With Diana Hoddinott (Annie Hacker), Ronnie Stevens, Frank Middlemass, William Fox and Donald Pickering.
Produced and directed by Sydney Lotterby.

One of Us (27.02.1986)
With John Nettleton (Sir Arnold), Diana Hoddinott (Annie Hacker), Michael Aldridge, John Normington, Miranda Forbes and Martin Muncaster.
Produced and directed by Sydney Lotterby.

SERIES 2

Man Overboard (03.12.1987)
With John Nettleton (Sir Arnold), Frederick Treves, Michael Byrne, Peter Cartwright, David Glover, David Conville, Philip Anthony, Philip Blaine, Geoffrey Cousins and Hilary Field.
Produced and directed by Sydney Lotterby.

Official Secrets (10.12.1987)
With Antony Carrick, Jeffry Wickham, Denis Lill, Tom Bowles, Sadie Hamilton, James Newall and Michael Shallard.
Produced and directed by Sydney Lotterby.

A Diplomatic Incident (17.12.1987)
With Diana Hoddinott (Annie Hacker), Christopher Benjamin, Alan Downer, Robert East, Mansel David, Nicholas Courtney, Bill Bailey, David King, Raymond Brody and William Lawford.
Produced and directed by Sydney Lotterby.

A Conflict of Interest (23.12.1987)
With Deborah Norton (Dorothy Wainwright), Peter Cellier (Sir Frank), Richard Vernon, Louis Mahoney and Miranda Forbes.
Produced and directed by Sydney Lotterby.

Power to the People (07.01.1988)
With Deborah Norton (Dorothy Wainwright), John Nettleton (Sir Arnold), Diana Hoddinott (Annie Hacker), Gwen Taylor, Jonathan Adams and Miranda Forbes.
Produced and directed by Sydney Lotterby.

The Patron of the Arts (14.01.1988)
With Deborah Norton (Dorothy Wainwright), Diana Hoddinott (Annie Hacker), John Bird, Antony Carrick, Geoffrey Beevers, Martin Milman, Myfanwy Talog, David Rose and Guy Standeven.
Produced and directed by Sydney Lotterby.

The National Education Service (21.01.1988)
With Deborah Norton (Dorothy Wainwright), John Nettleton (Sir Arnold), Diana Hoddinott (Annie Hacker), Peter Cartwright and Jerome Willis.

Produced and directed by Sydney Lotterby.

The Tangled Web (28.01.1988)
With Ludovic Kennedy and Geoffrey Drew.

Produced and directed by Sydney Lotterby.

YES, PRIME MINISTER (GOLD)

Main regular credits: written by Antony Jay and Jonathan Lynn; drawings by Gerald Scarfe; theme music by Ronnie Hazlehurst.

Main regular cast: David Haig (Jim Hacker), Henry Goodman (Sir Humphrey Appleby), Chris Larkin (Bernard Woolley), Zoe Telford (Claire Hutton).

SERIES 1

Crisis at the Summit (15.01.2013)
With Tim Wallers, Chandrika Chevli, Sophie Raworth and Chris Fawkes.
       Produced and directed by Jonathan Lynn and Gareth Gwenlan.

The Poisoned Chalice (22.01.2013)
With Pip Torrens, Sevan Stephan, Sam Dastor and Sara Carver.
       Produced and directed by Jonathan Lynn and Gareth Gwenlan.

Gentleman's Agreement (29.01.2013)
With Edward Baker-Duly.
       Produced and directed by Jonathan Lynn and Gareth Gwenlan.

A Diplomatic Dilemma (05.02.2013)
With Sam Dastor.
       Produced and directed by Jonathan Lynn and Gareth Gwenlan.

Scot Free (12.02.2013)
With Robbie Coltrane, Tim Wallers and Ilan Goodman.
       Produced and directed by Jonathan Lynn and Gareth Gwenlan.

A Tsar is Born (19.02.2013)
With Tim Wallers and Sam Dastor.
       Produced and directed by Jonathan Lynn and Gareth Gwenlan.

Acknowledgements

This book was Sam Harrison's courageous decision. He believed in it, and in me, enough to wait a remarkably long time until I was available to write it, and I am so grateful to him for his faith, his patience and his support.

I must thank Sir Antony Jay and Jonathan Lynn, of course, for their cooperation and insights. It was a pleasure to spend so much time reflecting on their extraordinary achievement.

I am also pleased to thank Kathryn Ferguson for ensuring that all of our various communications reached the right destinations. Her courteousness was as impressive as her competence.

Derek Fowlds could not have been more helpful, or more encouraging. It is always a delight to find that someone is as decent and kind as he is talented.

Sydney Lotterby was similarly enlightening. Probably the greatest producer/director of British sitcoms, his modesty is as notable as his talent.

Lord Donoughue was an invaluable, and very entertaining, interviewee. He is proof of the fact that the writers were as shrewd in their choice of ally as they were in their choice of opponent.

I am also grateful to all of the other people who provided assistance, advice and insights from within Westminster, including David Blunkett, Laurence Mann and Chris McCarthy, along with those who preferred to remain anonymous. The fact that several of my former students are now working within Whitehall was also rather welcome.

I must thank Lord Kinnock for the use of his and Patricia Hewitt's *Yes Minister* sketch, and Sir Bernard Ingham for Margaret Thatcher's *Yes*

Minister routine. No complementary Liberal, SDP or Lib-Dem sitcom skit, alas, was available for inclusion.

Valerie Warrender proved a fascinating source of information regarding the remarkable work that went into transforming bare studio sets into uncannily accurate replicas of the rooms inside Number Ten. She epitomises the brilliance of the team behind the scenes.

A number of friends, now sadly departed, deserve to be acknowledged here for the many insights they gave me about television, sitcoms and the BBC: John Ammonds, Eddie Braben, Richard Briers, Jonathan Cecil, Sir Bill Cotton, David Croft, John Howard Davies and Eric Sykes. They were genuinely kind and generous people, as well as expert in their arts, and I remain indebted to all of them.

I must also record my thanks to the staff of the following institutions: the Office of Black Rod; the BBC Written Archives Centre (especially Jessica Hogg); the National Archives; the British Library, Newspaper Library and Sound Archive; the British Film Institute Library; the Albert Sloman Library, the University of Essex; the Churchill College Cambridge Archive; and the University of Cambridge Library.

My agent, Mic Cheetham, was as helpful as ever. She made the whole process so much easier than it might have been.

My mother, as always, was a constant source of encouragement. There is no adequate way to express it, but my gratitude is immense.

Finally, my heartfelt thanks go to Silvana Dean, whose friendship is such a privilege. This book is for her.

Graham McCann
Cambridge 2014

Notes

Prologue

Frontispiece quotations:

Thomas Paine: *The Age of Reason* (New York: Dover, 2004), Chapter XVII, p. 76

Walter Bagehot, *The English Constitution* (London: Fontana, 1993), p. 251

Harold Macmillan: Letter to Reginald Bevins, the Postmaster General, 10 December 1962

1 Although microphones were added to the new Commons Chamber when it reopened in 1950 (after bomb damage during the war), it would take another thirty-eight years before they were used on a regular basis. In 1975, MPs backed the idea of public radio broadcasting and a month-long experiment began on 9 June of that year (television broadcasts were rejected by a margin of twelve votes). Following a report from the Services Committee on the experiment, MPs debated it on 8 and 16 March 1976, and voted for radio broadcasting on a permanent basis. Radio recording of proceedings within the House of Commons commenced on 3 April 1978, although only isolated occasions, such as Prime Minister's Questions or the Budget, actually went out live on the BBC and commercial radio stations, with the BBC broadcasting a summary of proceedings at the end of each day. In 1983, the House of Lords voted to allow television to broadcast live debates from its chamber. The first regular live television broadcasts from the House of Commons began on 21 November 1989. A channel dedicated exclusively to live broadcasts from both Houses was launched in 1992: called The Parliamentary Channel, it started

as a cable-exclusive channel (operated by United Artists Cable and funded by a consortium of British cable operators) but was purchased by the BBC in 1998, retitled BBC Parliament and relaunched under its new name on 23 September 1998.

2 Michael Marshall, Under-Secretary of State, Hansard, HC Deb. 25 February 1980, vol. 979 cc. 936–8.

3 Sir Keith Joseph, Secretary of State for Industry, Hansard, HC Deb. 25 February 1980, vol. 979 cc. 938–41.

4 William Whitelaw, Home Secretary, Hansard, HC Deb. 25 February 1980, vol. 979 c. 397W.

5 Lord Campbell of Croy, Hansard, HL Deb. 25 February 1980, vol. 405 cc. 1000–4.

6 The Lord Bishop of Blackburn, Hansard, HL Deb. 25 February 1980, vol. 405 cc. 1010–36.

7 Richard Crossman, 'The Real English Disease', *New Statesman*, 24 September 1971, p. 1.

8 Walter Bagehot, 'Physics and Politics' (1867), in Norman St John-Stevas, ed., *Walter Bagehot* (London: Eyre & Spottiswoode, 1959), p. 446.

9 Ibid. p. 456.

10 Mary Whitehouse, quoted in *The Times*, 29 April 1965, p. 8. See also my *Spike & Co.* (London: Hodder & Stoughton, 2006), the chapters on Johnny Speight and *Till Death Do Us Part*.

11 Anthony Trollope, *Can You Forgive Her?* 1864 (New York: Random House, 2012), Chapter LII, pp. 349–50.

12 Anthony Trollope, *Phineas Finn*, 1869 (Harmondsworth: Penguin, 1977), p. 68.

13 Anthony Trollope, *Phineas Redux*, 1874 (Oxford: Oxford University Press, 2001), p. 227.

14 Anthony Trollope, *The Prime Minister*, 1876 (Oxford: Oxford University Press, 2011), p. 145.

15 Winston Churchill, 'Cartoons and Cartoonists', *Thoughts and Adventures* (London: Odhams Press, 1947), pp. 11–12, 13, 15 and 17.

16 Thomas Carlyle, letter to C.G. Duffy, dated 29 August 1846. Source: *The Carlyle Letters Online*, vol. 21, pp. 33–4, ed. Brent E. Kinser, Duke University Press, 14 September 2007.

17 *BBC Variety Programmes Policy Guide for Writers and Producers* (aka 'The Green Book'), (London: BBC, 1948), p. 11.

18 Peter Cook, 'TVPM', *Beyond the Fringe*, Fortune Theatre, London, 1961. See *Tragically I Was an Only Twin*, edited by William Cook (London: Century, 2002), p. 51.

19 See Charles Dickens, *Little Dorrit* 1857 (Ware: Wordsworth Editions, 1996). Dickens used the Barnacle family to mock the nepotism, incompetence and inertia that he felt characterised the Civil Service in the nineteenth century: 'The Barnacles were a very high family, and a very large family. They were dispersed all over the public offices, and held all sorts of public places. Either the nation was under a load of obligation to the Barnacles, or the Barnacles were under a load of obligation to the nation. It was not quite unanimously settled which; the Barnacles having their opinion, the nation theirs' (pp. 103–4).

20 See Anthony Trollope's *The Three Clerks* 1858 (Oxford: Oxford University Press, 1990). Trollope based the character of Sir Gregory Hardlines on that of Sir Charles Trevelyan, who, alongside Sir Stafford Northcote, had been charged with the task of transforming Whitehall's bureaucracy from something amateurish and reliant on patronage into a modern professional organisation founded on proper examinations. Trollope wrote of Hardlines: 'Great ideas opened themselves to his mind as he walked to and from his office daily. What if he could become the parent of a totally different order of things! What if the Civil Service, through

his instrumentality, should become the nucleus of the best intellectual diligence in the country, instead of being a byword for sloth and ignorance!' (p. 68).

21 See Max Weber, 'Parliament and Government in Germany under a New Political Order', 1918, in Peter Lassman and Ronald Spiers, eds, *Max Weber: Political Writings* (Cambridge University Press, 1994), p. 159. See also his classic account of the phenomenon in his 1922 work *Economy and Society* (Berkeley: University of California Press, 1992).

22 William Haselden, 'The Evolution of a Government Official', *Daily Mirror*, 12 January 1918.

23 William Haselden, 'The Public Money and the Public Man – 2', *Daily Mirror*, 20 Mar 1919.

24 The original idea for the show's title had been '*M.U.G.*' – an abbreviation of 'Ministry of Universal Gratification' – but the increasingly common use by newspapers (beginning with the *Daily Express*, 2 May 1939, p. 1) of the phrase 'It's That Man Again!' to signal yet another report about Adolf Hitler encouraged the show's makers to adopt it as their title. The setting was originally a pirate radio ship, but this was changed to a Government Ministry early on during the show's run.

25 This Whitehall setting was later replaced by a seaside location called 'Foaming-at-the-Mouth', with Whitehall's civil servants replaced by local council bureaucrats.

26 Sir Edward Bridges, *Portrait of a Profession: The Civil Service Tradition*, the Rede Lecture, University of Cambridge, 1950 (Cambridge: Cambridge University Press, 1950), p. 33.

27 A further fourteen episodes of *The Men from the Ministry* (consisting mainly of old plotlines slightly revised) were made by the BBC Transcription Service in 1980 for broadcast in other countries, and were only aired for British audiences on BBC 7 in 2012.

28 'Birmingham is Revolting', *The Men from the Ministry*, first broadcast on BBC Radio 4, 24 August 1976.

29 See *The Men from the Ministry*, 'The Big Rocket', first broadcast on the BBC Light Programme, 30 October 1962; reprised as 'Boots', first broadcast overseas, 13 April 1980.

30 See *The Men from the Ministry*, 'The Great Footwear Scandal', first broadcast on the BBC Light Programme, 6 November 1962; reprised as 'Boots', first broadcast overseas, 20 April 1980.

31 *If It Moves, File It* (a sitcom that lasted for only one series of six episodes) was broadcast by London Weekend Television from 28 August to 2 October 1970.

32 Max Weber, *The Protestant Ethic and the Spirit of Capitalism* (New York: Charles Scribner's Sons, 1958), p. 128.

33 Walter Bagehot, 'Physics and Politics' (1867), in St John-Stevas, ed., *Walter Bagehot*, p. 449.

34 Walter Bagehot, *The English Constitution* (London: Fontana, 1993), Introduction to the 1872 Second Edition, p. 278.

35 Howerd's 1963 routine, a recording of which is available on the CD *Frankie Howerd At The Establishment And At The BBC* (Decca 2007), revolved around the lingering controversy that dogged the then Prime Minister, Harold Macmillan, following his dramatic decision, on Friday 13 July 1962, to carry out the most brutal reshuffle in British political history, known subsequently for that reason as the 'Night of the Long Knives'. The embattled Macmillan, responding to the Conservative Government's rapidly declining popularity among voters, had decided to radically change the composition of his Cabinet, removing those most associated with current unpopular economic policies and adding several younger, more dynamic ministers to revitalise the group as a whole. Spurred on by a script written mainly by Johnny Speight, Howerd gleefully eschewed the familiar analysis of the event and chose instead to discuss it as though it had been a domestic squabble largely between Macmillan's wife, Dorothy, and some of Macmillan's old colleagues, such as his Chancellor, Selwyn Lloyd. In an era when such irreverence towards political leaders was still deemed an audacious novelty, Howerd's performance caused a sensation and inspired many similarly iconoclastic routines. See my *Frankie Howerd: Stand-Up Comic* (London: Fourth Estate, 2004), Chapter 10.

36 See Plutarch, *Greek Lives* trans. Robin

Waterfield (Oxford: Oxford University Press, 1998), pp. 150–1.

37 Thomas Hobbes, Part 1, Chapter 4, *Leviathan* (1651), ed. Richard Tuck (Cambridge: Cambridge University Press, 1991), pp. 28–9.

38 Ibid. 'A Review, and Conclusion', p. 483.

39 John Locke, *An Essay Concerning Human Understanding* (1690), Book III, Chapter 10, par. 34 (Oxford: Clarendon Press, 1979), p. 508.

40 George Orwell, 'Politics and the English Language' (1946), in *Why I Write* (Harmondsworth: Penguin, 2004), p. 116.

41 The classic discussion of this topic is generally seen as being Michael Walzer's essay 'Political Action: The problem of Dirty Hands', first published in *Philosophy and Public Affairs*, vol. 2, no. 2, Winter 1973, pp. 160–80.

42 Jean-Paul Sartre, *Les Mains Sales*, 1948, translated as *Dirty Hands* in *No Exit and Three Other Plays*, trans. Lionel Abel (New York: Vintage, 1955), p. 224.

43 In Anthony Trollope's 1875 novel, *The Way We Live Now* (a biting critique of the corruption of late-Victorian morals), one of its central characters, the shamelessly shallow Lady Carbury, asserts her conviction that the praiseworthy deeds of the powerful escape the normal categories of morality: 'If a thing can be made great and beneficent, a boon to humanity, simply by creating a belief in it, does not a man become a benefactor to his race by creating that belief?' When accused of being 'an excellent casuist' in the defence of her position, she responds by describing herself as 'an enthusiastic lover of beneficent audacity'. See *The Way We Live Now* (Ware: Wordsworth Classics, 2001), p. 227.

44 Immanuel Kant, First Section, *Groundwork for the Metaphysics of Morals*, trans. Allen W. Wood (New Haven: Yale University Press, 2002), p. 15: '[A]n action from duty has its moral worth not in the aim that is supposed to be attained by it, but rather in the maxim in accordance with which it is resolved upon; thus that worth depends not on the actuality of the object of the action, but merely on the principle of the volition, in accordance with which the action is done, without regard to any object of the faculty of desire.'

45 See John Stuart Mill, *Utilitarianism*,

Chapter II, in *On Liberty and Other Essays*, ed. John Gray (Oxford: Oxford University Press, 1991), p. 137: '[A]ctions are right in proportion as they tend to promote happiness, wrong as they tend to produce the opposite of happiness.'

46 Isaiah Berlin, 'Two Concepts of Liberty', in *Four Essays on Liberty* (Oxford: Oxford University Press, 1969), p. 171: 'Pluralism [unlike either deontology or utilitarianism] does, at least, recognise that human goals are many, not all of them commensurable, and in perpetual rivalry with one another. To assume that all values can be graded on one scale, so that it is a mere matter of inspection to determine the highest, seems to me to falsify our knowledge that men are free agents, to represent moral decision as an operation which a slide-rule could, in principle, perform.' See also Thomas Nagel, 'Ruthlessness in Public Life', in *Mortal Thoughts* (Cambridge: Cambridge University Press, 1979) and Bernard Williams, 'Ethical Consistency', in Christopher Gowans, ed., *Moral Dilemmas* (Oxford: Oxford University Press, 1987).

47 Niccolò Machiavelli, *The Prince* (1532), eds Quentin Skinner and Russell Price (Cambridge: Cambridge University Press, 1988), Chapter XV, 'The things for which men, and especially rulers, are praised or blamed', pp. 54–5.

PART ONE

Header quotation: John Godfrey Saxe, in a lecture cited by *The University Chronicle* (Michigan), 27 March 1869, p. 4. The saying is often wrongly attributed to Otto von Bismarck.

1 The Writers

Header quotation: Ludwig Wittgenstein, *Culture and Value*, ed. G.H. von Wright with Heikki Nyman (Oxford: Basil Blackwell, 1980), p. 78c.

1 *Daily Express*, 25 January 1963, p. 8.

2 Hansard, HC Deb. 27 October 1955, vol. 545 c. 51W.

3 R.A. Butler, Hansard, HC Deb. 16 March 1961, vol. 636 c. 1412W.

4 Sir Frank Soskice, Hansard, HC Deb. 15 June 1961, vol. 642 cc. 698–702.

5 Wilson made this clear, shortly after becoming Leader of the Labour Party, in a speech at the annual meeting of the Society of Labour Lawyers. See also the report in *The Times*, 21 April 1964, p. 10, and the reminiscence in Tony Benn's *Out of the Wilderness: Diaries 1963–1967* (London: Arrow, 1987), p. 36.

6 Sir Frank Soskice, speaking in the House of Commons on 4 February 1965 (see Hansard, HC Deb. 04 February 1965, vol. 705 cc. 1256–7), also quoted by the *Daily Mirror*, 5 February 1965, p. 2 and 5 November 1965, p. 1.

7 Hansard, HC Deb. 04 February 1965, vol. 705 c. 1257.

8 Norman St John-Stevas, *Catholic Herald*, 4 June 1985, p. 4.

9 Ian Gilmour, Hansard, HC Deb. 4 February 1965, vol. 705 c. 1257.

10 Roy Jenkins, *A Life at the Centre* (London: Macmillan, 1991), p. 175. Sir Frank did eventually bow to pressure on 4 November 1965, allowing a new inquiry and granting permission to the surviving family of Timothy Evans to have his body exhumed from prison grounds and re-buried by his relations at Greenford, Middlesex. Roy Jenkins then replaced Sir Frank as Home Secretary in Harold Wilson's first Cabinet reshuffle, in December 1965. Sir Frank was made Lord Privy Seal and in 1966, upon being made a Life Peer, took a seat in the House of Lords as Baron Stow Hill of Newport. He died in Hampstead on 1 January 1979. Soon after becoming Home Secretary, Roy Jenkins recommended a Royal Pardon for Timothy Evans, which was granted in October 1966.

11 Thomas 'Tam' Galbraith was a Conservative MP, Government Minister and former Civil Lord of the Admiralty who was plunged into controversy when it was discovered, in September 1962, that his former Assistant Private Secretary, an Admiralty clerk called John Vassall, was a Soviet spy. Vassall, who was homosexual, had appeared so close to the married MP that – entirely unfounded – rumours began to circulate about a possible sexual liaison between

them. Encouraged by an Opposition that had raised numerous questions in the Commons about the modestly paid Vassall's extravagant lifestyle and frequent visits both to Galbraith's family home in London and also to his mansion in Scotland, the press, alarmed at the thought that a KGB spy had enjoyed privileged access to a Minister for several years without apparent detection, subjected both Galbraith and the Government as a whole to a prolonged investigation, designed to pressurise the powers that be into revealing the full extent of a presumed cover-up. Vassall had already been tried and sentenced to eighteen years in jail, but Galbraith, eventually, resigned from office, insisting on his innocence from any wrongdoing but admitting that his continuing presence in the Cabinet had become an embarrassment. The controversy, however, showed no signs of abating, with the press searching for more officials who might have been implicated. Rattled by the affair and furious with Fleet Street, the Prime Minister, Harold Macmillan, set up an independent inquiry, which, much to the anger of the media, ended up being just as critical of the press as it was of politicians and civil servants, and, in the bitter fallout, two journalists were sent to prison for refusing to reveal their sources. (See *The Times*, 26 April 1963, p. 18 and C. Andrew and O. Gordievsky, *KGB: The inside Story of its foreign operations, from Lenin to Gorbachev* [London: Hodder & Stoughton, 1990]).

12 On 12–13 July 1962, the Prime Minister Harold Macmillan, reacting with what he later admitted was panic over the poor performance of his Government, dismissed, or accepted the resignations of, the Chancellor of the Exchequer and six other Cabinet members, followed by numerous junior ministers. It was the most extensive reconstruction of a Cabinet by a Prime Minister since Ramsay MacDonald formed the National Government in 1931, but, on this occasion, it failed to have a positive effect. Macmillan's Conservative Party was confused, the public unimpressed and the Labour Opposition greatly encouraged. (See Harold Macmillan, *At the End of the Day* [London: Macmillan, 1973], p. 92.)

13 The Conservative MP John Profumo was Secretary of State for War when, in July 1961, he began a clandestine relationship

with a young model and 'occasional prostitute' named Christine Keeler. Although, as both a married man and a Government Minister, he soon realised the damage that would be done if the affair was ever exposed, his decision to end it after a few weeks failed to prevent it from being uncovered by the press, and Profumo then found himself caught up in a controversy. Soon after, however, another rumour surfaced, suggesting that Keeler had also had a relationship with Yevgeny Ivanov, a senior naval attaché at the Soviet embassy in London at the height of the Cold War, and, as a consequence, the size of the controversy thus suddenly grew from being merely a personal embarrassment into a full-blown national scandal. When pressed in private by Government officials to answer the allegations, Profumo vehemently protested his innocence and vowed to sue all of his accusers for libel. The story, however, refused to go away, and it was decided that Profumo would have to make a public denial in Parliament. The Minister duly stood up in the Commons on 22 March 1963 and, in a blatant lie, insisted that there had been 'no impropriety whatsoever' in his 'acquaintanceship' with Christine Keeler, and he repeated his threat 'to issue writs for libel and slander if scandalous allegations are made or repeated outside the House'. The sense of doubt and unrest, however, continued both in Parliament and in the media, and, on 29 May, the Prime Minister Harold Macmillan finally acceded to a demand for an inquiry into the matter. On 31 May, Profumo and his wife left for a holiday in Venice, where he confessed to her that he had indeed had an affair with Keeler. She advised him to return home at once and come clean – which he did. In his letter of resignation from the Government on 4 June, he admitted his lie, apologised, and said that he had lied 'to protect, as I thought, my wife and family'. He also stood down from his seat in the House of Commons, after which he dedicated himself for the rest of his life to doing good works, eventually receiving a CBE for his efforts in 1975. He died on 9 March 2006. (See Hansard, HC Deb. 22 March 1963, vol. 674 cc. 809–10 and HC Deb 17 June 1963, vol. 679 cc 34–176, and David Profumo, *Bringing the House Down: A Family Memoir* [London: John Murray, 2006]).

14 When Harold Macmillan's health deteriorated to the extent that, in October 1963, he decided to step down as Prime Minister, the 14th Earl of Home, who had been serving the Government from the House of Lords as Foreign Secretary, emerged after some widely reported infighting as his surprise successor. As it was, by this stage, deemed to be against constitutional convention (though not against the law) for a Prime Minister to be a member of the House of Lords (the last person to have been so was the 3rd Marquess of Salisbury, who resigned in 1902), the hunting, fishing, shooting aristocrat Home made use of the 1963 Peerage Act – which, ironically, had been prompted when a Labour MP, Anthony Wedgwood Benn, had been denied his current seat in the Commons when on 17 November 1960 he inherited his father's hereditary peerage and became, overnight and profoundly reluctantly, the second Viscount Stansgate. After a very public campaign by Benn and the Labour Opposition to change the law, the Conservative Government finally agreed to introduce the Peerage Bill in 1963, which would allow individuals to disclaim their peerages for their lifetime. Once passed into law on 31 July of that year, Benn was the first peer to make use of the Act, and (after the man who replaced him in the Commons, the Conservative Malcolm St Clair, stood down as a matter of principle) he was subsequently re-elected as an MP. It was therefore considered ironic when one of the next high-profile figures to follow suit was the Earl of Home, who gave up all of his hereditary titles (the Earldom of Home, the Lordship of Dunglass, the Lordship of Home, the Lordship of Home of Berwick, the Barony of Douglas and the Barony of Home of Berwick) became Sir Alec Douglas-Home, stood successfully for election to the Commons in the safe and vacant Conservative seat of Kinross and West Perthshire, and entered the Commons as the new Prime Minister. Defeated at the October General Election of 1964, he resigned as Leader of the Conservative Party in 1965 and was replaced by Edward Heath, but remained an MP for another nine years. On leaving the Commons in 1974, he returned to the House of Lords when (under the rules set out in the 1958 Life Peerages Act – another law that he had shown little interest in supporting) he accepted a life peerage, becoming known as Baron Home of the Hirsel, of Coldstream in the County of Berwick. (See the *Daily Express*, 24 November 1960, p. 1 and 18 October 1964, p. 10, and the *Daily Mirror*, 24 July 1965, p. 6.)

15 Jonathan Lynn, *Comedy Rules: From the Cambridge Footlights to Yes, Prime Minister* (London: Faber & Faber, 2011), pp. 31–2.

16 Jonathan Lynn, quoted in Michael David Kandiah (1994), '*Yes Minister* and *Yes, Prime Minister* (2): Jonathan Lynn', *Contemporary Record*, 8:3, p. 525.

17 Antony Jay, interview with the author, 1 February 2014.

18 Antony Jay, *Management and Machiavelli* (Harmondsworth: Penguin, 1967), p. 19.

19 Jonathan Lynn would say of Brian King's teaching: 'He did not define law as a system of rules, which was how most people defined it. Rules are not necessarily effective, he argued, and therefore not real rules unless society agrees to honour them. So a legal system is in reality, he said, a system of norms. International law, so-called, exemplifies this view' (interview with the author, 1 February 2014).

20 Antony Jay, *Confessions of a Reformed BBC Producer* (London: Centre for Policy Studies, 2007), p. 2.

21 Donald Baverstock, explaining the moral quality of the *Tonight* programme, wrote: 'Little things, [for example] where you put on a man you think is dishonest and he's made some witty remarks and the interviewer may have smiled in the middle and enjoyed it. You feel that's slightly immoral because you have endorsed this man's successful hypocritical projection of himself,' quoted by Grace Wyndham Goldie, *Facing the Nation: Television & Politics 1936–76* (London: The Bodley Head, 1977), p. 215.

22 Wyndham Goldie, *Facing the Nation*, p. 214.

23 Jay, *Confessions of a Reformed BBC Producer*, p. 1.

24 Terry Jones, quoted by Kim Johnson, *Life Before and After Monty Python* (London: Plexus, 1993), p. 37.

25 The episode of *Doctor at Large* was called 'Pull the Other One' and was first broadcast on LWT on 1 August 1971.

26 Lynn later acknowledged (*Comedy Rules*, p. 74) that his usual writing partner of the time, George Layton, 'had always been willing to go along with my satirical ideas, although temperamentally he was, I think, more in tune with [producer Humphrey Barclay's] cosier approach.'

27 Lynn, *Comedy Rules*, p. 78.

28 The most common criminology case study, on this topic, that was taught in Lynn's days at Cambridge would have been Johannes Lange's classic 1929 study of identical 'monozygotic' (MZ) and fraternal 'dizygotic' (DZ) twins. Thirteen pairs of MZ twins and seventeen DZ pairs were studied with regard to variety of 'criminal indicators', such as having a criminal record. The MZ twins had a concordance rate of 77 per cent compared to just 12 per cent of the DZ twins. This suggested strongly, in the context of the traditional 'nature versus nurture' debate, that there is a genetic element in criminality. As subsequent critiques pointed out, however, the sample sizes were very small, and the contentious nature of the findings thus inspired countless other experiments and studies in this area over the course of the next few decades. See Johannes Lange, *Crime as Destiny* (London: Allen & Unwin, 1929).

29 Jonathan Lynn, interview with the author, 1 February 2014.

30 Lynn, *Comedy Rules*, p. 78.

31 See *The Times*, 18 May 1973, p. 28.

32 Lynn, *Comedy Rules*, p. 81.

33 *Who Sold You This, Then?* won a Gold Award at the 1973 British Sponsored Film Festival.

34 Lynn, *Comedy Rules*, p. 82.

35 Antony Jay, interview with the author, 1 February 2014.

36 Ernest Jay was an actor whose best-known performances included such movies as *The House of the Spaniard* (1936), *O.H.M.S.* (1937), *Top Secret* (1952), *Grand National Night* (1953) and *The Curse of Frankenstein* (1957), while a certain generation of children would forever associate him more readily with the voice of Larry the Lamb's mischievous companion Dennis the

Dachshund in BBC radio's long-running *Toytown* series.

37 Lynn, *Comedy Rules*, p. 97.

38 Lynn, *Comedy Rules*, p. 83.

39 Antony Jay, speaking in *Comedy Connections*, series six, episode two: *Yes Minister*, first broadcast on BBC1 on 25 July 2008.

40 The transcript of Barbara Castle's speech was published (belatedly) in the *Sunday Times*, under the title 'Mandarin Power', on 10 June 1973, pp. 17–19.

41 See, for example, the *Guardian*, 14 January 1974, p. 9.

42 Antony Jay, quoted by Michael White, 'Men Behind the Ministry', *Radio Times*, 21–7 February 1981, p. 6.

43 Antony Jay, quoted in Michael David Kandiah (1994), '*Yes Minister* and *Yes, Prime Minister* (1): Sir Antony Jay, CVO', *Contemporary Record*, 8:3, p. 507.

2 The Situation

Header quotation: Lord Winchilsea, writing in 1875 on the occasion of the posthumous publication of Charles Greville's notoriously indiscreet diaries about the political affairs that he had observed at close hand while serving as Clerk to the Privy Council.

1 Antony Jay, speaking in *Comedy Connections*, series six, episode two: *Yes Minister*, first broadcast on BBC1 on 25 July 2008.

2 Jonathan Lynn, speaking in *Comedy Connections*, series six, episode two: *Yes Minister*, first broadcast on BBC1 on 25 July 2008.

3 Lynn, *Comedy Rules*, p. 83.

4 Antony Jay, interview with the author, 1 February 2014.

5 Antony Jay worked as series editor on *A Prime Minister on Prime Ministers*, a thirteen-part series in which Harold Wilson looked back at some of his predecessors and contemporaries at Number Ten. Made by Yorkshire TV, it was broadcast by ITV from 11 May 1977 to 22 February 1978.

6 Quoted by Lynn, *Comedy Rules*, p. 95.

7 Ibid. p. 96.

8 Quoted by Michael White, 'Men Behind the Ministry', *Radio Times*, 21 to 27 February 1981, p. 6.

9 Lynn, *Comedy Rules*, p. 96.

10 Richard Crossman, *New Statesman*, 21 March 1959, pp. 419–20.

11 Richard Crossman, *Diaries of a Cabinet Minister: Volume 1: Minister of Housing 1964–66* (London: Hamish Hamilton and Jonathan Cape, 1975), p. 12.

12 See *The Times*, 2 October 1975, p. 1.

13 *The Times*, 8 December 1975, p. 12.

14 *The Times*, 30 June 1976, p. 14.

15 *Guardian*, 8 January 1976, p. 11.

16 Richard Crossman, *The Crossman Diaries: Condensed Version*, ed. Anthony Howard (London: Magnum, 1979), p. 25.

17 Ibid.

18 Ibid.

19 Ibid.

20 Ibid. pp. 26–7.

21 Ibid. p. 40.

22 Ibid. p. 41.

23 See Kevin Theakston and Geoffrey Fry, 'Britain's Administrative Elite: Permanent Secretaries 1900–1986', *Public Administration*, vol. 67, no. 2, June 1989, pp. 129–47.

24 Crossman, *The Crossman Diaries*, pp. 41 and 64. (The then Head of the Home Civil Service was Sir Laurence Helsby.)

25 Ibid. pp. 92–4.

26 Ibid. p. 94.

27 Ibid. p. 92.

28 Antony Jay, quoted in Kandiah, p. 517.

29 Crossman, *The Crossman Diaries*, p. 25.

30 Lynn, *Comedy Rules*, p. 98.

31 Nelson Polsby, 'Where Do Ideas Come From?' lecture at the University of Chicago, quoted by Harry Kreisler, 4 September 2002, as part of the 'Conversations with History' series at the Institute of International Studies, University of California, Berkeley.

32 Lord Donoughue, interview with the author, 25 March 2014.

33 Antony Jay, interview with the author, 1 February 2014.

34 Jonathan Lynn, interview with the author, 1 February 2014.

35 Bernard Donoughue, *Downing Street Diary, Volume One: With Harold Wilson in No. 10* (London: Jonathan Cape, 2005), p. 51.

36 Lynn, *Radio Times*, 15 January 2013, p. 17.

37 Lynn, quoted in Kandiah, p. 527.

38 Lynn, *Comedy Rules*, p. 98.

39 Jay, quoted by Ben Duckworth in 'The Power of Comedy', *Total Politics*, 20 November 2009, online source: http://www.totalpolitics.com/articles/3313/the-power-of-comedy.thtml.

40 Leslie Chapman quoted in *The Times*, 9 May 1978, p. 2. (Shortly before Chapman retired, he sent the Department of the Environment a memorandum outlining his arguments for reform, citing some of the examples that would later feature in his first book. According to a spokesman for the Department at the time, an internal investigation was launched but it was found that 'the allegations were not supported by the evidence'.)

41 *World in Action*: 'In the Public Interest', broadcast on ITV on 8 May 1978. *The Man Alive Report*: 'Civil They May Be, But Are They Servants?', broadcast on BBC2 on 9 May 1978.

42 Leslie Chapman, *Your Disobedient Servant* (London: Chatto & Windus, 1978), p. 30.

43 Antony Jay, quoted in Kandiah, p. 518.

44 Antony Jay, quoted in Kandiah, pp. 511–12.

45 Lynn, quoted in Kandiah, p. 529.

46 P. G. Wodehouse, *Right Ho, Jeeves* (London: Penguin, 1999), p. 76.

47 P. G. Wodehouse, *Joy in the Morning* (New York: W. W. Norton & Company, 2011), p. 170.

48 Ibid. pp. 110–11.

49 See my *Spike & Co.* (London: Hodder & Stoughton, 2006), pp. 261–78.

50 Jay, quoted by Duckworth,

51 Jay, quoted in Kandiah, p. 508.

52 Crossman, *The Crossman Diaries*, p. 25.

53 Ibid. pp. 159–60.

54 Antony Jay, speaking in *Comedy Connections*, series six, episode two: *Yes Minister*, first broadcast on BBC1 on 25 July 2008.

55 This early name for Hacker is in some secondary sources rendered as 'Jerry', but documents in the BBC Written Archives Centre (henceforth abbreviated as WAC) confirm the spelling as 'Gerry'.

56 Lynn, *Comedy Rules*, p. 101.

57 Lynn, interview with the author, 1 February 2014.

58 Lynn, *Comedy Rules*, p. 101.

59 Jay, quoted in Kandiah, p. 511.

60 Lynn, quoted in Kandiah, p. 531.

61 See Theakston and Fry, 'Britain's Administrative Elite', pp. 129–47.

62 Lynn, quoted in Kandiah, pp. 531–2.

63 Crossman, *The Crossman Diaries*, p. 159.

64 Lynn, *Comedy Rules*, p. 112.

65 Lynn, quoted in Kandiah, p. 533.

66 Ibid. p. 532.

3 The Pitch

Header quotation: Anon, 'The Prayer of St Francis', submitted anonymously to the French publication *La Clochette* in 1912, and quoted by Margaret Thatcher outside Number Ten Downing Street on 4 May 1979.

1 James Gilbert sent a memo to David Gower at the BBC's copyright department on 13 October 1977, saying: 'Would you please go ahead and commission Tony Jay and Jonathan Lynn to write a 30-minute pilot script (as yet untitled). Delivery date 1.1.78'. Gilbert did actually know the writers' intention to call the programme *Yes Minister*, but at this stage he saw no need to confirm it. (Source: BBC WAC: Antony Jay Copyright File 1975–9.)

2 Lynn, quoted in Kandiah, p. 533.

3 Jay, quoted in Kandiah, p. 509.

4 Lynn, quoted in Kandiah, p. 527.

5 Lynn, quoted in Kandiah, p. 527.

6 See the 'Room 3' chapter in my *Spike & Co.* (London: Hodder & Stoughton, 2006).

7 See my *Dad's Army: The Story of a Classic Television Show* (London: Fourth Estate, 2001), pp. 102–3.

8 See Richard Webber, *Whatever Happened to the Likely Lads?* (London: Orion, 1999), p. 20.

9 See Chapter 2 of my *Fawlty Towers* (London: Hodder & Stoughton, 2007).

10 John Cleese, quoted by Lynn, *Comedy Rules*, p. 109.

11 Lynn, *Comedy Rules*, p. 109.

12 Lynn, *Comedy Rules*, p. 114.

13 Lynn, *Comedy Rules*, p. 110.

14 Lynn, *Comedy Rules*, p. 110.

15 Lynn, *Comedy Rules*, p. 113.

16 The episode in question was episode five in series 3, called 'The Bed of Nails'.

17 The script in question was from series three: 'The Bed of Nails'.

18 Lynn, *Comedy Rules*, p. 111.

19 See Crossman, *The Crossman Diaries*, p. 35.

20 Jay, quoted in Kandiah, op. cit. p. 509. (William Whitelaw, at the time when *Yes Minister* was first being written, was Deputy Leader of the Opposition and Chairman of the Conservative Party; Labour's Merlyn Rees had recently been appointed Home Secretary. Both men were widely regarded both inside and outside of the Commons as relatively reasonable, ruminative, moderate types who epitomised the kind of consensual politics that had characterised twentieth-century British politics before Thatcherism, briefly, challenged the orthodoxy.)

21 John Cleese, quoted in my *Fawlty Towers*, p. 54.

22 The pilot script had been formally accepted on 10 January 1978. (Source: BBC WAC: Antony Jay Copyright File 1975–9.)

23 Jay, quoted in Kandiah, p. 511.

24 Lynn, *Comedy Rules*, p. 103.

25 Antony Jay, speaking in *Comedy Connections*, series six, episode two: *Yes Minister*, first broadcast on BBC1 on 25 July 2008.

26 *The Good Life*, series one, episode four, 'Pig's Lib', broadcast on BBC1, 25 April 1975. Lynn played a window cleaner.

27 See *The Times*, 28 December 1985, p. 34.

28 Lynn, *Comedy Rules*, p. 103.

29 Nigel Hawthorne, *Daily Express*, 24 November 1984, p. 17.

30 Nigel Hawthorne, *Straight Face* (London: Hodder & Stoughton, 2002), pp. 247–8.

31 Quotes in *The Times*, 28 December 1985, p. 34.

32 John Howard Davies, interview with the author, 31 May 2007.

33 Source: BBC WAC: Antony Jay Copyright File 1975–9.

34 Source: BBC WAC: Antony Jay Copyright File 1975–9.

35 Source: BBC WAC: Antony Jay Copyright File 1975–9.

36 Lynn, *Comedy Rules*, p. 104.

37 Davies commissioned scripts five and six on 2 November 1978 for a joint fee of £725. He would not decide to commission a seventh script until after production on the show resumed after the 1979 General Election. (Source: BBC WAC: Antony Jay Copyright File 1975–9.)

38 See my *Fawlty Towers*, pp. 55–6.

39 See my *Dad's Army*, p. 52.

40 Derek Fowlds, interview with the author, 4 March 2014.

41 Derek Fowlds, interview 4 March 2014.

42 Derek Fowlds, interview 4 March 2014.

43 Source: BBC WAC: *Yes Minister* File T70/34/1, episodes one to seven, (series one).

44 John Howard Davies, interview with the author, 31 May 2007.

45 John Howard Davies, interview 31 May 2007.

4 The Preparation

Header quotation: Samuel Beckett, *Worstward Ho* (London: John Calder, 1983), p. 7.

1 Source: BBC WAC: *Yes Minister* File T70/34/1, episodes one to seven (series one).

2 John Howard Davies, interview with the author, 31 May 2007.

3 Jonathan Lynn, interview with the author, 1 February 2014.

4 Jonathan Lynn, interview with the author, 1 February 2014.

5 Lynn, *Comedy Rules*, p. 70.

6 Ibid. p. 71.

7 Antony Jay, interview with the author, 1 February 2014.

8 Paul Eddington, *So Far, So Good* (London: Hodder & Stoughton, 1995), p. 142.

9 Derek Fowlds, interview with the author, 3 February 2014.

10 Nigel Hawthorne, *Straight Face*, p. 248.

11 Quoted by Lynn, *Comedy Rules*, pp. 105–6.

12 Ibid. p. 106.

13 Ibid.

14 Ibid.

15 Derek Fowlds, interview with the author, 3 February 2014.

16 Hawthorne, *Straight Face*, p. 249.

17 Ibid.

18 Eddington, *So Far, So Good*, p. 142.

19 Derek Fowlds, interview with the author, 3 February 2014.

20 Antony Jay, speaking in *Comedy Connections*, series six, episode two: *Yes Minister*, first broadcast on BBC1 on 25 July 2008.

21 George Fox (1624–91) is commonly regarded as the founder of the Society of Friends, which is often referred to as the Quaker movement. Emerging in the 1650s in reaction to the corruption and obscurantism associated with the Anglican Church, the Quakers believed in the unique value of each individual, so they insisted on treating everyone equally. They believed in direct experience of God, so they regarded priests and rituals as unnecessary obstructions between the individual believer and God. Because of their spiritual egalitarianism, they resisted social hierarchies as well, refusing to raise their hats or bow their heads to anyone else regardless of title or rank. They were suspicious of any signs of affectation, so favoured plain and simple language, clothes and manners. Part of the power of Thomas Paine's radical political writings in the mid-eighteenth century, it is usually argued, came from his own Quaker background, which encouraged him to write more simply and accessibly than any of his eminent theoretical predecessors.

22 Eddington, interviewed in *The Times*, 28 December 1985, p. 34.

23 Eddington, quoted by Khan, 'The Men from the Ministry', p. 12.

24 Graham Greene, *The Power and the Glory* (London: Vintage Classics, 2001), p. 193.

25 Lynn, quoted in Kandiah, p. 524.

26 See, for example, the *Daily Express*, 11 November 1982, p. 23. (The actor Jonathan Cecil told me that Eddington had mentioned to him James Prior as a model for Jim Hacker.)

27 See the interview with James Prior, *Desert Island Discs*, first broadcast on BBC Radio 4, 11 January 1987.

28 See Lynn, *Comedy Rules*, p. 116. He told Lynn, 'I'm not interested in politics. Never have been.'

29 Jay, quoted in Kandiah, pp. 510–11.

30 Jay, 'Why *Yes Minister* is as true as ever', *Daily Telegraph*, 20 November 2009, p. 25.

31 Antony Jay, quoted by Lynn, *Comedy Rules*, p. 116.

32 Derek Fowlds, interview with the author, 3 February 2014.

33 Derek Fowlds, interview with the author, 3 February 2014.

34 Derek Fowlds, interview with the author, 3 February 2014.

35 BBC WAC: *Yes Minister File* T70/34/1, episodes one to seven (series one). No clear confirmation exists in the BBC archives regarding the authorship of the caricatures. Neither Antony Jay nor Jonathan Lynn could recall the name of any artist involved prior to Gerald Scarfe's arrival.

36 Nigel Hawthorne, in *Straight Face*, p. 248, recalled: 'they were so crudely executed, and, in any case, they didn't look like us'.

37 Ibid. p. 249.

38 BBC WAC: Ronnie Hazlehurst Artist File.

39 Jay, quoted in Kandiah, p. 510.

40 John Howard Davies, interview with the author, 31 May 2007.

41 It is sometimes – wrongly – claimed that John Cleese decided to use Lotterby's name in 'The Four Lotterbys' sketch, but Lotterby himself would recall that it was Feldman who 'rang me and said, "I want to use your name." I said, "Why?" He said, "It's such an unusual name." (Sydney Lotterby, quoted in the *London Evening Standard*, 28 July 2000, p. 48).

42 The first sketch was a delightfully whim-sical routine that saw four identically dressed Englishmen bump into each other while on holiday in Spain. As they talk to each other, they discover that all of them are called Sydney Lotterby, and three of them happen to be 'wholesale greengrocers' – while the fourth is a barrister who 'used to be a wholesale greengrocer'. The follow-up sketch appears to have been very similar, although, as a recording was rediscovered only recently, I have not yet been able to view it. 'Sydney Lotterby Wants to Know the Test Score' is more or less self-explanatory, and was apparently inspired by the fact that Lotterby did indeed often want to know the Test score.

43 Geoffrey Palmer, quoted in the *Daily Post* (North Wales), 20 July 2002, pp. 2–3.

44 See Ronnie Waldman, 'The Toughest Job', *Radio Times*, 4 December 1953, p. 5, as well as my *Morecambe & Wise* (London: Fourth Estate, 1998), especially Chapters 5, 13 and 14.

45 Source: BBC WAC: *Yes Minister* File T70/34/1, episodes one to seven (series one).

46 See my *Spike & Co.*, pp. 315–16. The question of stopping *That Was The Week That Was* in General Election year, according to Kenneth Adam, the then Director of Television at the BBC, began as a discussion between the Director-General, Hugh Carleton Greene, and himself. This was followed by further discussion at the weekly management meeting of BBC directors, after which the Director-General stated the intention to the Board of Governors at the beginning of November 1963, which they approved (see *The Stage*, 21 November 1963, p. 9).

47 The so-called Lib-Lab Pact was negotiated in March 1977 when the Labour Govern-ment, recently deprived of an overall majority due to a by-election defeat, was now facing a motion of no confidence. Needing the votes of some Opposition MPs to survive, an agreement was struck with the Liberal Party, whereby the Labour Party would accept a limited number of Liberal Party policy proposals in exchange for the Liberal Party's promise to vote with the Government in any subsequent motion of no confidence.

48 See, for example, the *Daily Express*, 7 February 1079, p. 1.

49 See the *Daily Express*, 15 February 1979, p. 1.

50 See the *Sunday Express*, 4 March 1979, p. 1.

51 Jonathan Lynn, interview with the author, 1 February 2014.

52 See the *Guardian*, 29 March 1979, p. 1.

53 Source: BBC WAC: Antony Jay Copyright File 1975–9.

54 Source: BBC WAC: David Jason Artist File.

55 Source: BBC WAC: *Yes Minister* File T70/34/1, episodes one to seven (series one).

56 Source: BBC WAC: *Yes Minister* File T70/34/1, episodes one to seven (series one).

57 BBC WAC: Ronnie Hazlehurst Artist File.

58 Source: BBC WAC: *Yes Minister* File T70/34/1, episodes one to seven (series one).

PART TWO

Frontispiece quotations:

Max Weber: quoted by Guenther Roth and Claus Wittich in their editors' introduction to *Economy and Society* (Berkeley: University of California Press, 1992), p. LIX.

Niccolò Machiavelli, *The Prince*, Chapter XIV: 'How a ruler should act concerning military matters', p. 52.

5 Series One

Header quotation: Walter Bagehot, *The English Constitution*, p. 61.

1 Conservative Party manifesto, 1979.

2 Naseem Khan, 'The Men from the Ministry', *Radio Times*, 23 to 29 February 1980, pp. 12–13.

3 This was actually a very late decision. In a letter dated 14 February 1980, Carol Vigurs, Manager of Facilities at the BBC, informed a colleague: 'A transmission date for this series has still to be arranged' (source: BBC WAC: *Yes Minister* File T701/34/1, episodes one to seven, series one).

4 Peter Fiddick, *Guardian*, 26 February 1980, p. 9. His complaint about Hansard was that, in one brief exchange, Sir Humphrey startles Jim Hacker by demonstrating that he has committed to memory a minor remark in the House by citing its place in Hansard as 'volume 497, page 1102, column B'. Fiddick complained that 'Hansard does not have page numbers – and each column is numbered. (And, judging by the volume number, our newly created Minister must have got into the Lords by mistake on the day in question but we'll let that pass)'.

5 David Sinclair, *The Times*, 25 February 1980, p. 25.

6 Source: BBC WAC: Viewing Barometer for 25 February 1980.

7 Roy Hattersley, 'Of Ministers and Mandarins', *The Listener*, 20 March 1980, pp. 367–8.

8 *Daily Mail*, 5 April 1980, p. 19.

9 Harold Wilson, quoted by Bernard Donoughue, *Downing Street Diary: With Harold Wilson in No. 10* (London: Jonathan Cape, 2005), p. 573.

10 Series one, episode three: 'The Economy Drive'.

11 Series one, episode five: 'The Writing on the Wall'.

12 Series one, episode six: 'The Right to Know'.

13 Series one, episode six: 'The Right to Know'.

14 Series one, episode six: 'The Right to Know'.

15 Series one, episode four: 'Big Brother'.

16 Series one, episode three: 'The Economy Drive'.

17 Series one, episode two: 'The Official Visit'.

18 Series one, episode 5: 'The Writing on the Wall'.

19 Series one, episode 7: 'Jobs for the Boys'.

20 Series one, episode 5: 'The Writing on the Wall'.

21 George and Weedon Grossmith, *The Diary of a Nobody* (London: Wordsworth Editions, 1994), p. 144.

22 Source: BBC WAC: Viewing Barometers and Viewing Panel Reports. In some publications and online sites it has been

claimed that the series' appreciation rating was 90 per cent or even higher. I have found nothing to corroborate this figure in the BBC archives. The final Viewing Barometer data for the series clearly states that the Reaction Index for this series (in other words, the average percentage of positive responses given via the BBC's own programme research poll) was 74 per cent.

23 It would also, in March 1981, win the Best Comedy award for 1980 from the Broadcasting Press Guild, with Nigel Hawthorne also receiving the Best Actor award.

Case Study 1

24 Sir Robin Butler, speaking on *Yes Minister: The View from Whitehall*, Part 1, first broadcast on BBC Radio 4 on 26 February 2005.

25 *Yes Minister*, series one, episode two: 'The Official Visit'.

26 The official, who requested anonymity, confirmed this in a private conversation with the author, 27 November 2013.

27 Lynn, *Comedy Rules*, p. 126.

28 Hattersley, 'Of Ministers and Mandarins', p. 367.

29 Hattersley, '*Yes Minister*', in Merullo, Annabel and Neil Wenborn, *British Comedy Greats* (London: Cassell Illustrated, 2003), pp. 179–82.

30 Kenneth Clarke, speaking on *Yes Minister: The View from Whitehall*, Part 1, first broadcast on BBC Radio 4 on 26 February 2005.

31 See Marcia Williams, *Inside Number 10* (London: Weidenfeld & Nicolson, 1972), p. 233.

32 See Joe Haines, *The Politics of Power* (London: Jonathan Cape, 1977), p. 183, and *Glimmers of Twilight* (London: Politico's, 2003), p. 154.

33 Quoted by Gerald Kaufman, Hansard, HC Deb 24 May 1995, vol. 260 c. 913.

34 Gerald Kaufman, *How to be a Minister* (London: Faber & Faber, 1997), pp. 68–9.

35 Jonathan Lynn, interview with the author, 3 February 2014.

6 Series Two

Header quotation: George Lichtenberg, *The Waste Books* (New York: NYRB Classics, 2000), p. 88.

1 Hansard, HC Deb. 26 March 1981, vol. 1 cc. 1180–6.

2 Michael White, 'Men Behind the Ministry', p. 6.

3 Margaret Thatcher, letter to Alasdair Milne, 31 December 1982 (accessed at the Thatcher Archive at Churchill College, Cambridge).

4 Michael White, 'Men Behind the Ministry', p. 6.

5 Oscar Wilde, *The Picture of Dorian Gray* (London: Wordsworth Editions, 1992), p. 6.

6 Barbara Castle, who served in Harold Wilson's Labour Governments during the 1960s and 1970s, published the first volume of her diaries, *The Castle Diaries 1964–1976*, shortly after the 1979 General Election, too late for Jay and Lynn to draw on for their first series but in good time for the preparation of the second.

7 Jonathan Lynn, speaking on *Desert Island Discs*, first broadcast on BBC Radio 4, 20 October 1984.

8 Sir Ian Bancroft, quoted in *The Times*, 7 May 1980, p. 18.

9 Jay, quoted in Kandiah, p. 518.

10 Jay, quoted in Kandiah, pp. 518–19.

11 Lynn, *Comedy Rules*, p. 122.

12 Ibid. p. 123.

13 Ibid.

14 Ibid.

15 Ibid.

16 Ibid. p. 124.

17 Ibid. p. 125.

18 Source: BBC WAC: *Yes Minister* File T70/33/1, episode one and filming (series two).

19 Hawthorne, *Straight Face*, p. 250.

20 Eddington, *So Far, So Good*, p. 168.

21 Hawthorne, quoted by Khan, 'The Men from the Ministry', p. 12.

22 Hawthorne, quoted by Garth Pearce, *Daily Express,* 24 November 1984, p. 17.

23 Hawthorne, *Straight Face*, p. 254.

24 Ibid.

25 Ibid.

26 Ibid. p. 253.

27 Ibid. p. 254.

28 Derek Fowlds, interview with the author, 3 February 2014.

29 Sydney Lotterby, interviewed in *The Stage*, 8 May 1980, p. 19.

30 Antony Jay, interview with the author, 1 February 2014.

31 Friedrich Hayek was a critic of all forms of centralised economic planning, arguing that centralised planning cannot work for an economy because complete knowledge of that economy is never available centrally. See *The Road to Serfdom* (Chicago: University of Chicago Press, 1994).

32 *Free to Choose* was a six-part television series produced by Video Arts and first broadcast in the UK in 1980 by BBC2. An American version of the series, which ran to ten episodes, was broadcast in the same year on PBS. See also Milton Friedman, *Capitalism and Freedom* (Chicago: University of Chicago Press, 2002).

33 As Buchanan put it in 'Contractarian presuppositions and democratic governance' in H.G. Brennan/Loren F. Lomasky, eds, *Politics and Process: New Essays in Democratic Thought* (Cambridge: Cambridge University Press, 1989), p. 174 (1986), politics is 'a process within which individuals, with separate and potentially differing interests and values, interact for the purpose of securing individually valued benefits of cooperative effort'.

34 Jay, quoted in Kandiah, p. 519.

35 Lynn, quoted in Kandiah, p. 523.

36 Lord Donoughue, interview with the author, 25 March 2014.

37 Lord Donoughue, interview with the author, 25 March 2014.

38 Derek Fowlds, interview with the author, 3 February 2014.

39 See the *Sunday Express*, 12 April 1981, p. 2.

40 *Observer*, 22 February 1981, p. 48.

41 *Daily Express*, 24 February 1981, p. 23.

42 Source: Broadcasters' Audience Research Board (BARB).

43 *Yes Minister*, series two, episode three: 'The Death List'.

44 *Yes Minister*, series two, episode seven: 'A Question of Loyalty'.

45 *Yes Minister*, series two, episode five: 'The Devil You Know'.

46 *Yes Minister*, series two, episode seven: 'A Question of Loyalty'.

47 *Yes Minister*, series two, episode six: 'The Quality of Life'.

48 *Yes Minister*, series two, episode two: 'Doing the Honours'.

49 This episode, called 'The Death List', was, as Antony Jay would recall, the only script in the series that caused the BBC to express any concern: 'The BBC only raised problems about one script and that was where we had a death threat against Jim Hacker. Their worry then was that it might go out on the same night as an assassination, like the March 1979 incident when the Conservative MP Airey Neave was killed by the IRA in the car park at Westminster. We overcame that, not by altering the script, but by agreeing that the programmes would be filmed well enough in advance, as they always were, for there to be a standby to put in that particular programme's place if anything were to happen' (quoted in Kandiah, p. 510).

50 *Yes Minister*, series two, episode one: 'The Compassionate Society'.

51 *Yes Minister*, series two, episode three: 'The Death List'.

52 *Yes Minister*, series two, episode five: 'The Devil You Know'.

53 Machiavelli, *The Prince*, Chapter XVIII: 'How rulers should keep their promises', p. 61.

54 Source: BBC WAC: *Yes Minister* File T70/33/1, episode one and filming (series two).

55 Source: BBC WAC: Viewing Panel Report, VR/81/142, 23 February to 6 April 1981.

56 Rosalie Horner, *Daily Express*, 24 February 1981, p. 23.

57 Dennis Skinner, Hansard, HC Deb. 29 January 1981, vol. 997 cc. 1071–2.

Case Study 2

58 *The Phil Silvers Show*, season one, episode two: 'The Empty Store', first broadcast on

CBS on 27 September 1955. The genius of the plot – surely one of the quintessential sitcom episodes of all time – was to have Bilko turn adversity into advantage by responding to gambling losses by renting an empty store, and then sitting back as all of his colleagues, convinced that, given this devious man's involvement, there must be something exceptionally lucrative in the empty store, start begging him to grant them a share in the non-business.

59 The 'Cheese Shop' sketch appeared originally in episode seven of series three, 'Salad Days', of *Monty Python's Flying Circus* (first broadcast by BBC1 on 30 November 1972) and was then featured in the 1973 Python album, *Matching Tie and Handkerchief*. A complete transcript of the version John Cleese and Michael Palin performed for Amnesty International's 1979 *Secret Policeman's Ball* is included in my edited collection, *A Poke in the Eye (With a Sharp Stick)* (London: Canongate, 2012), pp. 109–17.

60 Hansard, HC Deb. 15 June 1976, vol. 913 cc. 90–1W.

61 Hansard, HC Deb. 14 July 1983, vol. 45 c. 448W.

62 Jonathan Lynn, interview with the author, 1 February 2014.

63 See *Financial Control and Accountability in the National Health Service*, Public Accounts Committee report, 1981.

64 David Blunkett, speaking on *Yes Minister: The View from Whitehall*, Part 2, first broadcast on BBC Radio 4 on 5 March 2005.

65 See 'Memory Lane', *Wandsworth Guardian*, 23 November 2010, p. 10.

66 One reason for the now-defunct Putney Hospital's lack of redevelopment was the legal wrangling over the existence of a covenant, in the original deed of gift made by its founder, Sir William Lancaster, which stipulated that the land should 'be used in perpetuity as a general hospital'.

67 See Hansard, HL Deb. 16 June 1998, vol. 590 cc 128–9WA, for confirmation of the original decision to close the hospital following an NHS review. The plan to demolish the hospital and build a school on the site was widely reported in 2011, but was opposed by local groups due to environmental concerns. Another planning application was submitted in January 2013,

and was again challenged. In November 2013, the High Court rejected the judicial review made by the Friends of Putney Common against Wandsworth Council regarding the legality of their plans to develop on the former Putney Hospital site. A planning application was then given the go-ahead by the council's planning committee during a separate meeting soon after this decision. (See the *Wandsworth Guardian*, 8 November 2013, online: http://www.yourlocalguardian.co.uk/news/local/wandsworthnews/10797218.High_court_rejects_bid_to_block_school_development_on_Putney_Hospital_site/.)

7 Series Three

Header quotation: Friedrich Nietzsche, translated by Walter Kaufmann, *Beyond Good and Evil* (New York: Vintage, 1966), aphorism 146, p. 58.

1 According to Lord Donoughue (interview with the author, 25 March 2014): 'I heard from Jonathan and Tony that the BBC had been unconvinced that the books would sell. And then, when of course they did, and sold really, really well, they boasted about it as though it had been their idea!'

2 Lynn, quoted in Kandiah, pp. 530–1.

3 Ibid.

4 Sir Robert Armstrong, speaking on *Yes Minister: The View from Whitehall*, Part 1, first broadcast on BBC Radio 4 on 26 February 2005.

5 Records and cassettes featuring a selection of episodes started being produced by BBC Enterprises in 1981.

6 Source: BBC WAC.

7 Derek Fowlds, interview with the author, 3 February 2014.

8 Derek Fowlds, interview with the author, 3 February 2014.

9 Jonathan Lynn, interview with the author, 1 February 2014.

10 Derek Fowlds, interview with the author, 4 March 2014.

11 Paul Eddington, interviewed by Felicity Kendal on *Wogan*, first broadcast on BBC1, 13 January 1986.

12 Sources: BBC WAC and BARB.

13 *Yes Minister*, series three, episode one: 'Equal Opportunities'.

14 *Yes Minister*, series three, episode one: 'Equal Opportunities'.

15 *Yes Minister*, series three, episode three: 'The Skeleton in the Cupboard'.

16 *Yes Minister*, series three, episode two: 'The Challenge'.

17 *Yes Minister*, series three, episode four: 'The Moral Dimension'.

18 *Yes Minister*, series three, episode six: 'The Whisky Priest'.

19 *Yes Minister*, series three, episode six: 'The Whisky Priest'.

20 *Yes Minister*, series three, episode three: 'The Skeleton in the Cupboard'.

21 Source: BBC WAC: *Yes Minister* File T70/33/1, episode one and filming (series two).

22 Arthur Conan Doyle, 'A Scandal in Bohemia', in *The Adventures of Sherlock Holmes* (London: Harper Press, 2010), p. 3.

23 Sources: Rallings and Thrasher, *British Electoral Facts 1832–2006*; House of Commons Library Research Paper 10/36 General Election 2010.

24 Annie Hacker appeared in three of the seven episodes of series three: 'Equal Opportunities', 'The Moral Dimension' and 'The Whisky Priest'. In the first of these three she was politically engaged and eager for Jim Hacker to make his mark on Government policy until she felt threatened by one of his female colleagues; in the second she was a naive wife who was dazzled by a gift even though it plunged her husband into a scandal; and in the third she was a somewhat world-weary politician's wife who expected little in terms of principle and sat back and saw him serve up even less.

25 *Yes Minister*, series three, episode two: 'The Challenge'.

26 *Yes Minister*, series three, episode four: 'The Moral Dimension'.

27 Martin Bailey's *Oilgate: The Sanctions Scandal* (Sevenoaks: Coronet, 1979) was an in-depth examination of the 1965 Rhodesian oil embargo and how British Petroleum (BP), the company that, at that stage, was more than 50 per cent owned by the British Government, was party to an agreement that was in direct defiance of official Government policy which banned direct oil sales to Rhodesia.

Case Study 3

28 *The Times*, 30 January 1973, p. 2.

29 *The Times*, 30 January 1973, p. 1.

30 Antony Jay, quoted in Kandiah, p. 519.

31 Baroness Symons, speaking on *Yes Minister: The View from Whitehall*, Part 2, first broadcast on BBC Radio 4 on 5 March 2005.

32 Lord Donoughue, interview with the author, 25 March 2014.

8 Interregnum

Header quotation: Giuseppe di Lampedusa, *The Leopard* (London: Folio Society, 2000), p. 17.

1 Letter from Jonathan Lynn to Margaret Thatcher, 10 June 1983 (accessed at the Thatcher Archive at Churchill College, Cambridge). The full contents of the letter is as follows:

Dear Mrs Thatcher,

As co-author of *Yes Minister* I have often been delighted to read and hear of your admiration for our programme.

May I now return the compliment and offer you my congratulations and my good wishes on your magnificent and excellent election victory?

Yours sincerely,

Jonathan Lynn.

2 Letter from Margaret Thatcher to Jonathan Lynn, 15 June 1983 (accessed at the Thatcher Archive at Churchill College, Cambridge).

3 *Yes Minister* sketch, featuring Neil Kinnock and Patricia Hewitt, written in 1983. Source: The Churchill Archives Centre (Churchill College, Cambridge), The Papers of Neil Kinnock, KNNK 2/1/84.

4 Derek Fowlds, interview with the author, 3 February 2014.

5   Eddington, *So Far, So Good*, p. 170.

6   Lynn, *Comedy Rules*, p. 131.

7   Ibid. p. 130.

8   Ibid. p. 131.

9   Jonathan Lynn, interview with the author, 1 February 2014.

10 Antony Jay, interview with the author, 1 February 2014.

11 John Howard Davies, interview with the author, 31 May 2007.

12 The first radio series was aired on BBC Radio 4 between 18 October and 6 December 1983, with the second transmitted between 9 October and 27 November 1984.

13 BBC WAC: *Yes Minister* File T70/33/1, series two, episode one and filming.

14 BBC WAC: *Yes Minister* File T70/33/1, series two, episode one and filming.

15 Although Pete Atkin's adapted scripts were generally true to the spirit, as well as the letter, of the original television shows, there was, perhaps inevitably, the odd tiny detail that jarred. In the episode entitled 'The Quality of Life', for example, Atkin has Woolley call Hacker 'Jim', which the on-screen Woolley would never have done, famously resisting his Minister's attempts to get him to address him as anything less formal than 'Minister'.

16 Mary Whitehouse to Margaret Thatcher, 20 July 1983, National Viewers' and Listeners' Association Archives, Box 6, Albert Sloman Library, University of Essex.

17 See Bernard Ingham, 'Lady T's Favourite Yes Man', *Daily Express*, 7 November 1995, p. 7.

18 Ibid.

19 Ibid.

20 Jay, speaking in *Comedy Connections*.

21 Jonathan Lynn, speaking in *Yes, Prime Minister: Re-elected*, first broadcast on 15 January 2013 on GOLD.

22 Eddington, *So Far, So Good*, p. 191.

23 Ibid.

24 *Daily Express*, 21 January 1984, p. 9.

25 Lynn, *Comedy Rules*, p. 159.

26 Lynn, speaking in *Comedy Connections*.

27 Derek Fowlds, interview with the author, 3 February 2014.

28 Eddington, quoted in *The Times*, 28 December 1985, p. 34.

29 Interview with the author, 6 June 2000.

30 Interview with the author, 6 June 2000.

31 Lynn, *Comedy Rules*, p. 150.

32 Nigel Lawson would recall being the source for this in *Yes, Prime Minister: Re-elected*, first broadcast on 15 January 2013 on GOLD.

33 Source: BARB.

PART THREE

Frontispiece quotations:

Walter Bagehot, *The English Constitution*, p. 179.

Sir Edward Bridges, *Portrait of a Profession*, p. 29.

9 Yes, Prime Minister

Header quotation: *The Candidate*, screenplay by Jeremy Larner, Warner Bros, 1972.

1   As a phrase, there is some contention as to the origins of 'Prime Minister' in the British political context. It had been used, occasionally but invariably pejoratively, as early as the 1670s, in relation to Charles II's principal official, the Earl of Danby. Robert Walpole, when he heard himself so described in the 1720s and 1730s, dismissed it angrily, as did George Grenville in the 1760s and Lord North a decade later. The first use of the term 'Prime Minister' in an official document only came in 1878 when Benjamin Disraeli signed the final instrument of the Congress of Berlin as 'First Lord of the Treasury and Prime Minister of her Britannic Majesty'. The title did not appear in the Order of Precedence at Buckingham Palace until 1904, when it was given precedence after the Archbishop of York. The first statutory recognition of the title was the Chequers Estates Act (1917), which provided that the country house be occupied by the 'Crown's First Minister'. Even after this, however, there was no clear and entrenched constitutional

definition of the office and the proper extent of its powers. (See Peter Hennessey, *The Prime Minister* [London: Allen Lane, 2000].)

2 Antony Jay, interview with the author, 1 February 2014.

3 Jay, speaking in *Comedy Connections*.

4 Alec Douglas-Home, *The Way the Wind Blows* (London: Collins, 1976), p. 203.

5 Lynn, speaking in *Comedy Connections*.

6 The lines come from *Yes Minister*, series three, episode one: 'Equal Opportunities'.

7 Following the formation of a Coalition Government in December 1916, it was decided to establish a Cabinet Secretariat to record Cabinet decisions. Sir Maurice Hankey, the man appointed, established the precepts for a coordinating and record-keeping organisation, which led in 1920 to the creation of the Cabinet Office. (See John F. Naylor, *A Man and an Institution: Sir Maurice Hankey, the Cabinet Secretariat and the Custody of Cabinet Secrecy* [Cambridge: Cambridge University Press, 2009].)

8 Lynn, speaking in *Comedy Connections*.

9 The Conservative Party won the General Election of 1983 with a majority of 144 seats to retain power; with the Opposition vote split almost evenly between the recently merged SDP/Liberal Alliance and the Labour Party, and the Conservatives achieving their best results since 1959, the Government was returned with an increase in seats of 100.

10 Francis Pym quoted in John Cole, *The Thatcher Years: a decade of revolution in British politics* (London, BBC Books, 1987), p. 102.

11 Lord Stockton, quoted in the *Observer*, 17 November 1985, p. 11.

12 Lynn, *Comedy Rules*, p. 117.

13 Lynn, quoted by Kandiah, p. 523.

14 Lynn, quoted by Kandiah, p. 521.

15 Nicholas Ridley, *Industry and the Civil Service* (London: Aims of Industry, 1973), p. 3 and Leslie Chapman, *Your Disobedient Servant*, p. 122.

16 Antony Jay, quoted in the *Guardian*, 6 January 1986, p. 11.

17 Benjamin Disraeli, *Contarini Fleming*, Part VII, Chapter II (London: Frederick Warne and Co., 1832), p. 373. A related point was made by Edmund Burke: 'When bad men combine, the good must associate; else they will fall, one by one, an unpitied sacrifice in a contemptible struggle,' which can be found in his 'The Present Discontents', 1770, in Ian Harris (ed.) *Edmund Burke: Pre-Revolutionary Writings* (Cambridge: Cambridge University Press, 1993), p. 184.

18 Valerie Warrender, correspondence with the author, 29 November 2013.

19 Ibid.

20 Eddington, *So Far, So Good*, p. 148.

21 Ibid.

22 *Down Your Way*, featuring Nigel Hawthorne, first broadcast on BBC Radio 4 on 11 September 1988.

23 Sir Robin Butler, speaking on *Yes Minister: The View from Whitehall*, Part 1, first broadcast on BBC Radio 4 on 26 February 2005.

24 In 1985, for example, the imminent departure from the Cabinet of John Biffen, who was Leader of the House of Commons at the time, was touted in advance by Ingham, who referred to him off the record as 'a semi-detached member of the Government'. Ingham would later acknowledge that this and certain other quotes originated from him, when he answered questions from a Select Committee of Public Administration on 2 June 1998:

RHODRI MORGAN (CHAIR): In the history books of the 1980s, in some ways your two most famous contributions will be seen as negative briefing contributions. They were against Ministers of the Cabinet, not against the Opposition of course, but they were the references that you made unattributably to John Biffen and to Francis Pym and what I find fascinating about those in reading some of the things that you have written about that period is that you also said that you would rather commit *hari-kiri* – I am not quite sure of the correct Japanese pronunciation of it – than to have complied with the request from Colette Bowe, if I remember correctly, who was Leon Brittan's Head of Press and Information to leak the Solicitor General's letter in relation to Michael Heseltine at the height of the Westland controversy.

You said it was not your job to do dirty work; you were a civil servant. Now why was it your job to do dirty work as regards negative briefing against John Biffen and Francis Pym?

INGHAM: I did not think I was doing dirty work. What I thought I was doing was trying to bring some rationality to the argument and that is frequently difficult, if I may say so, in Lobbies. What was happening here was that Francis Pym had made an extremely gloomy speech in the same week that the Chancellor had said we were coming out of a deep recession. It turned out the Chancellor was right and the Lobby, not unnaturally, since Francis Pym was in charge of the presentation of policy, wondered how such a man could remain in the Cabinet.

MORGAN: He was not in the Cabinet?

INGHAM: Hang on a minute. He was certainly in the Government. What I sought to do at the end of a long and difficult passage, because neither Mrs Thatcher showed any signs of sacking him and he certainly did not show any sign of going, what I tried to do was to bring some rationality to the argument and explain it in terms of personality.

MORGAN: You were a civil servant and you were knocking a Minister of the Government?

INGHAM: I now wish I had not done it because that and John Biffen, which is exactly the same circumstance where I was trying to explain by relation to his position in the Government why he would do such a thing. I wish I had done neither, because it got me a reputation – in my view utterly undeserved, but nonetheless I got it – for rubbishing Ministers. Now rubbishing Ministers seems to be routine, several of them.

25 Simon Hoggart, *Guardian* (*Media Guardian* section), 1 November 2010, p. 2.

26 Derek Fowlds, interview with the author, 3 February 2014.

27 *Yes Minister*, series two, episode two: 'Doing the Honours'.

28 Sources: BBC WAC and *The Times*, 24 December 1985, p. 8.

10 Series One

Header quotation: Michael Oakeshott, 'Political Education', 1951, in Peter Laslett (ed.), *Philosophy, Politics and Society*, First Series (Oxford: Basil Blackwell, 1975), p. 15.

1 See, for example, 'Dumb . . . and it's getting dumber', *Observer*, (News section), 16 April 2000, p. 5. See also Pierre Bourdieu, *Distinction: A Social Critique of the Judgement of Taste* (Cambridge: Harvard University Press, 1985) for a broader contemporary consideration of the phenomenon.

2 Michael Heseltine, the Defence Secretary, resigned from the Cabinet on the morning of 9 January 1986. He had clashed with the Prime Minister over a rescue bid to save Britain's last helicopter manufacturer, the struggling Augusta-Westland. Heseltine had wanted to integrate Westland with Italian and French companies, while Thatcher wanted it to merge with the American firm Sikorsky. Heseltine – with the backing of the Defence Committee – claimed that the European deal, which was initially worth more financially, could form the basis of a strong arms industry to rival the Americans. His opponents claimed that the orders were based on aircraft still in the design stage. The debate, which had been rumbling on since April 1985, had been causing tensions within the Cabinet for many months before Heseltine finally decided to resign in protest. Upon leaving Number Ten, he said that the final straw had come when the Prime Minister insisted that all his public comments on Westland would have to be vetted by Civil Service officials before being released. In a statement to reporters later in the afternoon, Heseltine said: 'If the basis of trust between the Prime Minister and her Defence Secretary no longer exists, there is no place for me with honour in such a Cabinet.' Just fifteen days after his departure, the Westland affair provoked a second senior Cabinet resignation. Leon Brittan was forced to quit as Trade and Industry Secretary after admitting

that he had authorised the leaking of a Government law officer's letter that had been highly critical of Heseltine (see the *Guardian*, 10 January 1986, p. 1).

3 Lord Donoughue, interview with the author, 25 March 2014.

4 Bernard Donoughue, *Downing Street Diary: With Harold Wilson in No. 10*, p. 34.

5 Ibid. pp. 22, 23, 97 and 206.

6 Ibid. pp. 31, 61, 63, 76, 179 and 283.

7 Ibid. p. 35. (Donoughue's depiction of Falkender very closely echoes that of his colleague Joe Haines in *The Politics of Power* where, at great length, Haines notes both her good qualities – such as the exceptionally sharp mind that produced ideas 'fired off like rockets into the night' [p. 175] – and her bad ones, such as her many tantrums and sulks, her paranoia, her neuroticism and the shrill calls that she began by wielding the telephone 'like a slave driver his whip' [pp. 177, 187].)

8 Lord Donoughue would later remark (interview with the author, 25 March 2014): 'The character of Dorothy Wainwright obviously had some similarity with Marcia. That wasn't accidental. But Dorothy Wainwright seemed rather sensible to me, bringing some common sense to policies. And I'd heard that in the early days Marcia was a bit like that. But in my time she was just malicious, and when she interfered it was only about something that concerned herself, it was never about policy. So Dorothy Wainwright, although she grew from the same source, so to speak, struck me as a much more desirable character.'

9 Machiavelli, *The Prince*, Chapter XXI: 'How a ruler should act in order to gain reputation', p. 76.

10 In October 1983, the United States invaded the Caribbean island of Grenada, a former British colony that was now part of the Commonwealth. The action was ordered by President Ronald Reagan following a coup by a Cuban-trained military who executed Prime Minister Maurice Bishop and at least thirteen of his associates. The invasion angered the British Prime Minister of the time, Margaret Thatcher, whose attempts to stop it had been dismissed by the White House, with the Pentagon retaliating by expressing a 'sense of outrage' that she had refused to participate despite America's support during the Falklands conflict the previous year. Most other world leaders were angered by Reagan's action, and on 28 October the United Nations failed to get a motion passed deploring the invasion – because it was vetoed by the United States.

11 Bernard Ingham, quoted in the *Daily Mail*, 27 June 2009, p. 12.

12 In *Spycatcher*, Peter Wright claimed that he was assigned to unmask a Soviet mole in MI5, and he became convinced (although he never proved it) that the culprit was one of its former Directors General, Roger Hollis. Wright also told, among other things, of the MI6 plot to assassinate President Nasser during the Suez Crisis; of coordinated MI5–CIA plotting against the Labour Party Prime Minister Harold Wilson, and of MI5's covert surveillance of high-level Commonwealth conferences. Written by Wright in Tasmania, after his retirement from MI5, the first attempt at publication was in 1985, when the British Government acted immediately to ban the book in the UK. The ruling was obtained in an English court, however, which meant that the book continued to be available legally in Scotland, as well as other jurisdictions, and copies were put into circulation within Britain through personal imports.

13 On 13 October 1988, the British Government lost its long-running battle to stop the publication of *Spycatcher*. Law Lords ruled that the media could publish extracts from Peter Wright's memoirs, because any damage to national security had already been done by its publication abroad. They did agree, however, that Wright's book had indeed constituted a serious breach of confidentiality, which was the principle at the heart of the Government's case against him.

14 Bernard Ingham, quoted in the *Daily Mail*, 27 June 2009, p. 12.

15 Sources: BBC WAC and BARB.

16 *Secrets* (the newspaper of the Campaign for Freedom of Information), no. 11, January 1987, p. 1.

Case Study 4

17 This was confirmed by Kenneth Clarke when interviewed for *Yes Minister: The View from Whitehall*, Part 1, first broadcast on BBC Radio 4 on 26 February 2005.

18 Kenneth Clarke, interviewed for *Yes Minister: The View from Whitehall*, Part 1, Radio 4, 26 February 2005.

19 Joe Ashton, Hansard, HC Deb. 29 October 1986, vol. 103 cc. 335–8.

20 'No-Smoking Areas in Public Houses', Hansard, HC Deb. 29 October 1986, vol. 103 cc. 335–8.

21 *Choosing Health: Making healthy choices easier – Executive Summary*, Department of Health, 16 November 2004.

22 Information on the introduction and subsequent changes to the tobacco duty escalator is taken from the Institute for Fiscal Studies' *Green Budget* January 2001, 'Appendix C: Budgets Since 1979'.

11 Series Two

Header quotation: Stanley Baldwin, *Observer*, 20 May 1925, p. 10.

1 Robert Key, Hansard, HC Deb. 30 January 1986, vol. 90 c. 1171.

2 Lord Morton of Shuna, Hansard, HL Deb. 8 December 1986, vol. 482 c. 1045.

3 Lord Cledwyn of Penrhos, Hansard, HL Deb. 26 February 1986, vol. 471 c. 1113.

4 Denis Healey, Hansard, HC Deb. 16 April 1986, vol. 95 c. 951.

5 Sir Nicholas Fairbairn, Hansard, HC Deb. 21 May 1986, vol. 98 c. 394.

6 John Home Robertson, Hansard, HC Deb. 5 November 1986, vol. 103 c. 1011.

7 The Earl of Perth, Hansard, HL Deb. 18 November 1986, vol. 482 c. 195.

8 Dennis Skinner, Hansard, HC Deb. 16 December 1986, vol. 107 c. 1062.

9 James Naughtie, *Guardian*, 26 May 1986, p. 22.

10 See the *Canberra Times*, 26 November 1986, p. 1 and 5 April 1987, p. 1.

11 Derek Fowlds, interview with the author, 3 February 2014.

12 *New Straits Times*, 15 February 1986, p. 13.

13 Paul Eddington, *The Times*, 28 December 1985–3 January 1986, p. 34.

14 Nigel Hawthorne, *Straight Face*, p. 253.

15 Derek Fowlds, interview with the author, 3 February 2014.

16 Hawthorne, *Straight Face*, p. 253.

17 Derek Fowlds, interview with the author, 3 February 2014.

18 See, for example, the *Guardian*, 3 December 1987, p. 1.

19 Harold Macmillan, cited by Harold Wilson, apropos of the informal role of a Prime Minister, in *A Prime Minister on Prime Ministers*.

20 *Yes, Prime Minister*, series two, episode eight: 'The Tangled Web'.

21 *Yes, Prime Minister*, series two, episode seven: 'The National Education Service'.

22 *Yes, Prime Minister*, series two, episode seven: 'The National Education Service'.

23 *Yes, Prime Minister*, series two, episode seven: 'The National Education Service'.

24 *Yes, Prime Minister*, series two, episode one: 'Man Overboard'.

25 *Yes, Prime Minister*, series two, episode two: 'Official Secrets'.

26 *Yes, Prime Minister*, series two, episode two: 'Official Secrets'.

27 *Yes, Prime Minister*, series two, episode seven: 'The National Education Service'.

28 *Yes, Prime Minister*, series two, episode two: 'Official Secrets'.

29 See Bernard Donoughue, *Downing Street Diary: With Harold Wilson in No. 10*, p. 135.

30 This summary was by no means new. There is some debate as to who first wrote it. A version was certainly used by Dave Allen during the mid-1970s both onstage and in an edition of *Dave Allen at Large*, but authorship has also been attributed (without any specific date or place) to the former TUC President Cyril Plant, who is reported to have come up with the basic list and descriptions in 1976. See Denis MacShane, *Using the Media* (London: Pluto Press, 1979), p. 13.

31 *Yes, Prime Minister*, series two, episode four: 'A Conflict of Interest'.

32 *Yes, Prime Minister*, series two, episode four: 'A Conflict of Interest'.

33 *Yes, Prime Minister*, series two, episode eight: 'The Tangled Web'.

34 *Yes, Prime Minister*, series two, episode three: 'A Diplomatic Incident'.

35 *Yes, Prime Minister*, series two, episode one: 'Man Overboard'.

36 *Yes, Prime Minister*, series two, episode two: 'Official Secrets'.

37 *Yes, Prime Minister*, series two, episode two: 'Official Secrets'.

38 See *The Times*, 'Diary', 10 October 1986, p. 14.

39 Lynn, quoted in Kandiah, p. 522.

40 See the *Guardian*, 3 December 1987, p. 1. Heath was repeating his earlier attack on Thatcher's education policy now that her Government was returning to some of the old proposals in a new education reform bill.

41 See *The Times*, 24 July 1982, p. 3 and 22 June 1983, p. 20.

42 Lynn, quoted in Kandiah, pp. 521–2.

43 Ibid.

44 Jay, quoted in Kandiah, p. 514.

12 The End

Header quotation: Woodrow Wilson, 'A Wit and a Seer', *The Atlantic Monthly*, vol. 82, issue 492 (October 1898), p. 540.

1 John Naughton, *Observer*, 6 December 1987, p. 30.

2 Antony Jay, interview with the author, 1 February 2014.

3 Jonathan Lynn, interview with the author, 1 February 2014.

4 Derek Fowlds, interview with the author, 3 February 2014.

5 Jonathan Lynn, speaking in *Comedy Connections*.

6 Antony Jay, interview with the author, 1 February 2014.

7 Jonathan Lynn, interview with the author, 1 February 2014.

8 Jonathan Lynn, speaking in *Comedy Connections*.

9 *Guardian*, 29 September 1989, p. 6.

10 Peter Hall, quoted by Eddington, *So Far, So Good*, p. 221.

11 Eddington, *So Far, So Good*, pp. 230–1.

12 Eddington's performance as Justice Shallow in *Henry IV* was first broadcast on BBC2 on 28 October 1995.

13 Tricia Eddington, interviewed by the *Independent on Sunday*, 8 December 1996, p. 18.

14 *The Times*, 2 July 1994, p. 23.

15 *Mail on Sunday*, 26 June 1994, p. 30.

16 Michael Billington, *Guardian*, 22 June 1994, p. A4.

17 Paul Eddington, speaking in *Paul Eddington: A Life Well Lived*, first broadcast on BBC1, 15 July 2001.

18 John Howard Davies, speaking in *Paul Eddington: A Life Well Lived*, first broadcast on BBC1, 15 July 2001.

19 Nigel Hawthorne, quoted in the *Independent*, 7 November 1995, p. 10.

20 Nigel Hawthorne, *Daily Express*, 24 November 1984, p. 17.

21 Nigel Hawthorne, interviewed for the 'Cranky Critic' website: http://www.crankycritic.com/qa/nigelhawthorne.html.

22 Ibid.

23 Hawthorne, *Straight Face*, p. 291.

24 *Observer*, 5 September 1999, p. G14.

25 Hawthorne, *Straight Face*, p. 324.

26 Ibid. p. 290.

27 *Yes Minister*, series two, episode two, 'Doing the Honours'.

28 Nigel Hawthorne, speaking on BBC news, 23 February 1999.

29 Trevor Bentham in Hawthorne, *Straight Face*, p. 328.

30 Derek Fowlds, BBC Radio 5 Live, 6 November 1995.

31 Derek Fowlds, quoted in the *Daily Express*, 10 January 2002, p. 24.

32 *Inspector Morse*: 'The Settling of the Sun', first broadcast on ITV, 15 March 1988.

33 *Boon*: 'Best Left Buried', first broadcast on ITV, 4 December 1990.

34 *Van der Valk*: 'The Little Rascals', first broadcast on ITV, 6 February 1991.

35 *The Darling Buds of May*: 'The Season of Heavenly Gifts: part one', first broadcast on ITV, 23 February 1992.

36 Derek Fowlds, interview with the author, 3 February 2014.

37 Derek Fowlds, interview with the author, 3 February 2014.

38 Derek Fowlds, interview with the author, 3 February 2014.

39 *South China Morning Post*, 30 October 2012, p. 8.

40 The premise of the *Yes, Prime Minister* computer game was that, as Jim Hacker, one had to survive for one week as Prime Minister by overcoming various political crises and challenges, assisted by Bernard Woolley and undermined by Sir Humphrey Appleby.

41 Sky Television had begun a four-channel service of general entertainment (Sky Channel), movies (Sky Movies), sport (Eurosport) and rolling news (Sky News) on 5 February 1989, and British Satellite Broadcasting (BSB) brought several more channels to the air early on in the following year, but in November 1990, a fifty-fifty merger was announced to form a single company, operating as British Sky Broadcasting (BSkyB), but marketed as Sky. UK Gold was launched in 1992, but expanded its operation and increased its sitcom content in 1997.

42 Jonathan Lynn, interview with the author, 1 February 2014.

43 Jonathan Lynn, quoted by IGN Entertainment website, 25 August 2013: http://uk.ign.com/articles/2003/08/25/an-interview-with-jonathan-lynn.

44 The BFI 'TV 100' poll was chosen by members of the TV industry throughout the UK (1,600 programme-makers, critics, writers and executives were invited to give their professional opinions and personal tastes). Each voter was given a 'big list' of 650 programmes in six genres, along with spaces for any titles not included. The resulting top ten – announced in September 2000 – was as follows: 1 *Fawlty Towers*; 2 *Cathy Come Home*; 3 *Doctor Who*; 4 *The Naked Civil Servant*; 5 *Monty Python's Flying Circus*; 6 *Blue Peter*; 7 *Boys From the Blackstuff*; 8 *Parkinson*; 9 *Yes Minister/Yes, Prime Minister*; 10 *Brideshead Revisited*.

45 *Britain's Best Sitcom* was broadcast by the BBC in 2004. The top five were as follows: 1 *Only Fools and Horses*; 2 *Blackadder*; 3 *The Vicar of Dibley*; 4 *Dad's Army*; 5 *Fawlty Towers*.

46 *30 Greatest Political Comedies* was first broadcast on Channel 4 on 11 December 2006; an updated poll formed the basis of a second programme that was broadcast on 17 April 2010.

47 Armando Iannucci, speaking on *Britain's Best Sitcom*, first broadcast on BBC2, 7 February 2004.

48 *The Thick of It*, series one, episode one, first broadcast on BBC Four, 19 May 2005.

49 *Veep*, season two, episode two, first broadcast by HBO in the US on 21 April 2013.

50 Tony Benn, Hansard, HC Deb. 20 May 1992, vol. 208 c. 316.

51 Richard Spring, Hansard, HC Deb. 5 June 1998, vol. 313 c. 653.

52 Vince Cable, Hansard, HC Deb. 21 December 2000, vol. 360 c. 147.

53 John Major, Hansard, HC Deb. 13 July 2000, vol. 353 c. 1115.

54 George Osborne, Hansard, HC Deb. 1 July 2002, vol. 388 c. 49.

55 Peter Hain, Hansard, HC Deb. 13 January 2004, vol. 416 c. 668.

56 Michael Portillo, *Sunday Times*, 14 December 2008, p. 11.

57 Tony Blair, *A Journey* (London: Arrow, 2011), p. 516.

58 Lord Donoughue, interview with the author, 25 March 2014.

59 *Yes, Prime Minister*, series two, episode seven: 'The National Education Service'.

60 The so-called 'Granita pact' dated back to 1994, when Tony Blair and Gordon Brown were alleged to have had an after-hours tête-à-tête at the Granita restaurant on Upper Street, Islington on 31 May. It was there that the two frontbenchers were supposed to have forged the agreement that led Brown to announce the following day that he would not be standing for the vacant Labour leadership. The Shadow Chancellor duly announced that he would not be a candidate for the leadership, but would instead 'encourage' his friend, the Shadow Home Secretary, to run. In return for dropping out of contention, Brown was alleged to have secured an apparent 'guarantee' from Blair that a Labour administration would be driven by a Brownite 'fairness agenda'. Some sources also claimed that another agreement

was that Blair would eventually step down, probably by 2001, and allow Brown to succeed him. When the Blair Government subsequently veered away from the Brownite agenda, and Blair showed no signs of stepping down, the acrimony between the two men grew increasingly intense. Gordon Brown himself, however, addressed the whole story in an interview in 2010, three years after he had finally become Prime Minister. He said: 'There was no deal struck at Granita's. That's been one of the great myths and people have written about it. I'd already agreed with Tony before that dinner that he would stand for the leadership and I would stay on as the Shadow Chancellor, as the person in charge of economic policy. And there's an understanding that at some point Tony would stand down and he would support me if, when, that was the case. And that's where we left it' (*Life Stories: Gordon Brown*, first broadcast on ITV1 on 14 February 2010).

61 *Yes, Prime Minister*, series one, episode three: 'The Smoke Screen'.

62 David Cameron, quoted in the *Guardian*, 13 April 2012, p. 4.

PART FOUR

Frontispiece quotations:

Benjamin Constant, 'The Liberty of the Ancients Compared with that of the Moderns' (1819), trans. Biancamaria Fontana, *Constant: Political Writings* (Cambridge: Cambridge University Press, 1988), p. 326.

Alexis de Tocqueville, *Democracy in America*, vol. 2 (1840), trans. Henry Reeve and Francis Bowen, Fourth Book, Chapter VI (New York: Vintage, 1945), p. 339.

13 The Revival

Header quotation: John Lennon, speaking at the end of the live recording of 'Get Back' (1969).

1 Jonathan Lynn, *Financial Times*, 20 August 2011, p. 2.

2 Ibid.

3 Ibid.

4 Antony Jay, interview with the author, 3 February 2014.

5 Jonathan Lynn, 1 February 2014.

6 Jonathan Lynn, publicity interview, 2010.

7 Lord Donoughue (interview with the author, 25 Match 2014): 'I contributed three bits to it. One was the global warming bit, one was the BBC bit, and there was one other little subplot.'

8 Jonathan Lynn, quoted in *Saga Magazine*, 15 January 2013, pp. 58–61.

9 Antony Jay and Jonathan Lynn, *New Statesman*, 20 June 2011, p. 35.

10 Ibid.

11 *Daily Telegraph*, 5 September 2008, p. 1; *La Repubblica*, 28 April 2009, p. 1; *Corriere del Mezzogiorno*, 28 April 2009, p. 1.

12 Jonathan Lynn, interview with the author, 1 February 2014.

13 Jonathan Lynn, quotes in *The Times*, 7 May 2010, p. 12.

14 Quentin Letts, *Daily Mail*, 21 May 2010, p. 59.

15 Michael Billington, *Guardian*, 21 May 2010, p. 40.

16 Charles Spencer, *Daily Telegraph*, 28 September 2010, p. 31.

17 Quentin Letts, *Daily Mail*, 21 May 2010, p. 59.

18 Jeremy Kingston, *The Times*, 28 September 2010, p. 54.

19 Following the allegations about sexual abuse concerning the late Jimmy Savile, which started being publicised in September 2012, a police investigation dubbed 'Operation Yewtree' was launched in October. After a period of assessment, it was made into a full criminal investigation, involving inquiries into living people as well as Savile, about the alleged sexual abuse of victims ranging from prepubescent girls and boys to adults.

20 Myron Meisel, *Hollywood Reporter*, 14 June 2013, p. 14.

21 Jonathan Lynn, quoted on the comedy news website Chortle: http://www.chortle.co.uk/interviews/2013/01/04/16891/i%92m_perpetually_shockable._and_the_fact_that_i%92m_shocked_means_i_have_to_write_about_it.

22 Jonathan Lynn, interview with the author, 1 February 2014.

23 Antony Jay interview with the author, 1 February 2014.

24 Jonathan Lynn, speaking to Public Media for North Texas, 24 June 2013.

25 Source: BARB.

26 Tom Sutcliffe, *Independent*, 16 January 2013, p. 36.

27 Mark Monahan, *Daily Telegraph*, 16 January 2013, p. 32.

28 Sam Wollaston, *Guardian*, 16 January 2013, p. 21.

29 Comments quoted from Twitter, 15 January 2013.

30 Among those questioned by me were David Cameron, Ed Miliband, William Hague, Alan Johnson, Tessa Jowell, Jacqui Smith and Theresa May.

31 In March 1998, the 'unfair' imprisonment of Deirdre Rachid, a gravel-voiced fictional character in the ITV soap *Coronation Street*, moved the Prime Minister of the time, Tony Blair, as well as his Home Secretary and the Leader of the Opposition, to make public statements about her case. Blair, for example, was said to have urged the Home Secretary to investigate 'and is set to press for a rapid appeal or even a retrial' (see Mark Lawson, 'Stranger than fiction', *Guardian*, 4 April 1998, p. 21).

32 In November 2008, Gordon Brown, the then Prime Minister, took time out from perusing the works of David Hume and Adam Smith, and dealing with the country's economic crisis, in order to pen 'good luck' letters to his favourite contestants in the ITV revamp of *Opportunity Knocks*, *The X Factor*. 'Whatever the final outcome,' he gushed to one of them, 'yours is one of the great stories of this year's competition, and I know you will go on to great success in the future'. (See the *Daily Mirror*, 17 November 2008, p. 7.)

33 Derek Fowlds, interview with the author, 3 February 2014.

34 Antony Jay combined the two concerns in December 2011 when he took the opportunity at the launch of a report (for which he had written the Foreword) by the Global Warming Policy Foundation to claim that the BBC was biased in many ways, including over climate change.

35 *Yes, Prime Minister* (2013), series one, episode four: 'A Diplomatic Dilemma'.

36 *The Times*, 16 February 2013, p. 32.

37 Source: BARB.

38 I'm indebted to my editor at Aurum, Sam Harrison, for encouraging me to think about this point.

Epilogue

Frontispiece quotations:

Huw Wheldon, *The British Experience in Television* (London: BBC, 1976), p. 1.

George Orwell, 'Funny, but not Vulgar' (1945) in *Essays* (Everyman: London, 2002), p. 781.

1 Walter Bagehot, *The English Constitution*, Introduction to the 2nd edn (1872), p. 278.

2 See John Stuart Mill, *Considerations on Representative Government* (1861), section XII, in Gray (ed.) *On Liberty and Other Essays*, pp. 378–9

3 Ibid, section XII, p. 381.

4 Antony Jay, interview with the author, 1 February 2014.

5 Jonathan Lynn, interview with the author, 1 February 2014.

6 Derek Fowlds, interview with the author, 3 February 2014.

7 Sydney Lotterby, interview with the author, 8 July 2014.

8 Lord Donoughue, interview with the author, 25 March 2014.

9 Armando Iannucci, 'Yes, Minister: nothing changes', *Daily Telegraph*, 7 February 2004, p. 19.

10 See Bagehot, *The English Constitution*, p. 31.

11 See Hansard, HC Deb. 20 November 1985, vol. 87 cc. 277–366.

Bibliography

YES MINISTER

Primary literature:

Jay, Antony, *Management and Machiavelli* (Harmondsworth: Penguin, 1967)

Effective Presentation (London: British Institute of Management, 1970)

The New Oratory (New York: American Management Association, 1971)

Corporation Man (London: Jonathan Cape, 1972)

The Householders' Guide to Community Defence Against Bureaucratic Aggression (London: Jonathan Cape, 1972)

How to Beat Sir Humphrey: Every Citizen's Guide to Fighting Officialdom (Ebringdon, UK: Long Barn Books, 1997)

Confessions of a Reformed BBC Producer (London: Centre for Policy Studies, 2007)

Jay, Antony and Jonathan Lynn, *Yes Minister: Diaries of the Right Hon. James Hacker, Volume I* (London: BBC Publications, 1981)

Yes Minister: Diaries of the Right Hon. James Hacker, Volume II (London: BBC Publications, 1982)

Yes Minister: Diaries of the Right Hon. James Hacker, Volume III (London: BBC Publications, 1983)

The Complete Yes Minister (London: BBC Books, 1984)

Yes, Prime Minister: Diaries of the Right Hon. James Hacker, Volume I (London: BBC Books, 1986)

Yes Prime Minister: The Diaries of the Right Hon. James Hacker, Volume II (London: BBC Books, 1987)

The Complete Yes, Prime Minister (London: BBC Books, 1989)

The Yes Minister Miscellany (London: Biteback, 2009)

Yes, Prime Minister: a play (London: Faber & Faber, 2010)

'Oh no, minister', *New Statesman*, 20 June 2011, p. 35

Lynn, Jonathan, *A Proper Man* (London: Heinemann, 1976)

Comedy Rules: From the Cambridge Footlights to Yes, Prime Minister (London: Faber & Faber, 2011)

Secondary literature:

Adams, John, 'Yes, Prime Minister: "The Ministerial Broadcast" (Jonathan Lynn and Antony Jay), Social Reality and Comic Realism in Popular Television Drama', in *British Television Drama in the 1980s*, ed. George W. Brandt (Cambridge: Cambridge University Press, 1993)

Baker, Nick, 'Rise, Sir Humphrey', *Radio Times*, 4–10 January 1986, pp. 3–4

Barker, Dennis, 'How did they find the HP source?' *Guardian*, 23 February 1981, p. 9

Davis, Victor, 'It's the other lady inside Number 10', *Daily Express*, 21 January 1986, pp. 12–13

Donoughue, Bernard, 'Yes, Prime Minister: The Play, the History and Real Politics', in *Yes, Prime Minister* (theatre programme, 2010), pp. 10–11

Eddington, Paul, *So Far, So Good* (London: Hodder & Stoughton, 1995)

Gore-Langton, Robert, 'Yes again, Prime Minister', *Daily Express*, 30 September 2010, p. 13

Hattersley, Roy, 'Of Ministers and Mandarins', *The Listener*, 20 March 1980, pp. 367–8

'*Yes Minister*', in Merullo, Annabel and Neil Wenborn, *British Comedy Greats* (London: Cassell Illustrated, 2003), pp. 179–82

Hawthorne, Nigel, *Straight Face* (London: Hodder & Stoughton, 2002)

Hennessy, Patrick, 'The New Yes, Prime Minister', in *Yes, Prime Minister* (theatre programme, 2010), pp. 12–14

Iannucci, Armando, 'Yes, Minister: nothing changes', *Daily Telegraph*, 7 February 2004, p. 19

Ingham, Bernard, 'Whitehall's Wit', *Daily Express*, 7 November 1995, p. 9

Kandiah, Michael David, 'Yes Minister and Yes, Prime Minister (1): Sir Antony Jay, CVO', *Contemporary Record*, 8:3, 1994, pp. 506–20

'Yes Minister and Yes, Prime Minister (2): Jonathan Lynn', *Contemporary Record*, 8:3, 1994, pp. 521–34

Langley, William, 'Yes, Hacker's back again', *Saga Magazine*, January 2013, pp. 58–61

Leapman, Michael, 'Yes, Prime Minister, he's back', *Radio Times*, 28 November to 4 December 1987, pp. 98–9

Morgan, Kenneth O., 'The Common Ground', *New Statesman*, 7 July 1989, p. 36

Murray, James, 'The premier job that Paul would really hate', *Daily Express*, 4 January 1982, p. 23

'Politics? You can count me out, says the Minister', *Daily Express*, 11 November 1982, p. 23

Naughton, John, 'Hacker, PM', *The Listener*, 16 January 1986, p. 38

Pearce, Garth, 'Whitehall's sly old fox goes to earth', *Daily Express*, 24 November 1984, p. 17

Polsby, Nelson, 'Comic Truths', *Commentary*, September 1987, pp. 72–3

Waymark, Peter, 'The New Man in Downing Street', *The Times*, 28 December 1985, p. 34

White, Michael, 'Men Behind the Ministry', *Radio Times*, 21–7 February 1981, p. 6

General:

Amann, Ronald, 'The Circumlocution Office: A Snapshot of Civil Service Reform', *The Political Quarterly*, 77, no. 3, 2006, p. 340

Aristotle, *The Politics*, ed. Stephen Everson (Cambridge: Cambridge University Press, 1988)

Bagehot, Walter, *The English Constitution* (London: Fontana, 1993)

'Physics and Politics' (1867), in Norman St John-Stevas (ed.), *Walter Bagehot* (London: Eyre & Spottiswoode, 1959)

Barker, Ernest, ed., *The Character of England* (Oxford: Clarendon Press, 1950)

Benjamin, Walter, *One-Way Street* (London: NLB, 1979)

Benn, Tony, 'Manifestos and Mandarins', in *Policy and Practice: the Experience of Government* (London: Royal Institute of Public Administration, 1980)

Berlin, Isaiah, *Four Essays on Liberty* (Oxford: Oxford University Press, 1969)

Blunkett, David, *The Blunkett Tapes: My Life in the Bearpit* (London: Bloomsbury, 2006)

Brandreth, Gyles, *Breaking The Code: Westminster Diaries, 1992–97* (London: Weidenfeld & Nicolson, 1999)

Bridges, Edward, *Portrait of a Profession: The Civil Service Tradition* (Cambridge: Cambridge University Press, 1950)

Buchanan, James, *The Theory of Public Choice* (Ann Arbor: University of Michigan Press, 1984)

The Limits of Liberty: Between Anarchy and Leviathan (Indianapolis: Liberty Fund, 2000)

Burke, Edmund, *Pre-Revolutionary Writings*, ed. Ian Harris (Cambridge: Cambridge University Press, 1996)

Reflections on the Revolution in France (Oxford: Oxford University Press 1993)

Cardiff, David, 'Mass middlebrow laughter: The origins of BBC comedy', *Media, Culture and Society*, vol. 10, no. 1, January 1988, pp. 41–60

Carpenter, Humphrey, *A Great, Silly Grin: The British Satire Boom of the 1960s* (New York: Public Affairs, 2000)

Castle, Barbara, 'Mandarin Power', *Sunday Times*, 10 June 1973, pp. 17–19

The Castle Diaries 1964–1976 (London: Macmillan, 1990)

Chapman, Leslie, *Your Disobedient Servant* (London: Chatto & Windus, 1978)

Cockerell, Michael, *Live From Number 10: The Inside Story of Prime Ministers and Television* (London: Faber & Faber, 1988)

Cole, John, *As It Seemed to Me* (London: Phoenix, 1996)

Cotton, Bill, *The BBC As An Entertainer* (London: BBC, 1977)

Double Bill (London: Fourth Estate, 2000)

Crossman, Richard, *Diaries of a Cabinet Minister: Volume 1: Minister of Housing 1964–66* (London: Hamish Hamilton and Jonathan Cape, 1975)

The Crossman Diaries: Condensed Version, ed. Anthony Howard (London: Magnum, 1979)

Curran, Charles, *Broadcasting and Society* (London: BBC, 1971)

In the Public Interest (London: BBC, 1971)

A Seamless Robe: Broadcasting – Philosophy and Practice (London: Collins, 1979)

Donoughue, Bernard, *Prime Minister: The Conduct of Policy under Harold Wilson and James Callaghan* (London: Jonathan Cape, 1987)

Downing Street Diary, Volume One: With Harold Wilson in No. 10 (London: Jonathan Cape, 2005)

Downing Street Diary Volume Two: With James Callaghan in No. 10 (London: Jonathan Cape, 2008)

The Heat of the Kitchen (London: Politico's, 2003)

Douglas-Home, Alec, *The Way the Wind Blows* (London: HarperCollins, 1976)

Emerson, Ralph Waldo, *English Traits* (Cambridge: Mass.: The Riverside Press, 1903)

Finley, M. I., *Politics in the Ancient World* (Cambridge: Cambridge University Press, 1983)

Foot, Michael, *Loyalists and Loners* (London: Collins, 1986)

Friedman, Milton, *Capitalism and Freedom* (Chicago: University of Chicago Press, 1962)

Gambaccini, Paul and Rod Taylor, *Television's Greatest Hits* (London: Network Books, 1993)

Gowans, Christopher, ed., *Moral Dilemmas* (Oxford: Oxford University Press, 1987)

Grant, Ruth W., *Hypocrisy and Integrity: Machiavelli, Rousseau, and the Ethics of Politics* (Chicago: University of Chicago, 1997)

Greene, Hugh Carleton, *The BBC as a Public Service* (London: BBC, 1960)

The Conscience of the Programme Director (London: BBC, 1965)

The Third Floor: A View of Broadcasting in the Sixties (London: Bodley Head, 1969)

Haines, Joe, *The Politics of Power* (London: Jonathan Cape, 1977)

Glimmers of Twilight: Harold Wilson in Decline (London: Politico's, 2003)

'The right to know is not absolute', *British Journalism Review*, vol. 22, no. 1, March 2011, pp. 27–32

Hayek, F.A., *The Road to Serfdom* (London: Routledge, 1944)

The Constitution of Liberty (Chicago: University of Chicago Press, 1960)

Law, Legislation and Liberty, 3 vols (Chicago: University of Chicago Press, 1973, 1976, 1979)

A Free-Market Monetary System and The Pretense of Knowledge (Alabama: Ludwig von Mises Institute, 2011)

Hennessy, Peter, *Whitehall* (London: Secker & Warburg, 1989)

The Prime Minister (London: Allen Lane, 2000)

Hobbes, Thomas, *Leviathan*, ed. Richard Tuck (Cambridge: Cambridge University Press, 1991)

Hoggart, Simon, *The Hands of History: Parliamentary Sketches 1997–2007* (London: Atlantic Books, 2007)

Inglis, Fred, *Radical Earnestness* (Oxford: Wiley-Blackwell, 1983)

Johnson, Kim, *Life Before and After Monty Python* (London: Plexus, 1993)

Kant, Immanuel, *Groundwork for the Metaphysics of Morals*, trans. Allen W. Wood (New Haven: Yale University Press, 2002)

Kaufman, Gerald, *How to be a Minister* (London: Faber & Faber, 1997)

Kaufman, Herbert, *Red Tape: Its Origins, Uses and Abuses* (Washington, DC: Brookings Institution, 1977)

Lasch, Christopher, *The Revolt of the Elites and the Betrayal of Democracy* (New York: W.W. Norton & Company, 1995)

Locke, John, *An Essay Concerning Human Understanding* (Oxford: Clarendon Press, 1979)

Machiavelli, Niccolò, *The Prince*, eds Quentin Skinner and Russell Price (Cambridge: Cambridge University Press, 1988)

Macmillan, Harold, *The Past Masters: Politics and Politicians, 1906–1939* (London: Macmillan, 1978)

MacShane, Denis, *Using the Media* (London: Pluto Press, 1979)

Markovits, Andrei S. and Mark Silverstein, eds, *The Politics of Scandal: Power and Process in Liberal Democracies* (New York: Holmes & Meier, 1988)

McCann, Graham, *Cary Grant: A Class Apart* (London: Fourth Estate, 1996)

'Why the best sitcoms must be a class act', *London Evening Standard*, 21 May 1997, p. 9

'An offer we *can* refuse', *London Evening Standard*, 2 December 1998, p. 68

Morecambe & Wise (London: Fourth Estate, 1998)

'Sit back and wait for the comedy', *Financial Times*, 24 November 1999, p. 22

'Don't bury your treasures', *Financial Times*, 28 June 2000, p. 22

Dad's Army: The Story of a Classic Television Show (London: Fourth Estate, 2001)

'How to define the indefinable', *Financial Times*, 25 March 2003, p. 22

'Steptoe and Son', in Merullo, Annabel and Neil Wenborn, *British Comedy Greats* (London: Cassell Illustrated, 2003), pp. 179–82

Frankie Howerd: Stand-Up Comic (London: Fourth Estate, 2004)

The Essential Dave Allen, ed. (London: Hodder & Stoughton, 2005)

Spike & Co. (London: Hodder & Stoughton, 2006)

Fawlty Towers (London: Hodder & Stoughton, 2007)

A Poke in the Eye (With a Sharp Stick) ed. (London: Canongate, 2012)

McDonnell, James, *Public Service Broadcasting: a reader* (London: Routledge, 1991)

McFarlane, Brian, *An Autobiography of British Cinema* (London: Methuen, 1997)

Mill, John Stuart, *On Liberty and Other Essays* (Oxford: Oxford University Press, 2008)

Milne, Kirsty, The Advice Squad', *New Statesman*, 13 January 1995, p. 18

Muir, Frank, *Comedy in Television* (London: BBC, 1966)

Nagel, Thomas, 'Ruthlessness in Public Life', in *Mortal Thoughts* (Cambridge: Cambridge University Press, 1979)

Nathan, David, *The Laughtermakers* (London: Peter Owen, 1971)

Nussbaum, Martha C., *The Fragility of Goodness: Luck and Ethics in Greek Tragedy and Philosophy* (Cambridge: Cambridge University Press, 1986)

Political Emotions: Why Love Matters for Justice (Cambridge: Harvard University Press, 2013)

Orwell, George, *The Collected Essays, Journalism and Letters*, vol. 2 (London: Penguin, 1970)

The Penguin Essays of George Orwell (London: Penguin, 1984)

Essays (Everyman: London, 2002)

Ostwald, Martin, *From Popular Sovereignty to the Sovereignty of Law: Law, Society and Politics in Fifth-Century Athens* (Berkeley: University of California Press, 1986)

Paine, Thomas, *The Rights of Man* (London: Penguin, 1985)

The Age of Reason (New York: Dover, 2004)

Parris, Matthew, *Chance Witness: An Outsider's Life in Politics* (London: Penguin, 2013)

Podlecki, Anthony J., *The Political Background of Aeschylean Tragedy* (Ann Arbor: University of Michigan Press, 1966)

Polsby, Nelson, *Political Innovation in America* (New Haven: Yale University Press, 1985)

Ponting, Clive, *The Right to Know: The Inside Story of the Belgrano Affair* (London: Sphere, 1985)

Robinson, Nick, *Live from Downing Street* (London: Bantam, 2013)

Roth, Andrew, *Sir Harold Wilson: Yorkshire Walter Mitty* (London: TBS, 1977)

Sen, Amartya, *Commodities and Capabilities* (Oxford: Oxford University Press, 1999)

Seymour-Ure, Colin, 'The Media in Postwar British Politics', *Parliamentary Affairs*, 47, 1994, pp. 530–4

Shklar, Judith, *Political Thought and Political Thinkers* (Chicago: University of Chicago Press, 1998)

Sloan, Tom, *Television Light Entertainment* (London: BBC, 1969)

Smith, Adam, *The Theory of Moral Sentiments* (London: Penguin Classics, 2010)

Smith, Anthony, *British Broadcasting* (Newton Abbot: David and Charles, 1974)

Thatcher, Margaret, *The Downing Street Years* (London: HarperCollins, 1993)

Theakston, Kevin and Geoffrey Fry, 'Britain's Administrative Elite: Permanent Secretaries 1900–1986', *Public Administration*, vol. 67, issue 2, June 1989, pp. 129–47

Took, Barry, *Laughter in the Air* (London: Robson/BBC, 1976).

'Whatever Happened to TV Comedy?' *The Listener*, 5 and 12 January 1984

Walzer, Michael, 'Political Action: The problem of Dirty Hands', *Philosophy and Public Affairs*, vol. 2, no. 2, Winter 1973, pp. 160–80

'Philosophy and Democracy', *Political Theory*, 9, no. 3, August 1981, pp. 379–99

Weber, Max, *Max Weber: Political Writings*, eds Peter Lassman and Ronald Spiers (Cambridge University Press, 1994)

Economy and Society (Berkeley: University of California Press, 1992)

Wheldon, Huw, *British Traditions in a World-Wide Medium* (London: BBC, 1973)

The Achievement of Television (London: BBC, 1975)

The British Experience in Television (London: BBC, 1976)

Whitehouse, Mary, *A Most Dangerous Woman?* (London: Lion, 1982)

Williams, Marcia, *Inside Number 10* (London: Weidenfeld & Nicolson, 1972)

Wilmut, Roger, *From Fringe to Flying Circus* (London: Methuen, 1982)

Wilson, Harold, *A Prime Minister on Prime Ministers* (London: Weidenfeld & Nicolson, 1977)

Wittgenstein, Ludwig, *Culture and Value* ed. G.H. von Wright with Heikki Nyman (Oxford: Basil Blackwell, 1980)

Wolin, Sheldon S., 'Political Theory as a Vocation', *American Political Science Review*, vol. 63, no. 4 (Dec. 1969), pp. 1062–82

Wyndham Goldie, Grace, *Facing the Nation: Broadcasting and Politics 1936–1976* (London: Bodley Head, 1977)

Young, Hugo, *One of Us: Final Edition* (London: Pan, 2013)

Ziegler, Philip, *Wilson: The Authorised Life* (London: Weidenfeld & Nicolson, 1993)

Index